WITHDRAWN

D0980754

ALSO BY WILL FERGUSON

Beauty Tips from Moose Jaw:
Travels in Search of Canada

Hitching Rides with Buddha

WILL FERGUSON

CANONGATE
Edinburgh · New York · Melbourne

Previously published under the title: *Hokkaido Highway Blues.*

Published by agreement with Alfred A. Knopf Canada

Printed in the United States of America

FIRST AMERICAN EDITION

ISBN-10: 1-84195-785-2
ISBN-13: 978-1-84195-785-2

Canongate
841 Broadway
New York, NY 10003

Distributed by Publishers Group West

www.groveatlantic.com

06 07 08 09 10   10 9 8 7 6 5 4 3 2 1

All things considered, there are only two kinds of men in the world—those who stay at home and those who do not. The second are the more interesting.

—RUDYARD KIPLING,
as quoted in *The Honourable Visitors*

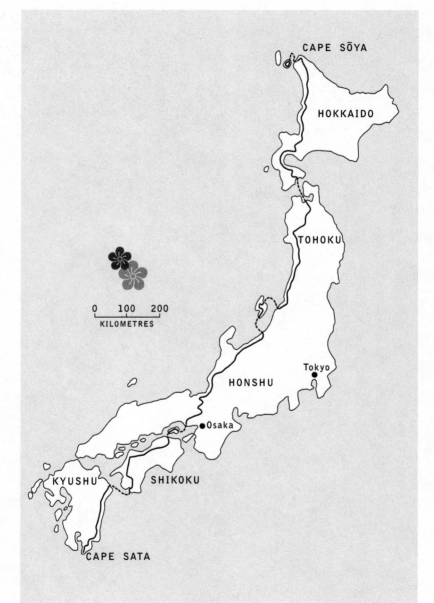

CAPE SŌYA

HOKKAIDO

TOHOKU

HONSHU

Tokyo

Osaka

0   100   200
KILOMETRES

KYUSHU

SHIKOKU

CAPE SATA

CONTENTS

Hitching Rides with Buddha

THE DEVIL'S WASHBOARD

Southern Kyushu

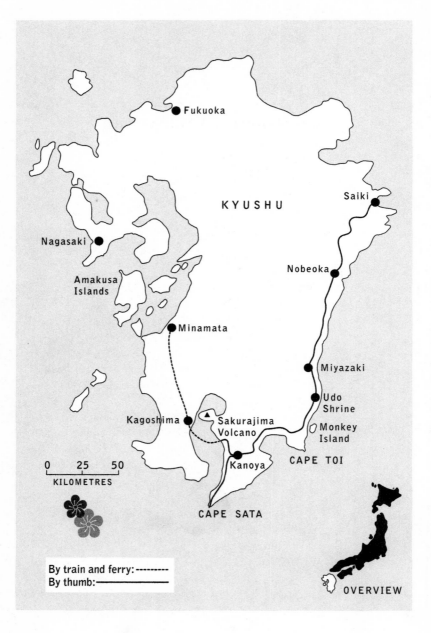

I

CAPE SATA is the end of Japan.

When you turn your back to the sea and look northward, all of mainland Japan is balanced, sword-like, above you. It is a long, thin, volcanic country: a nation of islands that approaches—but never quite touches—its neighbours. It is a land that engenders metaphors. It has been likened to an onion: layers and layers surrounding . . . nothing. It has been described as a maze, a fortress, a garden. A prison. A paradise. But for some, Japan is none of these. For some, Japan is a highway. And Cape Sata is where it ends.

A road winds its way in descending squiggles toward the sea. Tattered palm trees and overgrowths of vine crowd the roadside. Villages flit past. The road twists up into the mountains, turns a corner, and ends—abruptly—in a forest of cedar and pine. A tunnel disappears into the mountainside.

From here you proceed on foot, through the unexpected cool damp of the tunnel, past the obligatory souvenir stands, onto a path cut through the trees. Along the way, you come upon a hidden shrine. You ring the bell and rouse the gods and continue deeper into the forest green.

A faded cinderblock building is perched at the edge of a cliff, clinging to the last solid piece of ground. Inside, a tired-looking woman is selling squid that is skewered on sticks and covered with thick, sticky soy sauce. Somehow, you resist the temptation. Instead, you climb the stairs to the observation deck and, through windows streaked with dust and nose-smears, you gaze out at the majesty that is Cape Sata.

A few tourists mill about, uncertain what to do with themselves now that they've seen the view. They buy some squid, look through the coin-operated telescopes, and frown thoughtfully. "So this is Sata," they say. The end of the world.

Sata feels like the end.

Here, the mainland meets the sea. The coast tumbles into boulders. Pine trees lean out over dead-drop cliffs, waves crash and roll—almost soundless in their distance—and jagged rocks and sudden islands rise up like shark fins from the water. There is a perpetual wind at Sata, a wind that comes in from the open ocean and billows up the cliffside.

"Look," says Mr. Migita, herding his children before him as he comes. "Look over there."

He points back toward the mountains to a faint pink smudge in among the evergreens.

"*Sakura,*" he says. And the heart quickens.

The cherry blossoms have arrived. Now the journey has begun, now the race has started, now the challenge met. "Sakura! Do you really think so?"

He looks again. "Maybe not. You want some squid?"

2

EVERY SPRING, a wave of flowers sweeps across Japan. It begins in Okinawa and rolls from island to island to mainland. It hits at Cape Sata and moves north, cresting as it goes, to the very tip of distant Hokkaido, where it scatters and falls into a northern sea.

They call it Sakura Zensen—the "Cherry Blossom Front"—and its advance is tracked with a seriousness usually reserved for armies on the march. Progress reports are given nightly on the news and elaborate maps are prepared to show the front lines, the back lines, and the percentage of blossoms in any one area. "In Shimabara today they reported thirty-seven percent full blossoms."

Nowhere on earth does spring arrive as dramatically as it does in Japan. When the cherry blossoms hit, they hit like a hurricane. Gnarled cherry trees, ignored for most of the year, burst into bloom like fountains turned suddenly on.

The coming of the sakura marks the end of winter. It also marks the start of the school year and the closing of the business cycle. It is a hectic time, a time of final exams and productivity reports. Budgets have to be finalized, accounts settled, work finished. *Karōshi* (death by overwork) peaks in March. Deadlines, school graduations, government transfers—and then, riding in on April winds, come the cherry blossoms. And in one of those extreme shifts that seem to mark Japanese life, the nation swings from intense work to intense play. Crowds congregate beneath the flowers, saké flows, neckties are loosened, and wild spontaneous haiku are composed and recited.

These cherry blossom parties, called *hanami*, are a time for looking back and looking ahead, for drowning one's sorrows or celebrating another successful year. Toasts are made to colleagues, absent friends, distant relatives, and to the sakura themselves. Then, as quickly as they arrive, the cherry blossoms scatter. They fall like confetti, and in their passing they leave the dark green shimmering heat of summer, the wet misery of the rainy season, the typhoons of late August. At their peak—at full blossom and full beauty—the sakura last only a few days.

During their brief explosion, the cherry blossoms are said to represent the aesthetics of poignant, fleeting beauty: ephemeral, delicate in their passing. The way to celebrate this poignancy, naturally, is to drink large amounts of saké and sing raucous songs until you topple over backward. It is all very fleeting and beautiful.

It is also oddly formalized. In what other nation would you find a memo posted on a company's cafeteria notice board that reads: KEEP THIS AREA CLEAN. FINAL REPORTS ARE DUE FRIDAY. AND DON'T FORGET, WE ARE GOING CHERRY BLOSSOM VIEWING AFTER WORK TODAY.

In addition to the usual public parks and castle grounds, cemeteries are sometimes chosen as suitable spots for cherry blossom parties—as a counterpoint to the celebrations, and as a reminder that this beauty, this joy, like all things will pass. We live in a world of impermanence, a world of flux and illusion, a world brimming with sadness—so we might as well get pissed and enjoy ourselves. (Or at least, that's how I read the underlying Buddhist theology.)

In addition to Cherry Blossom Viewing, you have Moon Viewing, Snow Viewing, Wildflower Viewing, Autumn Leaf Viewing, and Summer Stargazing. All are formally engaged in, and all follow set procedures and seasons. As a service to readers, I have prepared a handy chart listing each phenomenon, the season in which it appears, and the correct manner in which to observe it:

PHENOMENON	SEASON	PROPER WAY TO VIEW
Cherry blossoms	Spring	Drunk on saké
Wildflowers	Summer	Drunk on saké
Harvest moon	Autumn	Drunk on saké
Autumn leaves	Autumn	Drunk on saké
Snow on ancient temples	Winter	Drunk on saké

In the late nineteenth century, a British scholar noted that if one could just reconcile the lofty heights of Japanese ideals with the earthy limitations of its people, one would truly understand the essence of this beguiling nation. Not surprisingly, he left Japan a bitter and frustrated man. Me, I don't even begin to understand the countless contradictions of Japan, but when the cherry blossoms come every spring I am swept away nonetheless.

My first two years in Japan were spent teaching English in high schools on the remote Amakusa Islands. The job had its perks. An absurdly large salary for one, and the camaraderie of my fellow teachers for another. The students, however, were another story. They studied English—or I should say, English was taught in their presence. Nothing ever seemed to sink in. Years of classes and endless tests and *still* they couldn't master the intricacies of a simple "How are you?" When I tried to have the most elemental of English conversations with them they looked at me with blank expressions, shrugged their shoulders, and said *"Wakaranai."* ("Huh?") They did this, I believe, just to annoy me. Don't get me wrong, these teenagers were polite and studious and well-mannered, but they were still teenagers, and teenagers are pretty well insufferable anywhere you go on this planet.

It was after school that I enjoyed myself. In Japan, teachers, priests, and policemen are traditionally the most lecherous, hard-drinking segments of society, and the teachers I worked with certainly lived up to their part of the bargain. The highlight of the year was the Faculty Cherry Blossom Viewing Party. We would crowd in under a stand of cherry trees, officially to view the flowers and reflect on the transience of life, but in reality as an excuse to blow off steam, spread malicious gossip, quaff great quantities, and flirt shamelessly with each other. At least, that's why I went.

The parties were always great fun—or until you sobered up the next morning and discovered that somehow you had managed to run up a two-hundred-dollar tab the night before. (That absurdly large salary came in handy at times.) The best parties were held at night, with the spray of sakura lit up by spotlights and with dozens of competing parties camped out beneath the trees. I even composed a haiku of my own while I sat, inspired by blossoms and beer, as all around me revelry and madness reigned. When I recited my poem, my Japanese colleagues were deeply moved:

> Early spring—
> Blossoms fall like rain.
> Pass me another beer, eh?

A fellow exchange teacher named Bill Robinson lived in a nearby town, and he wrote a haiku about school parties as well. His haiku is so subtle, so complex, so *deep* it actually requires footnotes. Heck, it even rhymes:

> School *enkai**
> You'll laugh, you'll cry—
> Kiss *ichi-man en*† goodbye.

One year, drunker than usual, I announced to my circle of Japanese teachers that I was going to follow the Cherry Blossom Front all the way to Hokkaido, at the northern end of Japan. Or rather, that is what was reported to me. I don't recall making this vow exactly, but I was repeatedly reminded of it. My supervisor, for one, constantly fretted over my plans.

"If you follow the cherry blossoms it will take at least a month. You should arrange a rail pass."

"Ah, yes. About my plan. When I said I would *follow* the blossoms, I was speaking figuratively. What I meant was—"

"The Principal is very impressed with your resolve. He says that you understand the True Heart of Japan."

These kinds of compliments are meaningless of course. Japanese lavish hollow praise on Westerners. If a Westerner masters the art of chopsticks he is complimented on his skilful hand-eye coordination; if he catches a lazy pop fly in left field he is complimented on his sports prowess; if he learns how to say *hello* in Japanese he is praised as being fluent, and so on. The phrase most often encountered in

---

*enkai: office party
†*ichi-man en*: ten thousand yen; approximately $115.

these situations is *jōzu desu ne!* which means, "Boy, are you talented!" but which might be more accurately translated as, "Not bad for a dimwit."

The best illustration of what *jōzu desu ne!* means is the way my next-door neighbour taught her five-year-old son to ride a bicycle. Eschewing training wheels, she simply put him on a bike and pushed him off, down the driveway, where he inevitably flipped over or hit a tree or skidded to a stop on his face. After a few of these lessons, the kid was a wreck: his knees scraped, his elbows bruised. But he kept getting back on and trying again and again, sniffling back the tears as he went. It was all very entertaining, and it provided me with hours of amusement as I sat at my kitchen table, sipping my coffee and charting little Taro's progress. I applauded his more acrobatic flips. Without fail, every time he set out on another foray, his mother would shout—in the brief moment he was in control— *"Jōzu desu ne!"* After which he would crash. Again. And again.

Whenever someone in Japan compliments my second-language skills with the exclamation "Jōzu desu ne!" I think of little Taro on his bicycle, barely in control and heading for disaster. Keeps me humble.

Anyhow, I had committed myself to discovering the True Heart of Japan. "William is going to follow the sakura all the way to Hokkaido," my supervisor would tell people at random, and I would grimace in a manner that might easily be mistaken for a smile. I stalled for three years.

When I finally did set out to follow the Cherry Blossom Front north, I went armed only with the essentials of Japanese travel: a map, several thick wads of cash, and a decidedly limited arsenal of Japanese, most of which seemed to revolve around drinking or the weather. ("It is very hot today. Let's have a beer.")

Japan is not a small country, no matter what the Japanese themselves may think. The main island of Honshu alone is larger than Great Britain. Were Japan in Europe, it would dominate the continent. Japan is larger than Italy, larger than Norway, larger than Germany. A journey from Cape Sata in the south to Cape Sōya at the north covers three thousand kilometres. In North America this would be a journey from Miami to Montreal—and at roughly the same latitudes.

So why this persistent image that Japan is a tiny little place? One reason is due to a cartographical optical illusion. On a map, Japan looks small because it is surrounded by the largest nations on earth: China, Russia, Canada, the United States, and Australia. But there is more involved than this. Japan is small because Japan *prefers* it that way. It supports the image Japan has of itself: the beleaguered underdog, small but mighty, the little engine that could. If you tell the average Japanese person that their country has a larger population base and a far bigger land mass than that of Great Britain, they will either resent it or refuse to believe you.

Oddly enough, despite their conviction that they live in a small country, my Japanese friends also thought of northern Japan as being hopelessly remote. For them, the island of Hokkaido was a world away, and when we discussed my travel plans they were not terribly optimistic about my odds. "It is very far," they warned. "Very far."

To make matters worse, I decided to go by thumb. Striking a heroic stance, I declared my intention to become the first person ever to hitchhike the length of Japan, end-to-end, cape-to-cape, sea-to-sea. This did not impress my Japanese friends as much as I had hoped.

"Why would you want to do that?" they asked, genuinely puzzled. "There is no reason to hitchhike. That's why we built the Bullet Train."

Others worried about my safety. "But," I would argue, "Japan is a very safe country, is it not?"

"Oh, yes. Very safe. Safest in the world."

"So why shouldn't I hitchhike?"

"Because Japan is dangerous."

And so on.

Now, I will admit that mooching rides across Japan is not a *major* achievement—I mean, it's not like I paddled up the Amazon or discovered insulin or anything—but I am the first person ever to do this, so allow me my hubris.

When I left my home in Minamata City aboard a southbound train, I felt suitably bold with my backpack and muscular thumb.

"I'm going to hitchhike the length of Japan," I told the man beside me.

He smiled and nodded.
"I'm going to follow the cherry blossoms."
He nodded.
"All the way to Russia," I said.
He smiled again, and soon after changed seats.

3

KAGOSHIMA CITY is the Naples of Japan. All the guidebooks say this. Having never been to Naples, I really couldn't tell you. The two do have a sister-city relationship, which is more of a suicide pact than anything, because both Naples and Kagoshima are known primarily for the imminent annihilation facing their people. Both cities, you see, are under the shadow of volcanic mountains.

Across from Kagoshima City, rising up from the bay and dominating the entire view, is the gothic presence of Sakurajima, an active volcano with a potential wallop far greater than that of Vesuvius. Over one million people live within a six-mile radius of Sakurajima, well within the Blast Zone. The volcano itself is extremely ugly. It seems to float on top of the water like a charred, smoldering mass of candle wax. Although originally an island, in 1914 one of its more violent eruptions spewed out enough lava to weld it onto the far side of the bay.

Incredibly, people continue to live on Sakurajima, even though an entire village on its east side was once buried under ash and stone. All that remains of the village is the top of a shrine gate, protruding out of the ground. The torii gate was over two stories high; only the top two and a half feet stick out. Undaunted, the people who fled returned as soon as the volcano calmed down. They rebuilt the town around the unnerving landmark of the buried gate. And life goes on. From the ash-rich soil of Sakurajima, the villagers harvest giant radishes that grow to the size of watermelons, and they hold their breath and they pray at their shrines and they wait for the next big eruption.

Kagoshima City is just across the bay. It will be destroyed by tidal waves and flaming rock-falls when Sakurajima goes. Not if—*when.*

As you can imagine, this adds an element of fatalism to the city. The grit and ash of the volcano lie like a funeral cloth over everything. Cars look old. Gardeners routinely dust their flowers.

I was on the beach of Kagoshima Bay one summer when across the water the entire mountain just, well, *shuddered*. If you're like me, you've probably never seen a mountain shudder. It got worse. Ominous dark clouds rolled up like bucket-throws of dirty water, and a muffled roar echoed across the bay and back again. *"Run for your lives!"* I said calmly. The others just shrugged. "Why bother? You can't outrun a volcano." (This, of course, did not stop me from trying.)

The Japanese word for volcano is *kazan*, "fire-mountain," yet the people of Kagoshima chose to name their volcano not for fire or thunder, but for the fleeting flowers of spring: Sakurajima, "Cherry Blossom Island." A rumbling volcano named in honour of a delicate blossom that symbolizes the transience of life. I used to think that this was all very poetic, but as I stood on the beach watching Sakurajima that day, I realized that the transience of life being alluded to was my own. The mountain shuddered again, like a grumpy old man shifting in his sleep, and then slowly returned to silence. The echoes were a long time dying. Only then did I exhale.

Southern Kyushu is divided into two peninsulas, and the quickest way to get to Cape Sata is to take a ferry from the western peninsula to the eastern and then travel south. Which is what I did. The ferry left with a sonorous, seagull-scattering blast of its horn, and I stood out in the wind on the upper deck and watched Sakurajima intently as it slipped by. (I was working on the "watched pot never boils" theory.)

An old man approached me. He was tiny and tidy and as wrinkled as my thumb after a bath. He seemed to be shrinking back into himself even as we spoke.

"American," he said. It wasn't a question.

"No."

"Where in America? Boston?"

I sighed. "I'm not American."

"New York? Chicago? San Francisco? Detroit?" He was evidently going to list every city in the United States, so I grabbed the next one that went by and adopted it as my new home.

"So," he said, "is it cold in Baltimore?"

"Very cold."

"In Japan," he said, "we have four seasons."

"Congratulations."

"Thank you. Are you married?"

"No."

"Can you eat Japanese food?"

This was Conversation by Non Sequitur, and I was thoroughly familiar with it by now. The trick was to answer with equally arbitrary statements, until you sound like a couple of spies conversing in code.

"Yes, I can eat Japanese food. Baltimore is very big."

"How long will you stay in Japan?"

"Until tomorrow, forever. It is very cold in Baltimore."

He shook my hand. We smiled warmly at each other, clearly this was an International Moment. He then motioned to the mountain. "You are watching Sakurajima very closely," he said. "It is beautiful, isn't it? How do you feel about Sakurajima?"

It's a volcano. It's named for cherry blossoms. It is mountain and sea and fire. "It is like Japan," I said.

He nodded thoughtfully. "You understand the true heart of my country." Then—and I don't mean to brag here—he assured me that when it came to speaking Japanese, I was pretty darned *jōzu*.

I had planned to take a bus down the peninsula to Cape Sata and begin hitchhiking from there, but there was no bus. At least, I don't think there was. I examined the bus schedule posted by the highway, but no matter how hard I squinted, it remained completely inscrutable.

The Japanese language is written in three separate alphabets, and I only know two and a half. The phonetic symbols (the *kana*) are easy enough, but the Chinese hieroglyphics (the *kanji*) are about as accessible to me as, well, Chinese hieroglyphics. If God had wanted me to learn *kanji*, He would have given me a bigger brain. So instead of catching a bus, I started hitchhiking earlier than planned, on a nondescript stretch of road cluttered with gas stations and appliance stores. Cars were flicking past in a steady tempo, the sun was out, and I felt good. It was under way.

Humming my own private theme music ("Mission Impossible"), I thrust out a thumb and smiled like an angel. I was trying to look innocent and non-violent. Westerners are perceived as being aggressive and vaguely threatening, and I was working hard to counter this impression. I had shaved my beard off before I left and got my hair cut in that hip Mormon style that is all the rage in Japan. I was even wearing a necktie. In Japan, the Mormon Look is definitely *in*, and the young male missionaries who are sent to Japan—clean-cut and polite and oh so Aryan—are considered sexy and suave by the Japanese. This is true. Now, I'm not claiming I looked as sexy as a Mormon, but I did look mighty clean-cut, if I do say so myself. (I was going more for a Jehovah's Witness effect.)

Within minutes a car pulled over.

When I say "within minutes" I mean, of course, "fourteen minutes," and when I say "car," I mean, of course, "white Honda Civic." I got it into my head that I would keep track of the time I waited and the make of each car that stopped; I even carried a little notebook and a nerdy clip-pen so that I could record this information, which I assumed would make excellent small talk at future cocktail parties. "Say, did I ever mention that the average wait time for a hitchhiker in Japan is seventeen-point-two minutes?" Fortunately, I had a flash of common sense and I threw the notebook away. I had made only the one entry.

The passenger door swung open and a young woman with black satin hair leaned over and smiled at me. "American," she said. It wasn't a question.

4

KAORI YAMAGUCHI was an English teacher at Ono Junior High, a small school up in the mountains. With only fourteen students, she *was* the English department. In the West, we are so captivated with images of crowded Tokyo subways and faceless salarymen that we forget how much of Japan is still rural and traditional. Granted, not much of it is out-and-out wild—there are precious few frontiers left—but farmlands and villages are still a big part of Japanese society. And the dominant colour of Japan, the colour that permeates the landscape and provides the backdrop of countless vistas, the colour that *is* Japan is green—a deep, wet, tropical green. You will find very little greenery in most Japanese cities, true. But you will also find very little of Japan in most Japanese cities. The urban cores are exciting, crowded, jaded, but they are also the most Westernized, standardized stretches of the nation. Another Japan exists a half-step away, along the back roads, in the provincial capitals, on the outer edges.

The highway Kaori and I were driving on ran low along the coast between Kagoshima Bay and the rolling green mountains of the interior. There wasn't a subway or a salaryman in sight.

"Where are you going?" she asked.

"Cape Sata."

"I used to live near Sata," she said. "There is nothing there and it is very hard to reach. It is maybe three hours away." You could see the burden of duty descend upon her. "I am sorry, but I cannot take you all the way to Sata. I am very busy. I'm sorry."

I have a cruel streak, and for a minute I was tempted to force her to drive me to Sata simply by asking. That's all it would have taken.

16

But I didn't. Maybe it was the necktie and maybe it was the crew cut; I felt strangely charitable. "You don't have to drive me to Sata. Really. Just down the road is fine."

She was almost sick with worry at this point. "But no one will stop for you. Japanese people don't pick up hitchhikers."

"But you're Japanese, and you did."

She ignored my powerful Western logic. "There are buses," she said. "You should take a bus instead. And after Sata, where will you go?"

"Hokkaido."

When I said this she laughed, covering her mouth with one hand in that highly annoying, yet oddly endearing way Japanese women have. Then her expression changed as she realized I wasn't kidding. Instead of shuttling me farther down the coast, she turned and drove inland. We came up onto a plateau and Kanoya City engulfed us.

"Is this the, ah, way to Sata?" I asked.

She smiled and said, "Can you eat Japanese food?"

Kaori drove me smack into the middle of town and, with a friendly wave and tally-ho, she abandoned me. Now I *was* lost. Trying to hitchhike out of a city centre is like trying to find an exit after being spun around three times with your eyes shut. My cleverly improvised strategy involved wandering about hopelessly in all directions with my thumb extended before me like a divining rod. It worked. I was rescued "within minutes."

His name was Mr. Migita and he was driving a big boat of a car, shiny-black and filled with kids. In the front seat was his daughter, a junior-high-school student simply agog at the sight of me, and in the back were his two sons, around seven and five years old.

Mr. Migita asked me where I was going and when I said Cape Sata, he told me I was heading in the wrong direction. He offered to take me back out to the coast, so I crawled in and faced the gaping stares of the two boys. You could tell what they were thinking: *Dad's gone mad.* It was as though their father had let a large bear into the backseat.

Mr. Migita looked at me in the rearview mirror. "Can you speak Japanese?"

"Sort of," I said. (Unless noted, the conversations in this book were originally in Japanese. Or at least something that resembles Japanese.)

The younger boy, Hidenori, was becoming suspicious. "Are you American?" No. "Then you're Japanese." No. "Well, if you aren't American and you aren't Japanese, what are you?"

Put like that, I wasn't quite sure. "I'm a *tanuki*," I said, and they burst into peals of laughter.

"You're not a tanuki!"

"Sure I am." Tanuki are creatures of folklore in Japan: raccoon-dogs with huge bellies and gigantic testicles who roam the forests drinking saké and trying to seduce young maidens by passing themselves off as noblemen.

The boys laughed and laughed, the daughter giggled behind her hand, and Mr. Migita eyed me warily from the rearview mirror. Hidenori then asked me with grave sincerity, "Are you really a tanuki?" His older brother biffed him one on the head. "You idiot, of course he's not a tanuki! He's an American." And everyone laughed some more, as the little guy rubbed his head and grinned sheepishly.

"Do you know how tanuki make music?" I asked them.

"Sure!" they yelled. "They use their stomachs like a drum!" Hidenori then proceeded to show me how by punching himself repeatedly in the stomach. "Very good," I said, but he kept on going.

"Ah, that's fine," I said. "You can stop any time." He continued pummeling himself in the stomach even as his eyes watered. "Come on," I said, and then, slipping into English, *"I get the picture, kid."*

His eyes widened with an audible *boing*. "English! You speak English! Say something, say something in English."

"Wayne Newton is the Antichrist."

"Wow! What does that mean?"

"It's a poem. Kind of a haiku."

When we reached the coastal highway, Mr. Migita pulled over and told me to wait in the car. (You could tell he was a real Papa; he talked to me the same way he addressed his five-year-old.) He made a call from a pay phone and when he returned he said, "I told my wife we'd be late. We're going to Sata."

The kids cheered and the three of us in the back did the Wave. Mr. Migita then told his daughter to change seats and he moved me up front. I had been promoted.

The highway twisted from one hairpin to another and there I was, sitting right up front like a big person. I swung my feet and watched the palm trees and villages spin by. There are no roads in Sata, just corners joined together. The corners kept coming and coming, and I began to get queasy. I could feel my stomach percolating—never a pleasant sensation—and soon I was threatening to erupt, volcano-like, across Mr. Migita's dashboard. Even in my stupor I realized that throwing up on your host was a bad way to start a relationship, and I fought hard to keep my lunch (pork and rice with a raw egg) from making an unexpected encore. We came to the parking lot just in time, and I bolted from the car and bent over, gulping down fresh air and trying not to faint. The littlest boy came up and punched me in the stomach. "You're not a tanuki!" he said.

"I'll kill you, you little shit."

"Hey," he called to his dad, "he's talking poetry again!"

When my inner ear had stopped spinning like a gyroscope and my stomach had ceased its amusing Spasm Dance, I joined the others at the tunnel. Mr. Migita had paid my entrance fee and there was no way I could talk him out of it.

"You are my guest," he said.

No, I am a freeloader hitching a ride. "Thank you," I said, as I accepted his generosity.

I did manage to decline the squid, however, even though Migita's daughter offered me her last tentacle. Standing at the top of the observation deck overlooking Cape Sata, I told her and her brothers about the mythical, faraway land of Ka-Na-Da, where children didn't have to go to school on Saturday or wear uniforms or even actually learn anything, and they sighed with understandable envy.

"Do you have a gun?" the youngest asked, and his older brother, Toshiya, immediately chimed in, "Yes, did you ever shoot anybody?"

"No," I said. "Only evil Americans shoot people. In Ka-Na-Da everyone lives in peace and harmony."

It sure is great being a Canadian. You get to share the material benefits of living next door to the United States, yet at the same time you get to act smug and haughty and morally superior. You just can't beat that kind of irresponsibility.

"Tell us more about Ka-Na-Da," said the children, and I obliged.

It was almost dusk when we left Sata. The sun was throwing long shadows across the road, and Mr. Migita had decided that I should come back to Kanoya City and have supper with him and his family. He pulled over to stock up on beer, and while he was gone his daughter leaned up and whispered in my ear, in English so soft I almost missed it, "My name is Kayoko. I am fine. And you?"

She then leaned back in her seat, obviously pleased with herself. Her brothers were dying to know what she had said. "Tell us, tell us!" they demanded, but she held her head high and proud and didn't say a word.

5

THE MIGITAS lived on the outskirts of Kanoya City, in a two-storey apartment block that faced an open field. Mr. Migita's wife welcomed me without batting an eye and, like a conjurer, she produced a full-course meal out of thin air. We nudged our way in around their low dining-room table and the food never stopped coming: raw fish with sinus-clearing horseradish, fried vegetables, noodles, more fish, salad, seaweed, soup, mini-sausages. It became a challenge to see if they could ever fill me up. Mr. Migita kept topping my glass with beer and encouraging my gluttony until finally, bloated to the brink of bursting, I conceded defeat. Mrs. Migita cleared the table of the wreckage and debris, and her husband and I settled back, sucking on toothpicks like a pair of feudal lords. This may sound sexist and insensitive and politically incorrect—and it is—but I had long since learned that had I offered to wash the dishes, or worse, had I *insisted*, I would only have humiliated Mrs. Migita. And anyway, I'm a lazy git and I was weighed down with forty pounds of excess food at the time.

The kids were doing their homework in front of the television. Which is to say, they were *not* doing their homework, they were watching television. It was clear that my presence had caused a lapse of household rules, and whenever their father absentmindedly looked over at them, they began to scribble away with feigned studiousness. A sci-fi animation show was moving stiffly across the screen. Everyone in it had huge blue eyes and ridiculous yellow hair and all the fluidity of a comic book being flipped through—slowly. Man, I hate Japanese animation. Give me some good live-action drama any day: Ultraman or Godzilla or Mothra. *Oh no! A giant moth!* Those were the classics. But you tell that to kids today and they just don't listen.

This isn't true, of course. Godzilla and Ultraman are still super-stars with Japanese children, and with adults as well. You know how Godzilla is always turning up to stomp on Tokyo? The filmmakers churn those movies out like clockwork, and Tokyo Tower has been destroyed so many times you'd think they'd have given up by now. *Rebuild it? What's the point? Godzilla will just come and knock it over again.*

Sometimes, Godzilla destroys other major metropolii, like Osaka or Nagoya, just for a change of pace, but mainly he sticks to Tokyo. The smaller cities in Japan have complained about this. They're jealous. The citizens of Fukuoka City even went so far as to circulate a petition asking—nay, *begging*—the producers of the Godzilla movies to destroy their fair city instead. Thousands of people signed these petitions and after years of pressure the producers relented and said, "All right, we'll destroy Fukuoka. Quit whining." Everyone in Fukuoka was delighted to hear this. Newspaper headlines boasted GOOD NEWS! GODZILLA TO DESTROY OUR CITY, and when it was later revealed that Godzilla would in fact rampage over all of Kyushu, the entire island was simply delirious with joy. So don't tell me the Japanese aren't a weird bunch of people.

Mr. Migita eventually did notice what his kids were up to, and they had that immortal parent-child conversation, one so innate I believe it is embedded right in the DNA. It goes something like this: Hey you kids, turn off the TV, it's bedtime. Just a few minutes more, please, Dad, please. No, you have school tomorrow. But the good part is coming, please, Dad, please. No! I said no, and when I say no I mean no, so the answer is no.

As usual, the children won. The animated characters blew up the planet and everyone was very happy, and the three kids filed off to bed. Mr. Migita and I, meanwhile, were on our sixth bottle of Yebisu Beer. He cleared a space on the table and began spreading out maps like a general planning a campaign.

"You can do it," he said. "But we must chart your way with great care."

We sat up late into the night, he and I, tracing highways with red pens, and with me making copious notes.

Eventually we came up with a complex course that zigzagged brilliantly across Japan and that made complete sense to us at the time. But the next day and miles away, when I unrolled Mr. Migita's maps, the routes we had marked and the cryptic asides I had jotted down with such conviction were now completely incomprehensible: "Good here, but not overland—highway changes to new one, must check to always see—Do *not* (and here I had underlined the word *not* forcibly several times) cross highway—wait at other places— West instead?—Check as I go."

It was two in the morning by the time Mr. Migita and I finished our cunning plan. We congratulated ourselves heartily and opened another bottle of Yebisu. By this point, he and I were blood brothers and we vowed eternal loyalty and friendship. He rolled up the maps with that careful deliberation people get when they have consumed too much alcohol, and we shook hands. Again. We did that a lot, often in lieu of coherent conversation.

Mr. Migita straightened himself up and said, with sudden determination, "You are my friend. You do not need to hitchhike. I will give you the money for a train ticket."

I was taken aback. "I'm not hitchhiking because I can't afford a train ticket." Had he offered me food and shelter because he thought I was broke? He was equally puzzled. If I wasn't short of funds, why was I hitchhiking? Why did I want to go all the way to Hokkaido in the company of strangers?

I assured him that the reason was not financial. Then I told him about Amakusa. For my first two years in Japan I lived in the most beautiful place on earth: the islands of Amakusa, south of Nagasaki. I taught in fishing villages lost in time, in misty coves with weathered temples and unexpected church spires. Amakusa is where the Jesuits of Portugal first landed in Japan, and it was in Amakusa that I first discovered the Power of the Thumb.

It was a discovery born of necessity. My work involved commuting between fishing villages without a car in an area where the buses apparently ran only on odd-numbered vernal equinoxes. Buses in Amakusa were like UFOs; I heard a lot about them but I never actually saw one. So I began hitching rides from school to school across the islands, much to the consternation of my supervisor. What began as a necessity soon became something else. It became a way *inside*.

The car is an extension of the home, but without any of the prescribed formalities that plague Japan. The hitchhiker in Japan slips in under the defenses, as both a guest and a travel companion. Bumming rides became its own reward, the journey its own destination.

In this spirit, I had set out for Hokkaido.

Arduous solo travel has a long history in Japan, and I was following in a proud tradition. The mendicant poet Matsuo Bashō wandered the highways of the deep north in the late fifteenth century and wrote a classic travel narrative about it. Three hundred years later an Englishwoman named Lesley Downer retraced his footsteps, and in 1980, Alan Booth *walked* the entire length of Japan, north to south, and wrote a travel narrative of his own. But these are solitary ways to see the country. I didn't want to travel among the Japanese, I wanted to travel with them. I didn't want to walk Japan, as Alan Booth had done, precisely because it is such a lonely, aloof way to travel. Also, it would have involved a lot of walking. Personally, I preferred zipping along in an air-conditioned car. Tromping down a highway all day often put Booth in a sour mood; but when you are constantly prevailing upon the kindness of strangers—as a hitchhiker must—it keeps you in a positive frame of mind. Call it Zen and the Art of Hitchhiking. The Way of the Lift. The Chrysanthemum and the Thumb. Heady on beer and the sound of my own voice, the aphorisms spilled out unchecked.

Mr. Migita had nodded off. The beer glass was empty, and it was time for me to crawl into one of those enormous cumulus futons that are always on hand for unexpected guests and other such freeloaders.

and said, "I'll take you through Osaki. Highway Two-Twenty meets Highway Four Forty-Eight, and you really should get past that inter-section before you start hitching rides."

Osaki came and went, we passed the intersection, but still Mr. Migita didn't stop. "We are almost at the coast now. I'll drop you off there."

It was five minutes to nine. "Won't you be late?"

"I'll call. Don't worry."

The highway crossed a river and there before us was the blue of Shibushi Bay. Palm trees filed by like telephone poles.

Nine o'clock passed. Mr. Migita said, "I'll take you to the next town. The rail line begins there. That way, if it rains, you can catch a train."

The sky was a clear, cloudless blue. "I don't think it's going to rain," I said.

"I'll take you anyway."

Houses began appearing at quicker and quicker intervals, the rice fields became smaller, a cluster of buildings and then we were through the town and back in open countryside. The train tracks fol-lowed the highway, crossing under and over it. A huddle of hotels appeared and beside them, oddly, a Ferris wheel.

Mr. Migita pulled into the parking lot. "I'll just be a moment."

Across the parking lot, the empty Ferris wheel was turning against a backdrop of sea and sky, carried by its own momentum. The trick with any Ferris wheel is to get the motion started and then maintain the spin. Momentum is the only force capable of defeating both inertia and gravity. Satellites in space do not orbit the planet. They are falling, continually falling, carried past the arc of the earth by the angle of their descent. And what is walking itself if not sim-ply maintaining a fall? It takes a great effort to set an object in motion, yet once you do, the motion becomes easier and easier to maintain. You strain to push a car but, once it's moving, it becomes almost effortless: You keep it going with its own momentum. Travelling is a matter of maintaining momentum. Resisting gravity. Free-falling past the horizon; falling, never landing.

Mr. Migita returned. "I told them I would be late."

"You already are."

"I told them I'd be more late."

We left the Ferris wheel receding behind us. The waves rolled in and broke along the bay. Mr. Migita didn't stop. "Just a little farther," he said, and then again, more to himself, "Just a little farther."

For a moment, I thought he was running away from home, but I was wrong. It wasn't about escape, it was a matter of momentum. He was caught in it, the centrifugal force of the traveller, the force that moves satellites, nomads, and Ferris wheels.

The southeastern coast of Kyushu is part of *Oni-no-Sentaku*, the "Devil's Washboard," a natural ridge-rock formation that runs in striated claw marks along the coast. It gives the entire region a just-finished feel, like pottery freshly thrown. Or wood unpolished, still showing the mark of the adze. The rain-forest green of Kyushu spills over the coast and then, suddenly, the scoured stone of the Devil's Washboard begins, as though the gods themselves had run out of sod.

It was low tide as we drove north, alongside the Washboard, to the Grand Shrine of Udo Jingū. Udo Jingū is built inside a cave overlooking the sea. To get to it, you have to leave the main highway and take a short side road in. Mr. Migita stopped the car at the entrance of the shrine grounds. A large torii gate divided the secular world from the sacred, and Mr. Migita—the momentum finally broken—said, almost apologetically, "I have to get back. Home. Family. You know."

We shook hands, and I promised to send him a postcard from the top of Japan. "When you get to Hokkaido, look for horses. They have horses in Hokkaido."

We stood in the shrill white light of a parking lot at noon. He didn't want to leave. Neither did he want to continue. Once interrupted, motion is hard to renew. We said goodbye and he drove away.

7

IN THE BEGINNING, there was Water and Chaos. The High Gods of Heaven, Izanagi and Izanami, God of the Male Aspect and God of the Female, stirred the brine with their spear, and the churning mud and falling drops formed the islands of Japan.

Thus begins the long and complex Shinto myth of creation, which is actually a surprisingly accurate description of how the Japanese archipelago itself was thrust up by the bubbling fires of an underwater volcanic rupture.

It was a time of great upheaval. Gods were born. Gods of the sky and the clouds and the trees and the earth. Gods of strength, of art, of love and anger—and of war. Until at last, the heavens and earth were filled with *kami*, god-spirits inhabiting every hidden corner and cranny of Japan, the Land of Wa, the Islands of Harmony. Key among them was Amaterasu, the Sun Goddess.

It was Amaterasu's grandson, Ninigi-no-Mikoto, who descended from the High Plain of Heaven to a windswept mountaintop in southern Kyushu. He brought with him the three Imperial Insignias of Divine Rule, still in existence today: a sword, a curved jewel, and a polished mirror. The immortal Ninigi-no-Mikoto had come to rule the islands of Japan, but through intrigue and insult his ancestors were cursed with a finite existence—immortality was lost—and from them came the human race, otherwise known as "the Japanese."

The Grand Shrine of Udo Jingū is dedicated to Ninigi-no-Mikoto's grandson. He in turn fathered Jimmu, the mythical first Emperor of Japan. And thus, through this long, convoluted family tree, the present Emperor of Japan traces his lineage directly back to Amaterasu, the Sun Goddess.

Shinto, the Way of the Gods, is Japan's homegrown religion. Buddhism came much later (via Korea), and in some ways remains an imported faith. Buddhism has a founder, a doctrine, and an historical basis: Shinto has none of these. Shinto's origins are lost in the mists of prehistory. As a faith, it grew from the natural awe, the fear and trembling, that humans have for the world around them: the fertility of womb and earth, the natural forces and the mysteries of life.

In Japan, the world is filled with primordial spirits. The kami are everywhere. The unseen world is pregnant with them, rich in life and charged with energy. Historical figures have been elevated to kami, and so have abstract nouns and animals.

Deeper still, Shinto is about *being* Japanese. One is not converted to Shinto. One is born into it. One simply *is* Shinto in the same way that one simply is—or isn't—Japanese. The idea of Shinto proselytizing is absurd. During World War II, the Japanese Empire built massive Shinto shrines in the countries it occupied: Singapore, Korea, Taiwan. But, removed from its Japanese soil, Shinto withers and dies. It is perhaps the only religion in the world that failed to convert the people it conquered.

Although it was used as a propaganda tool during World War II, and still contains heavy imperial connections, Shinto has largely returned to the more earthy, joyous roots from which it sprang. Shinto celebrates life. It is optimistic. Buddhism, in contrast, is gloomy. Shinto is for weddings; Buddhism is for funerals. Buddhist festivals are sombre. Shinto festivals are freewheeling, drunken affairs, intent on entertaining the gods. Buddhism worries about the afterlife. Shinto is concerned with the everyday and the here-and-now.

You will find Shinto shrines throughout Japan. Some are crumbling, some are well-tended. A few are lavish; most are small and humble. The object of veneration is often a polished silver mirror, a surface that reflects—and contains—the world around us. These mirrors, polished to a sheen, yet still clouded, are both reflective and obscure—a perfect symbol for the numinous nature of the religious impulse. Mirrors and local gods, the universal and the tribal.

You approach Shinto shrines through torii gates, and the entrances are usually guarded by a pair of stone lion-dogs. Like so many things Japanese, these lion-dogs came to Japan from China through a Korean intermediary. When they define themselves, the

Japanese tend to skip Korea, the middleman, and claim a connection to China that is direct and overemphasized. But here, in the shrine grounds of the gods, the Korean connection is acknowledged: the guardians are called *koma-inu*, "Korean dogs." That Korean icons should protect the repositories of all that is Japanese in spirit—the Emperor's Church in a sense—that Korean dogs should be given such a high-ranking position is something rarely commented upon by the Japanese. These stone guardians provide a telling clue about the ancient Korean roots of the Japanese Imperial Family.

The lion-dogs were originally a lion *and* a dog, and were very different in appearance, but over the years stonecutters found it easier to carve them to the same proportions. The two figures grew more and more alike, until their features blended. One lion-dog has a mouth that is always open, the other has a mouth that is always closed. The open-mouthed lion-dog is named *Ah*, the other is named *Un*, or more properly, *nn*. "Ah" is the first sound you make when you are born, "nn" the last sound you make when you die. "Ah" is the breath inhaled that begins life, "nn" the exhale of release, the breath that allows life to escape. Between the two lies all of existence, a universe that turns on a single breath. *Ah* is also the first symbol in the Japanese alphabet, *n* the last. And so, between these two lion-dogs, you also have the A and Z, the Alpha and Omega. In the original Sanskrit, *ah-un* means "the end and the beginning of the universe; infinity unleashed."

In Japan, people who are in perfect tune with each other, such as a pianist and a violinist playing in duet, are called *ah/un-no-kokyū*. *Kokyū* means "breathing," and the phrase suggests perfect, exquisite harmony: *ah/un-no-kokyū*, two or more breathing as one. If self-actualization is the ideal to which the Western world aspires, then common breath is the ideal to which Japan—and indeed, much of Asia—aspires. The word *harmony* in Japanese has the same cachet that the word *freedom* has in the West.

In Japan, the word for freedom, *jiyū*, carries with it the nuance of selfish or irresponsible behaviour. Group harmony is a higher value. This doesn't make the Japanese a nicer people. There are thieves and cheats and nasty characters in Japan, as there are anywhere. But the values that Japanese society subscribes to are starkly different from those of the West. If you had to embody the ideals of the West it would be the Statue of Liberty, or the Goddess of Jiyū as she is known in Japan, standing defiantly, the torch raised: a singular, powerful, one-of-a-kind presence. This is not the type of thing you would choose if you wished to give form to Japanese ideals. The ideals of Japan are captured instead in a thousand small stone guardians, in a thousand shrines, big and small, across Japan. A dog and lion so near in spirit that they have blended into one. *Ah/un-no-kokyū.*

On a less esoteric level, ah-un also refers to old married couples (or even old friends) who have been together for so long that they no longer have to finish their sentences. One begins with "Ah . . ." and the other agrees with "Nn . . ." (which is the Japanese equivalent of "uh-huh") and the entire meaning is understood.

As you enter a shrine ground, beyond the lion-dogs, you will find a fountain and a dipper. If you are planning to approach the gods you must first rinse your hands and mouth with water. Having made yourself presentable, you may now step up. You toss in a coin, bow, clap your hands once, and ring the bell. It is a rattle really, a dry hollow sound that nudges the gods awake. You bow again, make your silent petition, and clap twice more before you step away, making sure not to turn your back on the god enshrined within, behind the mirror.

Most of Japan's two thousand festivals revolve around the local Shinto shrine. The god is drawn from his inner sanctum by the shrine priest, coaxed out with a paper wand, and then paraded through the streets in a palanquin. It is thought that these processions were originally very slow and serious events, with the shrine priest himself carrying the altar through the village to ensure harvests, safety, prosperity. But, human vanity being what it is and the vanity of the gods being even stronger, the temporary containers of the gods grew larger and larger and more and more elaborate, requiring more and more people to carry them. Small armies of strapping young men were conscripted to carry the palanquin. And as these young men—girded with saké and priestly blessings—hauled the gods through the street on their shoulders, the rite descended into hilarity. The gods were bounced and jostled and ridden like runaway bulls, tipped over, sprayed with beer and saké. Competing gods even began jousting with one another in spectacular clashes. The gods, it was decided, enjoyed this. After all, they had spent the rest of the

year in fitful sleep, their slumber constantly interrupted by worshippers rattling the bell and asking for favours. That the festivals of
Japan are Latin in their revelry is a fact that takes many Western visitors by surprise. Shinto cajoles the gods into action. It entertains
them, and in doing so it celebrates the world around us.

Even here, at the Grand Imperial Shrine of Udo Jingū, the atmosphere is more festive than sacred. Souvenir shops and snack-food
stalls flank the approach, and visitors pass through a gauntlet of distractions on their way to the shrine. Men snap your photo and then
try to sell you a copy. Round-faced ladies in aprons offer soft ice-
cream cones and fried squid impaled on sticks. The smells swirl like
oil and water. You catch the sweet scent of octopus steamed in
dough. Snails, still in shell, simmer in broths. Trinkets and toys and
yells of welcome ricochet around you. Cartoon characters, super-
heroes, and the god-son Ninigi-no-Mikoto are rendered in the same
pink plastic and they all compete for the same jingle of coin in cup.
Stalls sell good-luck charms and talismans and sacred tablets. And
right smack beside them are fake doggy-do and large novelty buttocks. Everything is jumbled up in postmodern anarchy.

The approach to Udo Jingū bustles, and the closer you get to the
main altar, the thicker the crowds, the quicker the tempo. Touring
parties march through in phalanxes: schoolgirls in sailor uniforms,
boys in brush-cuts and school caps. There are couples, new and
unsure and excruciatingly aware of each other's presence, couples
comfortable, couples sullen, and couples past caring. They move like
tributaries through the main torii gate. The sound and scent of the
sea increases as you approach. A wooden boardwalk descends in
steps along the cliff face. Waves break below, rolling up against the
Devil's Washboard. People begin hurrying as they near the cave.

The sun is oppressive. It shimmers in a haze. The world is over-
exposed, reflective surfaces are painful to look at, the colours are
washed out. But here, inside the womb of the cave, the shadows are
damp and the air is wet. The cave breathes, and its exhalations are cool
against your skin. *Ah . . . Unn . . .*

Your eyes slowly adjust to the dark, and details emerge. The shrine
takes form, appearing from the murk like an image on a photographic
plate. Sounds: whispering voices, dry rattles, and the hollow plonk of
water dripping.

The shrine roof is in copper green, its angles fluid. It has the slope of a caravan tent. The style harkens back to the Mongolian steppes and the temporary tents of nomadic tribes. A message embodied in the very architecture of Shinto: The world is in flux, life moves, the rivers flow, and even the homes of the gods are but temporary shelters. Someday they, too, will be folded down like tents and put away.

I buy a bag filled with small clay pebbles and go outside to try my luck. In front of the cave a wooden balcony juts out over a jumble of boulders and salt spray. The sea throws herself up against the cliff face again and again, but the shrine remains just out of reach, tucked into its cave.

In among the sea rubble, at the bottom of the cliff, is a large misshapen boulder called "Turtle Rock," and atop the turtle's back is a *shimenawa* rope, looped in a circle. The rope signifies the presence of a kami and marks the area inside the circle as hallowed. Being (a) a Westerner and (b) a male, my first thought at seeing this holy circle, perched atop a large boulder at the bottom of a cliff, is to wonder, "How the heck did they ever get that rope down there?" I imagine it is one of the duties of the novice priests. "Send Hiroshi down, he's the new guy." Or maybe they tossed it, Hula Hoop style. The mysteries of the universe never held such appeal for me as the mystery of how they got that rope out there onto that boulder.

The circle on Turtle Rock is part of a sacred shooting gallery. Remember the clay pebbles I bought earlier? It is time to win favour with the gods. At Udo Jingū you lean over and toss the pebbles at the rock. If they land and stay within the circle you will be rewarded with great fortune, long life, good health—the usual stuff. People crowd the edge of the boardwalk, laughing and flinging pebbles. The sea is afloat with them, they cover boulder tops and rock ledges like rabbit droppings. Mounds of pebbles are inside the rope circle, but most have bounced out. Many are wildly off the mark. Not me. When it comes to tossing clay pebbles onto large rocks, I am pretty well the Omnipotent Master of the Universe. I try not to snort *too* loudly at the awkward misfires of my fellow worshippers. A voice beside me says, "He's cheating."

I looked around to see who was doing the cheating. They were referring to me.

"I beg your pardon," I said, scanning the crowd with a kind of How Dare You! look on my face, but no one would meet my eye. I continued tossing the pebbles. I was going for the world record slam-dunk pebble toss.

"What a cheater."

I spun around to face my detractors. Nothing. No one said a word. Finally, out of pity I suppose, an elderly couple stepped out toward me. She was wearing a trim blue elderly-aunt-type skirt, her hair suspiciously black. The gentleman she was with had heavy-framed glasses, a string necktie, and a balding head with strategically combed strands of camouflage.

The man smiled at me. He had his camera out and for a minute I thought he was going to ask if he could take my picture. This happens occasionally. Japanese tourists like to take snapshots of exotic white people in Japan, along with the usual pictures of flora and fauna. High-school yearbooks inevitably have photos of the school trip to Nara and Kyoto, with students posing first beside temple deer and then beside foreign tourists. In both cases, whether they are feeding the deer or feeding the foreigners, the students have the same nervous smiles. Personally, I hate posing for photographs. But no, the man didn't want my photo. He wanted to correct my error.

"You are not doing it properly," he said. "Men must use their left hand when they throw the pebbles. Women may use either, but it is better if they use their left hand also."

So I switched hands. I missed every shot. The crowd around me began chuckling and saying things like, "Jōzu desu ne," and other such derisive comments, so I decided to stop.

The gentleman who had corrected me carefully folded his handkerchief over and dabbed his forehead a few times. The Japanese don't seem to have any sweat glands. I know that sounds like a gross generalization, but it's true. I was sweating like the proverbial pig, beads dripping from my eyebrows, my shirt plastered to my back like a really bad job of wallpapering, and yet this elderly man needed only a few token dabs to mop *his* brow. As usual, I had forgotten to bring a handkerchief. He offered me one of his spares and I wiped my face and neck and forearms, stopping just short of my armpits. We both agreed that it was very hot out. His wife nodded deeply at my astute observations regarding current weather conditions (hot), and I knew that I had been adopted. I wrung out the handkerchief and then reached out to shake their hands. They seemed to hesitate.

"I am Professor Takasugi of Tokyo University," he said, and then paused. When I didn't react, he repeated his introduction. "Tokyo University," he said, and I realized that I was meant to be impressed by this, so I said, "Ah, yes, Tōdai, a great university."

He smiled modestly. "Thank you. My wife, Saori. She is also my assistant. We are in Kyushu for research. We are studying the social life of wild plates."

"Wild plates?"

"Not plates, *monkeys*."

"Ah, yes," I said. "That would make more sense."

The words for plate (*sara*) and monkey (*saru*) sound similar in Japanese, and for some reason I can never keep them straight. And like many Westerners, I also get confused by "human" (*ningen*) and "carrot" (*ninjin*), which once caused a lot of puzzled looks during a speech I gave in Tokyo on the merits of internationalization, when I passionately declared that "*I* am a carrot. *You* are a carrot. We are *all* carrots. As long as we always remember our common carrotness, we will be fine."

On another occasion I scared a little girl by telling her that my favourite nighttime snack was raw humans and dip.

Once Professor Takasugi and I got the wild plate thing sorted out, he explained that he and his wife were planning to travel south, toward Cape Toi, to visit a remote wild monkey island. They invited me along, and even though I was originally headed north, I accepted their invitation. After all, how often is it that you get to see plates in their natural habitat?

8

THE PROFESSOR'S CAR was cluttered with academic detritus. We had to move several boxes filled with loose papers to make a space for me in the back. All the while his wife was nodding with that painfully polite smile that many uninitiated outsiders mistake as being a sign of friendship. It is actually a sign of extreme unease.

Her husband slipped into his professor posture. "The social life of monkeys is very revealing," he said, with the air of a man who has spent his life studying something to the point where he has lost all perspective on its importance. (University does that to you.) "Japanese monkeys," he assured me, "are a unique breed."

He eased his car out of the parking lot. Did I know that Japanese monkeys were the most northerly in the world? No? Did I ever see monkeys in the wild before? No? Well, this would be a very interesting trip for a foreigner such as myself.

I tried to get the Professor to perform a monkey call for me, but he wouldn't take the bait. "I study the social life of monkeys, not communication," he said, so I did my own call and asked him if I was close. His wife giggled behind her hand.

The Professor spoke English exceptionally well, and he was clearly an expert in his field. His wife showed me a book he had written and nodded in deep agreement whenever I complimented him, shutting her eyes as she did so. She wasn't so much a wife as a fan. Unfortunately, I just can't take any bald man seriously when he oils his hair and combs it over, in long mutant strands, across his head. I was in the backseat as well, which didn't help, because I had this hardboiled-egg view of things. Instead of paying attention to the social life of Japanese monkeys, I was more fascinated with the Comb-Over Strategy itself. Do these people really think *anyone* is fooled? Don't they have mirrors? Or is it mirrors that are the problem? Straight ahead in your bathroom mirror must be the only way that combed-over hair looks even remotely natural. And even then, how often do you see people with hair growing horizontally across their forehead? The Japanese, who have a certain flair for comic description, refer to the comb-over look as *bar-code head*, in reference to the bar-code prices in supermarkets. Sitting in the backseat with this uncomplimentary view of a Tokyo University (pause) Professor, I was longing to pass a light wand over his head and see what kind of price would come up.

"And so, you can see how important the social life of the monkey is," he said in conclusion.

"Absolutely," I said.

South of Udo Jingū, the sea was the clouded silver of a shrine mirror. The highway unrolled low along the water, slipping and sliding and falling off the shore entirely at times in a series of bridges and causeways. The mountains crowded in, almost pushing the villages into the sea. Regimented forests, planted generations ago in straight lines for easier cutting, marched up the mountainsides in perfect formation. In Japan, even the trees behave themselves.

The Professor talked to me through the rearview mirror. I talked to the back of his head.

"Japanese monkeys are more advanced than other monkeys," said the Professor. "Foreign monkeys are individualist. They don't get along. But Japanese monkeys have very complicated social something-or-other and blah blah blah blah blah, therefore Japan is unique." (I'm paraphrasing.)

The Professor was a closet nationalist. The academic world of Japan teems with them. I have had experts tell me—straight-faced and sober—that the Japanese use a different side of the brain from other people (which is why the shrill cry of the cicada is a thing of beauty to the Japanese, while Westerners find the insect annoying); that their tongues are shorter (which is why they have trouble pronouncing English words); that their intestines are longer (which is why they have trouble digesting beef, especially foreign beef) and so on. In Professor Takasugi's case, it was monkeys he was interested in but the subtext was clear.

"Japanese monkeys have social patterns that are very different from foreign monkeys'. They prefer stability. Just like the Japanese. In the Oita Monkey Park," said the Professor, "a new leader has taken over. His name is Dragon and he has the respect of six hundred monkeys even though he has only one front paw. He lost the other in a train accident."

"A train accident?"

"That's right. I studied Dragon, and I believe that the experience of losing his paw taught him compassion for the other monkeys. Together with his fighting spirit, he could become leader even though he is handicapped. What does that teach us?"

"Perseverance?"

"Exactly. Now, Dragon's lieutenant is named Schola. Schola is larger and younger than Dragon, and could certainly beat him in a fight, but Schola knows his place and does not challenge the older monkey. Schola does not have a secret ambition for higher office. If a group has a strong leader and sincere lieutenants, the group will have unity and increased power."

"So Japanese monkeys like strong leaders."

"But there is much more to it than that. It is not simply a matter of raw power, as in foreign countries such as yours. In his book *The Frontiers of Monkey Studies*, Professor Tachibana"—he said the name as though I should recognize it—"has shown that the dominant-male theory does not apply to Japanese monkeys. It is more subtle. Professor Tachibana has shown that *consensus* is the key to understanding Japanese monkeys. The monkeys watch the actions of other monkeys very carefully, and when one moves, the others move in synchronized motion. This," he said with a satisfied smile, "resembles the behaviour of people in Japanese society."

I thought the Professor had used up his store of monkey anecdotes, but I was wrong.

"Now then," he said, "up in Shimokita, in northern Japan, it is very cold and the monkeys sit in hot-spring baths, just like Japanese."

I had heard this before, about how Japanese monkeys prefer Japanese-style baths. And a birdwatcher once told me that Japanese snow cranes bow to each other during their mating dance because, well, they are Japanese birds. Apparently, were they American birds they would shake hands instead.

"In Shimokita," the Professor said, "the monkeys form smaller groups. I once watched a monkey, named Momo, die from loneliness and stress. She was separated from her mother and thus could not fit in anywhere. The group rejected her and she died, not because she was hungry but because she was an outcast. It was very sad, even for an objective scientist such as myself."

"Just like the Japanese," I said.

"Pardon?"

"The monkeys in Shimokita," I said. "It's just like Japanese society."

"How do you mean?"

"Keeping strangers outside. The closed circle. Outcasts. The group picking on someone. Individually nice, but often cruel in a group. You know. Like Japanese society."

"That is not like Japanese society at all," he said, his voice brusque.

"But you were just saying it was like—"

"In this case it is completely different."

"No it isn't."

He clenched his jaw. "Completely different. Do you have monkeys in your country?"

"But what does that—"

"Do you?"

"No, I can't say we do."

"I have studied monkeys for more than twenty years. I am a professor at Tokyo University."

"Yes, but—"

"I have been on several government committees. Twelve years ago, Prime Minister Ohira invited me to take part in a Social Economic Committee. My advice on how monkeys organize their society was taken very seriously. I have been on Tokyo urban planning committees as well—as an expert."

That explained a lot. Tokyo certainly appeared to be a city designed by monkey-experts.

"But surely," I persisted, "monkeys and humans are completely different species. I mean, if your point is just that the Japanese people are supposedly some kind of separate race from the rest of us—"

The back of his head was flushed red and he was almost choking on his attempt to respond. I have this innate ability to step on people's toes, especially academic types, and being tossed out of the car and left by the side of a narrow, backwoods road was now a distinct possibility.

Then, just when things were at their tensest, the Professor's wife leaned over and said, with a painfully polite smile, "Can you eat Japanese food?" And for the first time ever, I was glad to hear the question and be back on familiar ground again.

We talked about Japanese food for the rest of the way, agreeing wholeheartedly that foreigners can't possibly eat pickled plums or fermented beans or raw fish or horseradish.

9

THERE ARE TWO ISLANDS. Kojima is the larger one. Torishima is half hidden behind it. Both are home to wild bands of macaque monkeys. At one time the entire Kyushu mainland teemed with them, but human encroachment has left only a few scattered groupings, mostly on remote islands such as these. The monkeys here are some of the least affected by man, and as such are the object of intense study by academics.

A few years ago, the monkeys on Kojima made international news (as far as monkeys go) when it was discovered that the females were *teaching* the younger monkeys how to rinse the sand off their food before they ate it. The monkeys of Torishima, meanwhile, did not rinse their food, so clearly this was not a case of instinct but of taught behaviour, something that was once thought to be the exclusive domain of humans. Then, suddenly, incredibly, the monkeys of Torishima Island began washing their food as well!

This sent the academic world into a tailspin, and teams of researchers descended. How was it possible that such a rare social trait should suddenly appear in two geographically distinct areas? Was there some recessive "food-washing" gene that had only now kicked in? Could the monkeys on Torishima have peered across the water and somehow understood what the other monkeys were doing and then copied them? Could this be some kind of simian extrasensory perception? Or were we witnessing a rare leap from one evolutionary plateau to another? The theories grew and grew, yet the mystery seemed intractable. Someone asked the local fishermen what they thought. "Well," the fishermen replied, "the monkeys do swim back and forth between the islands. Maybe that has something to do with it."

And that was how the Swimming Monkeys of Kojima were discovered. The mystery of the telepathic primates was over. It was
common knowledge to everyone in the area, of course, but it had
taken the Tokyo experts ages to figure it out.

The Professor drove down a narrow-laned road and we came to a
crescent of beach. Across the water was Kojima, a rounded cap of
deep jungle green. A few freelance fishermen were hanging about,
brown-skinned, young, almost lethargic. They exhibited a certain
jungle-cat conservation of energy; they barely moved when we
approached them. The encounter went something like this: The
Professor strides up. He wants a ride out to the island. It can be
arranged, they say. How much? There are shrugs. A price is given. The
Professor tells them that he is from Tokyo University. The fishermen
contain their excitement. The price is repeated. The Professor haggles
with them, first as a group and then one on one. They don't budge.
A professor from Tokyo is no match for a southern Kyushu fisherman.
We pay the initial, unchanged exorbitant fee to take the boat across.

Professor Takasugi was almost belligerent in his offer to cover my
cost, but I declined. It was the only time on the trip that I would
insist on paying my own way. The pilot of our boat was a study in
muscle and sinew. He had a long ponytail and an Errol Flynn moustache. I thought: If pirates attempt to board us on the journey over,
we will be in good hands. Unless of course our captain is a pirate as
well, in which case it is every man for himself.

The boat was paint-peeling white, and the motor was disproportionately loud for such a slow putt-putt of a vessel. Our captain had
to yell to be heard above it.

"There are about ninety monkeys on the island," he shouted.
"They are called the Wisest Monkeys in Japan."

"How so?" I shouted back.

"Well," he said, "they wash their potatoes before they eat them."

I was going to ask him how washing potatoes qualified one as
"wise." I mean, I wash my potatoes all the time but no one refers to
me as being particularly wise. Maybe "the Cleverest Darn Monkeys
in Japan" might be a more accurate title. But I felt I had annoyed
enough people for one day, and I wisely decided to keep my comments to myself. It is one thing to be kicked out of a car, it is quite
another to be kicked out of a boat.

"The monkeys of Kojima are wild, so whatever you do, *don't make eye contact*! If you have any food or drinks or valuables, make sure you leave them on board."

The boat snouted its way up to the slipperiest, roundest boulder the fisherman could find and we climbed out, the waves lifting and dropping the small vessel as we went. "I'll be back to collect you later," he said. He threw the boat into reverse and in a spew of black smoke propelled himself backward like a squid in a cloud of ink.

It was a long, scary scramble along the boulder-toss of Kojima's shoreline to a small clearing on the shore. The monkeys congregated on the beach, enticed out of the jungle by a scattering of seeds, potatoes, and what appeared to be old corn cobs. The monkeys were small—not much bigger than large house cats—grey, short-tailed, and obsessed with fleas.

This was the first time I had seen monkeys without a cage between us. They walked on their knuckles, just like zoo monkeys, and they looked just as smelly. I watched them for a few minutes, and I soon made an important social observation of my own: Monkeys are miserable little bastards. They spent their time biting, screaming, and picking on each other. The hierarchy was continually being reaffirmed, from the gnarly old ruler who prowled the beach looking for smaller monkeys to terrorize, to the toddlers who got battered about by everyone. There was little social interaction that didn't involve cruelty or intimidation; even the ones who were grooming each other were obviously gossiping viciously about their neighbours.

Monkey Harmony is about as smooth as it sounds. Every few seconds somebody would bite someone else and the bitee would run, screeching like a band saw on sheet metal. A barrelful of these vile little creatures would not be fun, it would be mayhem. *Loud* mayhem. I did like the babies; clinging to their mothers in wide-eyed wonder at the world around them, chewing fretfully on leathery nipples and hugging onto mom for dear life whenever one of the mean-spirited males chased their mothers away.

When not fighting, the monkeys crouched around, picking invisible bugs from each other's hair and then chewing them with great exaggerated jaw movements, as though they were eating wads of toffee and not, say, an insect the size of a speck of dust. (Do you even *need* to chew a flea? *Can* you chew a flea? You should be able to swallow the average flea whole, right?)

It was not a very holistic society. Many were picking at their anuses. Occasionally they would flick bum-gunge at each other just for spite. Sometimes they flicked it at us, the viewing public. Bullies and bad personal hygiene: It was high-school gym class all over again.

Not once, the whole time I was there, did I see a single monkey wash a single goddamn potato.

The Professor and his wife were making notes and counting monkeys. I wandered away. The beach had formed as a washout from a small stream, and I followed it back into a tangle of vines. In a clearing I came across an abandoned plyboard building. No one lives on Kojima, so this sway-backed, falling-down structure must have been an old research station.

The vines of the jungle were slowly embracing the shack, tendril-like, and it looked as though one good kick would take it down. A lordly old monkey was sitting on his haunches on the corrugated tin roof, eying me with undisguised hostility. I held his gaze a heartbeat too long and he lunged, teeth bared, with a horrible monkey scream. I fell over myself trying to get away, but it was a bluff and the monkey swaggered off, leaving me alone amid the green-leaf scent of the jungle, drenched in sweat and high on adrenaline.

The forest was thick with must and the smell of wet rot. A tree had fallen across the path, a great waterlogged, fern-festooned rain-forest turd of a tree trunk. And, as I stepped over it, something slithered through the tall grass below—and across my ankle.

I froze, foot raised, arms out, poised like the Karate Kid. I heard a voice squeak from somewhere in my chest, "Oh no." I was trapped, hopelessly trapped, until someone came along and rescued me or until my leg atrophied and fell off. A serpent was somewhere *down there*, near my foot. I stood in premature rigor mortis as my mind frantically flipped through its Rolodex of options. There didn't seem to be many.

I eventually solved my dilemma in the only rational way possible: I ran away without once touching the ground. That's not true, of course. I did touch the ground, but in a quick, high-stepping manner known among native islanders as the Humorous Panic Dance. I also screamed, "Get away get away get away get away get away!" on the off chance that this particular serpent had—freak of nature—evolved ears.

I would have made a piss-poor explorer indeed. The embarrassing thing is, I am a direct descendant (this is true) of Doctor Livingstone, the legendary explorer of "I presume" fame. The good doctor must have been spinning in his grave as his great-great-great-grandson ran screaming in terror not from a snake, but from the *sound* of a snake.

I made a mental note: Highways good, jungles bad. When you are on a highway, snakes get flattened by traffic and you have only to worry about the occasional head-on collision, which—although statistically more of a danger—is nowhere as frightening as the thought of a snake slithering up your pants leg. In most areas of Japan, it is the dreaded *mamushi* you have to watch out for. The other snakes—and there are lots of them—are not dangerous in the least, unless you count fear-induced coronaries. When I asked my fellow teachers how you can tell whether or not a snake is poisonous, they said, easy, just look for small brown circles the size and shape of five-yen coins. I thanked them for the tip and filed it away under "Utterly Useless Information." If they think I am going to get close enough to a snake to be able to recognize pocket change, they have vastly underestimated the power of my phobia.

With my heart still throbbing in my ears, I made my way back to the beach, and boy! wasn't I glad to see the Professor and his wife, and boy! wasn't I interested in what they were doing. "So what are you up to? Collecting monkey poop! Fascinating!" And I stuck to them like glue until the boat returned and took us back to shore.

The Professor and his wife were staying at a hotel farther south, at Cape Toi. To my surprise, they invited me along, though how much of it was simply a sense of duty was hard to say. "You will like Cape Toi," said his wife. "There is a nice view and a lighthouse, and there are wild horses there."

The wild horses of Cape Toi are free-ranging ponies that have grown so tame they eat out of your hand. I remembered Mr. Migita's parting advice ("Make sure you see the horses of Hokkaido!") and it struck me as odd that he found the domestic animals of Japan's far north exotic, while in his own backyard there were semiferal ponies. I suppose it has to do with the way that familiarity breeds myopia;

the people who live around Mount Fuji barely notice it any more. Distance has its own allure—this is what draws the traveller, magnet-like, toward the horizon, and the very fact that Hokkaido is at the other end of Japan from Kyushu must have captivated Mr. Migita.

I had never been to Cape Toi, and I was tempted. Maybe pitch my tent on the grassy highlands. But no, it would have involved too much backtracking. Cape Toi was halfway to Kanoya, and I think Mr. Migita would have been disappointed if I had shown up at his door again, my journey having been one from Cape Sata and then back to Cape Sata. This is the problem with destinations, they take over. They preclude a good deal of serendipity. They override every-thing. Far from being some free-flowing vagabond-type traveller, I was in fact being very linear. My route sliced Japan down the cen-tre. It was almost a straight line. End to End. Cape to Cape. There was something very obsessive about it, but I didn't have the courage to shake myself from my plans, and I said no to the Professor's offer.

They drove away, relieved to have disentangled themselves from being responsible for me, and I sat on the beach and watched the sky darken.

10

DUSK FELL as imperceptibly as dust. The fishermen slipped away, the small fading lights of their boats ineffably sad. As the land cooled, the sea winds began. A moon, half-full, took possession of the sky and, one by one, stars appeared, first Venus and then, slowly, scattered constellations. A single tall palm tree swayed sleepily on the wind like a servant's fan.

I didn't bother with a tent. The sky was clear and I had noticed a small torii gate earlier, marking a path that would lead to a hilltop shrine that could serve as an impromptu shelter, should the rain begin to fall. I had shared a roof with the gods before, and they were always quite accommodating—too accommodating at times. Once, in an Okinawan cloudburst, I sought refuge under a small shrine only to discover that every mosquito, frog, centipede, and lizard within a ten-mile radius had a similar idea. It was a regular creepy-crawly jamboree under there. Surrounded by this annoyance of creatures, I took a long time getting to sleep. Then, just as I was drifting off, a thought occurred to me: *I wonder if snakes mind the rain?* And that was it. I spent the rest of the night in rigid, wide-awake terror, listening to every snap and rustle.

Kojima's beach, fortunately, was far from any viper-infested undergrowth, and I unrolled my sleeping bag without fear. The moon gave the world a pale cast, as though I had fallen into a black-and-white photograph tinted blue. There were monkey cries across the water. I lay on the sand, looking up at the stars, and I could feel the earth turning beneath me. If you listened carefully, you could hear the groan and creak of pulley and rope, turning the earth and all the life that clings to it. In a single, vertigo heartbeat, it felt like I might slip off entirely and free-fall into nothingness.

—

I knew a girl once. Her name was Marion. She came to Japan from Scotland and we travelled through Korea and across the Japanese islands. We hiked along volcanic ridges. We island-hopped across Okinawa. We spent nights like this on empty beaches. We drank a lot of beer. Made a lot of love. And then she left and made her way back to Scotland. She left and I stayed, and that is pretty much where the story ends.

Sometimes I hate Japan. I hate it for not being an easier place to leave. And sometimes I fear that I *have* fallen off the earth. Maybe, when people fall off the earth, Japan is where they land.

It was not that I was lovesick or heartbroken. It was just that, on nights like this, under a full sky of stars, listening to the *ah* and *unn* of waves along an empty beach, on nights like this the mind turns naturally to a Scottish girl with brown hair and a warm smile. At night, when I dream, she is always laughing and turning into the sunlight. And I wake, feeling like a kite returning to earth because the wind it was riding has passed.

A moon, half-empty, had possession of the sky. Distant stars and islands near at hand. I lay there almost till dawn, on a Japanese shore, turning the image of Marion over and over in my mind, like you might with a stone in your hand. The edges blur and the features rub away, until all you are left with are scattered recollections and a vague sense of loss. Not feelings, but the memory of feelings. Longing. Nostalgia. Regrets so sharp they make your chest hurt.

11

I WOKE TO THE SOUND of waves and a sky of soft sakura pink. The morning wind had the smell of freshly washed sheets. In the forest, the birds were having their morning meeting and apparently things had degenerated into insults and name-calling. I sat up, stretched, and tried to flick the sand from my scalp. There was grit in my mouth, between my toes, and stuccoed to my skin. I rubbed my teeth with my fingers: morning breath. After crawling out and shaking my sleeping bag a couple of times, I jumped around trying to rub the sand from my body, but all I achieved in doing this was a kind of accidental aerobics. At least it woke me up.

The waves had receded during the night, and ebb tide had left a wide slope of wet, soft sand. I walked down to the water's edge, peed into the sea. Mused about life.

The forest bird committee abruptly ended discussion, their Bali music jangle stopping as suddenly as if a volume switch was turned off. The seabirds took over, flying in low, turning wide arcs above the water. In the distance, a piston-like chugging could be heard, growing nearer, louder—and then, in a flurry of seagulls, the fishing boats from yesterday reappeared, jostling into position along the pier. The young men turned off the engines and resumed the same postures as before. Strength in reserve. A boredom so intense it bordered on worldly disdain.

"Morning!" I said as I walked down the pier. This elicited a grunt here and a nod there, the most minimal forms of acknowledgement possible.

I wanted directions back to the highway but they were more interested in boat rides. How much to go across? It was half of what they had demanded from the Professor. Maybe it was because they knew me now. Maybe it was because they recognized the Professor's Tokyo accent. It didn't matter. I wasn't interested in visiting the island again.

A tour bus pulled in, crunching gravel under tires. The door slid open and a dozen or so men climbed out. They were members of an agricultural co-op—"potato boys" the fishermen said under their breath—and they were on an outing. A tour guide, with white gloves and a flag, marched them across the ten feet that separated the road from the pier, her flag held high should any of them lose their way. I watched the interaction of the agricultural co-op and the boatmen with interest. Farmers and fishermen, they have so little in common. The Harvest versus the Hunt, the sea versus the seed.

Japan is both fisherman and farmer. It is an island culture, but it also has the patience (and the suspicions) of a farmer: a fascination with seasons, with long-term plans, with harvests. The sea binds them. The fields define them. The cities of Japan are travesties precisely because Japan is still—at heart—an agricultural country. This is changing, of course. The cities are becoming cleaner, greener, more comfortable, and the villages are dying—but it is a slow death, and not an inevitable one. It is de rigueur among the overly romantic to wail and bemoan the death of the Japanese village, but Japan is simply finding a new equilibrium. The elegies are premature; there is strength in reserve.

The farmers were having trouble getting on the boats as the sea rocked and tilted them. The motors began with great bronchial coughs, and the fishermen's sons backed their beasts away from the pier. "There are about ninety monkeys on the island," I heard the fishermen begin, shouting over the motors. "They are called the Wisest Monkeys in Japan." And then, before anyone could ask: "They wash their potatoes before they eat them."

12

THE GLORY of the Japanese house is its roof. Heavy tiles; curved eaves; the embedded figures of Ebisu, God of Fishermen, and Daikoku, God of Farmers; dolphin-like tigerfish, backs arched to ward off lightning strikes: Japanese rooftops, at least the traditional ones that you encounter outside of the cities, are magnificent. The interlocking tiles are kept in place not by mortar but by design; when one tile goes, others soon begin to drop away, exposing the clay and straw beneath.

There is a fear in Japan that Japanese society is a tiled rooftop, held in place by the careful position of each member, that if one falters the entire structure starts to give way. It isn't true, of course. But the effectiveness of a fear has nothing to do with its reality. The tiles, held in place like standing waves, are stronger than they look. On older rooftops, moss and grasses grow, weeds, even the occasional batch of wildflowers.

These rooftops are liquid in design, but heavy in their mass. They transform even the humblest Japanese house into a castle. (At times, I suspect that the main purpose of the house itself is just to hold up and best display the roof.) Homes in Japan are even built from the rooftops down, without central support beams, in a design that has been described as "a book balanced on top of pencils." In many Western countries, the top-heavy nature of Japanese homes would not pass building regulations. But when the earthquakes rumble through Japan, they topple highway overpasses and split concrete, but the small, top-heavy wooden homes sway drunkenly and remain standing.

Japanese homes crowd the very edge of city streets. They squeeze in, cheek-by-jowl, almost wall-to-wall. Alleyways, only an arm's length wide, run between them. Neighbourhoods are a labyrinth of one-lane streets, narrow divides, dead ends. The Japanese usually cite the high cost of land for this closely packed effect, but there are other reasons at work. A typical Japanese village is surrounded by open, inviting areas: forests, rice fields, hills. But rather than spread the houses out and give everyone some elbow room, the Japanese wedge their homes into thickly clustered packs, as though huddled together for protection. The rice fields form a moat of green around them, and the Japanese live in each other's laps.

It is a habit born partly from geography—the fjords of the coastline naturally encourage villages to be clustered into coves. But it is also something else. The design of Japanese villages is born of a need that the West has largely disregarded as weak: the need for human company and the sadness of being left alone. In the West, we fear *insignificance*. In Japan, they fear *loneliness*. It is in this broad sense that Japan is described as being feminine and the West masculine. In the West we are obsessed with individuality. It makes us strong—in a very limited sense of the word—but like any commitment to an ideal it also requires a sacrifice. And what we have sacrificed in the West is our sense of belonging. In Japan, it is *privacy* that has been sacrificed. And it is this privacy that the Japanese home seeks to reclaim.

Japanese homes are often disproportionately large for the amount of land they occupy. It's the yards that are small, not the homes. Given a plot of land, the Japanese approach is to enclose as much space as possible within it. The yard, if it can be called one, is often a mere fringe of grass or a tiny miniature garden tucked in between the driveway and the front wall. In Japan the yard is still a semi-public place, and leaving it open is like making your house a public arena. Better to set the limits of your privacy as far as you can. You will often see houses along riverbanks cantilevered precariously over the river, trying to maximize the space contained even at the risk of losing it all. Japanese homes tend to slide into rivers a lot.

Even the entranceway of a home is not a completely private space. Salesmen, visitors, bill collectors, and metermen all step right into your entry unannounced. The entrance of a Japanese home is built on street level, that dirty, littered, lower *public* world. The private and the personal is above it. You step *up* from the entrance. The entire house is built on a higher level, and the rudest salesman in Japan, although he thinks nothing of barging right into your home, would never dream of stepping *up* uninvited. This is also why you take off your shoes. One leaves behind the dust of the world when you enter a home. You step up, you rise above.

There are more mundane reasons as well. Japanese homes are elevated because they are built for summer. The walls slide open, and the home opens like a magician's box to allow summer breezes and night winds to blow through. The raised floor provides a cool pocket of shade for the house to rest upon. Unfortunately, these same houses are horribly cold and drafty in winter. There is no such thing as insulation, and the floors are like sheets of dry ice. Any nation that chooses sliding paper walls over drywall and fibreglass insulation is not a nation that minds the cold. In most of Japan, it is the summer heat and humidity that are the real enemies. A sealed, thick-walled Western home would trap the moisture in and rot clothes in the closet. Japanese homes breathe.

I was standing on a corner in a tumble-down neighbourhood of Nango Town, admiring just such a home. Nango is a typical southern Japanese community, arranged without rhyme or reason, with the buildings flush against the main highway. Narrow alleyways lead off into hidden neighbourhoods, and the heavy-tiled rooftops are so close together they form a canopy.

The house I was standing in front of had a secret garden of bonsai trees and, in the absence of rides or even traffic, I had stopped to admire this tiny forest. Bonsai has been called the world's slowest sculpture. Living pine trees, their growth stunted by bound roots, they exist in miniature perfection, handed down from generation to generation. The technique came from China, but it is in Japan that it reached its apex.

That the Japanese have a special relationship with nature is one of the most misunderstood aspects of the culture. The Japanese do have a deep relationship with nature, but it is not with the wild, chaotic, untamed forces we think of in the West. It is nature controlled, contoured, perfected; this is what the Japanese mean when they speak of a love of nature.

I was standing there, captivated by this miniature forest, when a door slid open. It was the woman of the house; she had been watching me for some time. I said, "Good afternoon," and she returned my greeting, using the local dialect. I am always flattered when this happens, when they just assume I belong in this area, that I can understand the language of this valley, this island, this neighbourhood. Japan is like Britain in its rich variety of dialect and accent, and the Japanese spoken in southern Kyushu is an earthy one. I answered in dialect, or at least the little of it I knew, and she laughed, her eyes disappearing into crinkles.

"Your husband's bonsai is beautiful," I said. Although I did not know who shaped these trees, I knew that bonsai is a very male art. In Japan, women generally arrange flowers, men arrange trees.

She invited me inside for tea. I accepted and stepped up, removing my shoes. The house was cool and dark, but the main room looked as though it had been ransacked in years past and never straightened up. Corners were filled with folded newspapers, books piled in random stacks, clothes half-folded and forgotten, absently left bowls and cups and photo albums and bric-a-brac. It was like a museum that had been turned upside down and given a couple of good shakes.

The dust was as thick as dryer lint. The tatami mats were faded and soft underfoot. They had long since lost that fresh green scent of cut grass; many were threadbare and splitting at the seams. The walls were adorned with grandchildren's crayon art. The screens on the sliding doors were tattered, patched here and there with newer, whiter squares of paper.

This lady, alone in her disheveled home, was nonetheless wearing a freshly starched apron and a clean dress, as though she were expecting company at any time. She herself was perfectly graceful. I always feel like such a great ungainly mess of a person in Japan, a sweaty bull in a forest of deer, and whenever I return to North America I am surprised at how loud, large, and disorderly everyone seems. It's great. It's liberating to be back in my element. But it also increases my discomfort when I return to Japan—as I always do—and find that once again I am this clumsy, unwieldy figure, shirt untucked, shopping bags in disarray, hair uncombed, groping for a handkerchief that I do not have.

The lady who invited me into her home was so small it felt as though I were conversing with a hand puppet. We sat at the hearth and she stirred the ash in the fire pit. A cast-iron teakettle was suspended by a large hook—and even this was heavy with dust. She tilted hot water into a ceramic teapot, and we waited for the tea to steep. This is the most beautiful sentence in Japan. *The tea steeps.* A smell of topsoil and perfume rises up. It tastes the way that rice fields smell. And the final swallow, where the powder collects in the bottom, is also the most bitter.

In the adjoining sun parlour, she showed me further forests of bonsai. "The bonsai outside are in process. These are complete. His grandfather's." A pine tree clung to boulder, its trunk twisted, its branches curved by an imaginary wind.

"*Oi!*" It was the husband returning. He saw my boots in the entrance, but he wasn't prepared for a foreign face in his house. He recovered his decorum remarkably well.

"American, eh? What brings you to Nango?" He was wearing a spotlessly clean white undershirt and a pair of polyester jogging pants—there must be more polyester jogging pants per capita in Japan than anywhere else in the world. I liked him because he was unapologetically bald. His hair was combed straight back, defiantly; no comb-over camouflage here. A retired rice farmer, he was also an artist.

I admired his bonsai. He thanked me. I persisted. He thanked me again. There was one tree, a young one, still unshaped, that I particularly liked. I went on and on. His smile tightened. It really is a beautiful bonsai, I said, and then, before I knew it, I had gone too far.

"Please," said his wife. "Please take it. It is our present."

"No! Really, I just like it, that's all."

She persisted. "It is our present to you. Please."

Her husband was smiling as though someone were slowly tightening a vise on his nuts. His wife continued in her efforts to give me the tree, and he kept trying to throw her some of those *ah unn* non-verbal understandings, but she was oblivious. "I'm sure you would want him to have it, wouldn't you, dear? Such a nice young foreigner, travelling so far. It will make a nice memory of Nango. I can wrap it for you. It's very light. No, I'm sure my husband doesn't mind."

Fortunately, I managed to outlast her, and the man did not have to hand over one of his beloved bonsai. I always forget that in Japan complimenting something highly is good manners, but complimenting *too long* is gauche. True, no one is going to hand over his family sword or giant-screen Sony just because you keep prattling on about how much you like them, but he will be annoyed at the hints you are dropping, and as a hitchhiker, when you lose the goodwill of the people, you lose everything.

The husband in turn tried to give me one of his wife's flower-arranging vases. It was her turn to smile tightly, but I managed to decline his gift. The wife then offered me a ride out of Nango with her husband, and he graciously offered to have his wife make a box lunch for me. I half expected her to up the ante by offering me one of her husband's gold teeth, but it didn't come to that. They were a good couple, not exactly *ah* and *unn*, but close enough.

13

"GOODBYE, GAIJIN-SAN," said the lady of the house, bowing from the driveway as her husband and I drove away. "Goodbye and thank you."

There was a time I would have rankled over someone calling me *gaijin-san*. The word *gaijin* means "outsider," and is derived from the term *gai-koku-jin*, "outside-country-person." When the suffix *-san* is added to *gaijin*, it means Mr. Outsider. This was how the lady in Nango referred to me. Most Japanese insist that the word *gaijin* is strictly an abbreviated form with no undertone of racism intended, but they are wrong. Like *gringo*, the word *gaijin* has an edge to it. And when I ask my Japanese friends how they would feel if I were to refer to them in a similarly abbreviated form—*Jap*—their jaws harden and they insist that it is not the same thing.

Like most visible minorities living in Japan, I went through a hypersensitive phase. It happens after the initial euphoria has worn off and you realize, "Hey! Everyone is talking about me! And they're looking at me. What do they think I am, some kind of foreigner or something!"

We become Gaijin Detectors. It's like a silent dog whistle. It got so I could detect a whispered, "Look, a gaijin!" across a crowded street, and spin and glare simultaneously at everyone within a fifty-mile radius.

Even when I could understand the language, I ran into problems. The word for the inner altar of a Shinto shrine sounds exactly like *gaijin*. I remember visiting a shrine in Kyoto and having a tour group come up behind me. The tour guide pointed in my direction and said, "In front of us, you can see the *inner altar*. This *inner altar* is very rare, please be quiet and show respect. No photographs. Flashbulbs can damage the *inner altar*." Except, of course, I didn't hear *inner altar*, I heard *foreigner*. It was a very surreal moment.

Looking back, the biggest culture shock about Japan was not the chopsticks or the raw octopus, it was the shock of discovering that no matter where you go you instantly become the topic of conversation. At first it's an ego boost. You feel like a celebrity. "Sorry, no autographs today, I'm in a hurry." But you soon realize that in Japan foreigners are not so much celebrities as they are objects of curiosity and entertainment. It is a stressful situation, and it has broken better men than me.

And yet it seems so petty when you put it down on paper: They look at you, they laugh when you pass by, they say "Hello!" They say "Foreigner!" They even say "Hello, Foreigner!" But it's like the Chinese water torture. It slowly wears you down, and this relentless interest has driven many a foreigner from Japan.

It is still fairly mild. I tried to imagine what would happen if the tables were turned. I think of my own hillbilly hometown in northern Canada, and I wonder what kind of greeting the beetle-browed, evolutionarily challenged layabouts at the local tavern would give a lone Japanese backpacker who wandered into their midst.

I still hate the word *gaijin* and I still hate it when people gawk at me or kids follow, shouting, "Look, a gaijin! A gaijin!" But I have also learned an important distinction, and one that has made a huge difference to my sanity. It was explained to me by Mr. Araki, a high-school teacher I once worked with. "Gaijin means outsider. But *gaijin-san*," he insisted, "is a term of affection." Sure enough, once I started paying closer attention to who was saying *gaijin* and who was saying *gaijin-san*, I discovered that Mr. Araki was right. *Gaijin* is a label. *Gaijin-san* is a role.

In Japan, people are often referred to not by their name but by the role they play. Mr. Policeman. Mr. Post Office. Mr. Shop Owner. As a foreigner, you in turn play your role as the Resident Gaijin, like the Town Drunk or the Village Idiot. You learn to accept your position, and even take it as an affirmation that you do fit in—albeit in a very unsettled way—and you begin to enjoy Japan much more.

14

Ms. Mayumi Tamura and Ms. Akemi Fujisaki were on their way into the city to see a concert by a Japanese rock band called Blue Hearts. Mayumi and Akemi were young, high-spirited women, and together we managed to wedge my pack and my oversize self into the backseat of their Incredible Shrinking Car (it seemed to grow smaller and smaller as we drove). My knees were resting under my jaw. Akemi turned around to talk with me as Mayumi pulled out onto the highway and pointed us toward Miyazaki City.

Initially they wanted to talk about Japanese pop music, but my knowledge was limited to a handful of names. I asked them if Blue Hearts was a popular band. No, not really. Did they like Blue Hearts? No, not really. Then, laughing at my puzzled look, they explained that there was so little to do down here in this southern corner of Japan, so few distractions, that they take what they can get.

I asked them if they were good friends, and their eyes met, almost slyly, and a smile passed between them. "Best friends." Akemi reached over, lightly, and touched Mayumi's hand.

Great. I'd caught a ride with Thelma and Louise. Which was fine, as long as they didn't go driving off a cliff.

Mayumi, the driver, could speak English. She studied it with a determined passion, fitting her studies in during afternoons and work breaks and free evenings. She was a maid at an inn near Cape Toi. She was single, female, and gainfully employed—which in Japan translates as "world traveller." One of the acute ironies of the Japanese corporate-male philosophy is that the men of Japan do not have much time to enjoy themselves on extended holidays. Young women, on the other hand, may be underpaid and underappreciated, but in many ways they have more freedom. Their work is rarely their life, and it is they who are Japan's new breed of traveller. The men of Japan are lousy travellers and even worse expatriates. The women, in contrast, are more aware of the world: less xenophobic, more adventurous.

This newfound worldliness of Japanese women has also been partly responsible for a phenomenon known as "the Narita divorce." It begins during the honeymoon, when the young husband discovers—to his eternal chagrin—that his new wife is more sophisticated, more self-assured, and more at ease in a foreign country than he is. He also discovers that his samurai prerogatives are meaningless once he leaves the maternal bosom of Japan. The young wife, in turn, notices how *un*worldly, how bumbling, how *inept* her husband is, and by the time they get back to Narita International Airport in Tokyo, they can't stand the sight of each other. Fortunately, in Japan the marriage certificate is not usually signed until long after the ceremony, often not until the honeymoon is over. This acts like an escape clause. A couple returning from their disastrous first trip abroad can part ways at Narita, never to see each other again, and the marriage is effectively annulled.

Mayumi had travelled through Canada and Europe, and she was now planning a trip to London—and this time she was taking Akemi. The relationship between Mayumi and Akemi was, to a certain extent, one of *senpai* to *kōhai*, senior to junior, teacher to student. In Japan, absolute equality between two people is very rare. One person is always older or better-trained or more knowledgeable. This is true everywhere in the world, but nowhere is it quite so entrenched as in Japan, where the senpai/kōhai system is the basis of virtually every relationship. It is not always apparent, but the more attuned you become to the nuances of relationships in Japan, the more often you see it. The senpai/kōhai system is not meant to be an antagonistic master/serf relationship, though it does degenerate into this at times. More properly, it is the sense of a chain of knowledge being transmitted from one to another. In the case of martial arts or company training, the position is explicit, but even among friends there is usually an unstated understanding of who is to be the senpai and who is to be the kōhai. (And every kōhai naturally aspires to becoming a senpai one day.) Everyone in Japan is entangled—or nurtured,

depending on your bias—in an interconnecting web of uneven relationships, here the senpai, here the kōhai.

In Mayumi and Akemi's case, their friendship easily divided into
senpai (Mayumi) and kōhai (Akemi). Mayumi was the same age as
Akemi, but she had travelled more, done more, seen more. It wasn't
a matter of Mayumi dominating Akemi, it was simply a rapport that
they—like most Japanese—felt comfortable slipping into. Just as
Americans feel most at ease with unpretentious jocularity.

Mayumi and Akemi were a society of two. They had a secret map
that would take them away. They told me far more about themselves
than they really ought to (and more than I feel comfortable divulging).
When you are a hitchhiker, people spill their lives into your lap. Things
they would never tell their family they gladly surrender to a hitchhiker
precisely because the hitchhiker is a stranger, a fleeting guest, a temporary confidant. But there is also something about the physical position; there is little eye contact. Drivers watch the road and you talk
with parallel vision, without the extended face-to-face of normal conversations. It is almost like talking to someone at night in bed, when
the voices are disembodied and anything seems possible.

A sea change is under way, and Japanese women are the ninja
saboteurs. In Japan it is not a revolution, but sedition. It is not about
confrontation, but subterfuge. Together, Mayumi and Akemi were
charting a course. A trip to Britain and then a journey through
Europe, a change of jobs, whispers of work abroad. Secret passages.
Hidden dens. Escape.

Mayumi was unfolding the world for Akemi, like a glass gift in
layers of silk. I imagine that courtesans once opened the world for
their younger novices in much the same way. It is a sensual discovery to find yourself stepping from an isolated island into a global
bazaar of experiences and possibilities. Akemi had that impatient
panic of people on the verge of something new. It is like a first kiss,
this journey abroad, and she twisted in her seat, almost breathless,
and asked me about the world.

She wanted my advice about British society. Not being British,
I gave it. (It is one of those wonderful perks about being a foreigner
in Japan that you are accepted as an expert on everything from
Australian koalas to American gun laws.)

"Is Britain really so foggy?"

"Yes, very foggy," said I, suddenly an expert on fog and all things mist-related.

"But how can people breathe if it is so foggy?"

"Well, they're British, you see. Used to it."

"Is Britain safe?"

Mayumi answered this one, speaking in near exasperation. "Of course it's safe, I told you that many times. The world is not as dangerous as Japanese think."

But Akemi wanted to hear it from me. "Is it *really* safe?"

"Well," said I, "it *is* safe. Not as safe as Canada, of course, but still fairly safe, in a foggy British sort of way." And on I went, building up steam, flinging out cultural traits and pontificating about national tics, with Akemi all but taking notes as I went. When we exhausted Britain we moved on to France and then Switzerland—a country that I have not technically visited. Not that this stopped me.

"The Swiss are a very tidy people," I assured them.

By one of those odd quirks of life, it turned out that Mayumi and I had a mutual acquaintance: Paul Berger. Paul is a wry, perpetually perplexed New York exile who wrote his own book on Japan, *The Kumamoto Diary*.

"I met Paul in the Rock Balloon," said Mayumi. "Do you know the Rock Balloon? It's in Kumamoto City."

Do I know the Rock Balloon? The Rock Balloon is a "gaijin bar," where debauched foreign reprobates drink cheap beer and dance themselves into hormonic frenzies as they pursue equally debauched Japanese. Of *course* I know the Rock Balloon.

I tried to get some dirt on Paul—maybe he had tried to cruise Mayumi with a line about being Paul Simon's shorter brother, or maybe she poured her drink on his head and slapped his face or something—but no, Paul had been a perfect gentleman.

"He did talk a lot about spiders," she said. "There were giant spiders in his apartment. He was very afraid." (Paul has this irrational fear of spiders. It's embarrassing. Fortunately for Paul, I would never take it upon myself to expose this phobia of his in public.)

"So did he say anything about his bed-wetting problem?" I asked.

"Does he have one?"

"No. But I just thought I'd check."

15

MIYAZAKI IS A CITY of sighs. It carries a sense of faded grandeur. It was once the Budget-Minded Honeymoon Capital of Japan, a poor man's Guam. Guam in turn is a poor man's Hawaii, making Miyazaki a city twice removed from greatness. It is a city of also-rans, a favourite haunt of cardsharks and small-time mountebanks, a place for people starting over. Palm trees line the main streets. There are sad, romantic storefronts and bridal suite ads. (The hotels are still flogging the Honeymoon Horse, long after the beast has died.)

Miyazaki has the highest per capita number of gambling casinos in Japan. The game of choice is pachinko, a form of self-hypnosis, wherein people sit in loud, smoky, painfully lit parlours and feed silvery ball bearings into a spring-loaded trigger. The trigger sends the balls up, into the board—a kind of vertical pinball machine, but without the interactive quality that redeems pinball. The players watch, slack-jawed, cigarettes dangling from their bottom lips, as the ball bearings cascade down the board. The name is derived from the *pa-ching!* noise the balls make, a racket that echoes constantly through the parlours. It is the passion of prostitutes. There is exaggerated excitement, loud bells, and lights, and in the end a faintly dissatisfied feeling. You can almost hear the pachinko boards cooing, "Oh, yes, do it to me, baby. Gimme more."

Pachinko parlours are the scourge of the modern Japanese landscape. They are also the mirages of the city nightlife. You see their eye-catching Las Vegas signs a mile away, and they draw you in. They look exciting from afar, but as you approach you realize, *Damn!* It's just another pachinko parlour. The doors open, the place is deafening. The "Imperial Navy March" rouses the air, and the sound of balls bouncing down the boards has a stock-market frenzy about it—until you see the people, numb, transfixed. It's like walking into a bad zombie movie.

Miyazaki City is Pachinko Central. Akemi shrugs. What else is there to do in Miyazaki? I assume it is a rhetorical question. There is nothing else to do in Miyazaki, save the occasional Blue Hearts concert or overpriced disco.

Still, you have to love this city. It is like your favourite aunt, the one with the raspy voice and vodka breath, the one who has been divorced four times, the one who dates younger men. Jaded, slouch-shouldered, rough around the edges, but still able to turn heads. I liked Miyazaki in the same way some people like taverns and smoky pool halls.

The palm trees and wide boulevards, the scent of distant sea, and the faint taste of salt water and whiskey sours: Miyazaki reminds me of Miami, but without the handguns or shiploads of narcotics or Cuban exiles or ethnic tensions or—on second thought, Miyazaki is nothing like Miami. But both cities do share that same sun-bleached feel, where the colours fade into pastel shades of neglect and where the people are grateful for a breeze.

It was a muggy day in downtown Miyazaki, which is to say, things were normal. Once again, I was doing my impression of the Amazing Melting Man, the sweat as slick as oil on my skin. Mayumi and Akemi dabbed at their foreheads with handkerchiefs. They agreed that it was very hot out today. The cherry trees in Miyazaki seemed wilted, the flowers hung down like beads of perspiration, and when Mayumi and Akemi offered to take me to the park for cherry blossom viewing, I opted for draft beer and air conditioning instead.

Mayumi found a shop specializing in Chicken Nanban, Miyazaki's local dish. Chicken Nanban was, the shop owner told us with a certain amount of misplaced pride, invented right here in Miyazaki, though how much work went into thinking up fried chicken with mayonnaise is debatable. Every area of Japan boasts its local specialty. In northern Shimokita, it is wild boar meat. In Morioka, it is small mouthfuls of noodles, tossed back in what becomes more of a contest than a meal. In my own home prefecture of Kumamoto, the main dish is *basashi*, which is—this is true—raw horsemeat. As Paul Berger noted, the only problem Westerners have

with eating raw horsemeat is that (a) it is horsemeat, and (b) it is raw.
The first time I had basashi was at my welcome party, when I had
just arrived in Kumamoto. I asked one of the teachers what it was
I was eating and he struggled for a moment, and then said, in careful English, "This is a horse." I gently corrected him. "No, Mr.
Suzuki, in English it is called *cow*." He frowned and said, "No,
horse." And then he whinnied and imitated the sound of a galloping
horse by slapping his hands against his lap. "Horse," he said again.
But of course by that time I was already in the toilet with a finger
down my throat attempting to redeem my meal ticket, so to speak.

Where the other regions of Japan specialize in gourmet dishes such
as horsemeat or rolled seaweed, only Miyazaki has claimed Chicken
Nanban, the Big Mac of Japanese food. Poor Miyazaki. Even its
cuisine is second-rate.

Not that Chicken Nanban isn't tasty. It is. It is a popular dish
across Japan, and every take-out shop and box-lunch emporium has
Chicken Nanban on the menu. It is almost a staple of family restaurant chains such as Sunny-Land and Joy-Full. The name *nanban* is
from the characters for "south" and "barbarian," and it refers to the
Jesuit missionaries who landed in southern Japan in the sixteenth
century. Apparently these Portuguese missionaries, and the traders
who followed them in, were fond of fried chicken. Later, Dutch merchants introduced the concept of mayonnaise. Together, this gives us
Chicken Nanban—or more properly, "Barbarian-style Chicken."
That's right, barbarian.

You may want to pause a moment and wonder what sort of reaction
you might get in the West if you opened a restaurant offering "Jap
Noodles" or "Yellow Menace Sushi." The fact that restaurant chains
in Japan don't think twice about labelling a dish "Barbarian-style"
says a lot about Japanese sensitivity to outsiders—or their lack
thereof. Mind you, I suppose it could have been worse. They might
have named it Big-Nosed, Round-Eye, Butter-Smelling, Couldn't-
Make-a-Car-to-Save-Their-Life Chicken.

Mayumi, Akemi, and I finished our meal and said goodbye on the
walking mall outside the restaurant. The concert was starting soon,
though neither of them seemed thrilled about seeing any band
named "Blue Hearts."

16

HIGHWAY 10 north of Miyazaki City is one long extended aggravation of traffic lights and intersections. I walked forever. My tongue was thick with the taste of oil, diesel, and dust, and the traffic rattled by with bone-jarring persistence. At one point, above the haze of exhaust and cat's cradles of telephone wires I saw the Statue of Liberty advertising a muffler shop or a pachinko parlour. Or maybe it *was* the Statue of Liberty. Maybe I was hallucinating. Carbon monoxide will do that to you. To make matters worse, I was using a backpack apparently designed by astronauts. It had hooks and pulleys and compartments, and no matter what I did, it wouldn't sit straight. I began pulling straps at random, and it lurched on my back like a drunken sailor.

Rush hour came and went like a slow swell of ocean, but eventually a polished red sports car, low along the road like a hovercraft, pulled over. This car *purred*. Inside was a worried-looking man in a chef's jacket.

"Are you lost?"

"Not exactly."

"Where are you going?"

"Hokkaido."

I knew it was a long shot that he would be going all three thousand kilometres to Hokkaido. "I'll take you to the next town," he said. "That's as far north as I'm going."

Fair enough. I got in. There were plastic covers on all the seats, and when I started squirming about, trying to work my backpack onto my lap, he quickly offered to store it in the trunk. I stuffed it in beside a set of golf clubs.

"Do you play golf?" he said hopefully, and it just went downhill from there.

. The man behind the wheel was a chef named Kenichi Inada who had two great passions in life, neither of which had anything to do with cooking. His passions were (a) golf and (b) cars (more specifically *his* car). Now, I can hold my own in any Japanese conversation that concerns the weather, drinking, or chopsticks, but cars and golf are complete blanks to me. I can't even discuss them in English, let alone Japanese. When Kenichi asked me what kind of automobile I liked, I said "Blue." Pushed for more detail I said "Two-door." Yup, I would have to say that when it comes to automobiles I am a blue, two-door kind of man. Kenichi looked at me with an are-you-sure-you-are-really-a-guy? type of look. Then he asked about golf, and all I could contribute was that famous quip about golf being a good stroll ruined. I do not believe this endeared me to Kenichi.

His face had the creased good looks of a farmer, and he used polite Japanese, which was a nice change from all the "Hey you's!" and "Gaijin!" that had hounded me during my stay in Miyazaki. Unfortunately, he and I had zilch in common except for my needing a ride and his offering one. He was a hard man to faze. When I told him I was going to the very end of Japan he didn't blink, and when I told him I was following the Cherry Blossom Front he reacted as if it was the most common, sensible thing to do. It took the wind right out of my sails. So I started exaggerating.

"I might even continue across Russia." No reaction. "Maybe hitchhike through the Gobi desert. Hard, that, what with there being no cars or anything." No reaction. "Probably have to hitch rides on camels." Still no reaction.

He was more interested in explaining why his car was the best self-propelled piece of internal combustion on the road today. This involved a lot of technical car words that may well have been borrowed from English but which I wouldn't have recognized even if they were. It was a case of competing obsessions, dueling monologues: I would talk about cherry blossoms and he would nod and pretend to be interested, and then he would talk about dual-exhaust piston joints and I would nod and pretend to be interested.

For all his love of cars, Kenichi was an unusually cautious driver. We crept along well under the speed limit, and he'd begin braking miles ahead of any intersection. All that automotive power and he was afraid to use it. I tried to get him to open 'er up and see how fast she'd fly, but he said no. Then I asked him if I could drive. No. Are you sure? Yes. But I promise I'll be good. (I didn't actually have a driver's licence, but I didn't see the point in bothering him with such minor details.) There was a noticeable chill in the air after I made my third, summarily rejected request to take his car for "a little spin."

He dropped me off on an open stretch of highway west of Sadowara. We dutifully shook hands and exchanged addresses. He gave me his number and said, "If you have any trouble—if you become lost or if you want to play a round of golf or something—give me a call. Ask for Chef Inada."

"Thanks. And if you ever want to talk about haiku or cherry blossoms, that kind of thing, here's my number." I stepped back and looked down the highway that unrolled before me like tickertape. "Do you think I'll make it? You know, to Hokkaido."

"No. Japanese people don't stop for hitchhikers."

"Maybe I should *golf* my way across Japan instead."

And for the first time, his eyes brightened at the mention of my travels. "Wouldn't that be something?" he said, and you could see that he was picturing it in his head. "A round of golf on every course in Japan. That would be something, wouldn't it? You should do it and write a book about it."

He was still smiling as he drove—cautiously—away, the plastic seat covers shining in the sun.

My next ride was with a wiry young man named Kiminori Maruyama, who was impossibly thin and so grinningly young that he reminded me of my high-school students, even though he was several years out of school. Kiminori was driving a battered old box of a truck. I wasn't sure what the cargo was, but I thought what the hell, a gun runner or drug carrier might make a nice change of pace, so I climbed up and in.

He creaked open the door of his truck and shoved aside the take-out coffee cups, work gloves, and dust-bedeviled newspapers without so much as an arched eyebrow.

"Travelling, are you?" and he told me about his own long-distance hauls. Why, just last year he drove five thousand kilometres in one week, a solo trip from Tokyo to Nagasaki and back again.

"For business?" I asked.

"No, no," he assured me. "Strictly for pleasure."

He was completely discouraging about my own travel plans. There will, he assured me, be absolutely *no* rides once I got past Nobeoka, the next town up the road. It is empty up there. Just forests and hills. Nope, he didn't like my odds. Japanese simply do not pick up hitchhikers. Sure, *he* stopped, but that is just because he is a traveller himself and he understands my position. Why, just last year he drove from Osaka to Kitakyushu in nine hours flat. Not bad, eh? And another time he did a Tokyo–Aomori loop, solo. Straight through. Only stopped for gas and meals. No, no, it wasn't for business. It was a holiday.

Kiminori, it turned out, wasn't a professional truck driver. He worked for a pachinko parlour. When I caught a ride with him he was transporting a bunch of defective pachinko games (people kept winning on them) to a service centre in Nobeoka City where they would be, ahem, "repaired."

"My family"—he used the affectionate term for company—"is Twenty-First Seiki Pachinko. Do you know it?"

How could I not. They tore down a row of wonderfully dilapidated old shops in the middle of Minamata, the city where I lived, and they put up a sprawling Vegas-size monstrosity, with eye-socket-aching fluorescent lights and polished chrome. Brash. Big. Loud. Soulless. I know Twenty-First Seiki very well. I kept waiting for social activists and placard-waving protesters to picket the construction site, but no one ever did, and the heart of my sad tumbledown little city had another large bite taken from it. The word *seiki* means "century" in Japanese, and in some ways I suppose these towering, sleek, soulless buildings are the harbingers of the new millennium.

"Yes," I said. "I know Twenty-First Seiki. There is one where I live." He was pleased to hear it. His family was very big, they were everywhere.

—

Nobeoka City was to be my Waterloo. At least, that was how Kiminori saw it. He took me to the intersection nearest the Akadama Phoenix Pachinko. "You'll never catch a ride," he said with a cheery smile. I adjusted my backpack and tried not to snarl at him.

The last ride of the day, and the one that would take me straight through to the ferry port at Saiki, was with an older gentleman named Hiro Koba. He sighed more often than is normal and when I asked him about his work he said, "What's to tell?"

He was returning from a long day on the road, and he seemed tired, bone weary. "It's the job," he said. "I'm having a bit of trouble adjusting to it. I don't really belong down here. I'm from central Japan. Nagoya City. They have a castle there, with golden fish on top, do you know it? It's a beautiful castle. A reconstruction, of course. The war—well, you understand."

The highway north of Nobeoka ran through steep forests of evergreen and cedar. The heat wave that had stalked me the previous few days had ended and the sky was a softer shade of blue. We passed a temple, a side road, and a fleeting glimpse of cherry blossoms, faint against the green.

More than one hundred different strains of cherry tree grow in Japan. If you add the carefully crossbred substrains the number rises to three hundred. Some sakura are tufted like miniature chrysanthemums (*yae-zakura*), others grow on thin branches, in tight clusters (*Edohigan-zakura*). Some weep like willows (*shidare-zakura*). Some are tiny and delicate (*chōji-zakura*), others are garish and red (*kanhi-zakura*). Some sprout wildflowers from their trunks, others move on the wind like curtains. Some foam over like champagne, some grow in a web of tendrils. Some tumble early, some tumble late. Some tower high and lean, others are short and squat. Their trunks range from finger widths to gnarled girths more than eleven metres around. Some grow beyond their own strength and have to be propped up with wooden crutches to stop the branches from cracking. Hundreds have been designated gods and encircled with shimenawa ropes and honoured at shrines. Others have been designated Natural National Treasures. All are sakura.

The standard sakura (*somei-yoshino*) is not a natural blossom, but was crossbred from different strains to produce an artificially high number of blossoms per tree. This is why most Japanese insist that cherry blossoms in Japan are more beautiful than anywhere else in the world; they were created to be more beautiful. And yet, although these trees have now taken over the Japanese imagination, they are a relatively new addition, dating from the Meiji Period (1867–1912). Today, it is the man-made somei-yoshino that most people think of when they speak of cherry blossoms—when the Cherry Blossom Front is tracked across Japan, it is primarily somei-yoshino that are being monitored—but this wasn't always the case. The standard cherry blossoms were once those of the mountain, the *yama-zakura* with their smaller blossoms and leafier branches, the flowers sparser on the branch but deeper in colour.

The mountain sakura of Japanese tradition have been largely displaced in central Japan, but they remain strong in the south, and here, in the backwoods of Kyushu, it is indeed the yama-zakura that are still seen highlighting the forests like dabs of paint.

"There are cherry trees in Nagoya," said Hiro, "that take your breath away. We went every year to the castle, to see the flowers falling. I miss that castle. It had golden fish on top. In Nagoya." There were long pauses between everything he said, and his voice was so quiet it was almost like listening to his thoughts rather than his speech. "I used to visit the castle grounds with my wife. When she was young. I'm retired now. Semi-retired. I had to come south, for work."

Changing jobs is as traumatic in Japan as divorce is in the West. Hiro's company had gone out of business in Nagoya and he ended up here, in Oita prefecture, working as a salesman for a construction firm. He gave me his card. The company motto was in English: *Think of Space and Tomorrow.* I chuckled over the slogan and for a long time I didn't think much about it. But lately it seems to me that the motto might well be that of modern Japan. Not space in the sense of the stars, but in the sense of isolation and vacuums. This fixation with the future, with tomorrow instead of today, is strange in a nation with a two-thousand-year history. Stranger still in a country that gave us Zen Buddhism, haiku, and the tea ceremony. Japan seems hell-bent on modernity, and in the end I suppose it is for the best—or, at the very least, inevitable. *Welcome to the 21st Seiki.*

Almost a hundred years ago, a man named Wilfrid Laurier declared that "the twentieth century belongs to Canada." He was wrong, of course, and Canadians have spent a long time living down that remark. The twentieth century belonged to America. But the twenty-first century will belong to Japan. Not necessarily in the size of its GNP—not with the Japanese economy stalled like it is—but more in its outlook. Japan has no sweeping ideologies or founding philosophies. It is old-world nationalism and tribal alliances writ large against the future. Grounded in traditions, mesmerized by novelty, I can think of no nation better suited for the new postmodern world. Japan, almost by definition, is eclectic.

Think of Space and Tomorrow. It is a fine battle cry, but there are casualties along the way. Mr. Hiro Koba doesn't dream of the future, he dreams instead of Family and Yesterday. And Sunday afternoons in a park with a castle topped in gold.

"Does your wife miss Nagoya as well?" I asked.

"Oh, I suppose she does." There was a pause, longer than usual, and then: "I'm a widower. My wife passed away." And then: "Have you ever been to Nagoya? They have a castle there with beautiful golden fish. It's a reconstruction, of course. But I miss it. Have you been to Nagoya?"

It is the third time he has asked me this. Yes, I have been to Nagoya. What I didn't tell him was that I didn't especially like the place. It seemed to be just another large Japanese city, but then, I have never lived in Nagoya. I didn't go to school there, I don't have memories invested in it, I didn't work in Nagoya for thirty years, and my wife's ashes aren't buried there.

Hiro and I talked about the sakura and spring, but that only led back to the castle grounds of Nagoya, where the cherry blossoms are at their best. I could feel our conversation drowning in a series of sighs, so I changed tack.

"Hobbies?" he said. "I don't have any really."

Damn. But then, almost in passing, he said, "I like sumo, though."

Finally, I was back on steady ground. I am the equivalent of a Sumo Deadhead, following tournaments, keeping track of the stars, spending my money on sumo handprints and sumo playing cards and commemorative sumo banners. I love sumo the way some people love their country. It is, and I think I am being objective in my assessment, simply the greatest sport in the history of the universe.

In Japan, rotund pale flabby guys are considered the epitome of masculinity. Don't you just love that?

The *rikishi* of sumo ("wrestler" doesn't quite describe what a rikishi does) are objects of lust and adoration. Personally, I think it's the hair. Sumo rikishi were the only group allowed to keep their traditional samurai topknots when Japan went through its drastic modernization in the late nineteenth century. The rikishi's hair, oiled, pulled back, and combed into elegant fan-shaped roostercombs, gives them a Samson quality. (When a rikishi retires, his topknot is ceremonially cut away with a pair of golden scissors, his strength drained.)

The rikishi are massive, strong, obese, arrogant men. They are not especially bright. They drink heavy, play hard, and giggle like little kids. They are the last of the samurai. A scent of perfumed oil and sweat surrounds them like an aura of . . . well, perfumed oil and sweat. Women throw themselves at rikishi, and the rikishi get to eat as much as they want. I would give anything to be reborn as a rikishi.

Hiro and I discussed the previous tournament, the upsets, the triumphs. We picked our favourite fighters. Hiro naturally favoured the ones from northern Japan, I favoured the ones from the south. For some reason, a disproportionate number of rikishi come from either Hokkaido in the far north or Kagoshima in the far south. Even their styles of fighting have been described as "hot" and "cold," with the smaller southern rikishi known for their blistering arm-thrusting attacks, and the heavier northern rikishi tending more toward slow, walrus-like grapplings.

Sumo is the national sport of Japan. Part religion, part ritual, its origins lie in the contests of strength once held to entertain the gods during festivals. Even today, the high-level, professional sumo of modern Japan takes place under the suspended roof of a Shinto shrine, and the ring is blessed by a priest prior to each tournament. Sumo is replete with pomp and ceremony. The referees resemble priests, the rikishi toss salt into the ring in a purification ritual before each fight, and the Grand Champions, the *yokozuna*, wear white ropes—styled on those of Shinto shrines—around their midriffs during their elaborate entrance ceremonies.

Fights rarely last thirty seconds. It's a hell of a show. Explosive and yet, restrained. There are no weight divisions in sumo, which means that little ninety-kilogram halfpints can go up against two-hundred-fifty-kilogram giants, and the giants don't always win. Sumo requires a low centre of gravity—hence the force-fed diets and round, heavy bellies—but smaller, faster, smarter rikishi can get inside, grab the belt, and upset much larger men, who fall like toppled redwoods.

There was one rikishi who retired shortly after I arrived in Japan, and it was because of him that I got hooked on sumo. His name was Chiyonofuji, but they called him the Wolf. He was one of the smallest rikishi fighting. He was also the best.

Chiyonofuji was the son of a Hokkaido fisherman. Solid muscle. There was not an ounce of flab on the Wolf, and although technically a northern rikishi, in every other way he resembled the smaller Kagoshima fighters. While other fighters used sheer mass to win, Chiyonofuji used physics. His smaller body gave him a lower centre of gravity and he used this to fulcrum his opponents out of the ring. He was strong as a banshee as well. If he got hold of an opponent's belt, inside and on the right, the fight was pretty much over. Chiyonofuji would lean in, biceps rigid, legs low, and he would flip these giant oversize men ass-over-teakettle right out of the ring. And there he would be—still standing—at centre ring. It was a religious experience to see Chiyonofuji at work.

I met him once. True story. It was in Fukuoka City during the Spring Tournament. He was retired then; his topknot had been ceremonially cut off the season before (I *cried* when I watched it on television) and he was now a senior statesman of sumo. I was up the night before and was wandering around Fukuoka's notorious red-light district when lo! I ran right into Chiyonofuji. He was coming out of an exclusive all-girl topless cabaret. I recognized him immediately, and the following, now immortal conversation took place. (I have given it in Japanese as well, so that you can best savour the moment in all its authenticity):

ME: *Hora! Chiyonofuji deshō?*
   Hey! Aren't you Chiyonofuji?

CHIYONOFUJI (as he sweeps past):
   So da yo.
   Yup.

ME   (to the back of Chiyonofuji's head as he continues down the
     street):
     Komban-wa!
     Good evening!

THE BACK OF CHIYONOFUJI'S HEAD:
     No response.

There you have it, the Dumbest Conversation of the Decade.
When I told my Japanese colleagues about my encounter with the
Wolf, they cringed. For one thing, his name is no longer Chiyonofuji;
he has been given a name of higher respect befitting his position.
And for another, one does not just go up and talk to a man as great
as Chiyonofuji. (I was lucky he even responded at all.)

Mere moments after humiliating myself with Chiyonofuji, I ran
into several other rikishi. One stout fellow was getting into a cab and
I hurried over on the assumption that he would probably be thrilled
to shake my hand. It was Kotonishiki, always easy to recognize
because he looks just like Essa Tikkanen, a hockey player whom you
have never heard of either. I was a little more composed when I
accosted Kotonishiki. I thrust my hand into his and said, "Do your
best in tomorrow's bout." He nodded and said, "I will do my best."
And son-of-a-gun if he didn't go out and win the very next day.
I couldn't help but feel partly responsible. And needless to say, I am
now a *big* Kotonishiki fan.

Mr. Hiro Koba agreed that Kotonishiki had been very polite to
have stopped to chat. (It helped that I had a hold of his hand and
wasn't prepared to let go until he acknowledged me.) Kotonishiki,
meanwhile, went on to get caught in a twisted love-triangle sex-
scandal, with a pregnant mistress and a wife betrayed, which the
newspapers covered with an incredible eye for journalistic detail.
The life of a rikishi, you just can't beat it.

And so it was.

Instead of plumbing the depths of our souls, Hiro and I talked
sports like a couple of regular guys. I think there is a fear, somewhere in the mind of the traveller, an unease with emotions laid
raw and bare. I prefer width to depth, variety of experience to
intensity of experience, quantity to quality. And there is something

about Japan—the surface reflections and refracted lights—that allows you to skim across without having to sink below. Japan does not swallow souls whole, as do some countries. Countries like India. China. America.

Japan is a nation perfect for hitchhikers, and one of the great appeals of hitchhiking is that it is a transitory experience. You cut through lives in progress, the rides flip by like snapshots, and the people become a procession of vignettes. I was not searching for catharsis or murky depths, I was searching instead—for what? I suppose I was hoping, somehow, to find in this pixilation of people and places something larger, an understanding, if not of Japan, then at least of my place in it. It was not a quest—that is too grand a word for it. It was more of a need, an itch, quixotic at best, presumptuous at worst.

So I left Hiro Koba to the privacy of his life, to his own singular joys and small defeats. He liked sumo, he missed Nagoya. That was enough.

17

THE CITY OF SAIKI was built largely upon reclaimed land. This gives it a low, flat feel. The area around the port was arranged in a grid: square blocks, wide avenues, and box-like buildings. With several hours until the evening ferry, I wandered aimlessly through this forlorn town. It was the kind of place you expect tumbleweeds to roll through. Signs creaked on rusted hinges, and the stale smell of fish and diesel fumes had seeped into every house and plank. The paint was peeling, like eczema. Strangely enough, Saiki's straight-square gridwork of streets actually made it harder to get around. It was a confusing place. Every corner looked vaguely the same. I passed a red-lantern eatery, walked for a few blocks, and then, seeing nothing better, I circled back only to get hopelessly lost. Block after block and still I could not find it. It was getting dark, and I made a list of places in which I would not want to live: Saiki, Saiki Port, near Saiki Port, and Saiki. Harbour towns either hustle with excitement or reek with lassitude, old urine, and turpentine. Saiki is of the old-urine-and-turpentine variety.

As I passed one doorway, I startled a little boy, maybe four years old. He was buttoned up from neck to ankle, the sure sign of an overprotective mother. She proved me right by coming out hurriedly and telling him in a hushed, frantic whisper, *"Kiwo tsukete! Gaijin wa abunai yo!"* a phrase which always stings me when I hear it: "Watch out! Foreigners are dangerous!" But the little boy was having none of it. He stood, mouth open, his eyes a cartoon of surprise.

"Good evening," I said, first to him and then to his mother. She gave me a hypocritical little smile and a small bobbing bow. Her son, having regained the power of speech, burst out with "A-B-C-D! A-B-C-D! A-B-C-D-F-G-E!"

"Very good," I said. "Did you learn that in kindergarten?"

To which he replied: "A-B-C-D! A-B-C-D!"

This was getting real annoying, real fast. "Can you say Hello in English?"

"A-B-C-D! A-B-C-D!"

I congratulated him on his prowess with language and said goodbye. His mother bowed again, more deeply this time, and said with grave sincerity, "Thank you very much," though it wasn't clear whether she was grateful to me for speaking with her son or for not robbing her and leaving her and her boy for dead. At moments like these I have to fight the overpowering urge to yell *"Boo"* and see how high they leap and how loud they shriek.

Then, at the next corner, I came upon the red-lantern café I had passed earlier, and I went inside.

There was a plump, aproned lady behind the counter, and when I came in she exchanged glances with the only other customer in the place, a thin man slouched over his noodles. He slurped them up noisily, keeping an eye on me the entire time.

Above the bar were glossy photographs of Japanese battle-ships—not vintage Second World War destroyers, but modern, state-of-the-art vessels of prey. In one photograph a phallic grey submarine was emerging from the sea, the decks awash with foam and the Japanese flag emblazoned cross the aft or forecastle, or whatever the hell the correct seaman's term is. As the lady of the place hurried herself with my curried rice, I pondered the significance of these photographs. I was wondering how a nation that claims to be the "Switzerland of Asia," a nation whose constitution outlaws war and forbids it from ever having an army, I was wondering how such a nation managed to produce these lethal, sleek war machines. Except, of course, they aren't war machines. They are part of Japan's Self-Defense Force. Call it what you like, it is still a military buildup. I, for one, do not have a problem with this. Put yourself in Japan's position. You've got North Korea aiming its warheads at you with a certified nutball at the helm, and you've got your crazy cousin China babbling away beside you, armed to the ears with Communist-era nuclear bombs—which means that eighty percent of them won't work properly when fired. Unfortunately, twenty percent of Apocalypse is still Apocalypse. When you have neighbours like these, maintaining primed-and-ready armed forces would seem to make a lot of sense. But why can't they just come out and admit it? Why the big charade?

"*Oi! Gaijin!*" It was the other customer. He had addressed me in the rudest possible way. "Gaijin! *Chotto!*"

Shit. Just what I didn't need, a dyed-in-the-wool, one-hundred-percent certified Grade-A Japanese asshole. I tried to ignore him, but he became belligerent, speaking in what I think was a slurred Osaka accent. "*Oi!* You like that ship? You a sailor?"

"Sorry, I don't speak Japanese."

"Ha ha!" He called out to the lady, who was now bringing me my curry. "*Henna gaijin!*" ("Weird foreigner!") Then, his eyes narrowing, he said, "I am Japanese."

"Good for you."

"I am a Japanese sailor. That ship," he gestured with his jaw to one of the photos and in English said, "*Japanese, number one.*" And he sneered, his lips like eels.

There ought to be an archaeology of facial gestures. I am sure we could trace this particular expression—this eel-like sneer—all the way back to northern China. It is a mix of arrogance, utter contempt, and adolescent pride. In Japan it is usually more subtle than this caricature I was now up against. Sometimes it was so slight, you almost missed it. I once had a Korean customs officer sneer at me continuously for three hours straight as I was uselessly interrogated about nothing. When you get to China you see it more often. In Shanghai it is common even among young women. And by the time you reach Beijing, it is almost a permanent feature, more of an attitude than a facial expression. I do not doubt that somewhere out there, beyond the Great Wall in the outer steppes of Mongolia, there exists an old withered tribe, the wellspring of this sneer, the Ur-Sneerers, living in their huts, chewing skins, and spitting venom at one another. I was weary. I was weary of this tired old tune, this tinhorn anthem.

"*Oi!*" he said every time I tried to ignore him. He was drunk, or at least pretending to be. He switched back to English, "*Japan! Number One!*" and to emphasize his point he held up his index finger. I responded with my middle finger. "I agree," I said. "Number One!" But he didn't catch, or didn't understand, my insult.

I was trying to make this lizard man disappear but he kept inching closer to me, talking about how great, omnipotent, excellent, fully erect, etc., etc., the Japanese navy is. So I decided to take him down.

"Are you Korean?" I asked.

"What?"

"Are you Korean?"

He sputtered in disbelief. "Of course not! I am Japanese."

"Oh, that's right. You mentioned that. It's just that, well, you look kind of Korean. I think it's your eyes. Or maybe your mouth. Very Korean." And that was it. I had destroyed him.

It is one of the eternal mysteries of Japan: Are the Japanese arrogant or insecure? Deep down, deep inside: insecure or arrogant? Arrogant or insecure?

"Well, have a good night," I said with a smile. And, having driven the poor man to the point of apoplexy, and hopefully given him a lifelong complex—*Do I look Korean? Really? Do I?*—I paid for my curry rice and got up to leave. Just as I was about to go, I did the cruelest thing you can possibly do if you are a foreigner in Japan. I laughed at him. Not loudly, you understand. More of a chuckle, really. His face was purple with bottled rage, but fortunately—this being rural Japan—he did not follow me out of the café and beat me senseless. Instead he sat, seething in his own bile, and I left.

It was a hollow victory, of course. No doubt he now hates all foreigners on sight, and I have probably added to the already strained relationship between Japan and the West and created bad karma and misused my role as international ambassador of goodwill and poisoned the well of human kindness and killed the bluebird of happiness, but what the fuck, it was worth it.

I walked toward the white-bright phosphorous lights of the harbour, down to where the ferry was tethered. A group of boys, killing time on a spring evening in Saiki, were on their bicycles by the dock waiting for the ferry to leave. When they saw me, a mini-pandemonium broke out. They yelled, "Hello!" "This is a pen!" and other such witticisms. (Or more accurately, *Harro! Zis is a ben!*)

"Gaijin-san! Gaijin-san! Are you ging to Shikoku? You are? Did you hear that, he understands Japanese! Goodbye, Gaijin-san! Goodbye!"

The ferry bellowed once, twice, and the motor began rumbling. Cars were filing on, their headlights on low beam. "Say something in English! Gaijin-san, Gaijin-san, say something in English!"

"I have never eaten feces knowingly!"

And on that note, I said farewell to Kyushu.

TURNING CIRCLES

Shikoku and the Inland Sea

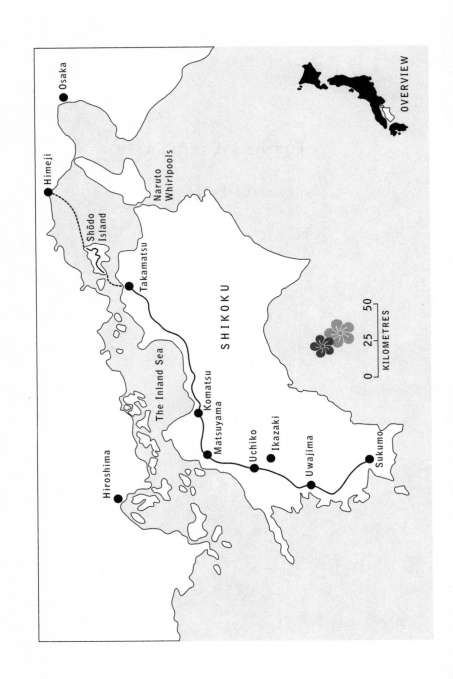

I

THE FERRY crossed a black sea to Shikoku. I stood on the deck watching dark shapes slide by in the night: islands and ships, clusters of lights, fishing boats like fireflies. The wind was billowing my jacket, and the moon above was an arc in the sky, a great luminescent toenail of God.

Just before the ferry was about to leave, a taxi had roared up to the dock and an elderly couple had scrambled out. The taxi driver hurried to get their bags out of his trunk. The ground crew, meanwhile, were already tossing the ropes free. The drawbridge was about to be raised. The couple could have made it—*would* have made it—but they stopped to bow to the taxi driver. He bowed back. They returned the bow . . . and at that moment they were lost. It was too late. The gate was closed, the dock workers waved them away, and they stood watching helplessly as the ship sailed without them. In the time it took to bow they had missed their ferry and were stranded on the wrong side of the strait, a husband and wife marooned by good manners.

Sukumo City is built deep in a fjord that forms one of the largest natural harbours in the world. I had expected Sukumo to be a bustling town—or at least one with a heartbeat—but from the deck of the ferryboat, all I saw were warehouses and a few forlorn streetlamps. As we slid into harbour, I went into the quiet controlled panic of the traveller who has just arrived at his destination and realizes he has no place to sleep, the notion of calling ahead and making a reservation having once again eluded me.

The ferry bellowed. Crew, on shore and on board, cast off ropes and hurried about, tying the ship down like Gulliver asleep in the land of Lilliput. I was one of only a handful of pedestrians. Everyone else had returned to their cars and, with headlights on, had begun filing off the boat. I ran to the head of the line and frantically held out a thumb, to no avail; the cars were gone, the few foot passengers had been whisked away by taxis and waiting relatives, and I was alone.

Sukumo Port is an eerie place at night. The waves were rolling in on ghostly groans along the pier. A shape—probably a cat, possibly a dog, perhaps a large wharf rat—slipped out from the shadows and across the alleyway. Japan is such a dark nation once night falls. Beyond the neon excitement of city centres, there are few if any streetlamps and, as an added obstacle, just to make things interesting—there are almost no sidewalks, and the gutters are a metre deep. (These sudden, open gutters are the bane of drunks and strangers.)

I groped my way toward a distant group of lights, but it turned out to be nothing more than a row of vending machines with a hover of moths and damselflies fluttering around the fluorescent glow. "Damn," I said to no one in particular. Then, just when things seemed hopeless, I gave up. I turned around and started back toward the dock, resigning myself to spending a night on the pier, huddled under a crate and fighting off wharf rats.

A voice from an alleyway called out in a stage whisper, "*Oi!* Gaijin-san! You're going the wrong way."

I couldn't see who was speaking, or even from which direction. "Pardon?" I said.

"The inn—it's farther down, on the other side of the street."

I looked all around but could see no one. Apparently I was conversing with the night itself. So I asked the night if the inn was very far, but this time there was no response. The voice had dissolved back into shadows, and I was left with a clammy sensation on my skin. *Deus ex machina.* It must have been the voice of God or Buddha or Saint Christopher, I decided, and I headed down the street with the renewed confidence that comes when you realize you are under divine protection. God is not such a bad guy after all, I thought, and I regretted the crack I had made earlier about His toenail.

2

THE DOOR STUCK. Warped wood and old ball bearings, I suppose. After a moment's effort, it relented and slid open. I stepped inside and checked the entranceway for footwear. Guests take off their shoes when they enter an inn and, by examining the type of shoes you see lined up in the entranceway, you can tell a lot about the place, its character, the kind of clients it attracts. If you see row upon row of polished businessmen's shoes, you know that you are in for a loud, sleepless night. (In Japan, male bonding generally involves a lot of drunken laughter.) Ditto if you see carefully paired men's and women's shoes. The moans of short-lived ecstasy are less obtrusive than the drunken shouts of salarymen, but they are also more disturbing to listen to—especially if you happen to be travelling alone. The walls in Japanese inns are notoriously thin. You can hear people snoring in the other room. And if you press your ear to the baseboard and listen carefully, you can't help but overhear couples making love. The worst entranceway sight, one that strikes terror into my heart whene'er I see it, is rows of children's running shoes. This signifies a school outing and you might as well forget about getting any sleep, what with the shouts and screams and flirting squeals and the play-fights and the constant treks to the bathroom. And that's just the teachers; the students are even worse.

The inn at Sukumo Port had a row of rubber boots in the entrance, a mixed blessing. These were fishermen's boots, and it meant that everyone would be sound asleep, but it also meant that they would be getting up at four in the morning when the only creatures dumb enough to be awake would be fish and other fishermen.

I called out, "Excuse me!" but there was no response.

87

It was an old, weathered inn, the kind that you can never imagine as ever having been new. A calendar in the lobby was dated from four years back and the floorboards had the only polish in sight, a shiny path down the middle, buffed by generations of feet walking to and from the rooms. The faint smell of mildew and mothballs permeated the place.

I called out again, louder this time, and I heard someone stir from a back room. An old woman shuffled out in slippers three times too big. She showed me to my room, explaining the bath times and toilet procedures and where the futons were stored, all in an accent as thick as stewed seaweed.

When I responded in Japanese she laughed with delight and clapped her hands once, lightly, in surprise. "You speak Japanese!" she said. "How clever of you, how very clever." (I speak Japanese the way a bear dances. It's not that the bear dances *well* that impresses people, it's the fact that the bear dances at all.)

Congratulating me again, she backed out of the room and left, still smiling. I looked around. It was a room that would have done Sparta proud: a pot of tepid tea, a wastebasket in case I was suddenly overcome with the urge to throw something away, and an alcove with a very tacky scroll of a tiger. There were cigarette burns on the tatami mats and water stains on the ceiling. Still, I liked the place. It had "character," as defined by the number of cockroach traps within sight. I changed into the cotton bathrobe, overstarched as always. (What is it with Japanese inns? Do they really think we like walking around as if we were suited up in cardboard?) I went downstairs to the bath and, finding the water still piping hot, I undressed, soaped and rinsed, and climbed in. *Ahhhhh.* If there is a Heaven and if I am going there, I expect it will be a hot Japanese bath with a bamboo cover and wisps of steam rising from the surface.

The Japanese find our habit of washing ourselves in the bathtub to be a bit disgusting, and they have a point. We do tend to wallow in our own dirty water. In Japan, you scrub yourself down first, rinse yourself off, and wallow instead in other people's residue. Not filth, of course, because you are expected to wash completely before you get in. Except that not everyone is as thorough about washing as they should be, and if you examine the water in any Japanese bath you will always find a hair or two floating on the surface and small flakes of soap or skin suspended in the water. There is a sense of communal baptism to it.

I am sharing water with strangers, I said to myself, and this seemed to be a very revealing metaphor of some sort, but I was too tired to work it out.

The next morning, I walked, besieged by yawns, down the street to Sukumo's Tropicana Café. The most glorious thing about it was its name. Remember the general rule, which I just now made up: *The grander the name, the blander the dame.* If you see a place called the Flamingo Club Caribana Coconut Inn you can expect K-rations, pineapple juice, and a ukulele solo. I ordered the Sunrise Festival Excitement Breakfast: fruit salad and a fried egg. Chewing thoughtfully, I scanned the room.

The only thing better than hitchhiking is *not* hitchhiking, and, whenever I can, I make a point of sidling up to potential car people in cafés and parking lots and other such public places. The man across from me looked like a good mark. He was well groomed, he had on a company jacket, and outside the window I could see the corresponding company truck. I leaned over and said, "Excuse me, do you know the way to the main highway?"

"Sure."

I waited. No answer. Apparently he thought I was taking a survey. "Is it far?" I asked, and then, dropping the hint like a wet bag of cement, I said, "I don't have a car, you see, and I was wondering if it was possible to walk to the highway from here."

He looked at me from across his bowl of miso soup. I grinned in what I hoped was a vulnerable but expectantly optimistic manner. He chewed his rice, sipped his tea. "All right, all right," he said finally, "I'll take you out to the highway."

The Travel Weasel strikes again. I revelled in my cunning.

3

S UKUMO IS A THIN, spear-like city contoured by the shape of its harbour. It is also a surprisingly rural place; we drove past marshes and fallow fields, well within the city limits. The company man dropped me off on the highway east of town and, pulling an impatient U-turn, drove back in toward Sukumo proper. I felt good. The road before me was a wide, easy one to hitch and, sure enough, the second vehicle that came by stopped. It was a minivan filled with sailors.

The driver cranked down the window and asked me where I was heading. When I said Hokkaido he answered *"Uso!"* a distinctly Japanese expression that can mean either "Really?" "No kidding!" or "Liar."

The sailors were wearing matching polyester track suits in synthetic blue, making them look more like a sports team than a fishing crew. They conferred with each other for a moment, and the driver nodded. I crawled into the van, over knees and elbows, and had to wake up a young man stretched out in the back so that I could sit down. He woke up with one of those startled "Where the hell am I?" looks, only to find himself staring up at my looming face. The van accelerated and I fell into him. By the time I had shifted my pack around and settled down, he was awake. Groggy, but awake.

His name was Yuichi Watanabe and he was just sixteen, the youngest crew member on the trawler *Myojin-maru*, outbound for the south seas of Okinawa. They were on their way to Nishiumi, a fishing port located on a spur of land an hour north of Sukumo.

Yuichi was a quiet boy, still a child really. It was hard to believe that he was heading out to open sea for a three-month voyage. Many ships went out, he acknowledged. Some never returned. By virtue of his age and inexperience, Yuichi was the kōhai to the entire crew, and the way he flinched when the other crew members yelled back at him to pass up cans of cola and balls of rice (none offered to me, I duly noted) seemed to suggest that Yuichi was having a hard time of it. Did he like his life? He gave a noncommittal answer. Was it difficult? Well, he said, it couldn't be helped, he had dropped out of school, and—realizing that the man in the seat in front of him was listening—he was very lucky to get this job. His senpai treated him—they were *kibishii*, he said, using a word that can mean anything from "strict" to "cruel."

"It's my fault, you see. Because I'm stupid. I'm still learning. Sometimes it's hard."

I asked him about the sea and he told me about waves that rose four stories high and storms that rocked the trawler like a cork in a bottle. He hated storms more than tangled nets. Did he still get seasick? He nodded. Yes, he still got sick. Some days he vomited so much he became *fura-fura*, light-headed. He lay in bed all day and the others, well, they treated him as can be expected. He was young, you see, and new at this.

He turned to watch the fields moving by outside. It must be nice to be a farmer, he said. The ground doesn't move—except in earthquakes, of course, but here in Shikoku they don't get many of those. Yes, it must be nice to be a farmer.

Of the four large islands that make up the Japanese mainland, Shikoku is the one most often overlooked and the one least travelled through. They call it "Japan's forgotten island," a place that gets so little attention it is almost invisible.

I know the feeling. The crew of the *Myojin-maru* dropped me off in what I believe is the geographic Middle of Nowhere. As their van pulled away they shouted, "Good luck!" and I was sure I detected a hint of sarcasm in their voices.

In front of me lay a starburst intersection where four roads and eight lanes came together, met in a confusion of arrows and traffic signs, and then splayed apart again, like a carnival fish pond where you grab a string on one end and hope that it's attached to something valuable on the other end. It never is.

With determined ignorance, I studied several road signs. My knowledge of the kanji alphabet is limited at the best of times, and all I could make out were sporadic bursts of words, none of which added up to anything that made any sense:

ATTENTION! ———— EAST ———— WILL BE ———— PLEASE ————
SOUTH ———— ———— IS ———— ONLY. THANK YOU.

"Ah," I said aloud. "East will be please south is only!"

Odder still, this ganglia of an intersection existed far from any town, deep in a forested valley, without a single gas station or house in sight. Obviously a government project. Curiouser and curiouser. The asphalt was new, the lines were freshly painted. The roads appeared out of nowhere, merged capriciously, and then disappeared around corners. It was maddening.

I wasn't anywhere near the sea, so I couldn't even use that as a rough guide. I assumed I wanted to go north, but that was just because I always hold maps so that my destination is at the top and north is always "up." I couldn't find a single road sign that read *north*, but eventually it dawned on me that if I found a road going *south* and then went the opposite direction, I would in fact be going *north*. (It takes me a while to catch on to such things.) Three different roads headed in a vague sort of "not-south" direction. I chose one at random and began walking.

I had just turned a corner into the woods when I heard the sound of a vehicle behind me. Desperate for advice, I ran back to Hell's Intersection, my backpack hallumphing on my shoulders like a Bedouin astride a camel, and I arrived just in time to see a truck fly by on a parallel road. I waved my thumb weakly in the air, much like a man on a desert island watching an airplane disappear over the horizon. It was no use. The moment had passed. Out of breath and disheartened, I let my backpack slip onto the ground.

Time passed. The sun inched its way up the sky. Waves of heat and humidity began to emanate from the asphalt. A bee appeared and tormented me a while, but eventually it too got bored and flitted off, presumably in search of shade. I began to ooze sweat. I felt a trickle down my back, then another. Time stopped. Not a single car appeared. I began to make lists of places I'd rather be, starting with the Black Hole of Calcutta and then eventually ticking off the inventory in descending grades until I got to a Japanese high-school English class. Anywhere but here.

I was sitting on my backpack, contemplating my shoelaces, when I heard a vehicle. Scrambling to my feet, I thrust my thumb out wildly in all directions, unsure from which road the car would appear. The noise grew louder and louder, like the pitch of a mosquito, and suddenly a sleek blue car whipped past me on the east-west axis. "Wait!" I cried.

At the last possible moment, the driver saw me. He slammed on the brakes and skidded to a stop. He then backed up, spun his vehicle around, and roared up beside me. He was wearing a mask.

I had always feared this: hitchhiking alone in a strange land and having a masked man pull up. Fortunately, this being Japan and not, say, Mexico, he wasn't a bandito with a handkerchief over his face. He was simply a man who happened to be wearing a white surgical mask. This is what people in Japan wear when they have a cold, to avoid giving it to others. Or when they fear *catching* a cold from others. Or when they *may* be coming down with a cold and are afraid both of giving it to others *and* of making it worse. Why this man was wearing a mask while alone inside his own car with the windows up, I couldn't say.

"I'm so sorry," was how he greeted me.

I found this reassuring. Bandits rarely apologize before they rob you.

"Please get in," he said. "I am so sorry."

He didn't remove his mask as we spoke, and it gave me the uncomfortable feeling that I had interrupted a surgeon on his way to some emergency operation. I imagined little Timmy lying on an operating table in dire need of a pancreas while his doctor was talking to me, but what the hell. It was a ride. I climbed in.

He handed me a business card. "I am Mr. Yamagawa. I am the mayor of Ipponmatsu Town. I am very sorry."

Cool. A mayor. I asked him if I was on the right road to Uwajima City and he shook his head. This didn't surprise me in the least. I am the world's worst scout. Had I been leading the pioneers in *Westward Ho!* we'd still be circling somewhere around Pittsburgh. I have gotten lost in elevators. You could almost use me as a "negative-example" navigator; just watch where I go and then chart a course along the exact opposite direction and you'd probably do just fine. How I ever became a travel writer is beyond me.

"Do not worry," said Mr. Yamagawa. "I will take you to Uwajima City. Don't you have a car? You should have a car. Please call my office tomorrow and we will arrange a vehicle for you."

I wasn't sure how to respond. After all, a car is a car, but in the end my better nature wouldn't allow me to accept the offer. That, and the fact that I don't have a Japanese driver's licence.

"Would you like something cold to drink?" He drove over a hill to a row of roadside vending machines and, with a quick "Please wait here," jumped out and ran across the highway, leaving me—a complete stranger—alone in his car with the keys in the ignition and the motor running. Such trust, such naiveté. I briefly considered a number of pranks I could play, but decided against them in the interest of international harmony. He returned a few minutes later with two cans of Kirin beer and a bag of peanuts. "Please, please," he said. "I am very sorry."

We were soon back on the coast, riding high above the ocean under a polished blue sky. Fishing villages were cluttered in the coves below us like jumbled driftwood washed in above the high-tide mark. Seawalls jutted out protectively. Fishing boats, tethered to docks, rose and fell on the swell of waves. There were even a few cherry trees, encircled by bands of petals that had fallen around them. But it was nowhere as impressive as the sakura I had travelled through in Miyazaki.

Mr. Yamagawa was very accommodating. "You want to see sakura? That is not a problem. We have a scenic route we call the Cherry Blossom Road. I'll take you through it." He turned onto a side road and the car climbed through forests, up to a ridge of mountain, and then—suddenly—cherry blossoms burst upon us on either side, the petals scattering across the windshield. It was like driving through a tunnel of flowers. Above us, the overhang met in an honour guard of spring, a triumphal arch in white and pink.

"I'm going to travel with the sakura all the way to Hokkaido," I said.

He laughed. "You want to leave Ipponmatsu Town?"

"I've never been to Ipponmatsu Town. I'm following the cherry blossoms."

"But what about soccer?"

"Soccer?"

"Yes, soccer. How do you like Japanese-style soccer? Is it different from England?"

He and I seemed to be reading from different scripts. "Well," I said, "I don't really care for soccer. It's too slow. I prefer ice hockey. And sumo. If you could just combine the two it would be great: Sumo on skates. I'd pay good money to see that."

"Ha!" he slapped his dashboard from the sheer mirth of it. "You don't like soccer. English humour. Very funny."

"I'm not English."

"Oh, you are Brazilian then? How do you like Japanese soccer?"

I was completely lost at this point. First he wanted to give me a car, now he wanted to discuss Brazilian soccer techniques.

He handed me a small pad and pulled down his mask for the first time. "Do you think," he said with sudden humility "I mean, do you mind? Would you sign your autograph? For my son. His name is Kentaro. He loves the Grampus Eight."

"Grampus Eight?"

"We are very honoured that the Japan Soccer League has chosen our town for its spring training. We welcome the players. Especially the foreign players, such as yourself." He glanced down at the note pad. "Kentaro," he said. "My son's name is Kentaro."

We came out of the flowers just then, in a kind of reverse-epiphany. I stared down at the pad. I was faced with a moral dilemma. Should I sign some illegible scrawl and let Mr. Yamagawa ascribe it to whichever imported soccer player he had mistaken me for, or should I confess my true (non) identity? Should I let the Mayor of Ipponmatsu continue to believe he was sharing his car with a celebrity, or should I bare my soul and admit that I had gained a two-hour ride to Uwajima, with beverages and a scenic side trip included, all under false pretenses?

I cleared my throat. "Before I sign this, I should tell you something. I'm not exactly a soccer player."

"You are one of the coaches?"

"Not exactly."

"Oh. You are a manager then? Or a trainer?"

"No. I'm a hitchhiker."

It was his turn to be confused. "A hitchhiker?"

"I've come from Cape Sata and I'm going to Cape Sōya. I've never played organized soccer in my life, I've never been to your town, and I don't know who the Grampus Eight are. But I'm sure they are a fine team and I am very happy for you."

"I see."

A horrible silence descended. I wished I was back at the Lost Intersection of Shikoku. A desert island, my dentist's, Pittsburgh— anything would have been better than this.

"Do you still want me to sign your notebook?"

"No," he said. "That won't be necessary." And for a moment I thought he was going to ask for his beer back.

The ride into Uwajima was the longest of my life. Mr. Yamagawa dropped me off at the train station, which I took as a hint of sorts, and my profuse thank-yous and apologies didn't seem to ease what was clearly a betrayal of sorts.

"Good luck," he said. "Please come to my town any time." But I don't think he really meant it.

The mystery remains. Who was I supposed to have been? Was there actually someone out there as stubby and out-of-shape as I, making a living at soccer? Or is it just that we Westerners all look the same? Honestly, my physique is about as athletic as Yogi the Bear's. Although I prefer to think of myself as "big-boned," especially around the waist, the Japanese have no compunction about calling me fat. "My, you sure are fat, aren't you!" They come right out and say this to me, just like that. Once, when I was attempting to charm a hostess in a night club, she smiled at me during a lull in the conversation and said, seductively, "How did you ever get so fat?" It kind of spoiled the mood.

If nothing else, that ride to Uwajima was the first and will probably be the only time in my life that I have been mistaken for a professional athlete. I just wish a beautiful woman and not a middle-aged mayor had made the mistake. Had a single female asked for my autograph, I would have signed it with a flourish and perhaps even thrown in some celebrity soccer anecdotes as well. Life can be so cruel.

4

THE CREATION MYTH of Shintoism begins not with an apple, shamed nudity, and original sin. It begins with the drunken, fumbling incest of the god Izanagi and the goddess Izanami, a pair of siblings who brought the first humans into existence not from clay and rib bone, but in the good old-fashioned way: they got drunk and jumped in the sack. From this came several thousand children, most of whom became gods as well; but a select few became Japanese.

As a folk religion, Shinto has a lusty enough history, replete with sex shrines, fertility rites, naked festivals, and rituals suspiciously similar to orgies. Most of that has since been cleaned up, alas, and only a few sex shrines remain. I choose the term carefully. To call them "fertility shrines" is too limiting; these shrines encompass all aspects of couplings, both human and supernatural. The sex shrines that have managed to survive various waves of puritanism in Japanese history have lost much of their original sensuality and are now treated more as titillating curiosities than as living religious sites. But they are not abandoned. Nothing historical is ever completely discarded in Japan, it is just added onto, like another layer of papier-mâché.

At Taga Shrine in Uwajima, the main object of veneration—or envy, as the case may be—is an enormous battering ram of a phallus. This massive, veined wooden penis is more than mere wishful thinking on the part of the Japanese; it is a bona fide cultural icon. As in, "Hey, get a load of that cultural icon."

Demure Japanese women, dressed in Western fashions and carrying Chanel bags, come to Taga Shrine to pray before the phallus. They pray for easy childbirth and good health, and it isn't in the least bit incongruous. Japan has a way of transcending incongruities. This easy eclecticism is one of the country's greatest strengths.

The only disturbing part of this ritual (if you happen to be male) is when these same demure women fold up the slips of paper their fortunes are printed on and then wedge them into the wood-grain of the phallus. The phallus has dozens of these paper slips jammed into it like acupuncture needles, some of them in areas so sensitive that it causes me to double over in sympathetic pain even now.

Taga Shrine is not lurid, it's rather subdued. Granted, the lily-pad ponds were decorated with stone penises, but tastefully. The land the shrine is built upon was first consecrated seventeen hundred years ago. And although none of the original structures have survived, the present shrine is still so old its origins have been lost. In fact, Taga is referred to as both a Shinto shrine *and* a Buddhist temple, syncretic not by design but through the blurring of borders. Like the union of man and woman, the point of contact between Buddhism and Shinto is a bit messy and you can't really tell what belongs to whom.

The mythology traces it back to Izanami, the archetypal goddess who died giving birth to fire. Transformed by death into a Goddess of Destruction, she roared out, "I shall kill a thousand lives a day." To this, the God of Life replied, "If you must. But know this: I will give birth to one thousand five hundred lives a day, and I will win."

They call Taga "The Shrine of One Thousand Five Hundred Lives." It rejuvenates worshippers, it cures illnesses, it helps married women get pregnant and pregnant women give birth. They come to pray at the stalk of life: the penis, from which life is transferred from man to woman to world. Suddenly, it didn't seem so strange.

Sex is religion, philosophy, morals, science, life. This is the creed of Taga Shrine, and it was here that the first Taga priest was spiritually awakened to the principal of opposites in union. And thus began his quest: to seek and find and gather symbols of this vital life principle.

Which brings us to the museum. The museum, beside the under-stated calm of Taga Shrine, is a three-storey box of a building, circa 1974: Disco Architecture. Appropriately enough, it is dedicated to sex.

I'm not sure what I expected. Soft lights, red wallpaper, sitar music, wafting incense, maybe an instructional diagram or two. Who knows, I thought, as I paid the exorbitant entrance fee (I have long since passed the point of caring about costs in Japan; I just open my wallet and let them loot it of whatever arbitrary amount they decide upon), I might even pick up a few pointers.

It was nothing but neurotic clutter, a novelty-cum-oddity shop lit in sickly green fluorescent and crammed to the corners with every sexual image you can imagine, and then some. It smelled uncomfortably of sour milk. Walking through it was like creeping through the attic of some sex-crazed ferret.

This has been going on for generations. The sex collection has been passed down from father to son, and the physiognomy of the current priest/curator fits perfectly with his occupation. He has a thin face, slicked-down hair parted on the side, heavy-rimmed glasses, and beads of sweat permanently affixed to his upper lip. His father started it all and was, in a way, the Doctor Livingstone of Japanese sexual exploration. He travelled the world, tromping among the hill tribes of long-necked Thai women, canoeing through Papua New Guinea, and hacking his way through the Amazon rain forests. He ranged the African savanna. He roamed the Persian plains. He even—and here's the scary part—visited Soho. And instead of T-shirts and postcards, our intrepid adventurer brought back stone vulvas, phallic fetishes, and wooden sex totems. Do you think the people at Japanese Customs were getting a little tired of this guy? *"Anything to declare?"* "Well, just this seven-foot stone vagina."

It was all jumbled together. The walls and the corridors, the stairwells, even the ceilings. Everywhere you looked there was sex, sex, sex. It was inescapable, it was obsessional, it was relentless. It was like being a teenager all over again.

Blow-up toys, love chairs, marital aids, the complete *Kama Sutra*, catalogued and unabridged, with positions basic, advanced, and impossible. Peruvian pottery, dolls from Nepal, figurines from Bali, wall hangings from India: endless variations on such a common theme. Leather straps hung like horse harnesses, and bondage paraphernalia cluttered shelves. There were groovy, black-lit nude zodiac charts from California (boy, am I glad I missed the sixties); there was even a display of "British erotica"—surely a contradiction in terms. Paintings from Pakistan depicted an assortment of fanciful bestiality, including a man and a camel, a man and a gazelle, a man and an alligator (don't ask), and a young princess with the entire Bronx zoo.

(What is that? A *giraffe?*) There was a woman with a giant octopus, her body covered with suction-cup hickeys.

Mind you, some of it *was* educational. A chart of Tantric hand signs demonstrated how to delay orgasm through finger position and breathing patterns. I was practicing one such arrangement when a tour group went by and I burned red from embarrassment. "Scientific interest," I mumbled, and hurried on to the next floor.

From Hinduism to pop-art porno. Marilyn Monroe over a steam grate, *sans* panties. Disney characters in flagrante. Anatomically correct versions of Mickey and Minnie. The Mona Lisa topless and the Statue of Liberty in a leather bra. There was something to offend everyone. The Seven Dwarfs had added a new member to their ranks, a well-endowed little chap named Sleazy. The trio of See-No, Hear-No, Speak-No monkeys had recruited a new participant: Feel-No-Evil. My head was swirling. How to make sense of this rummage sale of the psyche? There was even a collection of Cubist Nudes, which is possibly the stupidest concept ever in the history of art. "Is that a breast? I think that's a breast. Or maybe a chair." Cubist Nudes give you a headache; it's like watching the Playboy Channel after they've rescrambled the signal for nonpayment of bills.

A display case depicts the various fertility festivals still being held in Japan. They are disarmingly unabashed. In one, women pull portable altars containing enshrined decorated penises. They aren't in the least bit embarrassed to be doing this. One penis is made of stone and weighs two tons. In another festival, men in red demon masks, with suspiciously shaped sausage noses, run amok in the crowds, poking phallic staffs at women. In another, more solemn event, women in kimonos queue up, each with a giant wooden penis, and proceed down the street like soldiers bearing arms.

As I stood marvelling at the sheer weight of the museum's collection, a tour group came through. They were led by a requisite Perky Tour Guide in a perky outfit with white gloves, a perky stewardess-style hat, a perky smile, a very perky hairdo, and just a general all-round perkiness. She was leading a group of retired men and women through the museum and they dutifully filed past each display case with the same dulled half-attention one gives to any museum. "On our left we have erotic ukiyoe prints, or *shunga*, that date to the days of the Floating Pleasure World. Notice the careful attention to detail."

The tour group shuffled by and only a pair of grey-haired matrons held back, giggling like schoolgirls and pointing surreptitiously at various displays. I tried to imagine my own grandmother coming through this place and enjoying it as much as these two ladies were. I couldn't do it.

"Do you see anything you like?" I asked them.

"Oh yes," they said, and broke into fits of giggles. They fled, hands over their mouths and almost weeping with laughter.

By now I was growing numb, as though Novocain had been injected directly into my brain. I was getting awfully tired of looking at penises. Pound for pound, male body parts were overrepresented. Every second display case was stuffed with penises: strap-on penises, corkscrew penises, telescopic penises, penises with wings, penises with wheels, and penises in shapes truly imaginative—fish, deities, flutes, candles, saké bottles—all worked into that same familiar shape. One room contained hundreds and hundreds of wooden phalluses crowded into the centre of the floor like a crop of mushrooms. A rope partitioned the harvest from passersby, and you walked around clockwise as you might an altar. Or an accident scene.

Farther along, where certain photographs and woodblock prints of locked loins were deemed *too* graphic, the museum curators had simply glued tiny fluffs of cotton batting over the naughty bits. Thus, the engaging sight of men and women peering intently at cotton batting, straining their eyesight like art aficionados examining brush strokes on a Van Gogh. They would lean forward, craning their necks as they tried to see around the fluff, and then, with a satisfied nod, move on to the next print.

I did make one genuine historical/sociological observation that afternoon. So you can see that my trip to the sex museum was not some cheap ploy to pique reader interest and increase sales of this book. No sir. What I noticed was this: the old pornographic ukiyoe prints from the Tokugawa Era, with their ludicrously large and grotesquely detailed depictions of copulation, are not offensive to womanhood. They are graphic, certainly, and unappealing, perhaps, but they are not offensive. The women in them take a very active part, their kimonos fanning out as they climb astride noblemen and sumo wrestlers with the utmost decorum and at unthinkable angles. It is only later—after Japan's contact with the West, coincidentally—

that the depiction of women in Japanese erotica becomes more and more passive, until, finally, they have been transformed into the submissive offerings presented in Japan's adult comics and magazines.

"And here on the left we have the Seven Stages of Seduction as portrayed by the French artist Pierre la Préverse—" Another tour group was coming up and it was time for me to escape.

It was an exhausting experience. I never would have thought it possible, but I had reached my point of prurient satiety. Spend an afternoon in Uwajima's sex museum and the last thing you want to think about is sex. It's like gorging yourself on chocolate: you feel queasy for hours afterward and can't face sweets for a week. It is more of an *anti*sex museum, so mind-gnawingly incessant that it dims desires and mutes interest from sheer sensory overload. Force high-school students to make a field trip to this place once a week and you would end the problem of teenage pregnancy.

I staggered out, shell-shocked and limp—literally—and ate lunch in a small café near the shrine, where I shoveled rice into my mouth like a dazed automaton. "So," said the proprietor with a knowing yet sympathetic smile, "you've come from the sex museum."

5

THERE IS MORE to Uwajima than sex. The city is also home to one of Japan's few authentic medieval castles. I checked into a quaint (read: decrepit) hotel not far from the station, and I asked the owner—a man permanently attached to a television screen—where I could find the best place to view Uwajima Castle. Without looking up from the television, which was playing a particularly engrossing commercial for foot powder, the owner waved his hand in the general direction of Tokyo and mumbled something about a mountain. "There's a giant statue of Kannon at the top, you can't miss it."

Kannon is the multiple-formed Goddess/God of Mercy and is easy to spot. When I stepped outside I saw Her/Him high above the town like Christ over Rio de Janeiro. The only thing that stood between me and the Kannon of Uwajima was a small cluster of houses.

Trust me to lose a mountain.

I strode purposefully toward the Goddess of Mercy only to exit from the maze of narrow streets, minutes later and facing the opposite direction. Again I plunged in, and again I ended up chasing a mirage. First I would find Kannon on my left, the next time on my right. Cursing loudly and glaring about me at this conspiracy of city planning, I did what any intrepid traveller would do: I gave up.

Only then, as though a fog had lifted, did I notice the neighbourhood I had been trying to escape. It was one of those timeless villages-within-a-town-within-a-city that Japan contains like gift boxes within gift boxes. I abandoned any hope of obtaining Mercy. Instead, I walked deeper and deeper into the side streets and avenues. I turned randomly at every corner and I never found myself at the same place twice. The scent of spring and woodsmoke folded itself around me.

I followed an alley so narrow I could run my hands along the houses on either side of me. I looked in on people's lives. A man in an undershirt shakes his head at a newspaper. A student stops to sigh amid a stack of textbooks. Two old men sit motionless before a game of *go*, one plotting his next move, the other waiting; it is impossible to tell which man is doing what.

Vignettes: a woman raking the driveway gravel, a man tending a garden of bonsai, futons hung out to catch the sun from upstairs windows like seasick passengers slumped over the edge of an ocean liner. Clothes drying on bamboo poles, the pants legs strung up as if in mid-karate kick.

The alley ended at an arthritic cherry tree that was sweeping its blossoms into an old canal. The petals floated atop the water, soggy pink islands that broke over rocks and were washed away. School kids rattled by on bicycles, pursued by a squat little dog who followed, wheezing and sad. I crossed the canal on what would have been a footpath in North America but in Japan was part of a working residential street. Halfway across, a car squeezed past with only inches to spare. You could continue forever into Japan, turning corners, moving down alleyways, lost in the layers, captivated by vignettes.

Having abandoned my search for Mercy and the Mountain, I stumbled upon the way. It was like a Zen koan: when you pursue, it eludes, when you stop, it seeks you out. Or maybe it was just dumb luck. Either way, I was happy. I had discovered a path that ran behind a temple and wound its way through a wooded park and a cemetery, and then finally to the Goddess Herself/Himself.

Kannon is sometimes male, sometimes female, but after the bombardment of the sex museum this gender-shifting ability didn't seem that remarkable. The Uwajima Kannon is in the form of a woman. Chalk-white and marble-cool, she looks out with the deep serenity of Buddhist statuary, across a valley filled with city, to the castle, perched on a hill of its own. These two peaks are islands on an urban sea. The city flows below and around them: Kannon and Castle, looking at each other across a gulf, refugees separated by a flood of ferroconcrete.

6

THEY CALLED IT *Sengoku-Jidai*, the "Era of the Warring States." It was a time of civil war, when the samurai clans of Japan fought for control over the Land of Wa. It began with the uprisings of 1467 and didn't end until 1600, with the Battle of Sekigahara and the ascension of the first of the Tokugawa shōguns. With this, the longest, most successful totalitarian regime in human history began: two and a half centuries of isolation and central control. Japan was tossed from one extreme to the other, from anarchy to tyranny, and between the two you have four hundred years of human history.

The Sengoku Jidai, immortalized in saga and song, has inspired countless sword-and-samurai *chanbara* movies—so named because the hero's theme music is inevitably "chan-chan-bara-bara-chan-bara-chan." In the West, children play cowboys and Indians. In Japan, they play chanbara, chasing stray cats and younger siblings down alleyways while armed with only a pair of sticks, one long the other short, the sword and dagger of the samurai class.

Japan was once a chanbara country: a land of noble warriors, ninja assassins, feudal lords, beautiful courtesans, and lots of castles. Castles hidden in valleys, fortified on plains, buttressed behind walls, haughty atop mountain passes. Today, only a dozen are still standing. Many more have been rebuilt as tourist attractions, with varying degrees of accuracy, but it is the extant castles that are treasured.

A persistent myth holds that most were destroyed by the United States during the firebombing of Japanese cities. This is not entirely true. There were a few glaring examples: Nagoya Castle with its golden tiger-fish, and of course Hiroshima Castle. Both have since been rebuilt to original scale. (In Hiroshima City I once overheard a tourist ask his Japanese guide, "Hiroshima Castle, is that an original or a reconstruction?" I winced so hard I got a facial spasm.)

Most of Japan's castles were destroyed long before World War II, first during the feudal wars and then later during unification, when the Tokugawa shōguns systematically dismantled and destroyed hundreds of castles under an edict limiting each clan lord to a single fortress. (In typical bureaucratic fashion, lords without castles were required to *build* one.) The goal was to confine the clan lords and solidify Tokugawa rule. It worked, and two and a half centuries of relative stability followed—but at what a cost.

Only 183 castles survived the Tokugawa shōguns. Then came the modernizing forces of the Meiji reformers, and the real destruction began. Beginning in 1873, 144 castles across Japan were dismantled, sold, or razed as Japan sought to "Westernize" itself through a kind of cultural shock therapy, the effects of which are still being felt. By the end of the Meiji period only 39 castles were left standing. The American bombers of World War II destroyed two dozen more, and today only 12 are left.

Japanese castles are not the dread granite bastions one associates with Europe. Japanese castles are delicate in appearance, like decorative wedding cakes poised above the treetops. They look down upon the townspeople huddled below as a lord might look down upon a vassal. Indeed, to call them castles is a bit of a misnomer. They were manors as much as anything, and their design was based more on ostentation and pride than on tactics—or even common sense. The usual plan was to build the tallest wooden structure possible on the highest hill you could find. And they wondered why lightning kept hitting them. That's right, military strongholds built entirely of wood. They tended to catch fire, and any army close enough to pelt a castle with fireballs was close enough to burn the castle to the ground. In a hundred years of warring and fighting and dying, no one ever thought to build a single castle out of stone. The wonder is that any survived at all.

The real strength was never the castle itself, but the labyrinth of walls and moats that surrounded it. The walls of the Japanese castle are majestic. They sweep up above you like a wave about to break, rough-hewn rock made supple in design. They confound you. They lead you into dead ends, they force you through bottlenecks, they make you backtrack and hesitate. (Much like the average Japanese neighbourhood, now that I think about it.)

These walls within walls, ringed with corner watchtowers and sentry posts, helped keep the potential field of combat far away from the sequestered life of the courtiers and calligraphers inside. Once the walls were breached, however, the castle was practically defenseless. This is in stark contrast with the citadels of Europe, which are designed to be defended right to their very gates. Japan prefers to fight its wars at a distance, in outposts far beyond its walls, in Okinawa, Saipan, Midway. When the outer walls are taken, there is no Fortress Britain to fall back upon.

Uwajima Castle was built by Lord Tōdō, who began construction in the year 1595, at about the same time that Shakespeare was writing *Romeo and Juliet*. Tōdō's castle was later handed over to the powerful Daté clan, who began extensive renovations in 1664. Over the centuries, the castle's guard towers fell into disuse and were eventually torn down. But the central keep remains. It has stood for four centuries. It has survived wars, uprisings, political intrigue, Tokugawa edicts, and American bombers—solely because it lacks any strategic importance.

The irony is sweet. Consider Osaka's castle: It was once the sprawling power base of Japan's *second* most powerful family. The *most* powerful family destroyed them and razed their castle, and today all that stands is a concrete reconstruction, while Uwajima's castle, so tiny and so unimportant that no one ever bothered to siege or sack it, is now a protected cultural property. It stands just three stories high, with flying gables that are awkwardly large for its frame. Not so much a wedding-cake architecture as cupcake, it just may be the cutest little castle in Japan.

High atop its tuft of forest, Uwajima Castle is above the flow of time and history. To reach it, you follow a winding footpath through an ancient forest. No tree has been cut on Castle Mountain for three hundred years; wild tanuki roam its underbrush, and the entire hillside is now a national wildlife preserve, an ark for animals that fell back in retreat at the city's encroachment, seeking high ground in a deluge. The forest rings with birdcalls.

Crowds of children in bright costumes hurried past me as I clambered through the woods. With them came women in summer kimonos and men in traditional *happi* coats, kanji characters splashed across the backs. The nearer I got to the summit the thicker the crowds, until finally it became a single flow of bodies rushing in a current toward the top. I ran with the crowd up the last few steps and came out in front of the castle.

A festival was waiting to begin. Dancers milled about impatiently, taiko drummers shuffled their ranks, and a jerry-rigged PA system announced times and protocol in a steady, static-ridden chatter.

They were here to herald the spring. At Uwajima Castle the cherry blossoms hung heavy like grapes upon a vine. To entertain the gods and to honour these flowers, carnival revellers were mustering their forces. The scratchy voice on the PA kept countermanding previous instructions and the crowds rearranged themselves accordingly, amid grumbled complaints and scattered laughter.

I wended my way through and the crowds parted like the sea before Moses. Women eyed me with intent indifference. Schoolchildren openly gawked, jaws gaping. Men watched my every move as though I might pull out a handgun and start shooting at any moment. Old women bowed with perfect precision, not a degree too low, not a degree too high. You could use the bows of Japanese grandmothers to chart the entire Japanese social hierarchy, from outcast to outsider, from doctor to lawyer to Emperor.

"A foreigner, look!" A flock of high-school girls burst past in a flurry of nervous laughter, and boys, brave after the fact, whispered *"Harro!"* to the back of my head. "Ah, we have an international guest from America here today," said the disembodied voice of the PA system, the voice of a decidedly tinny god. "Maybe he will sing a song for us later."

That I, so very average and unexceptional, should cause a stir among these bright crowds of costumes gives a new perspective on the idea of exotic. I remember a trip to a Japanese zoo, and how the children turned their backs on the caged wildebeest and watched me instead. *More interesting than a wildebeest*, became my personal motto after that. It was oppressive at times. When your face doesn't fit the national dimensions you find yourself in an observer-affected universe; your presence alters actions, and the very act of observing changes that which is observed. You cannot slip by unnoticed. You cannot forget the pigment you present to the world. If nothing else, Japan has taught me what it is like to be a visible minority.

The crowd shifts. On some elusive cue, the drums begin, and the first group of dancers advances, a troupe of severe-looking women, their faces white as bone, lips lacquer red. They move from posture to posture with studied ease, their hands shaping the air in pre-ordained patterns, effortless, unsmiling. They are followed immediately by a confusion of schoolchildren who make up in enthusiasm what they lack in coordination. After the children, an electronics company's managers and sales clerks, misstepping and fumbling side by side—then another column of precision-bowing grandmothers, then one of junior-high-school boys, then one of insurance salesmen. The three central divisions of Japanese life are thus represented: age, gender, and the workplace.

Near the end, a ragged band of farmers comes down the line in drunken disarray, swigging from flasks and improvising lyrics and dance steps as they go. They are crowd pleasers and you can see the lacquer-lipped women absorb this usurpation with stoic indifference.

One by one, the processions continued, down to the castle and then a turn, falling in like army cadets in blocks of colour schemes: high-school blue, young-girl yellow, sakura pink.

When the last group of dancers reeled to join the ranks, the music stopped. Then came the deer.

From behind the wall of dancers and into the open field they came, young boys in gilded antlers, eyes painted wide, movements unsure. They were dressed like Asian princes, the avatars of the deer-child. Siddhartha afoot. They formed and dissolved patterns. They gathered in circles, they moved in half steps. The dance built slowly in a crescendo of motion, moving toward free-form, flirting with chaos.

Then, the hunters. Young girls, sashed in silk and armed with arrows: girls dressed as boys dressed as men. They stalked in stylized movements, and the hunt became a dance. Flowers fall from the stem. Youth comes to an end. The arrival of spring also marks its imminent departure. In pairs, the hunters and the deer moved in circles. They cross-hatched their movements, braiding pathways in wider and wider curves until at last the circle broke and the hunt ended.

I was never asked to sing my song. When the dance of the deer and the hunter had finished, the attention of the gods turned elsewhere and the crowds reverted to profane preoccupations: group photographs, salutations, the long walk home. Young girls and boys, no longer deer or hunters, the spirits having passed from them, chased each other around the castle in a series of squabbles and taunts. I passed one such deer as he demanded of his mother, "Chocolate! Give me chocolate!" When he saw me, he cried out, *"Harro! Harro!"* and soon the entire herd had joined in and I was chased down the hill by the human shells of magic past.

I never feel more like an outsider than when I attend a festival in Japan. Here is Japanese culture at full gallop, and all you can do is stand aside and watch it pass you by. As I left the castle grounds, the last of the drums were beating out a message, and the message was not for me.

It wasn't the lack of Western faces at the Uwajima Festival that made my chest feel so hollow. The truth be told, I prefer to be the only outsider; to have bumped into other Westerners would have reduced me in my pride to the level of tourist. I tell myself often that I am not a tourist. I exist somewhere else, in between voyeur and exile. Which is to say, my journey is almost complete. In Japan, the movement from Tourist to Exile to Insider is one that ends at Exile. There is no final step inside. We are kept at arm's length by the arc of a bow, by the sound of a drum.

The Japanese are not a cold-hearted people. Sometimes I wish they were, it would make leaving easier. The problem is not that you aren't welcome. You are. You are welcome *as an outsider*. The problem is not exclusion, the problem is *partial* exclusion. The door is open but the chain is on. One hand beckons and the other blocks. Like a hostess in a snackbar, Japan flirts its way into our hearts, it pours our drinks, it strokes our ego, it smiles and sighs and listens to our stories, and then in a moment of silence it asks: "How did you ever get so fat?" Japan is not the Land of the Broken-Hearted, it is the Land of the Wounded Pride. It is not that I want inside and can't that bothers me. I do not want to be Japanese. What rankles my Western heart is that *it doesn't matter what I do or do not want*. I could not be Japanese, anyway, even if I wanted to be, and this is so hard on the pride. We want to reject, but we do not want to be rejected.

For expatriates in Japan, the question is this: Do you really want to go all the way inside or are you just hurt that nobody asked you to?

Strangely enough, the closest I ever came to feeling I belonged to Japan—one does not belong *in* Japan, one belongs *to* Japan—was during a festival, when I laboured with an army of men from my neighbourhood to carry a shoulder-aching movable shrine, the size of a small house, in the city's summer festival. We were dressed in blazing red jackets and straw sandals. To gird ourselves for strength and stamina we wrapped mummy-cloths of white linen around our midriffs and twisted banzai headbands around our brows. The shrine was both our glory and our burden, like being born Japanese I suppose. A Shinto priest blessed it with a sweep of paper. We then hoisted it onto our shoulders and entered a traffic jam of other such shrines. We elbowed our way into the throng. We chanted challenges. We swerved and collided. We battled our way down main street and, as we went, people threw buckets of water at us and sprayed our heads with beer. We were running a gauntlet and at the end of it we collapsed, soaked in sweat and water and alcohol. We were triumphant. We ranted and raved. We congratulated ourselves hoarse and far beyond the level of actual achievement. Damn, it was fun. Then one of the men turned to me and said, "You foreigners are so much stronger than we Japanese," and instantly I was outside the circle again, looking in. Waiting. In exile.

7

THE UWAJIMA FESTIVAL did not degenerate into water balloons and beer baths. It was restrained to the point of sadness, and the only water that touched me was a faint mist that came down near the end. It shrouded the castle in soft-focus and reduced the crowds to outlines. Then the footlights came on and the castle glowed as though lit from within, like a paper lantern in the night.

Down below, in the town of tradesmen and alehouses, the neon was flickering on. The streets were slick with rain. Crowds of revellers spilled out, some still in costume, some already steeped in saké and song. A man yelled "Hey, foreigner!" and came over to present me with a can of beer. "For you, Mr. Foreigner. Japanese beer. Number one! Japan is an international country!" and he returned amid hoots and laughter to his circle of friends.

I dropped the can, unopened, into the first garbage bin I came upon.

There was an incident of aromas. I entered a side street lined with restaurants and noodle shops, and I was surrounded by smells. Ginger wrapped in soy wrapped in smoke. At the same time, under the shelter of a small roadside altar, incense sticks were burning, and even in the mist and haze you could smell it, the scent of spice and prayers. That, and the odour of urine from an alley and untreated sewage running under concrete slabs along the gutter. The smells met and mingled.

They call it the Seidensticker Complex, after the American scholar and translator, and it describes the ambivalent feelings that torment long-term foreign residents in Japan, a pendulum of emotion, alternating between attraction and repulsion, affection and anger—back and forth. But the image is false. These feelings do not alternate. They are inseparable. As inseparable as the scent of urine and incense on the same wind. The same festival that beguiles you also excludes you. One does not love and then hate and then love Japan like a metronome. One *lovehates* it, one wants to draw *nearfar* to it, to *gostay*.

For most Westerners, one urge or the other eventually wins, and instead of inseparable feelings you have only to go or to stay. But there are some who are caught in the middle, suspended by opposing desires. They are lost and not sure if they want to be found. They try to run in two directions at once and fail. Like a deer on a highway.

Such were the morose thoughts that pursued me through the drizzle and oily refractions of Uwajima. Just be glad you weren't keeping me company that night; I was as deep as I ever want to go. Everything was fraught with significance, every gesture portentous, every glance an omen.

I sought refuge from myself in a crowded bar and grill, and from the moment I stepped inside, I was everybody's best friend in the world. *"Welcome! Welcome! Come in!"* This was in the time-honoured tradition of Japanese blue-collar eateries: to be as noisy and as nonphilosophical as humanly possible. Everything is everyone else's business and you never whisper when you can shout. *"Ah, Mr. Foreigner! Welcome, Mr. Foreigner!"*

The Japanese call these places *aka-chōchin*, "red lanterns," what we in the West might call greasy spoons. But in red lanterns it is not just the spoons that are greasy. The chopsticks, the menus, the table-tops, the plates, the walls, the cooks permanently and the customers eventually, everything gets covered in a thin film of grease, what might otherwise be called "atmosphere."

No tea-ceremony subtleties here. It was in-your-face hospitality, back-slapping, boisterous, and very loud. I had learned to be wary of such welcomes. Westerners are often treated as sources of amusement and ridicule in Japan, and it can be difficult to spot the difference between derision and friendly chiding. The line is fine, almost invisible, between someone mocking you and someone genuinely curious. Tonight, thankfully, there was no mockery in the air. I sat down at the counter across from a choreography of cooks performing circus feats with knives and whisks, their hands a blur, dicing cabbage, stirring woks, and tossing up plate after plate of Japanese shish kebab.

One of the cooks, a haggard young man with a week's worth of stubble, leaned over the counter and screamed, *"What do you want!"* I was two feet away. I gave him a preliminary list and he announced to the room, "He speaks Japanese! The foreigner speaks Japanese!" but no one was much impressed save the cook himself. The owner came over and chased him away.

The shop was named Sasebo, after a city in the owner's home prefecture of Nagasaki. The Amakusa Islands where I used to work had once been a part of Nagasaki, and even now there is a sentimental bond between the people of the islands and those of the peninsula. When I told the owner that I had lived in Amakusa it was as though I had declared myself to be his long-lost brother come home with a winning lottery ticket in my pocket. "Beer!" yelled the Master of Sasebo like a wounded soldier calling for a medic. "Beer!"

The Master of Sasebo was a man of immense girth and good humour. The Uwajima City High School baseball team, which his shop helped sponsor, had gone to the national championships in Osaka and been thoroughly trounced. He gave me a souvenir baseball cap. His previous restaurant had burned to the ground last spring. He gave me a souvenir lantern from the place. I half expected him to present me with photographs of some distant dead relatives as well, but he didn't.

Instead, he ordered a plateful of deep-fried battered squid, which looked just like onion rings but tasted just like deep-fried battered squid. I hate accepting food at restaurants in Japan, because the people doing the proffering inevitably pick the least appetizing item on the menu. No one ever sends me pizza or french fries, it's always squid this and squid that. Later, for a change of pace, the Master ordered a dish of raw octopus and then, perhaps to make amends, he presented me with a plate of artfully arranged strawberries—which don't really go with fried squid and octopi, but I appreciated the gesture. Heck, it was on the house, and how many times can you say you have been handed a raw octopus as a gift and not as a practical joke?

Having taken care of my immediate material needs—baseball caps and multilegged sea creatures—the Master slapped his hand on his chest and said, "My name is Taiyano. And you?"

"William."

"Wi-ri-mu!" he cried. "His name is Wi-ri-mu!" He repeated this again for the benefit of the cooks, who passed my name down the line like a state secret. The disclosure of my father's name was a further cause for celebration, as was my age, my occupation, and my prowess with a set of chopsticks.

"You sure are talented with those chopsticks! More beer!"

I think Taiyano took a liking to me because he saw me as a fellow nomad. He was born on the Gotō Islands, even more distant and more wreathed in history than Amakusa. He grew up in Nagasaki City. Later his family moved to Sasebo, near an American army base, where he failed to learn any English beyond *"Goddamn it all to hell!"* which he peppered his speech with while talking to me. "More beer, goddamn it all to hell!" he would yell, which impressed his cooks to no end. "The boss speaks English! Did you hear that? He's talking to a foreigner."

After Sasebo, Taiyano had drifted east. He worked his way across Kyushu and southern Honshu, and eventually he found a wife and a livelihood here in Uwajima. We talked about baseball for a while, the scandal being that the Uwajima High School team had lost to Osaka Central because of a suspicious call made by one of the umpires, who just happened to be from Osaka and was clearly favouring the hometown team. The final score was 14 to 2. As this tale of treachery was retold, the cooks paused for a moment of silence. They shook their heads sadly at the injustice of it all. Then Taiyano told them to get back to work.

He asked me why I had come to Uwajima. "Foreigners never come to Uwajima. Never."

"But *I'm* a foreigner, and I did."

Once again my powerful Western logic was ignored. I told him about my own ongoing journey and suddenly I was a celebrity again, elevated to a level beyond that of any mere soccer player. "On his way to Hokkaido!" he roared. "More beer!" The cooks crowded around their side of the counter and fired questions at me about my journey: how long did I have to wait, what kind of cars stopped for me, could I eat Japanese food, that kind of thing. "Fourteen minutes and a white Honda Civic," I replied. "And yes, I can eat Japanese food." Taiyano shooed them away like alley cats.

Then, in a cryptic aside, he said, "Be careful. There are good people in Japan, but there are also bad people. Very bad."

For one skin-crawling moment I thought he was going to tell me about some lone Japanese psycho who was picking up hitchhikers and eating their livers, but fortunately that was not the kind of thing he was alluding to. "Most Japanese are kind," he said, "but some are very bad." And before I could stop him, he was spilling out his woes of how, in his first shop, yakuza thugs had threatened him and demanded money and how the police had brushed his complaints aside. How in one town the yakuza were practically a parallel government, and how he had settled in Uwajima mainly because it was small enough to be relatively free of extortionists, the bane of Japanese small businessmen.

Japan is a safe country. There is no word for "mugging" in the Japanese language, nor are there separate words for lock and key. Murders, drug trafficking, and burglaries are exceptionally rare; muggings are almost nonexistent, except in Osaka and Tokyo, where they are sensationalized by the press and cravenly ascribed to "foreign elements." A mugging in Japan is considered a major news story. That should tell you a lot.

Crime does exist, but it exists on another strata. Instead of robbing passersby on the street corner, the Japanese prefer extortion, bribery, embezzlement, cabals, monopolies, and price-fixing. It's not as messy and has a higher profit margin. What this means is that in Japan the politicians are all on the take, but you can walk down almost any street in any city at any hour of the night and be completely safe. After all, how many times has somebody jumped out of an alleyway and attempted to embezzle from you?

The Japanese, unfortunately, have derived the following flawed syllogism from all of this: Japan has a very low crime rate. Therefore, Japan is very safe. Therefore, the rest of the world is incredibly dangerous.

I remember the mother of one of my students fretting endlessly over the safety of her daughter who was going on an exchange to the United States.

"It is so dangerous," she said. "I am worried for her safety." And where was her daughter going? Which seething pit of savagery and disorder? "Iowa." The lady pronounced it with the same revulsion one might use when saying "Sodom."

Taiyano had seen enough of the outside world at Sasebo, though how accurately American GIs represent Western civilization is debatable. For him, Hokkaido was exotic enough. "Make sure you see the horses," he said. "They have horses in Hokkaido."

By this point we had renewed our celebrations—it having been discovered that my blood type was O positive—and a rumpled old man with a perfectly bald head slumped down beside me and insisted on shaking my hand. "*Ah, Gaijin-san,*" he said. "*Mamgrm kyogrf shrgoi deshne!*"

Which, translated, was: "Ah, Mr. Foreigner. Mamgrm kyogrf shrgoi deshne!"

It was worse than trying to read Japanese highway signs. I felt depressed; so many years in this country and there were still times like this when I understood less than ten percent.

"Pardon?" I said.

"Mugrmff gfrrmmg," he explained.

It got worse. The Japanese language has audible punctuation. To make a question in Japanese you just add *ka* to the end of the sentence. An exclamation point is made by adding *yo*. The bald man, gripping my arm like it was a lifeboat on the *Titanic*, mumbled something unintelligible that ended in *ka*. I knew I had been asked a question, but I didn't know what. "Doshda gffmm ka?" he repeated. When I didn't answer he became insistent.

"Doshda gffmm ka?"

"Sorry, I don't—"

He smote the table with his fist. "Doshda gffmm ka?!" he demanded. The *ka*s were now coming fast and furious and the man was purple with rage. The veins began to throb in his temples. "DOSH-DA-GFF-MM KA?"

In desperation, I hazarded what I hoped would be a noncommittal reply. "Yes," I said. "Absolutely. But then again, maybe not. Who knows?"

With this, his expression softened, he patted me on the back, and tears welled up in his eyes. "Grhhmm deshne," he said sincerely.

"I must apologize," said Taiyano. "He's my father. He can get emotional at times. He was in Nagasaki City when, well, you know."

Oh lord. I felt sick to my stomach. My throat tightened. Nagasaki. "What was he asking me? Was it—was it something to do with, you know?"

"No, no. He was talking about baseball. He's still pretty upset that we lost the championship."

"Grmmffda yo," grumbled the old man as he stared down at his beer.

8

THE RAIN FELL throughout the night and when I awoke the skies had cleared and the air was crisp. I folded my futon and packed my bags. In one night I had managed to disperse my belongings around the entire room, a feat that never ceases to amaze me. I walked down the hall to the lobby where Television Man was still rooted in place, staring intently at a morning weather report. I banged on a bell apparently provided for my amusement, because it brought no immediate response.

After several minutes of this the man yelled, *"Customer!"* Now I understood. He was Off Duty, though the difference was hard to see. A woman I assumed was his wife came out to serve me. As she wiped her hands on her apron, she looked me over. "You're a foreigner."

I conceded her point; I was indeed a foreigner. She seemed proud to have spotted it.

"He's a foreigner," she said to her husband, who, with a single one-syllable grunt, managed to say, "Piss off, I really don't care, can't you see I'm too engrossed in this morning weather report to concern myself with such irrelevancies, and fix me a sandwich while you're up."

She remained chirpy and undiscouraged by this. She said a word I didn't recognize, and when I looked at her blankly she simplified it for me. "Sumo," she said. "I suppose you are here for the sumo."

Sumo? At first I thought she was making a veiled reference to my weight and I was about to lunge across the desk at her when she elaborated.

"The bulls," she said. "You'd better hurry, the tickets will be sold out soon."

And that was how I found myself attending the Uwajima bull-fights, a competition held only seven times a year. Today was one of those seven days. My timing had never been better. I booked an extra night at the inn and, following a hastily drawn map provided by the innkeeper's wife, I went in search of Bull Sumo.

When I arrived, the banners of individual bulls were aflutter outside the arena and crowds had already formed. We filled the seats in a crush of bodies, and the air was thick with the dust and pungent smells of rodeos half remembered from my youth. The same raw energy, the same blue-jean crowds, the same earthen pit.

I had heard of bullfights when I was in Okinawa, but I didn't know they were held on the main islands of Japan as well. The sport itself is part pageantry, part parody. The bulls are ranked just as in real sumo, from Grand Champion (yokozuna) down in numbered levels. The bulls being larger than life, a new rank has been added specifically for them, one higher than even yokozuna and rendered, inexplicably, in English: *Super Champion*. These bulls were definitely on steroids. They were pumped up, swaggering, slicked-down, and barrel-chested.

"They feed them beer, you know," said the man beside me. "And eggs. Raw eggs."

"No kidding," I said. They certainly were impressive animals.

"And snakes."

"Snakes?"

"*Habu*. From Okinawa. Very poisonous."

"They feed them snakes?"

He nodded gravely. "Makes them fight."

The man behind me had been eavesdropping and could take no more. "*Oi!*" he said to the first man. "Not snakes, you idiot. Snake-*shōchū*. It's alcohol, they soak habu snakes in the bottle, you know, like worms in Mexican tequila. They don't feed them actual snakes. Where did you hear such a thing?"

The first man refused to acknowledge this and continued to address only me. "They eat snakes," he repeated.

The second man tapped me on the shoulder. "No, they don't."

"Snakes make them strong," said the first man.

Another tap on my shoulder. "It's not true. Don't listen to him."

And on it went, a running argument-by-proxy with me in the middle. I remained neutral.

"Welcome," said a loudspeaker, "to the second annual All-Japan Championship, pitting local Uwajima bulls against the best from Okinawa, Tokyo, and Kagoshima."

"Who owns these bulls?" I asked the man beside me, but the man behind me answered instead, as though my question had boomeranged.

"Farmers, truck drivers, anybody." He was speaking down the back of my neck. "It's a hobby sport. It began with the Dutch more than a hundred years ago. A Japanese fisherman saved a Dutch ship from sinking during a storm and they presented him with two bulls to show their thanks. The fisherman didn't know what to do with them, so he started staging fights."

"He didn't think to eat them?"

"Oh, no. Japan was completely vegetarian back then. Buddhist, you know. Over the years more bulls were brought in, and it really began to boom. Lots of gambling, drinking. People would bet their tax money in rice and lose everything. Some lost even their houses, so around Taishō ten—"

"I'm not good with the Imperial dating system. When is that?"

He thought a moment. "Around 1925. Anyway, the government banned it and everyone was very sad. The town just couldn't get any energy, you understand? Very sad. The city alderman who supported the ban lost his seat in the next election, and soon we had bull sumo again and everyone was happy. But after the war, it was banned again. General MacArthur. He said it wasn't good for public morality."

I twisted around halfway in my seat. "How do you know all this?"

"I'm just reading from the program. Look." He passed it up to me and pointed out a section in it. I pretended I could read it.

"See," he said, louder than was necessary. "Right there. They feed them snake-liquor, not snakes."

There was a pause. The man beside me leaned over and said, in an equally loud voice, "My father once saw a bull eat a habu, fangs and all. They eat snakes, these bulls. Makes them strong."

A clicking of wood and the long, wailing voice of a ring announcer marked the start of the tournament. Everything mimicked real sumo: the list of fighting "techniques," the ceremonial tossing of salt to purify the ring, the embroidered aprons thrown over the bulls like saddles, the white rope belts of the champions. The bulls had stage names as well—Iroha the Second, Shadowman—and they even had their own entrance ceremony filled with strut and pride.

Here's how it goes. Two bulls are led in on tethers. They circle. Their owners manoeuvre them toward centre ring. The bulls make eye contact and, because they are basically walking testosterone banks, they immediately want to fight. You can see much the same ritual in any country-and-western bar. The bulls snort, strain, and paw the dirt, and then, in a clash of egos, they lock horns and fight. They bellow and push, twist and struggle, but they do not gore each other. (Though one did get nicked.) It is a contest of strength and willpower, and it lacks the violence of a Spanish bullfight or a Texas rodeo.

The matches are gruelling to watch: the bulls eyeball-to-eyeball, steam rolling off their flanks, their backs knotted in muscled exertion. Then, almost mysteriously, it ends. One bull suddenly loses his courage and breaks away, and the crowds—depending on which way they wagered—either cheer loudly or smile. (The ones smiling have just lost a fortune; this is how you show calamity in Japan.)

Some bouts were embarrassingly short. One young bull stopped, took a look at his opponent, and ran away. Bull psychology is intriguing. Initially both bulls are aggressive, but wary. When one bull shows weakness and flees, the other immediately pursues. When it stops running, the other stops. When one squares off, the other does as well. And when two bulls are equally matched, the bouts can last over an hour. On one occasion, however, *neither* bull wanted to fight, and for all the shoulder slaps and cries of *"Yo-shi! Yo-shi!"* from their owners, the two bulls just stood there in centre ring and gently nuzzled each other. It was rather tender to see.

The final match of the day was an epic. One of the owners was a woman from Okinawa, and news cameras were there to cover the event. She was the first woman to compete professionally—though let's be fair, the bulls do most of the work—and she was also the first woman ever to be in a position to take the championship. The final battle lasted *four hours.* By the end of it the two grand champions were barely standing, their tongues lolling so low they were licking dirt, the sweat and steam coming off them like saunas. The scene ached with fatigue and something deeper than fatigue. It was *will,* pure and primal. Strength broken by strength and still strong.

Then, dream-like, one of the bulls swung his head away and loped off to the edge of the ring. The victor didn't have the energy to make even a perfunctory pursuit. The crowd roared, for it was the woman's bull that had won, it was now "Super Champion," and the woman was ecstatic. She leapt and shouted and performed an Okinawa jig at centre ring. People swarmed over the barrier cheering wildly. It was pandemonium. Through the crowd, the champion belt was passed along and then draped across the bull's weary shoulders. The woman climbed up on top of her bull, and she rode him around the ring. A spontaneous procession followed her. Newsmen waved their microphones like wands, trying to catch a comment for their listeners. I followed the crowds over the barriers and pushed my way through the tumult of bodies, across the soft loam of the ring. The bull was in his regalia, surrounded by admirers. I reached through and laid a hand on his side; it was hot to the touch and it reeked of pride, power, and victory.

The next morning Uwajima was sane again. The ghosts had dissipated and the city was pale in the sunlight. I still do not know if the Uwajima of the previous day ever existed; travel tends to heighten one's awareness to the point of delusion. Was it the same castle that had glowed like a lantern the night before? The deer, had they fled as well, leaving the woods to the tanuki, those half-mythic creatures of folklore and taxidermy shops? And what of the hunters? Had they grown up? Had they abandoned the hunt?

On the way out of town, I passed the Grand Shrine of Warei where one of the gods honoured is Ushi-oni, the Demon Bull, the central figure in the Uwajima Cult of the Bull. I stopped to pay my respects. As I returned to the street, I saw, across from me, another backpacker. It was the first Westerner I had seen since I left Minamata. He was heading in the opposite direction, and he looked just like me. Same haircut, same posture, same backpack. He smiled at me. I nodded. We passed.

On another stretch of road, in another state of mind, it would be a singularly unremarkable occurrence: two travellers pass each other on a road, surely as common an event as one could hope for. But it wasn't another road. It was Uwajima, it was here, and it was unnerving. I often think about him, the other me, and I wonder, did he get where he was going? Did I unnerve him as he had me? Did he see himself reflected back as well, the two of us caught in a momentary infinite regress?

With a mixture of reluctance and relief, I turned my back on Uwajima, a city where every extreme is possible and no one gets out unbruised. I chose a spot in front of a gas station and stuck out my thumb.

And that's when I met the Japanese mafia.

9

I DON'T KNOW for certain he was a member of the Japanese mafia. I was making an educated guess based on several important clues: he had on sunglasses, he was wearing a shimmering lime-green silk suit, his hair was in a tight "punch-perm," and—most telling of all—he was driving an American car. "Watch out for Cadillacs," my fretful Japanese friends had warned me as I set out. "And beware the black Benz!"

Japanese gangsters do tend to favour such vehicles, but I suspect that the connection between foreign cars and danger reveals more about the Japanese psyche than it does reality. Good people drive small white Japanese cars. Bad people drive expensive, black, non-Japanese luxury cars. And the Americans wonder why they can't seem to sell any Chryslers in Kobe.

I didn't care. After spending much of my time twisted like an amateur contortionist in cars the size of tin cans, it was nice to ride in a big, cigar-smokin' Yankee automobile. Whether my host was a gangster or not was still undetermined. Yakuza thugs have tattoos up their backs and they are often missing the joints of their little fingers, chopped off as an act of repentance each time they do something wrong. (You can spot the really talentless thugs. They're the ones with the nickname "Stumpy.")

I wouldn't be able to see a tattoo on the man unless he took his clothes off, and I couldn't think of a smooth way of asking him to do this. Instead, I surreptitiously counted his fingers and they were all there, which I found reassuring. If he was a gangster, at least he was an astute gangster. Polite too. The whole time we rode together he never once tried to extort money from me. He even bought me a can of apple juice.

In a cunning ploy to uncover his yakuza identity, I casually asked what he did for a living. He answered, cryptically, "I'm a city engineer for Ehime prefecture, Uwajima Department of Resources. Here, take my business card. It has my address and phone number right there." It was all very mysterious.

I was standing beside the highway, drinking said apple juice and having survived my brush with organized crime, when a figure approached on the other side. It was a man in a white robe with a bowl-shaped straw hat that covered his face. He was carrying a begging bowl, a pouch, and a pilgrim's staff. I watched him walk toward me, trucks rattling by in clouds of highway dust and noise; it was as though he were moving in slow motion against the backdrop of a speed-addicted world.

I wanted to run over and give him a *settai*, a donation, and receive his blessing, but I wasn't sure how to approach him—or even how to cross the multi-lane highway that separated us. (It is the fate of many of us to always find ourselves on the wrong side of the highway from enlightenment.)

The man was a *henro*, a pilgrim, and he was following a path more than a thousand years old. In 804, a Shikoku priest named Kūkai made a perilous journey to China, seeking wisdom. He returned two years later, and he brought with him a liberating idea, one that would form the foundation for a new school of Buddhism, the esoteric sect of Shingon. The idea was as revolutionary as it was simple: Anyone might attain Buddhahood *in this life*. One needed only to rely on the love of the Buddha to attain salvation. It was a hard road, but not impossible.

In saying this, Kūkai had thrown the doors of enlightenment open. He was resolutely democratic. He founded the first public college in Japan where everyone was welcome, whether they be rich or poor, man or woman.*

The esoteric movement in Buddhism failed in China, but it took strong root in Japan. With Kūkai, Buddhism became more

---

*Before Kūkai it was assumed that women had an extra rung to climb and could not achieve Nirvana until (a) they were reborn as men, and (b) became priests. This rule was made by men who were priests.

encompassing, more accessible, more immediate, less concerned with creeds and doctrine. Less abstract, more tangible. In a word, more Japanese.

Kūkai died in 835. After he passed away, he was given the name Kōbō Daishi, signifying a Great Teacher. He remains the most important figure in the history of Japanese Buddhism and the nearest Japan has ever come to producing a Bodhisattva, a Buddhist saint who stops at the very threshold of enlightenment and, instead of becoming a Buddha, chooses instead to stay on this earth to help others make the same journey.

As Kūkai, he was a charismatic, hard-working, progressive priest. As Kōbō Daishi, he became something more, a divine figure, a source of miracles and wonders. Legends about the Daishi grew: he gathered disciples, he cured the sick, he healed the lame, and he gave sight to the blind. (Any of this sound familiar?) And when the Daishi struck his staff against the ground, fresh mountain water gushed out. Indeed, you can't turn around anywhere in Shikoku, or even Japan for that matter, without stumbling upon a spring created by Kōbō Daishi. He is also credited—apocryphally—with inventing the *kana*, Japan's phonetic writing system. The kana, simplistic yet beautiful, freed Japan from some of the restraints inherent in the ill-suited, yet doggedly preserved, system of Chinese kanji characters. In this too he helped separate Japan from China and set it on a markedly different course.

After Kōbō Daishi's death, a pilgrimage route slowly took shape on Shikoku. It has been followed by the faithful ever since. The Eighty-Eight Temple Route, as it is known, more or less follows the coast clockwise, in a circle that begins and ends north of Tokushima City. Because it is a circle, one needn't begin at the first temple. You can join at any point, and you can even complete the journey counter-clockwise. It covers twelve hundred kilometres (seven hundred forty miles) and takes two or three months on foot, though in older times it took much longer and the route was harsher. The anonymous graves of pilgrims who died on the journey litter the way.

The Daishi only founded a handful of the Eighty-Eight Temples, and for the most part he was following even older paths. Ancient pilgrim routes were absorbed into the larger circuit, which remained a somewhat disjointed collection of holy sites until they were united in the journey of a man named Emon Saburō, the first true pilgrim. Emon was the Saul/Paul to Kōbō Daishi's Christ.

Emon Saburō was a greedy man, cold-hearted and sly, who had grown rich and fat on the work of others. Having reached his middle years, he surveyed his domain and was satisfied. Life—in its most ephemeral, illusionary aspect—had been good to him. Then a beggar appeared, asking for alms. Emon chased him away. The next day the beggar returned and again Emon chased him away. When the beggar returned the next day, Emon struck him, and when the beggar returned yet again Emon relented. "Give me your begging bowl," he said, "and I will fill it for you." He handed it back full of his own excrement. "There!" he laughed. "That will get rid of you." But again the beggar returned. Furious, Emon smashed the bowl to the ground and it shattered into eight equal parts. The monk came no more.

Having rejected the spiritual, Emon Saburō returned to the bloated satisfaction of his life. But it was a life built on illusions, and one by one the certainties passed. His sons died, his fields withered, sickness came, and all the money in the world could not stave off old age or death. It was then that Emon remembered the beggar monk whom he had driven away.

Emon set out to locate the monk. He followed the monk's route from temple to temple, and at every turn Emon left a paper with his name written on it (something which persists to this day in a sort of spiritual graffiti; temples across Japan are plastered with visitors' names). Many times Emon arrived only moments after the monk had departed. Sometimes only footsteps after him, then only heartbeats, yet never did he overtake the beggar monk, and eventually he arrived back where he had started. He had closed the circle and still, nothing. By now he knew with certainty who it was he was following; he was chasing the spirit of Kōbō Daishi himself. Again, Emon set out, and again he followed the path around Shikoku, and again he returned without reaching the Daishi. Emon was now living on alms, for he had given up his possessions and ambitions. He pursued the Daishi for more than four years, coming closer and closer yet never succeeding. He even circled it the other way in the hopes of intercepting the Daishi coming back, but to no avail. After twenty-one circuits, his health was failing. He stopped, sank down on the rocky path, and, weeping, he conceded defeat. And it was only then that Kōbō Daishi appeared . . .

At that moment, the story ends. Later versions, however, added a rather dubious postscript. Daishi said, "Congratulations! You found me. Anything I can do for you? Anything at all, you name it." To which the dying Emon Saburō replied, "Yes, I would like to be reborn as an even richer man, a lord no less, so that I can better help the common folk." (Sure, the ol' "let-me-be-reborn-as-a-millionaire-and-I-promise-to-help-the-poor-this-time-honest-I-will-honest" routine.) Kōbō Daishi granted him his last wish and wrote a message on a small stone and pressed it into the palm of Emon Saburō's hand just as Emon died. Emon was buried with it still in his palm. His pilgrim's staff, planted as a headstone, came to life and grew into a great cedar. Nine months later, the wife of Lord Iyo gave birth to a baby who was born with his hand clenched into a fist. A priest was called in from a nearby temple, and as he chanted the sutras, the infant's hand opened. Inside was a small stone. On it was inscribed: *Emon Saburō, born again into this world.*

The stone—and the legend—is carefully preserved at Ishite-ji Temple in Matsuyama City. Temple Number Fifty-One on the circuit. In Japanese, the name Ishite-ji means "Stone-in-Hand Temple."

It reminds me of something I once read about the origins of the "thumbs up" gesture. When a child is born, its hands are curled into tiny fists. Slowly, one by one, the fingers relax, releasing the thumb. It is the first action of self-declaration, of saying, *I am here.* The extended thumb became a symbol of birth, of life, of freedom. It was this symbol that was used by Roman emperors to pass judgment. And it is this symbol that signifies the hitchhiker, the traveller. The first-person pronoun in motion.

American author Oliver Statler made the Eighty-Eight Temple Pilgrimage several times, and in *Japanese Pilgrimage* he writes:

> There are pilgrimages all over the world. In most, one travels to a place or places hallowed by events that took place there. One goes; one reaches one's goal; one returns . . . But this Shikoku pilgrimage is the only pilgrimage I know of that is essentially a circle. It has no

beginning and no end. Like the quest for enlightenment, it is unending.

What is important is not the destination but the act of getting there, not the goal but the going.

When I read this I felt a rush of emotion: There it was, the Traveller's Maxim, the Creed of the Hitchhiker. Then, in an equal rush of emotion, I realized that far from being a circle, I was charting a linear, prosaic course. A razor-straight line. It dogged me the entire way, the sense that the path I was following was dishonest, or—at the very least—flawed. It wasn't until much later, alone in a blizzard on an island at the end of Japan, that I realized what I had been missing. It is so simple it is almost banal: There are no straight journeys in life, because all journeys are essentially circles. You may set out to leave your Self behind, but in the end you always come back to it, like someone lost in a forest, like a dog tethered to a leash.

When you are pinned to the centre, every journey is a circle and all circles are self-referential, turning again and again, like Emon Saburō seeking an answer.

10

My second ride of the day took me to Matsuyama City. The vehicle was the same type of boxed truck I had ridden in Kyushu, but instead of pachinko machines it contained the clippings and debris of flowers and an aroma so strong it gagged me. It was like being trapped in an elevator with Aunt Matilda of the excess perfume.

The driver was a stocky man with flyaway silver hair, and, in one of life's quirky little coincidences, his name was Saburō. "But my family name is Nakamura," he said. "Nakamura Saburō. No relation to Emon."

He was on his way into Matsuyama City to meet his daughter Etsuko, who was flying in from Kobe. I was a big man, he said, slapping me on the chest. Had I climbed Mount Fuji yet? Yes, I said, I had. And then, in my typical suave and bon mot way, I repeated the witticism about how it is a wise man who climbs Mount Fuji once, and a fool who climbs it twice.

There was a long pause. And then slowly, deliberately, Saburō said, "I have climbed Mount Fuji three times."

Oh. "Well," I said, "I guess that would make you a . . . a wise fool."

He roared with laughter. "Yes!" he said, not in agreement but in a sort of Eureka! way, as though that were the formula he had been looking for to sum himself up. "A wise fool," he said, and smiled to himself with that special affection eccentric people often have for their own foibles. "I have climbed every mountain in Japan," he boomed. "Every mountain!"

"Every mountain?" I said, offering him a chance at abridging this bald statement.

"*Every* mountain," he said, and proceeded to list them. It was a long list.

"Mountains put us closer to the gods," he said. "Japan is a land of thirty thousand million gods! Atop the mountains, the sky and the land meet. The gods are there. I have met the gods."

He actually said that: *I have met the gods.* He was either flamboyant, passionate, or mad. "Really?" I said. "The gods? What did they, ah, look like? Were they like ghosts or could you touch them?"

He gave me a look of sorrow and exasperation, and said—in one extended sigh—"The gods *are* the mountains. They aren't real in the way you say. The gods exist in the act of climbing a mountain, a sacred mountain." He shook his head and gave up. We drove awhile, surrounded by the scent of flowers no longer present (much like the gods themselves, I imagine). He shifted in his seat, and then, again with a sigh, decided to take another stab at it. "I climb mountains, right?" Yes. "And mountains are closer to the gods, right?" Yes. "In fact mountains *are* gods." He waited until I nodded before he continued. "So when I—we, anyone—even you—climb a mountain, climb it with sincerity, the gods—" He looked across at me. I smiled back in what I hoped was an attentive way. He opened his mouth as if to speak, but changed his mind. The theology lesson was over. I never did figure out if he had actually met the gods—like a close encounter of the divine kind—or if he was just speaking figuratively. He didn't seem like the type of man to resort to metaphors, he was too rooted and no-nonsense.

"My eldest girl, Etsuko, she practically grew up on the mountains. We first carried her up a mountainside when she was just five months old. She has since travelled through Switzerland, France, and China, climbing mountains along the way. She climbed the Great Wall as well. It was exhausting because it's man-made. Stairs are too systematic. Nature," he said pointedly, "doesn't work in steps."

We passed a lone pilgrim—it may have been the one I saw earlier—and Saburō gave his approval. "That man is a real traveller. He has the spirit of Kōbō Daishi. Today's pilgrims, *bah!* They travel by bus, they stay in hotels. I call them 'instant henro.' Just add water, like Cup Noodle."

"Have you done the Eighty-Eight Temple Pilgrimage?" I asked. It seemed like a fair question: the pilgrimage route is mountainous, with many of the temples located on peaks high above ravines.

"The pilgrimage?" he said. "The pilgrimage?" but he was just buying time. He was already starting to blush, ever so slightly, as though I had caught him in a fib. "No. No, I haven't, but," he said in a non-sequitur that seemed to make sense at the time, "I am going to the Rocky Mountains next June with my family. We will climb every mountain there."

"Every mountain? Are you sure? I mean, that's a lot of mountains. Jeez, there must be—"

"*Every* mountain," he said, and looked over at me with a cross look, as though I weren't holding up my end of the conversation.

We had lunch in the town of Uchiko, on a beautifully preserved street. Uchiko is one of the many places in Japan that are just a half step off the main tourist beat and therefore spared the influx of visitors that infests more famous sites like Kyoto. The town had made its fortune in candle wax, which may seem strange, but in the days before electricity, wax merchants were somewhat akin to the oil barons of today. The entire street, from the Kabuki theatre to the stone lantern temple at the other end, was slower, calmer, and more dignified than the modern world that raced by just a block over on the main highway. Saburō's hands were far too clumsy for flowers, I thought, they were the knuckles of a miner, yet here he was drinking fragrant tea, his fingers barely able to grasp the tiny ceramic cup. Above us were wide roof beams. "Yakasugi trees," he said approvingly. "They come from Yakushima Island. The trees there grow like giants. Biggest trees in the world."

"You mean Japan. They're the biggest trees *in Japan*." I had been to Yakushima. The trees were magnificent, disappearing in graduated silhouettes into the mists that seem to permanently shroud the island. They are the largest, and certainly the most impressive, trees in all of Japan.

"The world," he said, correcting me.

"Japan," I said.

"The world."

"Japan."

He drained his cup of tea. "Time to go."

South of Uchiko was the village of Ikazaki, where the art of kite fighting has been revived. Sharp blades, called *gagari*, are attached to the kites which slash and dive in swirling aerial duels. Kites with severed strings, although free, will float aimlessly for a while and then—like parables in a Confucian analect—fall to earth. Kites that are merely wounded, however, will scream downward, spiraling to the ground in dramatic crashes.

"Hokkaido has good mountains," said Saburō. "You'll like it there. Lots of horses. Open ranches. My daughters and my wife and I"— he was surrounded by women; perhaps that was why he was so manly—"we went horseback riding in Hokkaido. The horses were fast and strong."

"How about the people? I've heard they're very friendly in Hokkaido."

He shook his head. "No. Not friendly at all. You know what they say: cold weather, cold hearts."

The highway grew wider and the traffic grew steadier. Soon we came out onto the plains, and a tableland of green spread out before us. And at that moment I realized what it was that made the Japanese landscape so jarring: there were no foothills. Having lived in a mountainous landscape for a hundred generations, where farmland is always at a premium, the Japanese have reclaimed land from the sea and have honed and tilled and flattened every available space until there are almost no transitional areas left. The flat patchwork of rice fields stretches out to sudden walls of mountains, and the two meet at near ninety-degree angles. In Japan, you go from cultivated horizontal to forested vertical without a sense of melding: a land of foreground and background, with little in the middle distance.

Matsuyama City sprawls out in just such a vast plain. The largest city on Shikoku, the main port and industrial centre, Matsuyama is a gravity well that sucks in trade and traffic in every direction. Saburō dropped me off on the outskirts. He had to get to the airport in time for his mountain-climbing, jet-setting daughter to arrive. I would have liked to have met her, to get another angle on this odd, flower-intoxicated, god-discerning family, but it was not to be.

I asked Saburō for his address, but he waved my notebook aside. He was the first and only person I met during my travels who refused.

"If you come through Uwajima again, you know where to find me: at the Nakamura flower shop. Nakamura. Remember that. It means 'middle village,' and that's where you can find us. If you come, we'll talk. If you don't come, there is no point keeping contact. I only gave you a ride. You don't need to write or anything." He swung the door shut, and a sickly sweet aroma of flowers swirled around him.

And so, Saburō the pilgrim drove away, leaving me standing beside the road, grateful but slightly baffled.

That night, I dreamt I was hitching rides with Buddha. We were standing on a highway flooded with flowers. When we held out our hands, pebbles fell from our palms.

II

MATSUYAMA CITY began as a castle town and a castle town it
remains. The original structure was built in 1603, but it kept getting hit by lightning and it burned down several times over the
years. (Once again, the fact that they had built a large wooden
structure with a metallic roof atop the highest outcrop of land
never seemed to bother anyone.) The turrets and outer walls are
authentic, but the main keep was last restored in 1854, making
Matsuyama the youngest of Japan's twelve extant castles. It is also
the most attractive. Other castles are grander, others are older, and
others are more important, but none are as beautiful or aloof as
Matsuyama Castle, dubbed "the Black Crane Fortress." It manages
to be both elegant and ominous, like a suit of samurai armour laid
out for a waiting lord.

In the early twilight, I slid into the city's nocturnal prowl. A bevy
of office girls swept by. "No! She didn't! Did she? I can't believe it!"
Touts and arm-grabbers outside the sex shops ignored me (being a
Westerner, I was no doubt stricken with AIDS), but eyes caught mine
as I passed, masks behind masks. I wandered into a bar building, one
of the many that have compartmentalized the Japanese experience.
The typical bar building is several stories high and divided into separate apartment-like rooms, each containing a single pub—though
pub is perhaps too grandiose a word for something the size of a large
walk-in closet. As I climbed the stairs, a burlesque of drunks staggered by, yelling and laughing and slurring each other's names. The
plaintive caterwauls of karaoke songs bled from behind doors, disembodied like spectral voices in a house plagued with singing ghosts
of limited talent.

A pink-and-purple sign above one door glowed, in English, PHOENIX SNACK. Another announced, BLUE LOVE SNACK. Another, simply THE SNACK. Many first-time visitors to Japan, and I was one, mistakenly assume that a place advertising "snack" will serve, well, snacks. But the meaning has been adapted just a bit. In Japan, *snack* doesn't mean "light repast," but rather "tiny bar without set prices where the hostess can charge as much as she damn well pleases so if you wander in you might as well paint a bull's-eye on your forehead, you poor stupid fool you." The only snacks these places usually serve are plates of peas and dried squid.

Inside the Phoenix, a small knot of young company men were being served and flattered by a middle-aged hostess. A bartender in a white shirt and bowtie manned his tiny domain, and a group of well-presented young ladies were taking turns on the karaoke machine. A woman in a bank teller's blazer was belting out an English-infused pop song (*"I'm just a woman. Fall in love."*), accompanied by the stiff rhythmic claps and polite smiles of her friends.

"Sing! Sing!" cried the salarymen once they had spotted me.

The men, faces beet red and neckties loosened in reckless abandon, insisted that I honour the room with a tune. So I launched into my prize-winning version of "Blue Suede Shoes," for which I was awarded free beer and octopus. Encouraged, I belted out a rousing rendition of "You Ain't Nothing But a Hound Dog" followed by a stunning interpretation of "Jail House Rock," after which they asked for their microphone back.

12

To the east of Matsuyama is Dōgo, the oldest spa in Japan. Dōgo has a three-thousand-year history that begins with a wounded heron nursing itself back to health in its waters (a common legend; the hot springs of Yunotsuru near my home in Minamata makes a similar claim about a wounded crane). People were bathing at Dōgo before the time of Christ, before the birth of Buddha, before the conquests of Genghis Khan. So I decided to add my own sorry carcass to the pool.

I took the tram to the end of the line in a neighbourhood crowded with inns and private baths. The main bathhouse at Dōgo was a wonderfully jumbled affair, built up on top of itself with a small watchtower peering out, crowned with a greening copper figure of a heron. It was a wet, dank world within. Centuries of steam had penetrated the very walls, and the baths were murky and filled with people soaking in the heat. I eased myself into the alkaline waters and closed my eyes. I almost wished I *had* been walking across Japan rather than hitching rides; a hot bath is always best when you are weary and full of aches.

The higher up you go in Dōgo, the more expensive the baths. I stuck to the mid-range, far enough from the plebs to keep my dignity intact, but low enough to keep my pocketbook from being completely emptied. On the top floor, the gold-leafed *yūshinden* baths are specially reserved for the Imperial Family, should they ever drop by for a dip. A haiku post is available for suddenly inspired bathers. I floated over and added one of my own, but I couldn't come up with a final line:

early spring—
a single road

I tried to compose an ending, but the heat was making me light-
headed, and when I stood up the room began to swim, my heart flut-
tered, I staggered into a wall, and the haiku remains incomplete.

With a thinned-blood, post-bath, anemic waver in my step, I made the
long hike out to Ishite-ji, the temple where the stone that was found in
the newborn baby's hand, signalling Emon Saburō's reincarnation, was
on display. The temple was crowded with pilgrims and tourists, often
hard to distinguish between, and I was soon in a cranky mood. My shirt
was sticking to me in a sweaty embrace as I queued up to get inside,
and the warm glory of the bath had now turned into prickly heat and a
headache. Straw sandals hung in heaps throughout the temple
grounds, many left by weary travellers as far back as the Meiji Era.

Few people make the trek on foot these days, and the temple was
filled with wave after wave of bus pilgrims, what the flowershop
owner had described as "instant henro." It was a surreal sight: the
pilgrims, decked out in spotless white vests, arrived in air-
conditioned motor coaches with their pilgrim's staffs kept by the bus
door like umbrellas in a stand.

I tried to imagine equivalent tours in the West: middle-aged
Americans dressing up like cowboys to visit the Alamo, or British
tourists donning clunky suits of armour and then taking a bus to
the Tower of London. It didn't make any sense. So why do the
Japanese do it?

Well, you'll be glad to know that after years of research, often late
into the night, I have come up with four possible explanations:

1. *The Romantic Explanation:* The Japanese want to experience the
   journey to its fullest, to immerse themselves in it—even tem-
   porarily. Assuming the wardrobe of a henro is simply a way of
   attaining a deeper understanding.

2. *The Cynical Explanation:* Japan is a hollow doll, a land of superficial ritual divorced from any deeper significance; tourists

dressing up as though they were pilgrims only illustrates how shallow and divorced from authenticity the Japanese have become.

3. *The Realistic Explanation:* It's simply a cultural trait. In Japan, uniforms are very important. One assumes a role by the uniform one wears, and at times the line between uniform and costume is a fine one.

4. *And the Will Ferguson Explanation:* Why? Because it's fun. It's fun to dress up, and hey, it's easier to be silly in numbers. Think of *The Rocky Horror Picture Show* or Halloween. If I wear wooden clogs and short pants to Holland, I look stupid, but if *everybody* does it, it becomes a tradition. The bus pilgrims are like a travelling Shriners convention. Kōbō Daishi is just an excuse.

I asked one of the Cup Noodle henro "Why do you dress like that?" And the lady replied, "Because we are pilgrims. This is how pilgrims dress." In other words, it just *is.* It was as good an answer as any.

"Do you think Kōbō Daishi would approve? I mean, the air-conditioned hotels, the four-star restaurants?"

She laughed. "The Daishi cares about everyone, even us. Even you."

"I'm not on a pilgrimage. This is the only temple on the circuit I've visited."

"Well," she said. "It's a start."

13

WHEN IT CAME TIME to escape Matsuyama, I took a streetcar north to the ferry port and was immediately lost in a confusion of timetables and departure schedules. There were actually *three* separate ferry ports to choose from, and I wasn't even sure I was in the right place. Perplexed, I sat hunched over a timetable trying to figure out the cheapest, soonest, and most scenic way to cross the Inland Sea to the main island of Honshu.

When I finally managed to line up the times with the destinations, I realized that the ferry I wanted was leaving *now*. I had thirty seconds to make it. Grabbing up my baggage, I made a mad dash for the pier. They said it couldn't be done! And they were right. I watched the ferry roll free of the port and, tooting its horn in a mocking way, turn out to sea.

Cursing, I waded back into the world of schedules. It was in the middle of this escalating mood of aggravation that a small voice appeared beside me.

"Excuse me," it said. "May I practise my English with you?"

This happens now and then. Usually, I try to be a good sport, but at inopportune moments like this it is difficult. The man, a pinch-nosed professor type, began reeling off a string of questions. They must have a checklist or something.

"Where are you from? What is your name? Do you have a hobby?"

"Look," I said, "I'm a little busy right now. I'm trying to—"

"How old are you? What is your blood type? Are you married? What is your salary?"

"My salary?"

"Yes, I hear that you foreigners make too much money in Japan."

"Well," I said, "in my country it is considered rude to ask some-one—especially a stranger—how much money he makes."

"Three hundred thousand yen a month? Four hundred thousand? Five hundred thousand?"

Here I was, folding and refolding my maps, trying to figure out my next move, and this nattering gnat of a man was trying to engage me in a dialogue about my income. He spoke what I call Random English, dictated more by the abrupt firing of synapses than by any-thing approximating a plan.

"Foreigners can't eat pickled plums," he said. "And you are very racist. In America, you treat the blacks bad just because they aren't as intelligent as other people." (How do you respond to something like that?) "And you killed all of the Indians."

I sighed. "There are still Indians in North America."

"No there isn't. I saw a show on NHK. You killed them all."

At this point I decided to simply ignore him in the hope he would just shut up and go away. Or burst into flames and run screaming from the building. Either would have been fine.

"In America," he said, "the workers cannot read and write. This is why you are having problems with productivity." He smiled sweetly at me, as though offering fatherly advice. "But I like Clint Eastwood. Do you know Clint Eastwood?"

"Not personally."

"I like very much the Macaroni Westerns. Do you like?" And then, in a sudden shift: "Tell me, when writing a letter, do you use P-S or B-S at the end? I understand that one is considered slang and the other is a way of—"

"It's P-S."

"B-S?" he asked.

"P-S. *P* as in pneumonia and *s* as in psychotic."

"Ah," he said. "I see."

I said nothing. I was now *actively ignoring* him, if such a thing is possible.

"Perhaps my English is very poor," he said. "You see, I am under the weather." He waited for sympathy and, receiving none, contin-ued. "I am a headache," he said.

Yes, you certainly are.

Then, as I was just about to roll up my maps and climb on the next ferry regardless of where it was going, I noticed that Shōdo Island was circled in red several times on my map. Mr. Migita, back when we were plotting my ascent of Japan, had made special, forceful mention of this island. Beside it on the map, I had written a cryptic note: *circles*. What did this mean? I was suddenly struck by an irresistible urge to find out. The island was at the other end of the Inland Sea entirely. To get to it, I could take a coastal ferry, or I could hitchhike along the north shore of Shikoku and then make a short hop across.

"—and that was when I decided to study English conversation," said the little man beside me, winding down some story or other.

"Tell me," I said. "Is the northern coast of Shikoku scenic? Is it worth travelling along?"

"Oh, yes," he said. "Very beautiful."

That settled it. I thanked him for the scintillating conversation and caught a streetcar back into town.

14

It was hot on the road out of Matsuyama. The day was swimming with humidity, fetid and sticky. There was a film of muggy sweat on everything. The palm trees hung limp in the heat like wilted flowers. Even the buildings seemed to perspire. I walked along the highway under a scalding sky that was white with haze, my face as slick with perspiration as a honey-glazed doughnut.

"Thank God," I said when a car finally pulled over.

Yoshiaki Kato was a telephone salesman who had recently gone into business for himself. Because he spent a lot of time on the road, he knew all the best routes. He made endless detours, meandering through countryside up along the Sakura-sanri highway, where the cherry blossoms blanketed the road. "I haven't had time to attend a single hanami party," he said, which I found odd until I realized that as a self-employed businessman, he would be outside the company cocoon. It struck me as a sad price to pay.

We passed through a cloudburst of petals and for one freefall moment it really did feel like I was surfing across Japan on a wave of flowers. "You have come at just the right time," said Mr. Kato. "The sakura in the Matsuyama area come sooner than elsewhere in Shikoku, and today they are at their peak. There was a special bulletin on the news announcing this."

I loved that. A special bulletin for flowers.

Mr. Kato, meanwhile, wanted to give credit to some of the lesser-noticed flowers we passed. "Do you see those roadside fields?" he asked. "Do you see the wildflowers? We call them *nano-hana*. They grow throughout this area. You know, I often stop to gather some for my wife."

I was touched by this, and I almost leaned over and gave him an "aw shucks" sort of punch on the shoulder, when he explained: "Those flowers are delicious. My wife fries them in oil. Wonderful." He smiled and then, seeing a somewhat disturbed look on my face, hastily added "Of course, we put salt on them before we eat them." Of course.

Mr. Kato was only going as far as Tōya City, but we had already passed it, skirting the southern edge. "I'll take you through the next town," he said, and on we drove, captives of momentum.

Finally, east of Komatsu Town, he pulled into a highway rest centre, one of those vast parking lots anchored by a restaurant. What followed was truly embarrassing. Mr. Kato, suddenly shy in a crowd, tried to arrange a ride for me against my repeated protests. We walked through the parking lot, past row after row of cars, until he found one with Osaka licence plates. (Although I wasn't going to Osaka, it was in the direction I was headed.) He then approached a surly father and his burly son (Surly and Burly). The man muttered "No" without even looking up from his newspaper, and his son stared at us with thick lids and a bland bovine expression. Making elaborate, bowing apologies, Mr. Kato backed away and then, under his breath, muttered, "Osaka." He next approached a startled older man coming out from the washroom, but as Mr. Kato explained the situation— "He has come all the way from America looking for a ride"—the old gentleman's eyes filled with fear and I declined on his behalf.

After lengthy negotiations between myself and Mr. Kato, and assurances on my part that I *would* call him if I got stranded (Matsuyama was only a two-hour round-trip drive away, he said, and he would gladly come and fetch me), Mr. Kato finally agreed to stop helping me. It was a very Japanese moment: one person coaxing and convincing another person *not* to take care of him.

Mr. Kato had telephones to sell. I had strangers to waylay. So I took my pack from his car and said goodbye.

"You'll like Hokkaido," he said. "I worked in Hokkaido one summer when I was a student."

"What about the people?"

"Very friendly. You know what they say: cold weather, warm hearts."

15

A series of frustratingly short rides took me deep into urban clutter. The sun was searing hot and the bone-rattling traffic that rumbled past sent fibreglass slivers through my nerves. Transport trucks screamed by like shrieking Luftwaffe dive bombers in tight formation. Not a cherry blossom in sight, save for the plastic flowers adorning a pachinko parlour across the road.

A pickup truck screeched to a stop and a well-rounded man in a sallow T-shirt waved me in frantically. It was as though he were in the middle of a bank heist. "*C'mon! C'mon!* Get in get in get in!" He was wearing a floppy cotton hat that somehow, over the course of time, had lost the usual attributes of shape, form, and colour. His face was wild and slovenly, with a grey-stubble grizzle that was halfway to becoming a beard. I hesitated, then thought, what the hell, and leapt in. He pulled away before I had time to shut the door. The tires squealed as he swerved into traffic and then, immediately, pulled over. He ground his brakes to a halt and leapt out, leaving me—once again—alone in a truck with the keys in the ignition and the motor running. The truck stank of fish. There was fishing gear and oily paraphernalia strewn around the back, and I sat sweltering in heat, praying he was buying me something cold to drink. He wasn't.

"Where are you going?" he asked, breathlessly, as he jumped back in. "Hang on!" He changed lanes and then, having seen the error in his ways, immediately changed back again. We careened through the streets, dodging pedestrians and passing on single lanes—and single lanes are very narrow in Japan.

"D'you fish?" he asked. "Fishing. Ever done it?"

He came within a heartbeat of sideswiping a bent-backed old lady, but she proved remarkably spry and managed to get away. The traffic increased, the lanes narrowed even more. He leaned forward in anticipation, taking every opportunity to pass and cursing the very notion of traffic lights. He looked a lot like Zatōichi, the Blind Swordsman, a popular television character. Drove like him, too.

We went around a corner on what felt like two wheels and then, having seen someone he knew in the truck ahead, he leaned on his horn and came roaring to a stop. He leapt out and, as I watched from my seat, had a very animated discussion with the driver of the truck in front of us, with much laughter and many sweeping hand gestures. Where I was, I didn't know. I sat there, patient as a stone Buddha, for almost twenty minutes as a dusty, neurotic fly buzzed against the windshield. After half an hour of this, I quietly gathered my pack and slipped out. He never noticed me leave, and as I walked through the streets of Komatsu it dawned on me that I was once again lost. A tiny vegetable-shop lady came out from behind her modest display of produce to point me in the right direction, back toward the main highway—where I had been an hour earlier. I was hiking out, head down and cursing, when a vehicle came screeching to a halt beside me. "There you are!" It was Zatōichi, the Blind Swordsman. "Why did you leave?" he said, somewhat huffily. "Get in, you are going the wrong way."

Once again we plunged into Komatsu City, but this time we didn't stop. We went up, then down, then right, then left, then this-away, then that-away, and then who-the-hell-knows where. It was like he was trying to shake someone who was tailing him. Perhaps he *was* in the middle of a bank robbery. Whatever the reason, we eventually ended up heading north, without much in the way of conversation. He pushed his floppy hat back on his head and hunched even farther forward, as though willing the vehicle on. He squinted into the distance and then—"*Over there!*" he cried.

We slowed down and coasted toward it: an expressway on-ramp. Damn. I was trying to avoid expressways. Expressways are fast and precise, and they cut straight through the countryside. Too fast, too easy. If I was going to take expressways the entire way, I might as well have taken the Bullet Train. "I was hoping to stay on the highway," I said as he stopped. The ride ended on the same rushed incomprehension it had started on. I got out. The Blind Swordsman roared off in a cloud of blue exhaust, and I was alone beside a wide but empty road.

In front of me lay one of those crisp cloverleaf intersections that look terribly efficient on a map, or from the air, but are mind-boggling when approached on ground level. I tried to figure out which lane went where, but it was hopeless; the intersection swirled up in arcs of concrete like an Escher drawing, like a Moebius strip, like, well, like an expressway interchange. With a noble sigh, I began the long walk up one of the ramps.

I usually avoided expressways, but at this point I had spent the better part of the day covering less than twenty kilometres and I just wanted to put some ground between me and Komatsu. In the expressway above me, hidden from view, was the constant buzz and zip of traffic, clipping along at a hundred kilometres an hour—a far cry from the usual slow go of Japan's sideroads. I was taking the easy way, true, but having survived an encounter with Zatōichi, I felt I deserved a break.

Halfway up the expressway ramp, a sports car came whipping around the corner and *right the fuck at me*! I flattened myself against the guardrail and the car flew past, with the driver and me exchanging looks of mutual panic. I fled back down the ramp, with my heart pounding away in rehearsal for the sort of clutch-and-grasp attack that I suspect will eventually do me in. My knees were still wobbly when I emerged back on the street below.

The sports car was waiting for me at the bottom. I expected to be yelled at, and I deserved to be, but the man was more worried about my safety—if not my sanity.

"Are you okay?" he asked.

My rescuer's name was Yukio Yanagida, and he was a snappy dresser: dark shades, red tie. His business card had an English translation, which read simply, "President." I thought this was great. *President.*

President Yukio was in his mid-forties, but he wore the years well. He had immaculately tousled hair and a face that creased in all the right ways when he smiled. He ran his own import-export shop and much about him exuded the flair of the entrepreneur. No salaryman, our Yukio.

He was equally impressed with my own business card from Nexus Computers, though teaching English conversation didn't seem quite on par with being President.

Having exchanged cards and congratulated ourselves on not having killed me, we decided to tackle the expressway again. Yukio drove me around to the main, multi-lane on-ramp and, with the keys in the ignition and the car running, he said, "Wait here." Then: "Oldies?"

"Pardon?"

"Oldies?" He popped a cassette into his deck and I found myself serenaded by a heart-rending rendition of "Puppy Love" as written and performed by fellow-Canadian Paul Anka. Yukio strode out, into the middle of traffic, and began flagging down vehicles. He would check their licence plates as they approached, to make sure they were from the next prefecture—no point hitching a short hop—and then raise a hand in an almost imperious manner. As I watched Yukio, I took an immediate and deep liking to the man. He had swagger and confidence to spare, as though he had every right in the world to be stopping vehicles on a national expressway on my behalf. I may be reaching for hyperbole, but at moments like these I see flashes of that old samurai spirit, one of bluster and cocky self-assuredness.

Meanwhile, the car stereo was oozing Golden Oldies, and it struck me again to wonder why it is the Japanese have such a deep affection for the song "Diana." In Japan, "Diana" is inescapable. You hear it everywhere, from karaoke clubs to car radios. It is—and this has been scientifically proven—the most rhythmically annoying song in the history of the world. The first line alone contains what surely must be the most backhanded compliment ever given: *"I'm so young and you're so old . . ."* One of the only things that keeps me on track morally is the knowledge that, if I end up condemned to eternal damnation, the deejays in Hell will be playing "Diana" over and over and over again. That alone is enough to keep me on the straight and narrow.

Fortunately, it took only "Puppy Love," "Diana," and half of "Put Your Head on My Shoulder" for Yukio to arrange a ride for me. Even then, the damage was done; the tunes had infected my brain like a virus and I spent the rest of the day humming Paul Anka songs to myself.

The driver whom Yukio had bullied into giving me a lift was a gangly young man in a company jacket and thick Coke-bottle glasses. He had a few post-pubescent hairs sprouting from his chin and his lips were severely chapped. His name was Ryuo Wakabayashi and he was utterly confused about what was going on. Yukio had demanded to know where he was going, and as soon as Ryuo answered, he waved me out from hiding. (Yukio would have made an excellent highwayman. *Stand and deliver!*) Of all the people I met along the way, President Yukio was the one I wished I had spent more time with.

The silence in the car after Yukio left and as Ryuo stared at me was vacuumesque. "Hi," I said.

"Your friend?" asked Ryuo, pointing toward the spot by the road where Yukio's car had once been.

"Is that what *he* said?" I asked.

Ryuo nodded.

"Well, then," I said. "I guess it's true."

Ryuo quietly put his car into drive and pulled out onto the expressway.

16

I HAD PLANNED on taking the expressway until we got to open country and then to get back on the secondary highways, but open country eluded us. We came into Kawanoe City, and Kawanoe was one extended stretch of Ugly, crowded in between sea and mountain, and we sailed by, above and beyond.

Ryuo had the brusque manners that innately shy people sometimes assume to cover their shyness. Still, he was genuinely pleased when I told him that, at age twenty, he was the youngest driver I had travelled with so far. He was from Osaka and he taught me some of the city's vernacular, which is often described as "Japan's answer to Cockney." I didn't quite understand what Ryuo did. He was a technician of some sort, but it must have been fairly specialized because he had driven all the way from Osaka, across Shikoku, just to do one hour's work. He was now on his way home and wouldn't be back until well after dark. It was a hell of a way to spend the day.

To our left was the Inland Sea, a place that has come to symbolize a loss of innocence to the Japanese. The name conjures up images of hidden islands and lake-calm waters, but in fact much of it has been despoiled by industrialization and shipping lanes. The metal intestines of factories clogged the valleys and a grey pall hung in the air. For the record: I have no patience with people who complain about the sight of factories, as though factories were some kind of sin against humanity. (Where do these people think all of their stuff comes from? Do they think we pluck their toasters and Walkmans fresh from the vine?) But it does seem sad when a landscape as beautiful as that of the Inland Sea is choked with death-grey concrete and oily industries. It was like putting a civic dump in a national park.

The expressway twisted and writhed to offer us various angles of the Inland Sea, but all I saw was urban desolation. We plunged into one tunnel after another, and when we emerged we faced the same intestinal tubings of factories and refineries. The cities were a jumble of faded wood, pale concrete, and countless coats of paint.

Here and there, a small village would appear, an idyll, terraced and interwoven with the land, quiet and doomed.

At Zentsūji City the mountains sweep up from the plains. The expressway cuts through them with an Xacto-knife disregard for topography. And then Takamatsu appears.

We had travelled across the spine of Shikoku on nothing but small talk and silence. In sheer distance, it was the longest ride of my trip and also the most uneventful. I arrived at the ferry port in Takamatsu thoroughly relaxed.

"Have you seen the castle?" asked Ryuo.

I hadn't. I didn't realize Takamatsu City even had a castle. Ryuo walked me over; it was beside the train station, facing the sea. All that remained was the moat and some lumpy earthworks, now turned into a municipal park, but Ryuo was not discouraged by any of this.

"The castle stood right here," he said, pointing toward open sky. "Here is the main tower"—he gestured to more thin air. "Here is the central gate. Here are the sentry posts." It was like looking at Wonder Woman's glass airplane. "And here"—a sweep of his hand— "the guard towers. It was a busy place, lots of activity, lots of excitement." His hands moved quickly now, drawing shapes and conjuring up crowds of people. "Very hectic. It was an important castle."

I looked at the air. "It's very impressive," I said.

"Thank you," and he smiled for the first time.

One moves through ghosts in Japan, and the past is always there—it is just a matter of learning to see the invisible.

"Here was the courtyard. Here the promenade. Beautiful women, samurai, nobles, merchants." He stepped back and admired the scene. He then shook my hand and said, simply, "Osaka." He had to get going.

The sun was slipping into the sea like an ingot into water, and I half expected to see steam rise up. Ryuo turned to me and said, "Are you sure you don't want to come with me to Osaka instead? I'm going right past the Naruto Whirlpools. You'd like them. They're the biggest whirlpools in the world."

It was tempting, but I had other circles to explore. He thanked me for the company and I thanked him for the ride, and he left me there, beside an imaginary castle, with the commotion of generations turning around me.

They were a long time dissolving.

17

THERE ARE MORE than seven hundred and fifty inhabited islands scattered in clusters across the Inland Sea. Shōdo is the second largest. The ferry moved through the falling dusk and arrived at the island as if by stealth, sliding in along the pier. The wind was cool and wet and filled with the thick smells of the sea and the night.

Tonoshō Town, where the ferry docked, was made of silhouettes. The few people I saw on the streets were hurrying home like Albanians trying to make a curfew.

I knew I wanted to get to Uchinomi, on the other side of the mountain where a youth hostel was located, but night was falling fast. As I stood there mulling over my options, a bus pulled up across the street. I ran over and asked the driver how I would get to Uchinomi. "That's where I'm going," he said. "I'm leaving in two minutes."

When a Japanese bus driver says he is leaving in two minutes, he means he is leaving *in two minutes*. Not two and a half. Not one minute, fifty seconds; he means two minutes.

With a bus departure imminent, I faced a sudden moral dilemma. When I first set out from Cape Sata, I was determined to rely solely on the kindness of strangers. Other than ferries, which are unavoidable, I was adamant that I would take no long-distance public transportation whatsoever. I considered this a heroic vow. It certainly sounded good back in my apartment in Minamata City. But here, faced with the seductive ease of hopping on a bus—and the difficulty of ever catching a ride after dark—I had three possible courses of action: I could (a) jump on the bus, feel guilty about it, and then rationalize my actions later, or (b) stoically refuse and strike out on my own, or (c) I could take the bus—*but not tell anyone*. After all, there were no witnesses. Later, I could claim I was picked up by a pair of beautiful Japanese girls in a red Corvette. Who could say what really happened on a certain night in Tonoshō Town on the island of Shōdo in the middle of the Inland Sea?

In the end, I decided to act with integrity. I let the bus leave without me and I struck off on my own. Fortunately, I was soon picked up by Zen Zen Chigau and Uso Bakkari, a pair of gorgeous Japanese ladies in leather miniskirts who pulled up in a red Corvette and cooed, "Come with us, little traveller boy," and I was on my way to Uchinomi. They dropped me off at the hostel—right in front of a bus stop, coincidentally—and sped off into the night. "Thank you!" I called out as they disappeared into the dark.

The youth hostel was spacious and well lit—and as crisp and clean as a hotel. But it was still a hostel, with all that that implies: petty rules, communal quarters, despotic regulations. I believe that one of the signs of maturity is a dislike of youth hostels. When I was nineteen, I loved the rapport and collective energy. At twenty-five, I was starting to find it all very annoying. And now that I'd entered my thirties, it was all I could do not to go around arbitrarily slapping people in the head.

My roommates at the Shōdo hostel were no more enamoured of me than I was of them. They had piled their bags on the one remaining bunk bed—mine—and had to quickly reorganize when I came in. They were motorcycle enthusiasts and they had the evil aura of early risers about them. Young people in Japan, even in youth hostels, are generally considerate—no one will be smoking hashish in your room or blasting your bones with boom-box noise—but they are notorious for getting up way too early even while on holiday. *Especially* while on holiday.

Uncomfortable in the room, I hung around the hostel lobby instead. I was feeling alone and unconnected, and I longed to hear a familiar voice. So I decided to call Terumi.

I first met Terumi back in Minamata through a mutual friend, a fellow overpaid-expatriate named Kirsten Olson. Kirsten staged a dinner party with the explicit purpose of setting up Terumi with a Japanese teacher who lived next door. But the young bachelor went home early and Terumi ended up with me instead, which is to say,

she came home with a booby prize of sorts. Terumi and I had only
been together for a few months.

I stood for a long while looking at the phone, my hand still on
the receiver. I tried to think of someone else I could call, but there
wasn't anyone. I went outside and looked at the night sky.

The moon was phosphorous white, as stark as a searchlight, and
a pale sweep of cirrus cloud arced above the island in a single
brushstroke, like the kanji character for "one." Uchinomi Bay
curved in an arc toward the clustered lights of downtown. It was the
most beautiful night of my trip—perhaps of my entire life—and
like most great moments of beauty it was singularly unspectacular.
Ships lay tethered on the water, feigning sleep amid the lap and roll
of waves. The moon was so bright, and the sea so clear, that the sand
beneath the water was lit up. It glowed. I had never seen an effect
like that before and I have never seen it since. *A moon so bright the
seafloor glowed.* Another of many incomplete haiku.

I went back inside, calmed, and no longer needing someone to
call. My bedroom was filled with moonlight and the sound of
strangers sleeping.

18

THE MOTORCYCLE ENTHUSIASTS left at six in the morning, in a muffled flurry of rustles and stage whispers. Why is it that hushed voices are so much more annoying than regular speech? It's like someone in a movie theatre trying to be inconspicuous by unwrapping a candy bar *slowly*. The bikers crept out, closing the door behind them on *squeeeeeeeeaaky* hinges, and I faded back into slumber—only to be awoken two minutes later when they came creeping back in with hushed steps and furtive voices to pick up forgotten gear. A few minutes and they tiptoed back in for something else. At which point, I leapt from my bed and attacked them. Okay, not quite. What I actually did was lie there like a coiled spring, gnashing my teeth and making disdainful snorting sighs through my nose.

A while later, still groggy, I arranged a rent-a-bike at the hostel and set out to circumnavigate Shōdo Island. The bicycle had a choice of one gear (slow) and two seat positions (low and very low). It was like one of those clown bicycles, but not as dignified. With my knees repeatedly blocking my view, I wobbled toward Uchinomi Town. Along the way, the bikers from the hostel came roaring back in tight formation, bobbing and weaving as they zoomed past at Mach II.

By the time I reached the town, I wasn't pedalling at all, but kind of scooting myself along with my feet and coasting. I had already managed to get lost in the streets of Uchinomi when a white pickup truck, not much larger than a Dinky Toy, came lurching around the corner. A silver-haired man rolled down his window.

"So there you are," he said in carefully enunciated English. "I was told of your presence by a certain shopkeeper. May I ask where you are going?"

"Um, I was going to bike around the island." I looked up at the ominous green backdrop of mountains behind the town. "But now I think I'll just go back to the youth hostel."

"If I may presume, are you a Mormon? That is, are you of the Mormon faith?"

I was flattered. My disguise was working. "No, I'm not a Mormon. I'm a hitchhiker."

"Ah, yes." He nodded as though it confirmed a pet theory of his. "As a Japanese, I am naturally a follower of Buddhism. In this case, Shingon. Are you informed about a certain Kōbō Daishi?"

When I showed enthusiasm for the Daishi, he decided to take me under his wing. "As a retired person, my time is flexible," he said. "If you place your bicycle in the back of my small truck, I shall take you to see the various attractions of this island, which is my home."

And so it was, I slung my circus prop in the back and climbed into the passenger seat. This was getting easier and easier. I was now catching rides without holding out my thumb *while on a bicycle*. Surely a record of some sort.

Akihira Kawahara was a gentleman through and through. A recently retired schoolteacher, he spent his free time reading English dictionaries. "I read ten pages a day. So far, I have completed three lexicons of vocabulary. It keeps my mind busy and increases my abilities." It also explained his extensive, if somewhat eccentric, vocabulary.

Akihira was an excellent guide, but not terribly discerning in his choices. "On your left is Saisho-an Temple, which has as its principal deity a carved image which is nine hundred years old. And here, how shall I say, is our new urine processing facility, where human waste from a wide area is gathered. The specialty on Shōdo, I should add, is *tenobe sōmen*, a type of handmade noodle that is quite delicious."

He was very thorough. He even identified *smells*. When we came down an especially pungent stretch of road, he said, "What you are noticing is the smell from many seaweed and soy sauce factories, for which Shōdo is also famous."

The island was far bigger than I imagined. There was no way I would have been able to ride a bicycle around it, even with gears. Shōdo was also far more mountainous than I expected, with a cloak of forest covering the peaks like a blanket draped over sharp rocks.

These mountains, mossy green, provided the backdrop to every view, just as the sea provided the foreground. It felt Mediterranean, which was more than mere imagination. As Akihira explained, Shōdo was the only place in Japan where olives were commercially grown. The climate was so similar to that of Greece, with just the right mix of sea and sun and long parched summer days, that, while olives failed elsewhere, they flourished here. Olive branches, as Akihira pointed out, were a symbol of peace, and Shōdo was known as the Olive Island, a pocket of peace in an otherwise hectic world.

"It is often remarked upon that Shōdo Island is Japan in miniature," said Akihira proudly, as it was a great honour to be the miniature anything in Japan. "In Shōdo we will find the same percent of mountains to plains, agriculture to industry, and town to country which we find in Japan as a whole."

When Akihira noticed that I was taking notes, he concluded, "If I may so presume, your occupation is that of journalist."

"Ah, no. Not really."

Akihira suddenly veered to one side—his driving rivalled that of the Blind Swordsman himself—and took me down a steep side lane that plunged toward the water. We swerved into a driveway at the last possible moment and came to a skidding stop in front of a barn-like building tucked into a cove. It looked like some sort of clandestine shipyard.

We were met by Mr. Mukai, a tanned older man dressed in white coveralls. He had a golden smile—literally. His bridgework was extensive.

"Mr. Mukai owns a Honda dealership," said Akihira. "But that is not why we are here, as you shall see."

Akihira turned to Mr. Mukai and explained that I was an important journalist from America here to do a feature story on Shōdo, and Mr. Mukai slid open the doors of the building and there in the dusty dark, as inexplicable as coming across the Ark of the Covenant, was a high-winged seaplane.

Mr. Mukai was one of the few private pilots in Japan and practically the only one south of Hokkaido. (In a land as long and narrow as Japan, and with air lanes as crowded as they are, very few private air licences are handed out. It is almost the equivalent of getting your own space rocket permit.)

Akihira smiled with the pride that comes from having a friend such as Mr. Mukai. "This is Mr. Mukai's third seaplane, which he built by hand and of his own design. It is the only hand-built seaplane in all of Japan. Surely it is a remarkable work. The motor is that of a Volkswagen car. There is space for a passenger. Every Sunday, Mr. Mukai takes his plane out and flies high above Shōdo Island." There was a meaningful pause. "Today is Sunday."

Hot damn! An airplane ride! Hitchhiking a ride through the air was even more impressive than on a bicycle. If I could pull this one off, I would go down in the Freeloaders' Hall of Fame. But it wasn't to be. Mr. Mukai was working on the motor and the plane was grounded. I asked him if he might be able to patch it up for just one flight, you know, for the sake of international journalism, but he declined.

Not coincidentally, perhaps, on a hill behind a temple not far from Mr. Mukai's airplane hangar was a monument to the kamikaze pilots who had trained on Shōdo during the war. Maybe it was better that I missed the thrill of riding in a homemade seaplane with a VW bug for a motor, but I doubt it.

Everything after a lost airplane ride is bound to be anticlimactic, but Akihira did his best. He drove back up the road, popping in and out of gear like someone with double-jointed knuckles, lurching and bouncing until we reached a small, secluded village named Tanoura.

Tanoura was the site of one of Japan's most touching novels, *Nijūshi no Hitomi*, "Twenty-Four Eyes." Written in the 1920s by Ms. Sakae Tsuboi, "Twenty-Four Eyes" is the semi-autobiographical novel that tells the story of a young woman who comes to distant Tanoura to teach at a small rural school.

"Twenty-Four Eyes" was turned into a film using the original Tanoura schoolyard as a set, and it was here that Akihira now took me. We marched in, waving aside the 350-yen entrance fee—"He is a journalist from America, here to do a story on Tanoura." Although the day was humid, the interior of the three-room schoolhouse was shaded and the old wood beams and weathered floors exuded a quiet coolness. Akihira stood before the school shrine and recited the *Opening Proclamation of Fealty to the Emperor*, which he had learned as a boy.

"During the war, mines were dropped in the harbour," said Akihira. "After the war, the minesweepers came through, exploding the mines one by one. I was just twelve or thirteen and I remember, very vivid, the windows shaking. *Boom. Boom. Boom.* One man died, I believe."

In Tanoura School an old textbook showed students precisely how far to bow to their superiors (forty-five degrees) and the proper way for women and girls to kneel.

"One of the first phrases a child learned to write," said Akihira, "was *sakura ga saita*, 'the cherry blossoms have bloomed.'"

Tanoura was a melancholy place. For all its sudden and enduring fame, the village was slowly dissolving. A modern highway now joined this tiny community to the rest of Shōdo. It spared the villagers the long mountain walk to the next town, but it also siphoned off the young people.

"Twenty-Four Eyes" has become little more than nostalgia. There is no longer a school in Tanoura. The teachers and their dwindling number of pupils were moved from the village in the 1970s, and now all that remains are museums and movie sets. *Sakura ga chitta.*

19

SHŌDO ISLAND has a pilgrimage route of its own. According to legend, Kōbō Daishi visited Shōdo Island and founded several temples which would later become the backbone of a second, smaller Eighty-Eight Temple Pilgrimage. The route was laid out by Shingon priests either in 1686 or after 1764, depending on which source you consult. Where the Shikoku pilgrimage takes months to complete, the Shōdo route takes only days—and even less if you take a packaged bus tour.

Akihira drove me back to his house. It was a well-arranged Western building turned at an angle to fit in among competing plots of land. Inside, he showed me photographs of some of the temples on Shōdo's pilgrimage; none were singularly spectacular, yet all shared the cachet of the circle.

"Hundreds of people still come to Shōdo every year," he said. "But many are not real pilgrims but merely tourists. As a pilgrim, one must abstain from alcohol, one must practise asceticism and vegetarianism, one must not wander at night in search of entertainments, and, most vital of all, one must call upon Kōbō Daishi with true feeling. Without sincerity, the pilgrimage is—if this is the correct word—a sham. Or is it shambles?"

"In this case, either will do."

"A pilgrimage is meant to be difficult. It is meant to test you. Many of the pilgrims came for specific reasons; they were sick, or poor, or old. My family has a long involvement with the Shōdo pilgrimage. My great-grandmother used to take care of unfortunate pilgrims, tending to them free of any charge. It almost bankrupted the family, but the karma she collected has now returned, and my family has been blessed with security and longevity."

"Your family? Are you married?"

"I am alone now. My wife was— Did you want coffee, or perhaps a cold refreshment?"

He showed me some landscape prints by a visiting artist who had painted scenes from Shōdo. We sat in the clean silence of his house awhile before he said, almost as an afterthought, "She died . . . Not so long ago. A year. Less, less than a year."

He smiled. It was a smile of sadness, an expression that is deeply Japanese. I used to be baffled by smiles of sadness, but now I think I understand. These smiles reveal emotions even as they seek to conceal them. They say, I am sad and so I will smile in the understanding that you will realize that it is only a façade that hides a hurt too deep for tears. Entire essays have been written about the Japanese smile. It is a sigh deferred, and it is far more profound than weeping sobs or streaming tears. Akihira was the second widower I had met since Sata. In Japan, where the women live longer than any other group on earth, where the men—especially the men of an older generation—rely so heavily on women and are so lost without them, in Japan a widower is one of the saddest figures imaginable.

"I believe in Kōbō Daishi," Akihira said. "I believe that his benevolence encompasses everything. It makes sadness and loss more bearable, don't you think? Let me tell you of a certain incident many years ago. To be speaking more precisely, it occurred on April fifteenth, 1980. I was sitting at my desk, here, when a young and saintly man appeared hence like a ghost. It was Kōbō Daishi, of that I am certain, and he spoke to me, telling me to write a book in English to explain Shōdo's pilgrimage to outsiders. This I have done." Akihira handed a copy of his book to me. "Please have this, as a gift."

From Akihira's house, we drove up the wilder east coast of Shōdo, past corrugated tin shacks of uncertain structural integrity that looked more like metal tents than permanent dwellings. Akihira wanted to show me something called *zannen ishi* ("that's too-bad stones"), and we found them in a forested grove near the village of Iwagatani. They were rough-hewn blocks of granite that lay tumbled throughout the woods like massive dice. Some had sunk partway into the soil and were half covered with moss and matted grass. Some bore faded kanji characters, still faintly visible, that were the family crests of once great overlords. In the 1500s the rock quarries of Shōdo had supplied the stonewall defenses of Osaka Castle (the walls still stand in Osaka, though the castle itself is a reconstruction). These jumbled stones left behind on Shōdo had been deemed imperfect or poorly cut and were rejected. They remain to this day, *zannen ishi*, lined up near the shore, or half forgotten in quiet forests.

We continued up the northeast coast with the expanse of the Inland Sea below and beyond, and Akihira pointed out the smaller uninhabited islands, one of which was evocatively named Kaze no Ko, "Child of the Wind."

Shōdo Island is again being eaten. The quarries that supplied Osaka Castle were now supplying the raw rock for further construction at Osaka's newest glory—an international airport built on an artificial island. Osaka has always considered Shōdo to be a colony, in the baldest sense of the word: a place to be exploited, not developed. As we drove north toward the Shōdo quarries, trucks rumbled by loaded down with crushed granite. The convoys roll day and night, and Shōdo has once again been inflicted with economic leprosy: a chunk here, a chunk there, to please new Osaka lords.

Great dry, bloodless bites have been taken from Shōdo, and the dust drifts up in a fireless smoke. Amid the chalk-like powder, moving like harnessed elephants, are massive trucks, their din and roar as loud as any minesweeper. Blasting caps and sudden monochrome firework explosions puncture the air. Quarries are such primal places: man and rock and machine. I was fascinated by it, as I always am when I see large equipment digging up chunks of earth. I am one of those weird construction-site groupies you see peering through fences in rapt attention.

We stopped for a light lunch at the Fukuda ferry port, with Akihira somehow managing, in a vast, near-empty parking lot, to box in one of the only other cars there. From the restaurant's window, the view was once again sea-saturated. Even the farmers tilled their land within sight and scent of the sea. It was such a compact, manageable landscape.

From the restaurant we drove—south? north? I wasn't paying attention any more. I had slipped so comfortably into the role of pampered guest that I no longer took note.

Along the coast, we came upon a small community that was gripping the hillside. Above it was a rocky promontory named *kabuto iwa*, after the helmets worn by samurai warriors. The road twisted and turned to get through the village, dropping low and skimming the water to get around a large, drab cement-block apartment building that had, apparently, dropped from the sky.

"I'm sorry," said Akihira. "It isn't very clean."

"Pardon?"

He grimaced. "I'm sorry."

And I knew then what we had just passed through. I knew it very well, because I had taught in schools in towns just like this one. It was a *burakumin* town. Those were burakumin shops and burakumin apartments, and those were burakumin children playing in the streets.

Japan has a caste system. Japan has a caste system and burakumin are at the bottom. Their ancestors were butchers and leatherworkers, shunned by a Buddhist society that had learned to eat meat but not to accept those who processed it. This stigma, incredibly, has been handed down for generations and is firmly entrenched. Circles include and *exclude*, they create outsiders and insiders, and outcasts.

But it goes beyond the burakumin. Not long ago, I read a newspaper report about a Chinese businessman who was named to the head of a local PTA in Japan. The media trumpeted this as a breakthrough in "internationalization." An official in the Japanese Ministry of Education agreed, saying, "This demonstrates that any qualified person can serve as president of a PTA union, no matter what nationality he or she may be." On it went, rounds of self-congratulation over the first "non-Japanese" person ever to head a PTA. The man was quoted as saying, "I hope to include many people in our program, including foreigners such as myself." A wonderful and warm story. Except for one small detail. This particular non-Japanese person was born in Japan, educated in Japan, had lived in the prefecture for thirty years, and had a son—also born in Japan—who was now attending the school. But his *grandparents* were from China, and thus he would always be a foreigner, a "Chinese resident of Japan," and would never be a citizen. Nor will his son.

There is an even larger subclass of Koreans in the country, many of whom are the descendants of slaves (sorry, "forced labourers") taken to Japan from their Korean colony, a practice which started centuries ago and which lasted right up until 1945. These Korean families have been in Japan for generations. They speak Japanese. They work and live and die in Japan, and most have never even *been* to Korea. Yet they will never be treated as "true" Japanese citizens.

None of these three Japanese subcastes—burakumin, Chinese, or Korean—are what we would call visible minorities, but they are easy enough to detect. A six-hundred-page blacklist of burakumin communities was circulated among companies well into the 1980s. The list was eventually suppressed (or at least, better hidden), but the practice still persists. Japan has an extensive Orwellian system of public records. Every marriage, divorce, and relative is recorded by the local town hall. One cannot separate from one's past, or from one's family, or its past. You are trapped. It is like inheriting your grandfather's reputation or your uncle's nickname. Corporations routinely acquire these family records to screen out "undesirables," and parents expect to check over their children's suitors' backgrounds. A boy who falls in love with a burakumin girl, or a girl who wants to marry a Korean boy, is in trouble.

The Japanese never talk about burakumin; they are the ghosts of the society. If you ask a colleague about this lower caste, he will either brush it off or frown thoughtfully and try to change the subject. Those in even deeper stages of denial will insist that there is no such thing as burakumin.

Akihira was very uncomfortable when I asked him about them on Shōdo. (Burakumin towns traditionally did not exist; they were not marked on maps nor were they signposted, a habit that lingers in present municipal attitudes if not in the actual cartography.)

"Some burakumin are very good," Akihira conceded. "But some are very bad. Most, however, are just average people like you and me."

What a wonderfully evasive statement: some are good, some are bad, most are average. This could apply to any group of people on earth. It was a non-answer, but it did mark Akihira as being at least sympathetic to their plight.

East Indians in England. Aborigines in Australia. Natives in Canada and the United States. We have our own castes as well. It is a human urge, I suppose, this need to create outcasts; you will see it on Indian reserves and South African homelands. And in the buraku-min villages of Japan.

20

AFTER A FULL DAY of exploring the island, my ride with Akihira was coming to an end. This was not necessarily a bad thing. I don't want to sound ungrateful: Akihira was a gracious man, patient, generous, intelligent. But he was also—and I say this with the utmost respect—the worst driver in the history of the universe. He ground gears the way some people pull chainsaw cords. His truck never moved ahead in a linear fashion. It rolled backward, it lurched, it balked, it took running starts and made false stops and had second thoughts. It bounced and bucked across winding mountain roads and along sheer-drop coastlines. Perhaps it was a form of spiritual guidance; by the time it was over, I had taken to whispering the mantra *Namu Daishi Henjo Kongo* as we went around corners. When I climbed out, my vertebrae were out of line, like a stack of broken dishes, and for days afterward my back was racked with muscle spasms. I am not exaggerating. The Blind Swordsman had been the most dangerous driver of my trip; Akihira had been the most physically punishing.

At a fork in the road, halfway up Mount Hoshigajō, we left my bicycle behind and then drove deeper into a gorge to where cable cars ran up the mountainside. (I left my bicycle so that I could get it on the way down.)

The Kankakei gorge was magnificent. It's odd, but my memory of Kankakei is in black and white, like the muted layers in a Chinese ink brush painting, with pine trees leaning out over straight-down crags of rock. Below the cable car, sheer crumbling walls and stone arches moved by.

The cable car didn't go right to the peak. When I disembarked, I was greeted—if sullen silence can be called a greeting—by a few loitering monkeys, castaways from a larger group farther inland. They were better behaved than the monkeys of Kojima; continual contact with humans had made them almost tame. Several were sunning their fur, eyes half shut, in the warmth of the early evening. Below them, Shōdo Island was spread out like an estate before a lord. I had no doubt that the monkeys of Shōdo, looking down on their realm, felt a certain proprietary pride. Humans were merely endured. The heights belonged, in a lazy way, to them.

I hiked up a sweeping grassland hill and then into a forest of pine trees. It was a long, thigh-straining walk, but well worth it. When I reached the summit, a break in the forest offered a panorama of Shōdo even grander than that admired by the primate potentates below, though it did bother me—as I arrived panting and sweaty and out of breath—that there were no monkeys up here. Hey, they seemed to be saying by their absence, we may be lower-order primates, but we aren't *stupid.*

I was all alone at the top with the ego-inflating vertigo that comes whenever you find yourself at the very highest point of land available. It enlarges you to stand atop a mountain; you feel like a giant tottering on the peak and you hold out your arms, instinctually, trying to maintain balance. I leaned into the wind and almost took flight, over the Inland Sea, a sea the colour of hammered gold.

From these deluded Olympian heights, I followed an obscurely labelled footpath down the other side. The trail had the alarming habit of forking every few feet, and I ended up in a tangled thicket, from which I finally burst out of the woods and onto a highway, much in the manner of the Monty Python hermit.

There was only one road up here—a forestry road tarted up as a "Scenic Skyline Highway"—which greatly limited my choices. I walked south, through the unnatural silence of replanted forests. There was no traffic.

This did not bother me in the least because I knew, on a road as remote as this, that the first ride by would stop. And so it did. A surprised-looking forestry worker took me farther down the mountain to the site of Shōdo Island's Greek Shrine.

This shrine, this "Greek" shrine, is routinely scoffed at in most guidebooks and is consistently misunderstood by most Western travellers. The important thing to remember is that Shōdo's incongruous

Greek structure, complete with columns and stark rectangular lines, is, nonetheless, a working, consecrated Shinto shrine. It isn't simply a tourist attraction. Classic Greek architecture is starkly beautiful, as elegant and stately as Japanese architecture is fluid. Combining the two is a feat that should be applauded, not sniffed at, and Shōdo's Greek Shrine is a deft example of syncretic architecture. In this it has much in common with the historic homes in Nagasaki and Kobe, where Japanese and Western styles blended.

I walked through the shrine and over to the Greek-Buddhist Bell where the 108 sins of mankind are tolled out on auspicious occasions. Greek paganism meets Buddhist theology meets Shinto animism.

There is no point debating whether such structures are examples of synthesis or kitsch. It depends entirely on how you focus your attention.

I would have stayed for hours on the olive-green heights of Shōdo, but the sun had dipped behind the horizon and the lightscape had shifted from gold to dark blue. In film, they call this the Magic Hour, the moment just after the sun has disappeared and just before night falls, when the light is still reflected across the upper atmosphere. It is diffused, a time without shadows, when the landscape itself seems to be emitting its own illumination.

The lady who was closing up the shrine gave me a ride down the mountain to where my bicycle was parked. She wanted to wedge it in the back of her Mini-Car hatchback but it was a lost cause and, reluctantly, she abandoned me. No matter. I coasted down the hairpin turns of the mountain highway into a faceful of wind. The road was steep and my brakes were half-hearted at best, so what began as a pleasant ride became something of a suicide run. As I turned a corner in the descending forest, a Buddhist temple suddenly came into view. An excuse to stop. I skidded to a halt off the highway, and right across freshly raked gravel. My arrival caught the attention of the temple priest.

"Hullo," I said breathlessly.

The priest smiled and, without a word of explanation, waved me over. He took me by the arm and pulled me up a slippery earthen hillock beside the main building. Puzzled, I followed, pulling myself up on a grappling chain. I asked him where we were going. He didn't reply, just urged me onward.

At the top of the hillock was a mobile-like sculpture made of hanging sheets of slate. The priest was now almost entirely lost in the darkness, his black robes dissolved into the falling night, his face disembodied and faint. Picking up a small hammer, he tapped the sculpture once, lightly. A single metallic note sounded. The note lingered, like that of a tuning fork. He struck another hanging slate; another note, lower than the first. Then another, softer, and then, in overlaying veils of sound, he struck several more and stepped back to listen to them disappear, one by one, in slowly fading layers.

The priest handed me a wooden stick and together we managed to produce a shimmering version of "Jingle Bells," after which he clasped my hand and called on the name of Kōbō Daishi to protect and bless me.

This was a splendid chance to scam a ride and I succeeded brilliantly. We wrestled my one-gear rent-a-bike into the back of the priest's truck, and he transported me back down the mountain.

The road descended suddenly from dark forest into narrow streets. Instead of dropping me off at the hostel, the priest waved his hand in dismissal and took me instead to another temple. Every time I took a stab at conversation, he stopped me with a raised hand and a small embarrassed laugh and said, *"No English. Sorry."* "But—but I'm speaking Japanese, really I am." *"English. No."* It was demoralizing.

We entered the lower temple through a two-storey wooden gate, and a young priest came out to greet us. He had a Jiminy Cricket face and a shaved head. The older priest nodded toward him and said with deep satisfaction, "America."

Shuhō Jishi, the young priest at Seiken-ji Temple, spoke English fluently. He spent six years at a Shingon mission in San Francisco and had adapted well to life in America but, when his father died, he was forced to return to Shōdo Island and take over the family temple. "I'm the oldest son," he said simply. Priesthood is not a calling in Japan; it is a hereditary post. Training and proper knowledge are absolutely necessary, but a deep spirituality is not mandatory. As in so many things in Japan, it is proper behaviour that is the essence of worship: how to follow the rituals, how to recite key sutras, how to avoid making errors of protocol. Buddhist priests are not celibate and Shuhō was no exception. He was married with three small children, and after his time in America he was still adjusting to the elevated but sombre position of temple priest. Seiken-ji Temple was over three hundred years old, and its treasury contained sutras, lacquerware, and Buddhist statuary that were more ancient still. It was a heavy responsibility.

Shuhō invited me to stay at his home. His young son was in elementary school and the kid took an immediate liking to me, in the same way that some kids like big friendly Saint Bernard dogs. I was obviously not very bright. After all, here I was, all grown up, and I spoke Japanese with a terrible, thick accent. But I was, he decided, harmless.

He was a gangly kid, all arms and legs and ears, and endearing in his very gawkiness. While Shuhō's wife prepared a vegetarian supper, I sat with their son on the floor and played noisy absurdist games with his collection of Transformer Robots.

You've got to love the way children make robots and toy soldiers fight. Shuhō's son would pick one up, like someone holding a mallet, and deliver a series of complete body slams to the victim. *Wham! Wham! Wham!* Correct me if I'm wrong, but wouldn't this hurt the person delivering the blow as much as the one receiving it? I tried to explain this to him, but he just looked at me like I was stupid and continued the bout. *Wham!* Kids can be so illogical.

The Transformer Commando, having body-slammed the evil villain into unconsciousness, folded himself into a rocket ship and flew away. Another Transformer turned into a submarine, another into a rocket-launching tank. These toys, now standard fare, were invented in Japan and they strike me as being very Japanese, a form of "identity origami" that alters itself from one context to another. You change yourself completely to suit the role. Shuhō himself was living a transformer life, first in San Francisco and then, flip-flip-*bam*, a temple priest upholding an ancient way of life. In Japan, heroes transform themselves. In the West, they have "secret identities" (Superman/Clark Kent, Batman/Bruce Wayne, etc.), and I think this is a key distinction. The Transformer approach to things is very different from hidden greatness and secret identities. A secret identity is a superficial mask. Superman fools people, Batman wears a hood, but the Transformer changes *completely*. He doesn't hide his true self, he rearranges it entirely to fit the situation.

By now I was studying these toys like an anthropologist. Shuhō's son was bored and had moved on to other things. Shuhō leaned over to me and said, "If you like that toy you can have it." I was tempted—the dual-identity Transformer was a perfect talisman for anyone travelling in Japan—but I declined the offer. Even I have my limits, and taking toys from children, even incredibly cool toys, was something I usually tried to avoid.

21

THE FOLLOWING AFTERNOON, Shuhō took me up the mountain to see a Buddhist chapel. It was built inside a dark, alcove-like cave just behind the main temple. Sticks of incense, glowing like impaled fireflies, were arrayed in pin-cushion arrangements deep in bowls of ash. The smoke uncurled in thin filaments and hung, wavering, in the air. Over time, the smoke had laid down extra layers of darkness inside the cave, a patina of soot and old prayers which made the small gilt statues seem that much more lustrous. The golden statues stood in a half-circle around a thick stone column, a spatial mandala with the central stone pillar forming the focus.

Shuhō and I lit incense, waved away the flame, and bowed deeply. He then turned to me and said, "This cave began as just a small hollow in the rock. My father was convinced that a deeper cave lay within the mountain. He spent years chipping and digging, looking for it. The stone was like a spider's egg, there were bubbles and gaps in the rock, and the deeper he went the more certain he became that somewhere within this there was a greater cave. A magnificent cave hidden deep inside this mountain. He knew, one day, he would find it." Shuhō smiled with satisfaction.

"Did he?"

"No. He never did. But he never stopped chipping away. And eventually, he ended up making a cave of his own. This cave."

We stood for a moment without speaking. Shuhō looked to the back wall of the cave, where the chipping and cutting had finally come to an end. "My father," he said.

22

NAME DROPPING works wonders in Japan, and having a Shingon priest as a reference opened many a door for me while I was on Shōdo Island. I spent several days hitching rides and cadging free meals, most of it on the strength of Shuhō's good name.

I used Akihira Kawahara's book, *The Eighty-Eight Pilgrimage Sites on Shōdo Island*, as my guide and it was as thorough as Mr. Kawahara himself. The book had overlapping maps and detailed information on the prayers and poems to be recited at each site. Some passages were hard to decipher, but that just added to the appeal. Here, for example, is one of Kōbō Daishi's creeds, which appears in what can only be a verbatim translation (if you figure it out, let me know):

> Since we go astray, the three worlds are castles. Since we are enlightened, all the directions are non-existent. In fact, there are no norths, nor souths. Where on earth are the east and west?

The song of Shōdo is the hollow *tonk-tonk* of wooden Buddhist clappers and the low mantra of pilgrims. Where Shikoku's pilgrimage is epic, Shōdo's is intimate—and varied. The temples of Shōdo Island are hidden in secluded forests, tucked inside bamboo groves, deep within caves, down narrow footpaths, and beside busy streets. There are springs with miraculous curative powers, there are temples for love, temples for marriage, temples for childbirth (to put them in the proper chronological sequence). There is even a temple of wisdom, with a stone ring through which laughing children squeeze in the hopes of becoming wise. One temple has a live dragon trapped inside, behind a stone ceiling that is suitably claw-marked (the dragon had been captured by Kōbō Daishi himself, naturally). Another temple had imagery embroidered in human hair donated by one hundred thousand people, including past prime minister of India Jawaharlal Nehru. Another had once been a nursery for a captive tiger, another had as its altar a piece of Buddhist statuary that washed up onshore from the bottom of the sea in 1651. There was even a newly erected giant statue of Kannon, several stories high, with stairs inside it for devout pilgrims to scramble up and look out at the world through the eyes of enlightenment (literally).

However, the sakura had begun to scatter and it was time to move on. Shuhō took me to Fukuda Port to catch a late-night ferry, and— convinced that we were late—he flew along at breakneck speed, taking American risks on narrow Japanese roads, using the centre line as a crosshairs. Shuhō was right. We were late, but fortunately, at some point we hit Warp Speed and managed to arrive five minutes before the ferry set out. Convoys of granite-laden trucks were already filing on as Shuhō came zooming in, and I scrambled on board, my pack having grown even heavier in the interim. I was the last person on, and I didn't stop for any farewell bows. Shuhō waved from the dock as the ropes were tossed down.

A Transformer Priest. A San Francisco farewell. Sad rocks, a Greek shrine, and a Mediterranean landscape. None of it made any sense. *Since we go astray, the three worlds are castles. Since we are enlightened, all the directions are non-existent.*

The ferry slid free of the island and into the night, past the peaks of drowned mountains, other islands. Somewhere to the east was the churning whirlpool of Naruto, where currents meet and collide just below the surface.

There is one last story of Shōdo to tell, and it is appropriate to save it for now, for it was on a night like this, on a ferry departing Shōdo for the mainland, that an eighty-four-year-old man—a pilgrim— walked out onto the deck and, quietly, unobtrusively, slipped away. His name was Ichikawa Danzo VIII, a Kabuki actor of note, and in his death he gave his last and greatest performance, a performance that would assure him immortality.

Ichikawa first appeared onstage as a child in arms. When he retired in April 1965, it was celebrated as eighty-two years onstage. After the fetes and final farewell performance, he travelled to Shikoku and set off, alone, to follow the Eighty-Eight Temple Route of Kōbō Daishi. It was a remarkable undertaking for a man in his late years, and there are suggestions that he never expected to finish the pilgrimage, that he expected to die on the road. But Ichikawa finished his trek at the end of May, after the sakura had fallen and the circle had closed. He was at a loss over what to do. He sailed for Shōdo, apparently to complete that island's pilgrimage as well—but something changed his mind.

Why he chose to leave the final circle unfinished remains a mystery. Perhaps he was simply tired. He spent the last days of his life alone in a small inn on Shōdo before boarding a midnight ferry for Osaka. Rain was washing across the deck as Ichikawa made his way to the stern and stepped over the guardrail into a dark sea. He was never seen again. It was as though his body had vanished. He had chosen the moment of his exit carefully; the ferry was crossing the strong eastern currents of the Inland Sea and he was swept away into the whirlpool of Naruto—and the endless circles it spins.

Ichikawa's death became legend, the ultimate act of autonomy, the pilgrim deciding for himself how the journey would end. In *Japanese Pilgrimage*, Oliver Statler writes, "His was not an act of desperation but of resolution. He walked out of life as he had walked off the stage, with composure."

Which is not quite how I intend to go when my own circle comes to a close. I plan on being dragged into that great abyss by my fingernails, screaming and kicking all the way. Ichikawa, you're a better man than I am.

As the darkness fell on the ship's deck, I retreated inside, looking for voices and well-lit rooms.

CROSSING OVER

Central Honshu

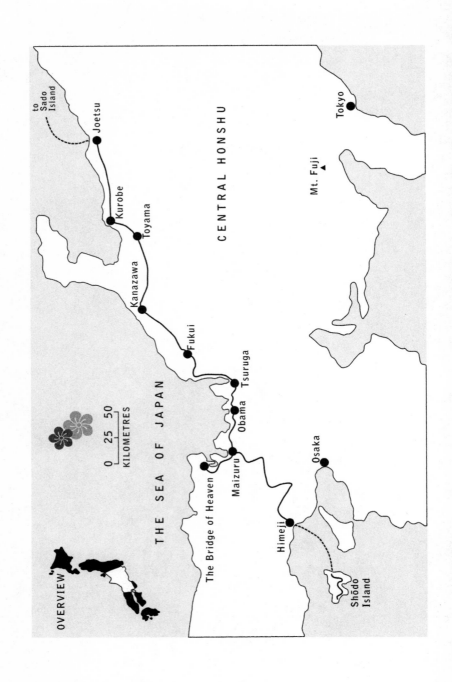

I

ON THE FERRY to Honshu, I had the misfortune of making friends with a group of truck drivers. They were huddled in the empty cafeteria on the ferry's upper deck drinking beer. The cafeteria itself was long closed but the vending machines were still running, and the truckers were sitting about eating dried fish and kicking back the beer. They soon spotted me, and I was hailed like a returning general. "*Oi!* Gaijin!"

They were headed for the big bad city of Osaka, their trucks loaded down with shipments of crushed granite, their clothes dusty and grey. The leader was a neckless man, heavy-browed with close-cropped hair, who took an immediate, antagonistic liking to me. He spoke in rapid bursts, in a thick Osaka accent: "Gaijin! Don't go! Stay and—drink this beer and—tell us where you're going and—what you think of Japanese women and—can you eat Japanese food—talk to us, Gaijin!" I shook his hand, or rather, he clutched my hand and whipcracked it something fierce. He handed me a beer and dragged me down to the seat beside him. The rest of his crew wedged in. "Look! The gaijin likes our beer. He's drinking it, so quick, get another can. We'll get this gaijin drunk, if it's the last thing we do."

Normally, my instincts are to avoid drunken, unruly truck drivers. *Avoid drunken, unruly truck drivers:* that's my motto. But in this case I made an exception. Shūho, the priest on Shōdo Island, had warned me that the ferry port at Himeji was far from downtown, that there would be no buses this late, and that a taxi would be exorbitant. I had hoped to wheedle a ride into Himeji with one of the passengers on board, but most were sound asleep in their cars, and the only lively, approachable group were these Osaka truck drivers. So . . .

"*Ha ha!* Gaijin wants a ride. Of course we will give him a ride! Are we not truck drivers? Are we not Osaka men? Quick—get him another beer so we—can toast our new gaijin friend! *Kampai!*"

"Isn't it illegal to drink and drive?" I asked with contrived innocence. I knew quite well the answer. It was *very* illegal. Japan had the strictest laws of any modern, industrial nation. Zero tolerance. If you drove after even one drink, you would lose your licence. If you worked in the public sector, you would also lose your job.

"Tonight's drivers are below, asleep. We drive in shifts and now—it is time to drink!" He emptied the can directly into his gullet, without swallowing, and then wiped the back of his hand across his mouth with a grandiose flourish. "We drink!"

Great, of all the people I had to latch onto, I ended up with Zorba the fucking Greek. At any moment, I expected him to toss down his beer can and leap into a dance. I tried to squirm away but he had a death grip on my shoulder at this point and I was trapped. Even worse, he pounded my back in exaggerated mirth every time I did anything even remotely entertaining. This wouldn't be so bad except that—as a foreigner—he found my very existence entertaining, so I was getting my back pounded an awful lot.

At least I had a ride. Or so I was led to believe. At some point during the festivities, I realized that Zorba was arguing with his minions over which bar to take me to—in Osaka. "Excuse me," I said. "Osaka?"

"You will *love* Osaka!" It was not so much a promise as it was a threat.

"But—but I'm going to Himeji."

"No, you're not." Then, loudly, "More beer!"

"Now wait a sec. I have to get to Himeji. It's very important. I have to see a doctor. Very serious. Life or death."

"Forget Himeji! Himeji is nothing. The women of Himeji—*bah!*—ugly, like this." He screwed up his face. "But Osaka women! Ah, Osaka women!" He threw his hands heavenward and grinned, convinced he had won the debate.

"Osaka women are horny," said one of the other truckers. "Yes, yes," they all agreed. "Horny, very horny. They wear red, bright red. They just don't care."

Jeez, how do you argue with that? Again, I tried to escape. It was hopeless. They had me in their clutches. One man, slurred beyond comprehension, kept grabbing my arm and pulling me in to whisper some reeking gibberish in my face. Another kept up a steady round of toasts, raising his beer at the slightest provocation. But the most unnerving man was the one who kept bringing up the American soldiers who had assaulted a young Japanese girl in Okinawa. He looked pissed off. The more he drank, the more he stared at me. And the more he stared at me, the angrier and more persistent he became. My few instincts dedicated to self-preservation were screaming. Run. Jump. Hide.

"Excuse me, I have to go to the washroom," I said.

"Me too! Ha ha! We can have a pissing contest!"

To which another trucker immediately yelled, "Ten thousand yen on the gaijin!"

"Yes, but first I have to go get my backpack. It's on the lower level."

"No, it isn't. It's right here." They slid it over.

"Yes, but I need to get my *other* backpack. I'll be right back."

Somehow I slithered free and disappeared down the stairs, dragging my pack behind me. I frantically looked for a place to hide. I found a corner behind a closed magazine stand and I squeezed in. Through the ferry windows I could see the docks of the mainland approaching, and I soon heard various voices calling out, "Gaijin! Gaijin! We have to go. Gaijin, where are you?"

The voices came and went from various distances, until one truck driver walked into the very room I was hiding in. I held my breath. There was only the throb and shudder of the ship's engines. "Gaijin?" With a heart-skipping seizure, I realized that I was standing in front of a light and my shadow was cast far across the floor, beyond my hiding nook. Fortunately, the man was too drunk to notice. Seeing no one about, he continued the search on the next level. "Gaijin! Gaijin! Where are you?"

They sounded genuinely worried, and I felt a small pang of guilt. Not enough to come out, you understand, but enough to make me feel sort of bad, especially after all the free beer.

The ferry bumped up against the pier, and I watched from above as the convoy of granite trucks rolled off the dock. They drove slowly, backing up traffic, and I saw Zorba looking this way and that from the passenger window of the lead vehicle, still trying to spot me. The trucks rumbled clear of the ferry and turned toward Osaka. Only then did I make my exit.

I was congratulating myself on my cunning escape when I realized, with a flood of all too familiar despair, that once again I was alone in the middle of the night, facing yet another dingy expanse of warehouses and empty dockside streets.

A taxi was waiting in front of the ferry office, but the pickings were slim. As near as I could tell, I was the only pedestrian to disembark. I would have had to compromise my integrity as a freeloader if I took a taxi into town, but as luck and duplicity would have it, Zen Zen Chigau and Uso Bakkari reappeared in their red sports car and leather miniskirts, and drove me all the way into the city. Very fortuitous, that.

2

CAPSULE HOTELS are a Japanese invention, and who else but the Japanese could have invented them? Instead of renting an entire room, you rent a small, space-age pod and crawl inside like an astronaut preparing to be frozen in suspended animation. Each unit has a control panel, a radio, an alarm clock, and even a television set. The rows of capsules/pods are arranged like storage bins, but the rest of the hotel is more spacious. There is a large, smoke-infested common room full of coughers, lots of vending machines, a coffee shop, and a spacious Roman bath where you soak in luxury before crawling into your space pod for the night. In the West, our beds are big and our baths are small. In Japan, it is precisely the opposite.

The clientele at your average capsule hotel is made up largely of riff-raff, ruffians, college students, shady characters, late-night pachinko players, and overworked salarymen who missed the last train home.

Capsules cost half as much as regular hotels, they are open twenty-four hours a day, and no reservations are required, which makes them ideal for the independent traveller. The bad news? Many capsules don't like to rent to foreigners. We make their other clients uncomfortable, we walk around in our shoes, we soap ourselves inside the bath, we rarely speak Japanese, we can't understand how anything works, we keep pushing the red emergency button on the control panel, and the pyjamas never fit us. The list of our transgressions is long.

Which is why, when I caught a taxi to the Hawaii Capsule in Himeji City, I made a big show of taking off my shoes and putting on the plastic slippers laid out for guests. I wanted the man at the front

desk to realize that, although I was a big clumsy barbarian, I knew
enough not to go tracking dirt through the hotel. But before I got two
steps toward him, he stopped me cold, holding out a hand in traffic-
cop fashion. "Japanese," he said with a voice full of gruff. "Do you
speak Japanese?"

His name was Ogawa and he was trying to look stern, but it didn't
work. He was a square-faced, middle-aged man with his hair slicked
straight back in a style that was appropriate for someone associated—however circumstantially—with the seedier side of life.

"Yeah, I speak the lingo," I said in what I hoped was an equally
gruff Osaka accent. It worked. His face spread into a wide grin,
his gruffness being the thinnest of charades, and he happily checked
me in. He went over the various charges and options and the endless rules, and then in a whispered aside he said, "There is an extra
charge of five hundred yen if you want the 'special' videos."

I had seen Japanese "special" videos before. "Are the good parts
scrambled out?"

He shrugged philosophically. "They are. But if you squeeze your
eyes together like this"—he showed me how—"you can kind of see
what's going on."

"The capsules don't have karaoke machines as well, do they?"

I was kidding, of course, but Ogawa didn't brush the suggestion
aside. He sighed. "Not yet. Maybe someday."

And he was probably right. I could well imagine a Japanese
salaryman, lying prone in a pod no bigger than a coffin, singing soul-
fully about his old hometown and the woman he left behind.

Ogawa didn't have much use for karaoke. He was one of the few
Japanese people I ever met who was openly hostile to it. Karaoke, it
turned out, had cost him his livelihood. He hadn't always been a capsule hotel manager. No, he was once an entertainer who travelled
the showbiz circuit of Japan as—I swear I'm not making this up—a
freelance accordion soloist. He had been involved with bands, but
his rugged spirit and the constant back-stabbing power plays among
the performers soured him on the group experience. No, he had to
be free. Just him and his accordion. But, alas, karaoke had driven
travelling musicians, such as himself, out of business. And the way
he said it, you couldn't help but agree that the end of barroom accordion artistry had been an irretrievable loss to Japanese culture.

"Nowadays," he said, "when I try to play my accordion music, people tell me to stop. I blame karaoke for this."

Having checked in, commiserated with the manager, and forced my much-beleaguered backpack into a locker, I went out to explore Himeji by night. The streets were alive with activity. At the end of the boulevard, lit up like a neon mirage, was Shirasagi-jō, the White Heron Castle, the finest castle in Japan—and possibly the world.

The city of Himeji was firebombed into ruin during the war. The castle survived—scorched, but intact. When, through the fire and smoke, the people saw that the White Heron was still standing, the castle became a symbolic rallying point. What they didn't know was that the Americans had spared the castle. They needed it as a reference point for their bombers. Turn right at the castle and you were soon over Osaka's shipyards. Turn left and you would be over Hiroshima.

Whatever the reason, the castle's continued existence is a miracle worth celebrating. Built in 1581, and expanded in 1609, it remains the pre-eminent example of warlord architecture in Japan. It stands perched on a small bluff of land, like a bird about to take wing, and the nearer I got, the thicker the crowds became. Most were leaving, streaming out from the grounds, heady with cherry blossoms and rice wine, their faces a deep red—almost purple. So many Japanese get red-faced when they drink alcohol, because of a hereditary lack of the liver enzyme that breaks down acetaldehyde. It is this chemical by-product of alcohol that causes their features to become flushed.

Some were singing, many were staggering; a few were hurrying to make the last trains; others, flagging down taxis. It was the type of charged atmosphere you find in a parking lot after a rock concert. I crossed the moat and entered the castle grounds. Stubborn party-goers were still active in the pockets of light beneath the sakura.

At Himeji Castle, the flowers were in full bloom and everywhere there was activity and laughter. Hands waved me in. Voices cried out. It was such a wonderfully friendly atmosphere. Long-lost friends I had never before met clasped my hands and smiled nostalgically. I made a few guest appearances, drank a bit of saké, shared a few laughs, and cadged a couple of cans of beer, but everyone was too far gone and I was still distracted by the castle itself, rising up in all its glory above the pink-and-white spray of sakura.

There are three thousand cherry trees around the castle, and I stood looking up in something akin to reverence. Fringed with flowers, it was so well presented, so impressively arrayed in spotlights, so *perfect*, that it was all I could do not to applaud.

Downtown in Himeji, the bars were closing and customers were being turned out. I headed back to the Capsule Hawaii. Along the way, I passed a man in a crumpled suit, reeling drunkenly. He was defiantly keeping his balance, as his eyes focused on mine.

"You," he said, "are a foreigner."

"And you," I replied, "are drunk."

But even as I walked away, I knew full well that in the morning *he* would be sober, and I felt deeply depressed.

Farther down, I came across something you rarely see in Japan: a fistfight. Well, it was more of a lapel fight, really. Two very drunk salarymen were grappling with each other's jacket collars, while a third man, even drunker than they, was trying to get between them as he repeated, unconvincingly, "Stop it, stop it."

There is a sad lack of profanity in the Japanese language. Just about the only bad thing you can call someone is "fool." So around and around these two went, yanking at each other's lapels, shouting abuse at each other as best they could.

"Fool! Fool!"

"I am not a fool. *You* are a fool!"

"Fool!"

I sidled up beside one of the spectators and asked, "Do they know each other?"

"Sure. Same company. Different departments."

"Really? So what's the problem?"

"They are having a disagreement about next year's sales plan."

And for once I was able to say, with no small amount of pride, "Well, you would never see two people getting violent over something like that back where I come from."

Ogawa of the Lone Accordions was still at his post, and he gave me a grin and a wave when I came back in. (We were now old friends.) I went to the Roman bath, a luxurious affair with pseudo-European décor: fake marble, fake gold leaf, fake frescoes, and very real scalding water. After simmering myself for a while, I changed into the hotel pyjamas and went down the rows of capsules until

I found my number. I wasn't really tired and I would have liked to lounge awhile in the common room, but it was filled with the hacking coughs of chain-smoking reprobates, so I declined. Instead, I purchased some clean underwear from a vending machine—just for the novelty of purchasing underwear from a vending machine—and climbed up into my space pod. It was a tight fit, what with the television set hanging down in my face, but I eventually worked my way in. Capsules are not for the claustrophobic.

Fascinated with the futuristic control panel, I pushed various cryptically marked buttons, I turned the radio WAY UP and then way down, I fiddled with the air conditioner and its sinus-numbing face-blast, and I set the alarm for exactly 06:48. I then clicked on the television set and I was suddenly staring at a huge pair of hooters. Mr. Ogawa, apparently, had decided to treat me to some adult entertainment. This would have been fine, except that I hate watching smutty movies. Everyone in them is always having so much more fun than I am. Hell, in most movies, the actors have more fun in the first ten minutes than I have had in my entire life. (I've suspected that the reason so many tight-lipped types get worked up over pornography is primarily sour grapes. "If I'm not going to get invited to a *ménage à cinq*, no one is!")

Even worse, the movie Ogawa had chosen for me was an American flick, which meant everyone was completely naked within five minutes and there were at least four people in the frame throughout. This might have been exciting were it not for the fact that in Japan the naughty bits are video scrambled, so what I was staring at was in essence one big writhing abstract rendering. A Cubist orgy in my little capsule. From what I could gather, it was a religious experience of sorts. ("Oh, my God!" "Oh, my God!") I tried squinting, which did focus the images but also gave me a severe headache and some very bizarre dreams.

3

LORD TOKUGAWA was the inspiration for the James Clavell novel *Shōgun*, and Himeji Castle was featured prominently in the miniseries.

When Lord Tokugawa defeated his enemies in 1600, he established himself as shōgun (or ruling generalissimo) of a united Japan. His rule was still shaky, however, especially in the rebellious Western provinces, so he sent his son-in-law, Lord Ikeda, to take control of the trade routes and assert the Shōgunate's authority.

The booklet from the Himeji Tourism Board described the castle's long and illustrious history:

> Before this castle galloped warriors on the feudal chessboard who fought with furious gusto and were parties disjointed and clashing, subject to no central or effective secular authority. Most of the men were inured to brigandage and found a life of gain by the sword irresistible.

Can't you just see it? Samurai armies clashing on the plains, warriors inured to brigandage, the swords irresistible, the occasional high-pitched lapel fight. By the time I reached the main gate (named, I noted with approval, *Sakura Mon*, the "Cherry Blossom Gate"), I was quite taken with the drama of it all.

You approach Himeji Castle through a maze of stone wall canyons that lead you astray by their very lack of apparent logic or overriding plan. Labyrinthine inner walls send you through narrow passages, past ambush points, and up to the main doors and then, just as quickly, turn you around and force you to make a 180-degree rotation so that—Zen-like—the only way to get to the castle is to walk *away* from it. These complex ground plans at Himeji are unparalleled anywhere in the world.

No one has ever taken Himeji Castle by force—or even bothered trying. One of the reasons the Tokugawa shōguns lasted as long as they did, and stamped their oppressive mark on Japanese society so effectively as they did, lies within these complex walls.

There are legends, scandalous, sexual, and supernatural, associated with the castle. Himeji has ghosts the way some places have mice. The best-known legend is centred on a stone drinking well, inhabited by the spirit of a young maid. Her name was Okiku, and she was tossed down the well for breaking one of her lady's plates. At night, when the winds blow through, you can hear the voice of Okiku counting, endlessly counting, her mistress's plates: *ichi-mai* . . . *ni-mai* . . . *san-mai* . . .

From the main tower, I made my way back down to the main gate, and I was about to leave when a thought struck me, much in the way that a gong is struck. I looked up at the walls that swept above me like a wave about to break, and I thought to myself, *Ninjas had it easy*. The walls at Japanese castles are made of irregular boulders, and though the stones at the corner edges fit as tightly as joinery, the sheer face of the walls—often four stories high—is a rough-and-tumble jigsaw puzzle that doesn't look particularly difficult to scale. As a teenager I had read books about ninja assassins and I was always amazed at how they were able to "scale castle walls by their bare hands." But castle walls in Japan have all sorts of handholds.

To prove my point, I decided to climb up. To make sure I had evidence of what I assumed would be a triumphant feat, I accosted a Japanese tourist and asked him to take my picture. He was a bit nervous because his tour group would soon be departing, but I assured him he could just take the picture and leave my camera on the bench. Before he could protest further, I scampered over and quickly made my way up the face of the wall. It was easy. Incredibly easy—at first. I had failed to notice that, although the walls began on a gentle curve, they soon turned and ran straight up—where overhanging eaves blocked a final ascent. I got about three stories up in the air when I suddenly realized I was clinging to what was, in effect, a sheer vertical surface. I couldn't go up, I couldn't go down, and—

in the middle of this—the Japanese tourist had called security guards who were now yelling at me to return. I was a cat up a tree. Coming down would be much more difficult than going up, and I was now in a state of barely contained terror. Slowly, painfully slowly, I descended, groping for space with my feet and refusing to look down, or up. I was hugging the wall the entire way, and as soon as I was back on stable ground, my knees went weak.

The Japanese tourist handed back my camera, angrily—and rightly so—and then raced off in search of his group, which had long since vanished and had probably already visited a dozen temples, several museums, and at least one souvenir shop by now. The guards, meanwhile, were berating me for pulling such a stupid stunt, and all I could say was, "I was trying to be a ninja."

4

THE FOLLOWING MORNING, I tried to outwalk the urban clutter of Himeji City, but after hiking for over an hour I was still beside a traffic-choked, exhaust-bathed, stop-and-go disaster. I stood there with my arm held out, fighting to keep a smile on my weary, dusty, sticky face, and wishing desperately someone would pick me up. Someone did.

He was a repulsive little man, and I will change his name to—ah, fuck it, he'll never read this. His name was Sukebe Hashimoto. He was a carpenter and—he claimed—a world traveller who had sailed the Seven Seas and visited every brothel and flesh house from Bangkok to Amsterdam. "Women like it as much as men," he said within minutes of our having met. "You just have to remind them who's the boss."

When he grinned his mouth curled up past his ears and his brow furrowed like the Grinch in the Seuss book. His teeth were yellowed piano keys and his breath reeked of stale cigarettes and old fish. Every time we passed a female, whether she was sixteen or sixty-one, he would nudge me in the ribs and ask me if I wanted to have cheap, meaningless sex with her. *Of course* I wanted to have cheap, meaningless sex, but he made it sound so dirty.

Hookers, young girls, strippers, women, sex: the man had a wide repertoire of topics. And as he detailed his imaginary exploits and molested passersby from afar, I thought to myself, *Wow, guys really talk like this.* I thought they only did in comedy skits and feminist films.

The day was hot and the traffic was terrible. We crawled away from Himeji, slower than continental drift, and along the way we passed a Japanese gas stand with its well-groomed fleet of attendants who ran out like cheerleaders every time a car pulled in. One girl waved cars back into traffic and bowed to departing customers.

Sukebe grinned at me. "What d'you think of her, eh? *eh?*"

She had a nice bum. "She has a nice bum."

"Haw! You pervert!" He was almost squealing in delight. "You like our women, eh? Like to screw, eh?"

He then pointed to my crotch and said, "You must have a big dick. I bet you do, all you gaijins are big. *Big!*" He made a fist and held out his forearm.

This was not the first time I had been leered at like this. In Japan, white males have all the nasty sexual innuendoes surrounding them that blacks do among whites. At first, I took it as some kind of lewd compliment, but it isn't. What it says is this: You are animalistic, a caricature, abnormal. When I was teaching high school, one of the gym teachers was absolutely obsessed with my dick. At parties he would make juvenile jokes and ridiculous gestures. I tried to defuse him first through bravado. When he held up his hands, like a fisherman exaggerating the size of his catch, I would say, "No, no, that isn't true, I am much bigger than that." But this only egged him on, until finally I decided to hit back, below the belt so to speak. The next time he started carping on and on about how well-endowed white men were purported to be, I said, "That isn't really true. It's not that our penises are big, it's just that Japanese penises are so small." His smile withered. The joking ended. He never hung out with me much after that, which suited me just fine.

My present travelling companion, meanwhile, was all but slavering. He was, I realized, less a man than he was a slug, a sack of phlegm that had somehow assumed human form. At one point he came dangerously close to actually grabbing my crotch. I smiled grimly and considered bouncing his forehead off the dashboard. That such an invertebrate had learned to operate a motorized vehicle was rather amazing.

Finally, I thought, to hell with it. No ride is worth this. "Big?" I said. *"Big?"* My little friend's eyes gleamed. "It isn't true," I said. "It isn't that we foreigners are *big*, it's just that—"

And once again I saw a smile wither and a once jocular rapport chill. He stared ahead, snarling at traffic, and then, abruptly, stopped the car and let me out. It had been a very short ride.

"Thanks for the lift!" I said in an overly singsong manner.

He muttered some reply, "Yeah, yeah, yeah, whatever," and drove off. I was quite proud of myself.

Although it was the type of encounter that makes you want to wash your hands afterward, this short hop had put me far enough away from the downtown core to allow me to breathe a bit freer. The city had thinned out by this point, and the traffic was no longer bumper to bumper. The Human Slug had barely disappeared when the next driver pulled over. It was a large freight truck. Large by Japanese standards, you understand. Which is to say, it was quite small. You don't see the fourteen-wheel, rocket-fuelled, amphetamine-powered cannonball rigs we have back in North America.

The driver, a young man in his mid-twenties, gave me a hand to shake even as he pulled his truck back into the flow of traffic. "Going to Osaka?" he asked—ominously.

5

JAPAN IS A LONG twisted rope. To cross over, to traverse the spine of the country, is to go against the grain. No roads go straight across. To get from one sea to the other, from the placid Inland Sea to the cold and stormy Sea of Japan, I had to zig and zag from one route to the next.

The truck driver I hitched a ride with dropped me off on the side of an expressway. "Are you sure this is legal?" I asked as I got out.

"Sure. Completely legal. Don't worry."

I was on a high curve of asphalt, miles from the nearest town. A silver river ran through the valley below like a trail of mercury. Farther out, railway tracks cut a suture line across green fields, adding to the sense of space and distance.

I walked into the landscape. I was on the watershed of Japan; to one side the mountains sloped toward the Inland Sea, on the other they sloped north toward the colder, wilder Sea of Japan. The air was clean and the views were panoramic. As long as the highway patrol didn't drive by, I was fine.

I walked toward what I thought was a small village. It turned out to be a graveyard, stacked up along the side of an embankment. There was a scattering of farmhouses nearby, but little else.

"What on earth are you doing way out here?"

It was the first question asked of me by a couple in a large family sedan when it pulled over. He was puzzled. She was concerned. "Are you lost? Are you in trouble?"

They were Masaru and Teruko Ito. Masaru was a kindly man, with a heavy face and gentle eyes. His wife, Teruko, although in her fifties, had the energy of a schoolgirl. They were on their way into

Maizuru City, and they welcomed me into their vehicle and fretted over me like parents anywhere. They had a daughter my age, they said. She could speak English, a little, and wasn't it a shame she wasn't here to meet me.

In lieu of her daughter, Mrs. Ito flirted with me instead. Did I have a girlfriend? Sort of. Was she Japanese? What did I think of Japanese girls? "Well," I said, "like you they are very attractive."

She laughed. "He's charming," she said to her husband, and he gave me a congratulatory nod.

We compared our countries, our lifestyles, our differing approaches to dating and romance. And wasn't it a shame that their daughter—who was single, by the way—wasn't it a shame she wasn't here to meet me.

The Cherry Blossom Front was only now coming to this side of Japan. "They use officially designated cherry trees," said Mr. Ito. "The trees are planted at one hundred and two different weather stations across Japan, and the degree of blossoms is carefully monitored. That's how they decide the percentage of flowers and the location of the Front itself." It sounded very scientific. And it was.

Mr. Ito warned me that the cherry blossoms were late this year. The radio had announced that they were only at sixty percent bloom. His wife paused, suitably worried on my behalf, and then immediately launched into an inquiry about Western weddings. Was it true that the bride and groom kissed, right up there in front of everybody?

We began our descent in lazy looping corners, down from the mountains and into a patchwork of fields and rolling foothills. We passed stands of top-heavy bamboo, listing in the wind like giant feather dusters, and soon came upon the naval port of Maizuru and the Sea of Japan. I had expected to see the cold blue colour of slate, with relentless waves and windswept houses perched along its shore, but for all the foreboding images, it wasn't that bad. A few waves, yet not much worse than the calm, flat waters of the Inland Sea.

"You should see it during a storm," said Mr. Ito. "It *attacks* the coast. Frightening."

"But exciting," said Mrs. Ito. "Storms are full of life."

A flutter of cherry blossoms flitted by outside the window. Mr. Ito frowned. "Those don't look sixty percent in bloom," he said, and we then had a long, guy-oriented discussion about whether the flowers were fifty percent in bloom or only forty percent. We compromised in the spirit of friendship and decided that they were in fact forty-five percent in bloom. Mr. Ito formally apologized to me on behalf of the cherry trees.

"The younger trees blossom later," said Mrs. Ito, making it sound almost poetic. "The older flowers are pink, the younger ones are whiter—purer."

"So there is beauty in age," I said.

And both Mr. and Mrs. Ito laughed. "You are too charming," she said, accusingly.

They were supposed to drop me off outside of Maizuru, but when I told them I was heading to the Bridge of Heaven, they decided, with that unspoken agreement that married couples have, that they would take me up the coast, I made a perfunctory protest, but they insisted, and we swept through Maizuru without stopping, swinging in and out of inlets, up along the coast, and then, coming up quickly on my right, was Ama-no-Hashidate, the Bridge of Heaven.

It is a natural, wooded causeway, a thin ribbon of forest unrolled across the bay. It began as a sandspit, created slowly over thousands of years as grass took root and then pine trees. This narrow bar of land divides Miyazu Bay almost in two. On the one side are choppy waves, rolling in from the Japan Sea. On the other side, in the lake-like lagoon silted with sand, is a calm mirrored surface. When viewed from above, it forms a trestle of forest that seems to float just above the water, an "avenue of pine trees." The Bridge of Heaven.

It was here, in the murky depths of time, that Japan was born. It was here that the drunken sexual forays of the siblings Izanagi and Izanami brought forth the thousands of deities and countless islands of Nippon. A male jewelled staff was plunged into the primordial wetness, withdrawn, and then waved, scattering its drops of seed across the void. When Izanagi and Izanami met—here on the Bridge of Heaven—they made the first, primal observation. "You have something that I do not have," said the sister.

"And you have a hidden place that I lack," replied the brother. Not the best pickup lines in history, but soon there were babies poppin' out all over. The two were so fertile that children were born from tears, sweat, sighs. The land was ripe, and everywhere moist life bloomed. The world began in forest and sea and rain, thick, wet, and humid, pregnant with possibilities.

"The Bridge of Heaven is three-point-five kilometres long," said Mr. Ito. "According to the official tally, four thousand seven hundred and sixty-three pine trees grow along it." We had parked the car and were now waiting for the pedestrian swing bridge to be brought into position. "No cars are allowed on the Bridge of Heaven," said Mr. Ito. "But we can rent bicycles."

Against my further protests, they paid for the rental and we set off down the Bridge of Heaven. Mrs. Ito kept swerving in and out ahead of me, almost crashing, gasping in laughter, as Mr. Ito trudged on, straight as an arrow and just as unwavering. The sand slowed us down now and then, and the wind came in with determined blasts.

The pine trees we passed had been shaped by the wind, forming a forest of gentle curves, and even the sandspit itself, while appearing straight, arced slightly. Framed by the banks on either side, the entire Bridge of Heaven forms a long, languid S shape. It is one of Japan's "Three Most-Scenic Spots," as ranked by tradition and tourist board promotions.

A research team from Meiji University spent several years analyzing the site. The scientists studied infrared images of the landscape, and a newspaper report—without the slightest hint of irony—made the following proclamation: "Using photographic computer analysis, researchers have succeeded in isolating the specific elements of beauty that compose Japan's most scenic locations . . . They have discovered that the famous white sands and blue pine trees of the Bridge of Heaven are relatively minor features of the view. A scientific breakdown shows that pine trees compose just 8.2 percent of the overall picture and the sandy beach a mere 0.4 percent. Sky, on the other hand, is more prominent, taking up 31 percent of the scene. Mountains make up 23 percent." (Who says you can't put a number on beauty?)

"There are *two* Bridges of Heaven," said Mr. Ito. "One that you ride through and another that you see from above. The two views are completely different."

"And you look through your legs," said Mrs. Ito. "Shall we go?"

I had heard about this. The proper way to view the Bridge of Heaven was to climb a mountain and then turn around, bend over, and look at it from between your knees. With your head upside down and your senses disoriented, the effect was said to make the bridge seem to float in air. I couldn't wait to see, first-hand, Japanese tourists striking these ungainly poses.

The brochure went one better and had a picture of a cute Japanese girl in a miniskirt bent over, smiling to the camera from between her legs. Directly above her derrière were the proud words: *One of the Three Natural Wonders of Japan.* Another pamphlet urged visitors to "enjoy the beautiful view between your legs," and the local tourist souvenir is a wooden carving of a very flexible man who appears to be attempting self-inflicted fellatio. He looked more like a novelty act in a burlesque show than a nature lover, but Mrs. Ito bought one for me, insisting that the man was, in fact, "contemplating the Bridge of Heaven."

A chairlift took us up to the viewing platforms at Kasamatsu Park and, sure enough, standing on special "looking-between-your-legs" platforms, a group of sightseers filed through, bending over and admiring the view. I did the same and, yes, the bridge did kind of, sort of, almost float, but it wasn't really worth the embarrassment and dizzying head-rush that followed. I suspect the whole idea was dreamt up by bored locals. "These tourists are so gullible, I bet we could get them to kiss their own ass. I bet we could make them *stand in line* to kiss their own ass."

Having viewed the Bridge of Heaven (which, by my estimation, composed 8.9 percent of the beauty and not 8.2 percent as reported), we drove back around the bay to find an inn. The Itos had adopted me with the paternal instinct and affection that couples often get once their own children have grown up. I think Mrs. Ito liked me because I seemed a little devilish; she liked storms and adventures and bad boys. We dined in the hotel restaurant, overlooking the view and enjoying a meal that must have cost a small fortune, but the Itos waved away my proffered wallet. "You are our guest." "A friend." "A very nice boy." We talked until nightfall, and the lights of the bay glimmered across the water. The Bridge of Heaven was now a silhouette and the Itos were saying goodbye.

Mrs. Ito sighed and said, "It is a shame our daughter wasn't here. I'm sure you would have much to say to her." Later, when I checked out, I discovered that her husband had covered the cost of my room.

When a child is born in Japan, the umbilical cord is saved and carefully stored, creating a dry, fragile relic—a personal piece of archaeology—that soothsayers and psychics muse over on special occasions. Umbilical cords contain a certain visceral magic in Japan, and as I looked out across the bay from my hotel window, out to the Bridge of Heaven, it hit me in a surge of recognition: I was looking out at the lifeline itself, the connection between god and earth. I was looking at the umbilical cord of Japan.

6

I CAUGHT A RIDE into the port city of Maizuru with a man who worked for a furniture-shipping company. Maizuru has a confusing, split personality, with two separate downtowns divided by a peninsula. Above the city, rain clouds were lying heavy on the mountaintops, and when the first raindrops hit, I retreated into a bookstore for a bit of *tachiyomi* (reading while standing up). This is something of an art form in Japan. Store owners never scowl or say, "This isn't a library, y'know." You will see crowds of people—men, women, and school-children—standing in bookstores reading for hours, reading entire magazines, cover to cover, with nary a murmur of protest. It's great (although some magazine publishers in Japan have recently taken to wrapping their more popular wares in shrink-wrap plastic).

It was while I was milling about in the language section that I came across a textbook and cassette entitled *Porno! Learn English by Yourself!* I had heard of this but until now had never seen it first-hand.

The Japanese fascination with studying English is virtually endless, and *Porno English!* combined two great passions: English and porn. It was inspired (I kicked myself for not having come up with the idea first), even if it was poorly executed.

There was, of course, a language tape and a lesson plan, as read by someone using the pseudonym Susie Bright. The content varied wildly from archaic Victorian erotica—"presently he glided my hand lower, to that part, in which nature and pleasure keep their stores in concert"—to the crudely direct—"let's do tongue-sex!"

As far as second-language learning goes, it covered new ground, a whole cornucopia of human perversion—everything from golden showers to bondage—all politely presented in standard textbook style, with grammar points, tips on pronunciation, and explanations of correct usage (i.e., when to use *screw* and when to use *amorous liaison*). Some of it was, well—let's just say I'm not sure what kind of response an earnest student of English would get if he ever tried to employ it.

The pickup lines, for one, were even worse than those used by Izanami and Izanagi. Here are some examples of the cool, sophisticated talk offered through the *Porno English!* language course:

> *You've got a good box. Let's go to bed.*

Or how about:

> *I'm an ass-man. Will you love me?*

And the always effective:

> *You're a cheese, darlin'.*

(Calling someone "a cheese," the text explains, is a sexual compliment.) A few more bon mots from the textbook:

> (a) *So, you're a horny tomato.*
> (b) *Try and trip around the world.*
> (c) *You're actually an oomph girl!*
> (d) *The dildo! So perfect for tonight.*

All are duly explained in grammatical detail, recited sombrely on the cassettes. And you just know that out there—somewhere—some poor Japanese businessman is sidling up beside a young lady and whispering in her ear: *Say, you're really an oomph girl, aren't you?*

7

It was a dark, overcast day and he was wearing sunglasses. He drove a metallic grey van and his hands were huge. He had cracked, callused knuckles, and he gripped the steering wheel with oversized fists. I don't remember what he was wearing or whether he was bald, thinning, or decked out in a pompadour; all I remember are those large leather-skinned hands.

His name was Shigeki Ōishi. It meant "big stone" and it suited him. "Any relation to Ōishi the samurai?" I asked with a forced laugh.

He turned and levelled his unblinking gaze at me. My laugh turned into a weak chuckle. "I'm the twelfth generation," he said.

"Really? *The* Ōishi?"

He didn't deign to respond.

This was like meeting the twelfth son of Richard the Lionheart. The saga of Ōishi is Japan's greatest epic. It's a tale of loyalty, bloodshed, betrayal, and honour. It began in 1701 with a simple breach of protocol and led, ineluctably, to a midnight assault, a brutal murder, and a mass suicide. In short, it had all the elements that make for great literature in Japan. Even better, it was a true story.

A quick summary: Lord Asano, a naive young man from the provinces, comes to the Imperial Court as an envoy. It is the duty of Lord Kira, Master of Protocol, to train Asano in the ways of the court. But Lord Kira mocks the young man and refuses to teach him the proper behaviour. Unable to take Kira's taunts any more, Asano strikes with his sword, slashing Kira's forehead. It is a fatal breach of etiquette; no weapons are permitted to be drawn within the Imperial Palace. At Kira's shrill behest, the reigning shōgun orders Asano to commit ritual suicide, and he does, slitting open his belly and then bowing down to be decapitated. Lord Asano's property is confiscated. His manor is sold, his family evicted. His wealth is taken and his loyal retainers are scattered. They become masterless samurai, *rōnin*, but they are rōnin in name only, for they continue to serve the memory of their master. In secret, they plot revenge. Led by Kuranosuke Ōishi, forty-seven samurai make a midnight pact and then disperse.

To deflect suspicions, Ōishi becomes a drunken wreck, brawling in the streets and abandoning his wife and children. Kira grows complacent. Memories fade. And then, on a snowy winter night, the rōnin march on Kira's manor and launch a devastating attack. They find Kira cowering in a closet and, with one sure blow, they cut off his head. Taking this as a trophy, they make their way to Asano's grave and present it to the spirit of their late lord. The rōnin do not run or hide or become fugitives. And after a lengthy trial, they are ordered to commit suicide. One by one, they perform the ritual, cutting open their stomachs and then bowing forward for beheading.

Vengeance, sincerity, loyalty, and an utter lack of fear when facing death: these are the core values of *bushidō*, the samurai code of ethics that has shaped Japan in one form or another for more than five hundred years. The tale of Ōishi is the epitome of these codes.

Knowing this, I was now more afraid of my driver than ever. I desperately wanted him to like me. "The teachers at Minamata High School performed the story of the forty-seven rōnin at the school festival," I bubbled breathlessly. "I played Ōishi's right-hand man. I got to say, '*Look! There's Kira!*'"

Ōishi was not as impressed by this as I had hoped. The fact that I had performed in a high-school production about his esteemed ancestor did not create a sense of kinship between us. How, then, to tell him that the other teachers and I had played it for laughs, that Kira's head was a pink papier-mâché balloon we lopped off and tossed into the audience. Or that our ritualized suicide was so silly the students were hooting and laughing and calling out, "More suicides! Do it again!" How to tell this samurai descendant, with the broken knuckles and the unblinking eyes? I decided not to.

"I have studied the martial arts of Japan for many years," he said. "I have a third ranking in judo and in kendo." Kendo is Japanese fencing, the model for the light saber fights in *Star Wars*. That would explain his knuckles, I thought.

He looked over at my notepad. I had been trying to jot things down surreptitiously. "I used to be a journalist," he said. "Based in Osaka. I travelled all over Southeast Asia. I hitchhiked as well"—he was not in awe of me and he wanted to make that clear. "I hitchhiked in Malaysia, Thailand, Indonesia. You ever hitchhiked there?"

"Once, in Bali, I—"

"I travelled to Singapore. I travelled to the Philippines. I travelled to Hong Kong. You ever been to Hong Kong?"

"No, but once I was—"

"It's hot. Very hot. I like the heat. It disciplines the mind. The Philippines were very hot as well, and the people were kind to me. I went there as a student—1974. You probably weren't even born yet."

"Actually, in 1974, I would have been nine or ten years—"

"The Vietnam War was still going. Tensions were high. The Americans used Japan like an amusement park, like a brothel. They took shore leave in Tokyo or Okinawa." Suddenly he said, "Look at you! You fear nothing."

"Well," I said, thinking of snakes, "that's not entirely—"

"Japanese people study English for three years in junior high, and four years in high school, and another two to four years if they go to college. Ten years of English, and they can't even tell a foreigner the time if he asks. We Japanese are too timid," he said. "We need to be fearless. We no longer take chances. Japanese don't want to make mistakes. They are too proud. They are," he paused and then carefully enunciated, *"too shy."*

Shyness: in Japan, it's the universal excuse. If I am ever hauled into a Japanese court, I plan on using it as my defense.

ME: Awfully sorry about the manslaughter charge, m'lord. But you see, I am very shy.

JUDGE: And do you feel ashamed about what you've done?

ME: Yes, Your Honour. I feel great shame. Shame and shyness.

JUDGE: (to bailiff) Release this man at once!

Don't knock it. In Japan, an expression of sincere remorse will usually take years off your sentence.

"Shyness is a form of weakness," said Ōishi, last of the samurai. Outside the window, rice fields ascended the hillsides in long, low steps. The landscape was cold and damp, with the scent of a coming storm, and static electricity lifted the hairs along my forearms.

We skirted the edge of narrow bays, where the coast doubled back on itself and the shoreline rippled in folds along the sea. In the small city of Obama, even in the chill and mud, spring was slowly seeping in; brown was transmuting into green.

"Obama is a little Kyoto," said Ōishi. "There is history everywhere." He took me to a few spots, showed me some historic markers, and then—just when I thought he was about to say goodbye—he turned back onto the highway. "I'll take you just a little farther down the road," he said.

Outside of Obama we passed a beautiful old farmhouse that was sinking into a slow, dignified decay, the thatched roof the colour of altar dust. More farmhouses appeared, packed tightly together. The fields came right up to their front doors, and I wondered how it felt to be hemmed in like that, facing thick lush harvests, dusty autumn stubble, wet spring mud. I wondered how that affects your world view.

They called this side of Honshu the "Back of Japan." It was the weather-beaten face of Nippon. Old wood, old tiles, old dreams.

Faint wisps of mist hung in the air. We were running one step ahead of the rain; behind us, clouds had begun to collapse. Caught in the momentum, Ōishi ended up driving me all the way to Tsuruga City, over an hour out of his way. The sky had been threatening rain, but once Ōishi dropped me off and drove back down the road, the darkness receded. Through the clouds shone a clean blue sky. Like Heathcliff in *Wuthering Heights*, Ōishi had brought the storm with him.

Later, back in Minamata, one of the teachers I used to work with was disturbed by my meeting with Ōishi. "The children of the original Ōishi were killed by the Shōgun to prevent further vendettas. It was standard practice to wipe out your enemy's entire family line. I don't see how the man you met could have possibly been a direct descendant of *the* Ōishi. He was either pulling your leg—or he was a ghost."

"But I have his business card," I said, brandishing it triumphantly. "How many ghosts carry these?"

"In Japan," the teacher assured me, "even ghosts carry business cards."

8

THEY DROVE BY TWICE to check me out. They were laughing each time, and I wasn't in a good mood.

Like so many pairs of friends, one was short and talkative and the other was big and good-natured. Ren and Stimpy. Timon and Pumba. "Hey, you! Where you going?" It was the little one. He was calling from the passenger window of a white rent-a-car. I was across a very busy intersection from them.

"North," I said curtly. "I'm going north."

"North! *North?* Where north?" They were laughing it up at my expense.

"Just north."

They had a quick huddle. "Okay," they said. "You can come with us, but you have to help us meet girls."

Their names were Makoto (Mac) and Tomoyuki (Tom) and they were cruising the backroads of Japan. "We came all the way from Hokkaido," said Mac, as I lifted my backpack into their trunk. "We've been driving the coast. We were going south, but we can take you north. We don't care. We have no schedule. We're free!"

"Free," echoed Tom, the bigger, quieter one.

"Look at that!" said Mac, stepping back and pointing as though he had just now noticed it. "Hokkaido licence plates! Take a picture. You can show it to your friends back in Kyushu. They'll be amazed."*

"Tunes," said Li'l Mac as I climbed into the backseat. "What kind of tunes do you like?"

They scanned the radio until they found something loud and

---

*I did. They weren't.

cacophonous and then plied me with drinks and snacks until they had thoroughly won me over. Tsugaru City dissolved into rice paddies, wet and newly planted, and the rice paddies dissolved into mountains. Somewhere along the way we passed the Statue of Liberty holding a banana.

Mac had been to America and his English was good, but idiosyncratic. "Florida was hot excellent. They had alligator crossing signs down on the highways. Crazy wild. And in Denver I show up and they have a stock car rally. It was just chance. Luck. I love cars. I drove in the States at one hundred kilometres an hour. Excellent." He swept back his hair. It was parted down the middle and flipped up in pop-idol waves that kept getting in the way whenever he turned his head.

The road banked from turn to turn and each vista became more dramatic. But Mac and Tom didn't want to talk about scenery or even cars. They wanted to talk about girls.

"What is your technique?" asked Mac. "How do you meet them?"

I don't have a technique. So I lied. I told them what my college roommate used to do. He would go to a laundromat and—in plain sight of a lady he liked—he would prepare to pour Mr. Clean floor polish into the washer. The woman would rush over to stop him, and he would act dumb and helpless, saying, "I thought cleaner was cleaner." She would then scold him in a playful manner and, next thing you know, they're in bed together.

"Japanese women love Americans," said Mac. "They think you're exotic. We'll take you with us, as bait."

Big ol' Tom agreed, and when we finally reached Fukui City, we pulled up to the local Mr. Donut. "Girls who like Americans come to Mr. Donut," said Mac knowingly. The three of us sauntered in and flopped down in a booth, cool as all get out. Mac started talking to me in English in a *really big voice*. This was to (a) establish our presence, (b) demonstrate that we were cosmopolitan, international English-speaking dudes, and (c) scare away any competition. Having defined our domain, we scoped the room. At the counter were a pair of college girls sipping milk coffee. Mac stared at them until they noticed our throbbing presence. He then jerked his head in my direction and said with a cocky grin, "American." Tom smiled in a shy yet vulnerable manner. I tried to look cool, dark, and American (as opposed to clumsy, pale, and Canadian).

The two girls, as if on cue, dropped their smiles and gave us looks that were utterly devoid of any expression. It was beyond disdain, it was a look of absolute indifference. Slowly, they turned back to their coffee and continued their conversation. My face was burning. Children laughed. Strangers stopped to point. Crowds were bussed in from neighbouring cities. Satellites shifted their orbits to capture the moment on film.

My charm as a woman magnet having failed, the ride came to an end. Mac told me to call him when I got to Hokkaido, but there was a lack of conviction in his voice that I found disheartening.

"We could try again," I said. "I just needed to warm up. Look, some more girls are going in! *Hey! Are you a horny tomato? Do you wanna love me?!*"

But Mac and Tom exchanged significant glances and my pleas were ignored. "Here's how to get out of Fukui," said Mac. "Walk down to the first set of lights. Turn right and then left. You can start hitchhiking after that. It won't take long. Very easy."

The weather was good; the traffic, steady. What could go wrong? I thanked them for the ride, we shook hands, and off they drove. I took a deep breath, briefly reconsidered making another sally into Mr. Donut, and set off down the road.

And so began the longest day of my life . . .

9

WHEN I WAS YOUNG, I wanted to be Alexander the Great, not because he had such a nifty nickname. (How many people do you know called "the Great"? *Hey, guys, Bob the Great called. He wants to know if he should bring cheese dip?*) No, I wanted to be Alexander the Great because he had his own conquering army. I always thought a conquering army could come in handy. For example, if Alexander didn't like a particular place—say the service was bad or he couldn't find a parking spot—he would simply turn his army loose and they would raze the buildings, salt the fields, and enslave the general population. It sounded like a lot of fun.

The point being, had I my own conquering army, Fukui City would no longer be standing.

What a hole. The citizens are actually proud of their reputation as Japan's rudest people. "We are very rude in Fukui," they will say. "May I spit in your coffee?"

The day started out just fine. I was on the perfect stretch of road: wide, uncluttered, just beyond the city limits, and several hours ahead of the evening rush. Surely one of these stalwart citizens would stop. They didn't. They did swerve, however, *in my direction*. Ostensibly, this was to get a better gape at the strange foreigner, but had they managed to clip me as they passed I suspect they would have pumped the air with their fists and shouted, "Awwright! Ten points!"

The sky darkened, the wind picked up, and these bloated, bottom-heavy clouds rolled in, looking like large wads of wool that had been soaked in a mud puddle. A raindrop splattered to the ground in front of me. A moment later another splatted on my right, then another on my left, like a sniper trying to find the range. Finally one hit me on the head and you could hear the distant gods of Fukui yell, "Awwright! Ten points!"

At first I was overjoyed. *Rain!* Surely I would now look so pitiable that people would stop out of sympathy. I changed my expression from non-violent Mormon to puppy-eyed orphan and looked wistfully at each car that passed.

Which leads to Ferguson's First Law of Hitchhiking vis-à-vis the Japanese: A foreigner standing by the side of the road in the rain with his thumb thrust out does not look sad or forlorn; he looks deranged. Cars sped up when they saw me and drivers' eyes watched me recede in their rearview mirrors just to make sure I hadn't leapt onto the bumper. Then the clouds opened up, and the rains came down as in the days of Noah.

Having given up on an early rescue, I struggled to get out my handy fold-a-pac plastic rain poncho—which was clearly intended as a novelty item, because it stopped approximately zero percent of the rain, while still managing to cling to my body like a wet sarong. The rain was coming down so hard and fast that it bounced up off the pavement in ricochets. The road was awash. I thrust my thumb at cars in a wild frenzy. No one stopped. I began cursing as they passed, alternating between my thumb and middle finger. Not a good hitchhiking strategy. "Gee, honey, let's stop for that rain-soaked wildman who is giving us the finger. Why look, he's wearing a novelty item over his head." I was out there in the rain for three hours. Let's pause a moment and reflect on this. Three hours. In the rain. And not a single Fukui person stopped. Get out the salt, boys! Burn the fields! Unleash the hounds! You remember Carthage? The sack of Fukui City would have made Carthage look like a romp in the park. *Fukui delenda est!* Though I doubt whether even Alexander's troops could have ignited anything in this downpour. Still, it was nice to imagine and it helped take my mind off the bone-chill of advancing hypothermia.

Like so many things in life, it got worse. Rush hour began: bumper-to-bumper cars hydroplaning by, dousing me with great sheets of water as they sailed past. Trucks went by like snowplows, pushing the rain before them, and one driver laughed at me as he passed. His licence plate: Fukui prefecture, naturally. The sun went down. Or rather, the rainstorm darkened. Headlights came on. Now I was a wildman ranting at traffic, illuminated by passing vehicles—

like Frankenstein in a lightning flash. Nobody was going to stop for
me and it was ten kilometres back into town.

I dragged my backpack up onto my shoulders. It was soaked
heavy with water, its space-age zephlon NASA waterproofing having
proven ineffectual in the face of a Japanese rainstorm. I turned and
was about to begin the long walk back into fun-loving Fukui City
when a low-slung sports car pulled over. The vehicle was practically
afloat. It was so low, it resembled a red life raft.

"Are you okay?" asked the driver. I squeezed in, dripping rain over
everything. I was wedged into the passenger seat, my backpack
across my lap.

"What the hell's *wrong* with you people?" I yelled. "Three hours
I waited, *three* goddamn hours!" I put my glasses on and they immediately fogged over.

"Where are you going?" he asked.

"Well, I *was* going to Kanazawa, BUT THAT WAS THREE HOURS AGO!
Now I'll be lucky to get to the next town." I pulled a soggy map from
my jacket pocket and peeled back the pages until I got to Fukui.
"Just get me out of this goddamn prefecture. What's the first town
after the border? Let me see. Kaga City."

"I can take you to Kanazawa," he said.

"Good. Then take me." I mopped my face with an already wet
handkerchief and wiped the fog from my glasses. For the first time,
I saw my driver. He was young, well dressed, and very dry. "Are you
from Fukui City?" I asked.

"Yes?" he said, hoping that was the right answer. It wasn't.

"Well, what is it with you people? Doesn't anybody care about
anybody else any more?" (You ever notice how personal affronts
inevitably signal the downfall of civilization as we know it?) "Fukui
City people," I said, "are not kind." This is a really mean thing to say
in Japanese, trust me.

We drove into the night. The car was deathly quiet, just the
sound of the rain drumming across the car roof, like fingertips on
Tupperware, and me hyperventilating. Slowly I calmed down enough
to realize that perhaps it was not a good idea to verbally abuse the
person who has rescued you. It might even be considered rude. To
tell the truth, as soon as the adrenaline subsided, I was overcome
with guilt.

"Say," I said, suddenly cheery, "it sure is rainy tonight."

The poor man eyed me fearfully, as one might well eye a mood-swinging lunatic. I introduced myself, he did the same.

"Shoichi Nakamura," I repeated. "Swell name, that. It means 'middle village,' right? My name means 'son of Fergus,' but who Fergus was I couldn't tell you. Somebody's father, I suppose, ha ha, just a little joke there. It sure is rainy, isn't it?"

Shoichi nodded and smiled as though speared in the stomach. A few minutes later he turned on the radio.

The familiar having failed me, I switched to ultra-polite Japanese. "And may I ask what you do for a living?"

"I work for Nexus," he said. "We make computers."

"You work for Nexus? No kidding? Me too!" But he clearly did not believe me, and the conversation drowned in its own bad beginnings. We arrived in Kanazawa City, hours later, after enduring the sluggish ordeal of a traffic jam and a harrowing glimpse of a four-car wreck. It was almost midnight. By now my guilt had reached pathological levels and I was trying anything, even money, to convince him I wasn't really such a bad person.

"Let me give you something for gas," I said, offering him roughly a hundred zillion dollars' worth of yen.

"No, no," he said. "You are my guest. It is my"—and here his voice caught in his throat—"pleasure."

In a way, I envy Catholics. I'm not sure I understand the details, but from what I gather, if you're Catholic you just go into a closet and mumble your sins to a priest, he gives you some punitive tongue twisters, and all is forgiven. Then you go out and find some more sins to commit. It seems very circular and holistic. Protestants, however, are stuck with their guilt forever, and if you happen to be *Presbyterian*, well, forget it, you might as well just go shoot yourself.

"Fukui is very beautiful," I said, flip-flopping like a politician on a campaign trail. "Lovely prefecture."

"Yes," he said, "but the people are not kind." Ouch. Talk about twisting the blade.

"Oh, that, I was just kidding. Listen, why don't we go out for supper? I'll treat."

"Thank you," he said, "but I have to get back to Fukui City, my friends are waiting for me."

"Your friends are waiting for you?"

"Yes, I was on my way to a goodbye party for one of my co-workers. He was transferred today."

"You mean, you weren't on your way to Kanazawa?"

"No, I was just going around the corner."

I began frantically rummaging in my wallet for more money. "Please. Here, for your troubles," I said, pressing fistfuls of cash at him, but it was no use. He wouldn't accept any of it, and I just wanted to crawl under a petri dish and die like the piece of primordial slime I was. This wasn't hitchhiking. This was bullying. I had browbeaten my way to Kanazawa and all my talk of Zen and the Art of Hitchhiking, and travelling *with* the Japanese and not among them, came back at me with unusual clarity.

"You are very kind," I said. "Very kind. You are a kind man." I repeated this like a mantra every few seconds until we arrived at Kanazawa Station.

"Enjoy your stay in Kanazawa," he said.

Fat chance. "Listen," I said, "give me your address and I'll send you something, a present, some money, just to thank you."

"No," he said. "That isn't necessary."

You son of a bitch. "Well, thanks again for the ride. I really appreciate it."

And off he drove, leaving me with several large burdens, only one of which was my backpack.

Kanazawa Station was ringed with bright neon signs and massive, contemporary slabs of hotel. You know the kind; they have names like The Hyatt Royal Regent Davenport Imperial Overpriced Inn, and are lit up at night as though they were the Parthenon itself and not simply a large filing cabinet for humans. I wandered into one such hotel. It was decorated according to standard middle-class notions of upper-class décor: glass chandeliers, leather couches, paisley carpets, superfluous lamps, and lots of brass and mirrors.

Like every hotel in Japan, it was ridiculously overstaffed. Entire fleets of doormen circled the lobby, searching desperately for something to do. They were trying to look busy so that the manager wouldn't notice he had fourteen people to open two doors and empty three ashtrays. Then again, this hotel probably had fourteen managers as well. Heck, it even had escalator girls. That's right, *escalator girls*. They stand beside the hotel escalators all day long and bow to every honourable guest who passes by.

I went up to the front desk where a man in a blazer had the comical idea that I would be willing to pay two hundred and fifty dollars for a single room. "I don't want the President's Suite. A single room will suffice." But the man at the desk persisted in his humour and I left. On the way out, I counted the number of bows I triggered: seven. Seven different people bowed and thanked me, and I hadn't spent one dime in the place. Had I actually rented a room, would they have prostrated themselves before me and offered to shine my shoes with their neckties? Japanese service can be so overbearing.

I wandered away from the bright lights and big-city atmosphere of downtown Kanazawa—a city the Japanese routinely refer to as "quaint" and "traditional"—and found a room a few blocks back in a charming concrete-and-concrete arrangement. It was called a business hotel, but the sign out front didn't say what kind of business. My guess would be cockroach exterminators. A steal at sixty dollars a night. And boy, didn't I get my money's worth. Every room in the hotel was provided with the following: a bed.

When I asked for a wake-up call the man handed me one of those big wind-up alarm clocks that no one has used since the forties. When I asked him for a towel, he charged me extra. I was going to ask for the time, but I wasn't sure I could afford it.

Once I got up to my room on the fourteenth floor—and I wasn't at all worried about being caught in a firetrap, no sir—I realized that I didn't really need the alarm clock. I had asked for it out of habit. My plan was to spend a couple of days in Kanazawa; for the first time in almost a week, I wouldn't be hitting the road at dawn. I could sleep in. In fact, I could go out all night and not have to worry. So off I went, having wrung out my jeans and dried my hair and splashed myself generously with aftershave, to prowl the mean streets of Kanazawa. Many hours later, I crawled back into bed, reeking of cigarette smoke and stale beer, just before sunrise—only to be woken from my pre-REM slumber not half an hour later by someone pounding on my door. It was the night clerk; he had noticed that I hadn't come down and was worried I had overslept. I couldn't even tell him to piss off and get lost. I had to get up and *thank* this man for disturbing me. He was just being concerned. "Thank you," I croaked.

At least I was in Japan, so I didn't have to tip him. All I had to do was leave large satchels full of cash with the hotel management when I checked out. This is to save us the embarrassment of evaluating service with anything as crass as money. Instead of something as vulgar and unbecoming as a tip, Japanese businesses prefer to slip in an automatic service charge of, oh, about seven hundred percent I would imagine, which is a small price to pay for such a face-saving device.

10

KANAZAWA IS an old castle town renowned for its old streets, old buildings, old pleasure quarters, an old villa, an old garden, and an old theatre. It is a very old city, except for the parts that aren't. All that was missing was the actual castle. Only the rear gate remained, imposing even in its quixotic lack of mission. The fortress it once guarded had long been lost to time and city planning.

I was disappointed with Kanazawa. I'm not sure why. It was a prosperous city, and I didn't begrudge the town its success, yet Kanazawa is quaint only if you are approaching it from Tokyo or Osaka. After the side roads of Shikoku and the fishing villages of Kyushu, Kanazawa felt too big, too congested, and—more importantly—too expensive. It was also the halfway mark of my journey and I had expected to enter the city triumphantly, amid cheering crowds and confetti. Instead, I had staggered in, exhausted and whimpering, and racked with a persistent cough and a lingering guilt. I hadn't been this tired or numb since my visit to the Uwajima sex shrine.

Beyond the generic Japanese-city look of its downtown (also known as "Really Big White Boxes Arranged in Confusing Patterns") much of Kanazawa is surprisingly well preserved, with neighbourhoods that date back to the days of the Tokugawa shōguns. And after Fukui City, the people of Kanazawa were downright hospitable. The whole time I was in Kanazawa not a single person attempted to spit in my coffee.

But where were the cherry blossoms? I saw a few scraggly flowers here and there, nothing to pen a haiku over. I went to Kenroku Gardens, across from the solitary castle gate, and searched for sakura but found none. The Cherry Blossom Front had not yet

arrived. A sombre-looking newsman pointed to a satellite map of
Japan and explained that in Kanazawa the sakura were only at eight
percent blossom, a full thirty-four percent less than last year. Or
maybe it was the other way round. Anyway, he was very concerned
about this and, to prove it, the television station showed an assortment of maps covered with contour lines and whorls and complicated grids, as if to say, "We paid a lot for these maps, so you're damn
well going to see every one of them."

I tried very hard to like Kanazawa, but I was impatient. I kicked
about for a couple of days. I ate at some wonderfully snooty restaurants where thin fish was arranged in papery designs and the waitresses moved about in a delicate kimono shuffle. These restaurants
were the very antithesis of the red-lantern dives I usually frequent. In
Kanazawa, the restaurants exuded a certain high-class ambience. They
also cost an arm and a leg, but were worth every limb if you ask me.
Anyway, I was getting a little tired of scuzzy joints and I enjoyed the
chance to try some of Japan's more unusual offerings. I even considered eating *fugu*, the poison puffer fish that can kill you if not prepared
properly. Still, you never know when you'll run into a Japanese fugu
chef whose home was destroyed during the war, so I gave it a pass.

I played, half-heartedly, at being a tourist. I read several pam-
phlets yet retained very little, other than the fact that Kanazawa
was—and here I quote for accuracy—"old." I wandered through a
dozen temples strung out along the city's many Temple Rows, where
I took heaps of confusing slides that my family and friends have
come to hate with a passion. ("This is Daimon Temple. It was—wait,
no. This is Jomon Temple and it was built—wait a sec, sorry, *this* one
is Daimon, the slides before were of Jomon—shall I go back?"
Family members: "No! No!")

One did stand out: the infamous Ninja Temple, built in 1659 or
1643 depending on which guidebook was consulted. What a great
place: A labyrinth of narrow corridors and sudden large rooms with
unusually high ceilings (the better to do chanbara in), it was riddled
with secret tunnels and hidden passageways. It even had a creepy
suicide-room with, appropriately enough, no exit.

By now I had checked off most of the sites in the guidebooks,
except of course the museums. Kanazawa is infested with them,
all with heavy, yawn-inducing names: the Prefectural Museum of

Traditional Culture, the Cultural Museum of Prefectural History, the Traditional Museum of Cultural Crafts, the Craft Museum of Historical History . . . I'm proud to say I didn't go to a single one. I have a theory about museums: they suck. People *say* they like museums, but they are lying. What they are really thinking about is, What's for dinner? and When will this be over? You don't enjoy a museum, you lump it, like cough medicine or opera. The only compliment I will accept about a museum, and only a particularly good museum, is that it is not as boring as most.

I stopped going on field trips when I was twelve, and now that I'm a grown-up I don't have to do anything I don't want to. I don't have to eat Brussels sprouts, study algebra, dance for Grandma, or raise my hand when I have to pee. And I sure as heck don't have to go to museums. You can say what you want about my lack of culture, but stick with me and I can guarantee you, I won't drag you through any museum that doesn't feature giant stone vaginas. How many can promise you that?

Not that I wasn't dying for some diversion. After endless, interchangeable days that featured me keeping myself company by not going to museums, I was getting a little stir crazy. I was bored. I was restless. I began asking strangers if they wanted to practise speaking English with me. I started sitting up at the front of the bus and talking to the driver. I even considered opening my Japanese language textbooks; that's how desperate I was for something to do.

And then it arrived: the Sakura Zensen, up from the south like a tidal wave. Trees came alive. The streets frothed with colour and the tile rooftops of Kanazawa were buoyant, adrift on pink and white. The tsunami of spring, a typhoon of flowers. Suddenly Kanazawa didn't seem so bad.

Vignette: I am walking through Kanazawa's ancient pleasure quarters when I see a geisha, wrapped in a silk kimono, just as she disappears through a doorway framed in cherry-blossom pink. A single-frame motion picture, a ukiyoe print—there, and gone.

Geisha still exist in small elite numbers. They study art, music, conversation, and lovemaking. They are not prostitutes. Even the highest-class Monte Carlo call-girl would pale in poise and pride beside a Japanese geisha. Although many geisha are now aging dragons, the one I caught a glimpse of was as beautiful as porcelain.

I wanted to follow her into that shadow world, through the gate, down the lane of cherry trees, to where her wealthy patrons awaited her arrival. But I didn't feel quite like getting the shit kicked out of me just then, so I left my vision as it was, untouched and unspoiled. *Geisha passing, early spring*—another uncompleted haiku by Will Ferguson.

II

I RETURNED to Kenroku Gardens in the evening. Everything had changed. Crowds of revellers had staked out their trees. People were singing and laughing and tumbling together under overhangs of blossoms. I wandered among the celebrations, uplifted. "Come! Come!" Hands waved me toward their circle, if only as an honourary, temporary member. Men, faces pink, pranced about with neckties around their foreheads. Women egged them on, clapping hands in time and all but yelling, "Take it off! Take it all off!"

Then, from out of the tumult, an English voice. "Excuse me please, are you from America?"

It was an elfin man, a few years older than I, dressed in a corduroy jacket and a conspiratorial smile. He was wearing his necktie half undone, clearly the mark of a rebel. And so he proved to be.

His name was Mr. Nakamura, thankfully not related to the one I had coerced into driving me to Kanazawa. Nakamura Two was an English teacher at a local high school, and he and the other teachers were having their annual Cherry Blossom Viewing Party.

I was invited over to meet Mr. Nakamura's circle of teachers, and I kept having these ambivalent flashbacks to my own tour of duty as a high-school teacher. Any minute I expected the *kōchō sensei* (like a principal, but with more power) to break into a long, ponderous speech exhorting the students to be ambitious and international and so on. But Mr. Nakamura's colleagues were a relaxed bunch, and they welcomed me under their tree without a single speech.

"My name is Yoshihiro," said Mr. Nakamura. "Please call me Yoshi. You are from Canada? I was there once, in my college days. I went by train through the Rocky Mountains. You know," his voice dropped, "my dream is to ride a motorcycle across North America, to see the Grand Canyon, the open sky."

I liked Yoshi. He had a soft, almost soothing voice and he spoke as though he were confiding in me at all times, as though everything he said was a secret and I was his accomplice.

He showed me a picture in his wallet. "This is my little girl, Ayané. She's three years old. Very cute. And this is my beautiful wife." He held the photo out for me to see. "I became a teacher by accident," he said. "I wanted to marry my wife, but at that time I had no steady job and I was sleeping on the floor of different friends' apartments. It was very fun at the time. I had only my motorcycle and a beard. Well, kind of a beard. My wife thought I looked like an adventurer, but her family was dubious. They wanted me to have a good job. In Japan, being a teacher is a very respected job, and I enjoy English, so I became a teacher."

Yoshihiro was originally from Kumamoto City in Kyushu, and his wife was from the Amakusa Islands, where I used to live. It really is a small world: Yoshihiro had once taught English at Amakusa Nishi High School, where I too had worked. This common set of reference points created an instant and durable camaraderie.

He tipped back his beer and, as I refilled it, he said, "My real dream was to be an animator. You know, for Japanese television. In Japan, this is a high-pressure job. My college friend drew animation for the television series *Dragonball Z*. Three times an ambulance had to come to our dormitory because he overworked so much." Yoshi laughed; overwork is somewhat endearing to the Japanese. "I love science fiction. Do you know Japanese animation?"

"Sure, I think it's great," I lied.

He brightened at this. "Really? How about Godzilla? Do you know Godzilla?"

Do I know Godzilla? The conversation shifted into high gear. We exchanged monster tales with that same breathless excitement sports fans get when they discuss their favourite teams, agreeing incessantly and interrupting each other's stories. "Mothra! Did you see the time—" "Yes, when Space Godzilla—" "Right, and Monster Mogira!" At one point we even sang the "Gamora Monster Theme Song" (*"Gamora is friend to all the children"*), for which we received a hearty round of applause from the other teachers.

"What's the deal with Gamora?" I wanted to know. "A giant turtle that flies through the air by spinning like a Frisbee. Who could navigate like that? And after you land, you'd be too dizzy to fight."

On and on it went. I'll spare you the details. Except one: did you know Godzilla can fly? It's true. He fires a blast of energy from his mouth and projects himself *backward* through space, a method only slightly less stupid than Gamora's. (Come to think of it, I've had morning breath that probably could have achieved the same effect.) Oh yes, one more detail I learned from Yoshi: The name *Godzilla* has no connection to the word *God*, that is simply a misrendering of it in English. In Japanese his name is Gojira, from the Japanese words for "whale" (*kujira*) and "gorilla" (*gorilla*), making him a Gorilla-Whale. Isn't that just the most fascinating thing?

"My wife scolds me," Yoshi said. "She scolds me because I buy my daughter Godzilla toys. But Ayané-chan likes them. She sleeps with Meca-Godzilla just like it's a teddy bear. I don't know. Maybe I should get her some dolls."

"Stick with Godzilla," I said. "How many dolls have saved the universe, beaten up Mothra, *and* knocked over Tokyo Tower? Godzilla makes a much better role model."

"You should meet my wife," he said. "She speaks English better than I. She studied Arabic in university. That is how she learned English."

"She learned English by studying Arabic?"

"At that time there was no Arabic-Japanese dictionary. First she had to learn English. Then she translated everything from Arabic to English to Japanese."

"So why bother?"

"It is a long story," he said. "When she was young she saw *Lawrence of Arabia*. The film, do you know? It moved her very much. Her dream was to visit the Sahara someday, to see the pyramids, the Nile, and—how do you say it, like a temple, but Islam?"

"Mosque?"

"Yes, to see the mosques and caravans . . . It was her dream."

The past tense was revealing. "She never went?"

"No," he said, his voice as soft as a sigh. "She never went. Maybe someday."

Dreams. In Japan the word carries with it the nuance of illusion. To admit something is your dream is almost to admit that it is unattainable. Motorcycles across a continent. Housewives who dream of caravans. Outsiders who dream of stepping inside. Japan is filled with such dreams; dreams pervade it like the countless deities that inhabit every mountain, every rock, every island in every bay. They dwell in homes. Altars are built to hold them, they are appeased with small offerings, they are as intangible as mist, as unavoidable as air. Dreams deferred. One of the Japanese ideals is self-sacrifice, and the first thing sacrificed is usually one's half-secret, intensely personal, unattainable dream. I remember a graffiti message on a temple wall, one of the first Japanese sentences I ever deciphered: *Japan is a nation powered largely by sighs.*

Yoshi looked up at the blossoms above us. "We grow," he said. "We grow and we compromise." Then, after a pause, "I love my family. Japanese people are shy to admit such a thing. We think that if you say it, it loses some of its truth. But I don't think so. I love my family, but someday I will drive across America in my motorcycle."

"And your wife?"

"She will travel with caravans. Someday."

Someday. I used to think that in Japan "someday" meant "some-day soon," or "eventually," but I was wrong. In Japan, someday does not exist in the future, it exists in an entirely different sphere of existence. It means "in another life, another time."

"And your daughter?"

He laughed. "She will learn how to fly. Just like Godzilla."

"And destroy Tokyo?"

"Oh, I don't think so. She will be a cheerful monster. She is too kind to smash such things."

A Bedouin. A long-distance rider. A cheerful monster.

"Wait till you meet my father," said Yoshi. "He is very cheerful. Too cheerful. He speaks English. My mother doesn't speak English, but she is very kind. Why don't you come to meet them?"

So we slipped away from the party, walking past pools of laughter and flowers lit in the night. His parents lived not far from the park, down a maze of narrow avenues, in a house tucked in beside a temple. The last time I met someone's father was in Uwajima, and he turned out to be an A-bomb survivor. I hesitated at the threshold of Yoshi's home.

"Your dad," I said. "He wasn't in Nagasaki or Hiroshima or anything, was he?"

"No, no," said Yoshi. He slid the front door open and we stepped inside. "But he was a POW."

Damn. "Listen, Yoshi, your father's probably asleep. I'll go, okay? Maybe another time."

"Don't worry," said Yoshi. "I'll wake him. *Tōsan!*" He called out to the dark, sleeping house. *"Tōsan!"*

A moment passed, and then a light flicked on and a silver-haired, sturdy-looking man came out. He was wrapping his bathrobe around his waist like a samurai answering a distress call. "Yoshihiro?" He put on his glasses and smoothed down his futon-tousled hair.

"Ah!" he said when he spotted me, his smile as broad as Yoshihiro's was soft. "Come in, buddy!"

Soon we had roused the entire household. Yoshihiro's wife came out and welcomed me with a sleepy bow. His mother smiled and fussed with her nightgown. Even little Ayané staggered out, rubbing her eyes lazily and peering at me with a rather annoyed expression.

Yoshihiro's dad was ebullient. "Sit down, sit down. We speak, okay? I study English every day, you want to see my notebook? I write English sentences and words, new words, proverbs, everything. 'A penny saved is a penny earned.' I show you my English notes." He went to get them, but halfway across the room he was distracted by a photo album and he forgot all about his original errand.

He came back with a stack of albums and opened one onto my lap. The photos inside were gloriously jumbled, completely out of order, much like the flow of the conversation.

"Here, you see. This is Yoshihiro as a young boy, just a baby. Here he is on motorcycle in Kumamoto City. That's where we are from, Kumamoto. Yoshihiro looks thin in this picture. Now he is fat a little, his wife is too good cook. Here is my wedding. Japanese wedding, very formal. Nobody smiles, too serious. This is Ayané, very cute. Here is Yoshihiro and Chiemi-san's wedding. She speaks English, you know?"

Green tea and sweets appeared as if having condensed out of the air. I was the only one who drank the tea. This is common; tea and small snacks are presented to guests as one might offer oranges to an altar—more in spirit than for actual sustenance. For a long time in Japan I had the uncomfortable suspicion that the tea was poisoned because no one else would touch it when I was around. It is a test as well. You know you have crossed the threshold from guest to friend when they join you in tea and snacks.

Old Mr. Nak wanted to know if I was married. "You have a wife? No? Everybody say get a Japanese wife, right? Tell you Japanese wife is good, right?"

I nodded, it was true. Everyone from street sweepers to company presidents had advised me on the merits of marrying a Japanese woman.

Mr. Nak had other ideas. "Don't marry Japanese woman. Whatever you do, don't marry them. Japanese wife is very good—*before the wedding*. After the wedding—" He threw his hands heavenward in defeat. "Very strong." Everyone laughed on cue, even Yoshihiro's mother, who didn't follow the English but was tickled to see her old hubby chattering away in another language. When she laughed her eyes disappeared into two perfect crescents, like upside-down u's.

"Before my marriage, wife is very gentle. Always bowing to me, saying 'You want tea, you want saké?' And if she need to—" He made a hand-burst gesture from his rear.

"Fart?" I said.

"Yes, when she need to do such thing, she goes into washroom. She turns on the water. She locks the door. And—*poof*." He made the tiniest of sound effects. "But now she don't care. Big noise—*boom*—just like thunder. You see the crack on the wall, over there? My wife make that."

By now we were all in stitches, especially Mrs. Nakamura, who enjoyed his fart gestures immensely. When Yoshi translated the above, she laughed herself into tears and then leaned across and swatted her husband on the arm.

"*Da-mé,*" she said. "Stop it."

But he continued, lamenting with Chaplinesque expressions the fate of men married to Japanese women. He changed his face from pathos to stone face as he switched from husband to wife, like a one-man vaudeville act. "Now I am old man. I am tired. When I say to my wife, 'I am thirsty, please a little saké, please, please,' she just look, like this"—he pulled a haughty face—"and she say, 'So? Cup is over there, saké is in kitchen.'" He heaved a noble sigh and sadly shook his head. "Oh, Mr. Will, don't marry a Japanese woman, they are like cats. They hide their claws."

Then he delved back into the photo albums. "You are going to Sado Island?" he asked. "Yes? Sado is good place. I went to Sado with my terrible wife last year," and he opened another album. "See, we are here. In the round boat like a washing tub."

Sado Island is famous for a legend of a young woman who crossed the sea from the mainland in a large, barrel-like tub to visit her exiled lover. (I don't remember how the story ends, probably in tragedy.)

Among the tour photos were pictures of serious Japanese men in short-sleeve shirts, buttoned right up to the top, with cameras hung like albatrosses around their necks. There was only one woman in the group, Mrs. Nakamura, and there was only one person smiling—grinning, really—and that was Mr. Nakamura. The two of them stood out as clearly as real people in a wax museum.

I looked at the photographs. "Why didn't the other men bring their wives?"

"Who knows?" said Mr. Nak. "Maybe they don't like their wives. Maybe their wives don't like them. It is old custom. Japanese men don't travel with their wives so much. But not me. How can I go to Sado without my terrible wife?"

"She doesn't seem very terrible," I said.

"Ha! We have company, so she is hiding her claws!" and again the house rocked with laughter, and again Mrs. Nakamura leaned over and swatted her errant husband.

One of the biggest sources of humour in Japan is the discrepancy between the public and the private person. Everyday life requires small, daily acts of hypocrisy, and these are a source of endless amusement.

A typical example—a comic haiku cited by Jack Seward in *The Japanese* (the translation is my own):

> as she gathers her loved one's funeral ashes
> she weeps and weeps—
> and searches for gold teeth

I tried to recite it to the Nakamuras, but it came out wrong, and they thought I was relating some sad personal story. They became very quiet. When Japanese tell it, it always gets a big laugh (it must be my delivery).

Fortunately, Mr. Nak soon had the room full of laughter again. You had to stay on top of the conversation when Mr. Nak was around, lest it veer out from under you like a runaway horse. His wife insisted that he show me his calligraphy; he had once been a prefectural champion.

He got down a big stack of his work and then instantly changed his mind, not from false modesty but from sudden inspiration.

"Every day I die," he said. "And every morning I am reborn. Every day is a lifetime. When I go to sleep I thank my god, thank you for this day."

He translated this into Japanese and his wife nodded thoughtfully and everyone paused out of respect, and then we were off again.

"You like fish? I went fishing yesterday, do you see my sunburn?" He showed me his forearms, as dark brown as polished leather. "I caught twelve baby fish: one, two, three, like that. Now when the mother comes home, she ask, 'Where are my babies? Why somebody take them away?' Sad, maybe."

He used the same forlorn face for the mama fish as he used for the henpecked husband earlier. It was highly entertaining. I had never met anybody quite like Mr. Nakamura. He was breathless in his excitement, as though he had a lifetime of small quips and every-day wisdom to share, as though he had only this one night to impart it, as though time were running out and he was picking up the pace.

"Guam," he said. "My wife and I in Guam." He showed me the picture of them in their Sunday best, smiling in front of a coral reef, an American flag in the distance. He had his official Japanese retired man's cotton hat on. He and his wife stood side by side like a pair of Buckingham Palace guards who didn't know they weren't sup-posed to smile. The Japanese use the world as a backdrop for photographs of themselves; the important thing is not the place, but the fact that you were there. Whether this is shallow or just more honest is hard to say.

"Australia," said Mr. Nakamura. "Look, a koala in a zoo. Looks like Yoshihiro." I looked at the photo and then over to Yoshi. He was right. And Ayané looked just like a little baby koala, clinging sleepily to her mother.

"I do not look like a koala," said Yoshi. He appealed to me as a dis-interested judge. "Tell him. I don't look like a koala."

"Sorry," I said. "Your dad's right, you look like a koala. But in a nice way."

"Ha," said his father, "I told you. My son is a koala."

Mr. and Mrs. Nakamura's next trip was to be a tour of Europe. Mrs. Nakamura was nervous, but her husband would hear none of it.

"My wife said she didn't want to go to Australia either. Too dangerous. Everyone hates Japanese, she worried. But we went." He chuckled. "And now she wants to go back."

"Really?" I said to her, switching over to Japanese.

"Oh yes," she said. "Australians were so fun and lively. Japanese are too shy, I like lively people."

"Like Pop," said Yoshi.

"Yes, your father is very cheerful," she said, using that ineffable, untranslatable, multipurpose term—*genki*. It is one of my favourite words in any language. It means healthy, energetic, optimistic, high-spirited, filled with life. When Japanese greet each other, it is not "How are you?" met with a hedged "Not bad." In Japan the question is "Are you genki?" and the answer is "Genki yo!" And when you part, "Stay genki!"

All languages have their blind spots. The Japanese can distinguish between *this* hotel and *that* hotel, but they cannot suggest *a* hotel or *the* hotel. English speakers can't describe *savoir faire* without slipping into French, and the French can't say hot dog without sounding silly: *chien chaud*.

Certain words just fit. The Americanism *OK*, with its many varied uses and easy-tripping rhythm, has been adopted by all but the most remote tribes in the world. Go to a bazaar in Istanbul or a village in Tierra del Fuego and you will hear native residents using *okay* among themselves, making it the most common word in human history.

The Japanese, meanwhile, can't distinguish between shame and embarrassment; in Japan, to be embarrassed *is* to be ashamed, the two are inseparable, which may or may not signify something about the Japanese value system as a whole. Yet at the same time, the Japanese have a pair of words, *wabi* and *sabi*, which together signify the beauty of the ephemeral and the fleeting; the aesthetic of decay, asymmetrical detail, and natural colour; and an appreciation of the incomplete, the impermanent, the imperfect. It takes a mini-essay in English to sum up what can be said in four syllables in Japanese.

"My father," said Yoshi, with the affection of a son who has given up ever trying to reform his father, "is *too* genki."

"Australia was genki," said Mrs. Nakamura. "I liked it. Very big. Very wide. And lots of koalas."

"Enough with the koalas already," said Yoshi.

Saké had appeared and we were exchanging drinks. "Your parents are world travellers," I said to Yoshi.

"It is their time to travel. My mother worked as a nursing instructor at the Woman's University in Kumamoto; my father is retired from his work at City Hall. It's their chance."

"We must see many countries, to see their ideas, to learn," said Mr. Nak. "Me and my terrible wife."

"Together?" I asked.

Mr. Nak was genuinely surprised by my question. "Of course, together," he said. He would be lost without her, to be apart was as inconceivable as to be alone. She touched his hand gently, in a gesture that was both soft and steadfast.

Chiemi and Ayané had gone to bed and Yoshi's eyes were at half-mast, but Mr. Nakamura was wide awake and so was I. We started in on a second round of saké. We sang a couple of songs, with Mrs. Nakamura giving a haunting rendition of a traditional ballad and me replying with "Blue Suede Shoes." I tried to talk Yoshi into a reprise of the "Gamora Monster Theme Song," but he was too tired, so I performed an encore of "Blue Suede Shoes" instead. Then it was back to the albums and a photograph of a nondescript beach and a dull blue ocean. "Guam?" I guessed.

"Saipan."

"Why would you want to go to Saipan?"

The smile on Mr. Nak's face shifted ever so slightly. "To see my old place. I go to Saipan before, many years ago. In the war. American army captured me, in Saipan."

"Well, look at the time," I said, turning to Yoshi for help, but he had nodded off. "I really should be going."

"I am only guy alive from my platoon. Imagine. Everybody dead in Saipan." He spoke with the same blithe voice he used to describe his lonely mama fish coming home to a house without children. "Have some more saké," he said.

Yoshi woke up with one of those sudden body jerks that are

always so disorienting and frightening. He looked about the room, smacked his lips drowsily, and then stumbled off to bed. Mr. Nak filled my glass. The tenor had changed.

"We said, 'Die for the Emperor. *Banzai! Banzai!'* You know banzai? It means, 'Live ten thousand years, Emperor.' We study to be soldier. Everybody promise, 'Die for Emperor!' I thought it's just to be polite, you know? But no, the other men, they believed it. Imagine. They said, 'Now we must die.' We are in a cave, you know, like a hole. Almost no trees. Everything fire, only ash." He kicked back his drink and his face became flushed. "We had no bullets. So I thought, time out. It's over. We tried hard, but we are lost. My friends"—he cleared his throat—"they began to sharpen sticks. They want to charge machine guns. Sticks against machine guns. Imagine.

"I saw Hell," he said. "Not in other world. On this world. In Saipan. Eight hundred American ships made a circle around the island. Every day, the bombs falling. We hid in caves. A baby was crying and a Japanese soldier took it away—so Americans don't hear it. Killing a baby. Can you imagine? On the cliffs, families—soldiers, mothers, everybody—jumping into the rocks. Now they call it Suicide Cliffs. Many people die. Today, it is popular for tourists. Nice sunsets, that cliff."

He filled his cup. "I remember," he said. "I remember Hirotsu-sensei, a schoolteacher. He was captured early, in the village. The Americans bring him out at night over loudspeaker. He says to us, 'Come out. Nothing will happen. Come out. Don't do the suicide.' But soldiers inside the caves are angry. They say teacher is a traitor. And they . . . they began to make circles. Small circles, close together, around a grenade. Then they pull the pin."

Another drink, sloppier than before, another quick toss back, and another wipe of the mouth. "I stayed behind. I didn't charge. I didn't do suicide. I surrendered." Suddenly his face wrenched in pain and the words came out in a cry of anguish. "*I surrender!*" Then a smile. "Just like that. That is how I say it. I surrender."

His wife sat in perfect silence, her eyes on her hands, her hands on her lap.

"Bobby," he said to me, "I wasn't ready to die that day, you know? On such a little island, far away from home, my family. I was eighteen years old. Not even a man, and now die?" Another drink, the same ritual. "In school, back in Japan, I study to be architectural engineer. So they send me to Saipan, to make barracks and schools—and prisons. Only eighteen. I wasn't ready to die that day. You understand?

"I cleaned my uniform but still it was dirty. In Japan to be dirty is the most bad thing. We must be clean, for our pride. I was Japanese, but my clothes were dirty. We ate weeds. No rice to eat, just weeds and sugar cane. Maybe sugar cane save my life. Maybe sugar cane should be Nakamura Family Symbol!" Big smile. "I became skinny, you know, like a stick. *Ha.*" But the laugh wouldn't come. It turned to wind somewhere in his chest. "I was young once. Before. In Saipan."

"I really should be going," I said.

"I expect they will do bad things to me, the Americans. We hear they are demons, like how Momo-taro fought, but real. You know Momo-taro? He is a little guy, he is born from a peach. Little guy, but he fights big demons on an island. It is very popular story, Momo-taro. But it is just a story for children. The Americans are not demons. And we—we are not Momo-taro. Nothing. I came down with a white flag, alone. They push, like this, not so hard. They are yelling, 'Don't move, Jap! Don't move!' But they never hit me. Nothing. They gave me some little food. Later, shoes. They are kind, not like us, not like what we did, not like—" He reached for the bottle, his hand shaking as I have never seen a human hand shake before. He spilled the saké as he poured it. "I didn't die in the POW camps. I didn't. I didn't die. I woke up."

"I should be going. It's very late."

"I didn't die."

"I should be going."

Mr. Nak spoke again, almost in a whisper. "I woke up."

"I should be going."

He swallowed the past like hot saké. "In the POW camp is where I first learn English. From Bobby. You know, Bobby?" He had had too much to drink and was slurring his words and time frames. "He is a private, D-Company. He the same age like me. You know Bobby? Sure, Bobby. From Oklahoma."

He was waiting for me to answer. I had trouble forming sounds, and when I did, my voice came out like smoke. "No, I don't know Bobby."

"He taught me English: 'How are you? How are you?' Bobby always smiling guy. One time they bring candy, our officers make a line, they think to eat first. 'No,' Bobby says. 'No. First child. Then woman. Then private. Officer last.' Our officers were humiliated. I study that word: *humiliated*, you know? Like ashamed. The women try to give their candy to the officers, but the officers say no. Very sad, the officers don't speak, just look away. 'Our world is over,' they say. But not me. I woke up in the camps. I didn't die. *I didn't die.* Bobby teach me, 'Hello, mister. What time now? One o'clock, two o'clock, half past five. Hey, buddy, how are you today? Chow time, lights out, fall in.'"

He stopped in mid-recitation. "I will show you something." He pulled out the bottom photo album in the pile. He opened it to the last page and carefully took out an envelope from a pouch. He unfolded it in layers: tissue paper wrapped in wax paper, wrapped in soft white cloth. At the centre of this was a photograph, small like the palm of a hand, without a crease on any corner. A black-and-white image, turned sepia over time: a teenager in a GI's uniform, dog tags, short hair, and a huckleberry grin. Across the bottom was written, in printing too careful to be anything except that of Mr. Nakamura: "Robert. Oklahoma, U.S.A. My friend."

"He look like you," said Mr. Nak.

He didn't look like me.

"He have your eyes," said Mr. Nak.

He didn't have my eyes.

"I don't know where Bobby is any more. One day, just gone. Maybe," said Mr. Nakamura. "Maybe he is old man like me." He carefully refolded the photograph into its wrappings and put it back.

"I think," I said, more to myself than anyone, "I should go."

"Ha, ha!" roared Mr. Nak. "I sing you a song! A very good Japanese folk song, but together with a dance. My dance. I make this dance." He lurched to his feet and pushed the low table to one side, toppling glasses and rattling plates. His wife moved the cushions out of the way and cleared the dance floor, as though a drunken jig at two in the morning was a perfectly normal occurrence in their household. I think she was happy for the change of mood.

"You must clap," he said. "Like this." I caught the simple rhythm and his wife helped me out. Mr. Nakamura took down the sword hanging over the entranceway. "Very old sword," he said, pronouncing the *w*. "My family sword. My father, next father, and so forth. Time and tide. You like this dance, Mr. Will. This dance is a samurai. He is too old to fight. He is not strong so much any more. He must use his sword like a walking stick, because he is too weak to hold it high."

Mr. Nakamura, awakened, turning slow circles in his bathrobe, his sword like a cane, his body bent in dance, a stylized posture representing old age: hand on lower back, shoulders stooped. A samurai too old to fight, he was also too drunk to stand, and he stumbled and bumped into the cabinet, knocking over a few knickknacks, staggering like a sailor. He stumbled back into the cabinet, but this time he held on to it and didn't move. I could hear him breathing, in effort. The dance was over.

With great dignity, Mrs. Nakamura rose and helped her husband steady himself.

"I should be going," I said. She nodded. I had stayed long enough as it was.

Mr. Nakamura stumbled over to see me off. "Come on, Bobby. We drink some saké with my lovely wife, you never met my wife, I want you meet my wife. Don't go." He reached out and held on to me. "Thank you come my home. I am an old man. Thank you."

I slid free of his embrace and stepped off the entrance platform into my shoes. They had been turned around for me, facing the door, in that ambivalent gesture of hosts in Japan.

From the entranceway, Mr. Nak looked at me, his expression no longer Chaplinesque. "Why?" he said. *"Why?"*

I understood the question, but I had no answer. How could I? Me, a milk-fed pup who has never cowered in caves with a sharpened stick, who never surrendered anything, never died and was never reborn every dawn.

I couldn't even say goodnight. My throat tight, I bowed deeply. When I came up, Mr. Nakamura had straightened himself into a perfect soldier's stance. He looked at me from across generations, from across oceans. His jaw was set like a man's fighting back fear. He raised his hand.

"No," I said. "No. Don't."

He saluted me. Crisp and precise, and I fled, fumbling with the door, bowing hurriedly a few more times, stepping on my shoe heels, pulling the door closed behind me. He didn't have to do that. He didn't.

I hurried through the streets blindly, and for the first time in years, I began to cry.

12

THERE IS a cherry tree in the village of Asamimura they call *Uba-zakura*, the Milk Nurse Cherry Tree. It is said to blossom on the same day every year: the sixteenth day of the second month of the old lunar calendar, the anniversary of the death of O-sodē, a devoted wet nurse who offered her soul in place of a sick child's. The child survived; the nurse died. Her spirit lives on in the tree. In *Kwaidan: Stories and Studies of Strange Things*, Lafcadio Hearn writes, "Its flowers, pink and white, were like the nipples of a woman's breasts, bedewed with milk."

Another tree blossoms on the anniversary of a samurai's ritualistic suicide. Yet another contains the soul of a child. Another, the soul of a young man.

The imagery of the sakura is problematic. It has long been entwined with notions of birth and death, beauty and violence. Cherry blossoms are central to the Japanese worship of nature, a mainstay of haiku, flower vases, and kimono patterns, and yet . . . the sword guards of samurai warriors also bore the imprints of sakura as a last, wry reminder of the fleetingness of life just prior to disembowelment.

But the starkest image of sakura is that of the *Ishiwari-zakura*, the Stone-splitting Cherry Tree, in the northern city of Morioka. Here, a cherry tree took root and grew in a small crack in a very large boulder. Over the years the tree has grown, splitting the vast boulder in two and emerging from it like life out of stone-grey death. The power of beauty to shatter stone; as brutal and sublime as any sword.

—

I returned to the Nakamura house the next afternoon just as they were stepping out.

"Hello, Willy-chan!" said Mr. Nakamura, without a flicker of what had passed between us the night before. In Japan, saké time is dreamtime; all is forgotten in the light of dawn. Mr. Nakamura, I noticed, no longer addressed me as Mr. but as "chan," a suffix reserved for friends and small children. As a Westerner, I would always be a bit of both.

"You stay our house tonight," said Mr. Nakamura. "Hotel is too expensive. You stay with us. I see you after, okay, Willy-chan?"

Chiemi and Ayané were on their way out. Ayané was dressed in the standard uniform: a pink sundress, little purse, and a straw sun hat with a ribbon around it. There is nothing cuter in this world than a little Japanese girl in a sun hat with Meca-Godzilla under her arm. Chiemi was carrying a parasol and a boxed lunch tied up neatly with a scarf.

"Ayané and I are having our cherry blossom picnic today, why don't you come?"

It was the third time I had been to Kenroku Park in as many days, but I didn't tell her this. It was a nice enough park. Same old pond, same old waterfall. Ayané was ahead of us, examining an especially interesting bunch of pebbles, having granted me joint custody of Meca-Godzilla. Which is to say, I got to carry him while she was out on her geological expeditions. Chiemi and I were near the water's edge when Chiemi pointed out the lantern.

"Do you see the lantern?" she said, and we stopped to look. "This is my favourite place in the park. That lantern is my favourite view. Do you see how it is? Half in the water and half out. When you look at it, what do you see?"

I hate these kinds of questions. I always come off sounding stupid. "Ah, *wabi-sabi?*" I guessed.

She was kind enough to pretend I was kidding. "No, really, what do you see?"

"Japan?" (Always a good second choice. Japan is a common theme in Japan.)

"Yes," said Chiemi. "That lantern is like Japan. Halfway between Asia. Halfway between the West. One foot in the past, one foot in the present. Now, does it look stable?"

"No," I said. "It looks like it might topple over any minute."

She nodded. "That lantern was built two hundred years ago. And it's still standing." A single cherry blossom fell into the water, lightly, in a ring of circles.

Ayané picked up a pebble and showed it to us. We all agreed it was the most amazing thing, a pebble, and right here in the middle of a park. Who would have guessed it?

Once Ayané had hurried off on another spontaneous but very serious scientific quest, I turned to Chiemi. "Tell me about Arabia," I said. "What's this I hear about you and Peter O'Toole?"

She blushed, ever so slightly. "Yoshihiro said to you?"

"Yup."

"That was a long time ago."

Chiemi loved Arabia from afar. She loved it because it was so different from Japan: arid where Japan was lush, nomadic where Japan was agricultural, dangerous where Japan was safe. Arabia was passionate; Japan, reserved. Arabia was united by Islamic monotheism. Japan was polytheistic. Arabia was stark, Japan was subdued.

Chiemi knew the names and tribes of the Sahara, she knew which way to circle the pillar in Mecca, she knew the title of Mohammed's wife, and the five creeds of Islam. She knew everything about it except how it tasted, how it smelled, what it felt like. It was an unfinished landscape because she had not entered it. Until she did, it would always be unfinished.

I had been to Arabia only nominally—a two-hour stopover in Dubai—but this alone was enough to incite Chiemi.

"What was it like?" she said. "Was it hot? Did they wear traditional dress?"

"Well, I only saw the airport. Lots of people in Arabian dress, armed soldiers, flowery writing—can you read it?"

She nodded. "What else?"

I had such a paltry story to tell. "Some women in veils. Lots of Mercedes. That's about it."

But it was enough; Chiemi smiled deeply to herself. Every story of Arabia seemed to corroborate its existence, proved it was real, separate from any dream. We walked on, trailing behind Ayané's meandering route through the park. Ayané seemed inordinately interested in pebbles. She gets it from her mother.

After the bentō lunch had been tidily consumed and the dishes just as tidily put away, and after the cherry blossoms had been dutifully admired, Chiemi turned to me and said, "Is Japan still exotic to you?"

"It used to be." I remembered the geisha disappearing. "There are moments still."

"How long will you stay?"

"In Kanazawa?"

"In Japan."

I laughed. "Until they kick me out."

13

THE GUIDEBOOK I was using spent less than a page on hitchhiking (about as much space as it dedicated to Japanese toilets), and the little that it had was wrong. The authors advised hitchhiking at the entrance ramps of freeways. Which I did. Which is how I got arrested.

The only time I had ever had a run-in with the law was when I was fourteen and I spray-painted GRAD '79 slogans across a rival junior-high school—a Catholic school no less, which means serious time in Purgatory once this is over. Since then, I have been a scrupulously law-abiding citizen. I even turned down marijuana proffered *at rock concerts*, which not only got me labelled King Dweeb Forever but also greatly reduced my enjoyment of the music presented (Das Vömit-Burger and the Highly Annoyed Power Tools).

I have this vestigial respect for policemen; I tend to call them "sir" a lot and I almost never jaywalk unless it's an emergency or no one is watching. In Japan, I am even more respectful. Japanese police have frightening powers, no one having the courage to tell them that Japan's feudal age has ended and that Japan is now a democracy. When I was taken in for a genuine Japanese police interrogation I was quivering like a sack of gelatin and ready to confess to anything before they even had time to apply the thumbscrews.

"Tell us!" screeched police officer Bone Head (I have changed their names to protect their identities). "Why were you hitchhiking on the Japanese National Freeway?" Bone Head was a highly-strung, wiry prepubescent in a police suit several times too big for him and a hat that stayed above his eyes only because his large, batlike ears were holding it up. His partner, Old Tired Guy, was stocky and taciturn. He had a crew cut, no visible neck, and knotted muscles in his forehead. Old Tired Guy dragged out a chair and motioned for me to sit upon it. The interrogation had begun.

"Have some tea," he said, as he offered me a cookie.

The police station was a small trailer beside the highway, little more than a parking lot for highway patrol vehicles. They had never had a stir quite like this and were leaning across desks, piled high with folders and reports, to get a better look at the foreigner.

I finished my tea. They poured me another. And so went the interrogation.

The younger officer was champing at the bit. He had caught a real live American and a lifetime of Hollywood movies was bubbling in his brain. He had even wanted to frisk me, but the older officer had given him a look of barely concealed contempt and had brushed him aside. The young officer's voice kept breaking whenever he tried to get tough with me, which tended to diminish his potency. The old guy was much kinder. They weren't so much Good Cop/Bad Cop as they were Good Cop/Really Annoying Cop.

The older man took down my name and address and then, with a world-weary sigh, he pulled out a big book of rules and began laboriously to flip through it. You could tell that a couple of times his mind had wandered and he was thinking about something else, then he would remember with a jolt and begin studying the book with heightened concentration, only to drift away a few minutes later.

"Ah, here we go," he said finally. "Walking on a national highway. Obstructing traffic. That's a thousand-dollar fine, a court appearance, and a revocation of work permit."

One hundred forty-one thousand yen. I almost gagged on my cookie.

"We'll need your Foreign Registration Card, your passport, two pieces of—"

Right about then I went into Dumb Foreigner Mode. "I was lost," I bleated. "I was trying to find a shortcut. I can't speak Japanese. The sun was in my eyes."

"Do not speak!" squawked the young officer.

The older man decided to give me one more chance. "Why were you on the freeway?"

It was hard to deny I was hitchhiking. The police had driven right up to me while my thumb was out and, when they stopped, I moronically assumed that they were merely concerned about my well-being. They were about to arrest me and there I was, grinning away like the dumbest kid in daycare. "Don't worry about me," I had said just before they hustled me into their patrol car and drove me here: Highway Patrol Station 71.

Outside the window, trucks and other traffic rolled by. The air conditioner in the station was one of those audible units, more rattle and hum than actual temperature modification. The room was muggy and hot. Maybe they were going to sweat it out of me. I drank my tea. They hadn't even offered me a phone call like on TV. Then it dawned on me: This wasn't TV. They were serious.

My trip might be over. I might lose my work permit. I might have to leave Japan and say goodbye to my paycheque. What was it I had said? "Until they kick me out." Never tempt the gods. My worst fear was staring me right in the face: I would have to go home and get a real job.

So I confessed.

My Lonely Planet guidebook had assured me that "the rules for hitchhiking are similar to anywhere else in the world." It also advised expressway entrances. I had waited outside just such an entry, beside the automatic toll booth, as cars sped past, just meters away on the main road. Other than perhaps inside a tunnel, expressway entrances are just about the dumbest places to hitchhike. Memo to Lonely Planet: nobody stops at expressways, *that's why they are called expressways.*

People zipped up, punched in their tickets, and then zipped off; sometimes they didn't even notice me standing there. During a lull in the traffic, I saw a single car coming down the freeway, so I ran out, through the toll entrance, and stuck out my thumb in a bold manner. The car stopped. It was a patrol car. And that was my whole sordid tale.

The older officer leaned back in his chair, and for the first time he smiled at me. He seemed genuinely amused with my story. "You came out to the road because you saw us coming?"

"That's right."

"And when did you realize that we were in fact the police?"

"When you turned on your flashing lights."

"You tried to hitch a ride with the Japanese police on a national expressway?"

"Yes."

It was all he could do not to slap his desk and laugh out loud. His mouth twitched with suppressed laughter.

"Ah, yes. Well—" He started to giggle and tried to stop himself. He wiped his eyes. "Well," he said. "This time I—I'll just give you a warning, but don't—don't do it again, okay?"

I thought back to when I crossed Japan from the Inland Sea to the Bridge of Heaven via expressways and considered confessing to that as well, but fortunately a few extra brain cells kicked in just about then and I kept my mouth shut.

"Foreign Registration Card!" said Squeaky Voice.

I didn't have my passport but I did have the above-mentioned FRC (a.k.a. the Gaijin Card). In Japan, foreign residents have to submit to being fingerprinted and registered and must carry their ID cards with them at all times. It stops just short of having our ears tagged. It's nothing short of bureaucratically entrenched xenophobia, true. But I kind of like my Gaijin Card. It makes me feel like an émigré in a spy movie, stopped at border patrols and mulled over by security men who eye you suspiciously and say things like, "Your papers are not in order," in deep Slavic accents. Not that this has ever happened. This was the first time that any Japanese policemen had ever asked to see my card. I was delighted.

The older officer typed out an arrest report and asked me to sign it. When I pulled out an *inkan* instead, he raised an eyebrow. The Japanese do not sign things. When they formalize agreements, cash checks, draw up contracts, or hand in office reports, they use inkans, little sticks with their names carved on one end. They use these to stamp their imprint on the paper in red ink. Some are made of cut stone, or even ivory, but most inkans are plain bamboo. I love my inkan. It makes me feel like a medieval lord, sealing letters with a signet. I wish I could get my inkan put onto a ring that I could press into red wax. It feels so aristocratic. *Gentlemen, my personal seal!*

Many Westerners had their names put in simple phonetic *kana*, but mine was in genuine Chinese hieroglyphics and it drew a crowd. Officers came over and tried to decipher it. My inkan was designed by one of the clerks at my first high school, using symbols that roughly corresponded to the syllables in my name. I had my heart set on using *Fugu-san* (Mr. Blowfish) for "Ferguson," but my supervisor thought it undignified for a teacher. Instead, I ended up with an *inkan* that combines the initial kanji characters in *Fu*ji, *A*so (from Mount Aso, a volcano in Kumamoto), *ga* (me), and *son* (village), making it Fuji-Aso-Me-Village, or *Fu-a-ga-son*. As the officers unraveled its meaning and made the connection to "Ferguson," they laughed approvingly and congratulated me. Then they remembered I was this dangerous, foreign-type criminal and they clammed up and returned to their desks.

Old Tired Guy let me finish my cookie and tea and then he and his annoying partner drove me down the highway to the next exit. It was the first and I hope the last time that I have ever been in the back of a patrol car. They dropped me off on a secondary road and, with a pair of curt bows and one last ridiculous glare from pre-pubescent Patrolman Bone Head, I was once again a free man.

And then it hit me, in a rush of pride, a thought so large I could not contain it: I had hitched a ride with the Japanese Highway Patrol! Possibly the first person in history to have pulled it off and gotten out alive.

Consider the facts: I thumbed down a police car, they gave me some tea, and we chatted for a while, and then they drove me ten miles down the road in the direction I was going and said goodbye. If that wasn't hitchhiking, what was? Had they thought about it, they would have dropped me off right back where I started, but they didn't. In fact, *they broke the law.* They stopped for a hitchhiker. *I win! I win!*

I was planning on using my copy of the arrest report in waste-paper basketball, but now I realized what I had done and the crumpled carbon copy in my pocket seemed like a personal citation. I might even get it framed. I really must send them a thank-you note, I said to myself. That and some pimple cream for Junior, ha ha! I did a little victory dance and whooped it up some more, and then I realized that I did not have a clue in hell where I was.

14

GRASSY FIELDS and cracked, overgrown pavement. A few farmhouses and a low line of mountains on the horizon. That was about it. I didn't know where I was or even what city I was pointed toward. I was shuffling through my maps when a single white car appeared in the distance like a lone horseman in a Macaroni Western, shimmering in the heat, growing larger. "Please oh please oh please don't go by," I whispered, and at the last minute I lost my nerve and instead of thumbing I leapt out and flagged him down. All I can say is, thank God it wasn't another patrolman. Blocking traffic is probably a violation of some bylaw.

"I'm sorry," I said. "I'm lost. Can you tell me where the road to Joetsu is?"

Inside was a bewildered-looking man in a denim shirt. "I will take you to Joetsu," he said, but I had learned my lesson.

"Where are you going?" I asked.

"I'll take you to Joetsu, don't worry. Please get in."

"Don't say you're going to Joetsu unless you really are going to Joetsu."

"I don't mind. Please get in."

"Not until you tell me how far you're going."

"Toyama."

"Ha! That's nowhere near Joetsu. I will get in, but only if you promise that you won't go any farther out of your way than Toyama. Agreed?" Hitchhiking in Japan can be so surreal.

Hitoshi Kusunoki was an art teacher at a small-town junior-high school. He spoke English about as well as I spoke Japanese, so we communicated in a mix of the two, with both languages often thrown into the same sentence. It worked out quite well.

The landscape expanded. The plains were wider, the fields emptier, the mountains more distant, the ocean out of view. It was, in a way, monotonous, a strictly functional landscape, pared down to the minimal requirements: mountains, field, road, sky.

Incredibly, Hitoshi had come to this very scenery for artistic inspiration. He had a carton of coloured pencils and paints and was hoping to stop along the way. He was going to Toyama City for a teachers' conference—"We must strive to be ambitious and international"—but was taking it slowly along side roads, enjoying the view.

"The view?"

"It's so open," he said. "Spacious."

"I don't know, I kind of miss the usual Japanese clutter, the small villages, the little valleys."

"Hokkaido is even more spacious," he said. "You will see." He then asked me how many cars it had taken so far.

"I think you're number twenty-seven."

"Twenty-seven cars. Twenty-seven 'Hellos.' Twenty-seven 'What is your names?' It must be, every time, the same questions, right? Can you eat Japanese food? Do you like Japan? What do you think of Japan? You must be tired, to always talk about Japan."

"Sometimes."

"Don't worry," he said. "I know about Japan. Tell me something else."

"Like what?"

"Other places."

I tried to trace back the routes and tangents that had brought me here, to this particular place at this particular time. It seemed as random as the path rain takes across a car window. How to pick the one definitive place, the one image that shaped you above all others?

The aurora borealis of my childhood? Being robbed at knifepoint in Amsterdam? (A terrific anecdote, that, but in truth a horribly emasculating experience.) A certain pub in London's Soho. An apartment in Quebec City. The week I spent camped in that large bog sometimes referred to as Scotland. And what else? Korea. Indonesia. The Great Wall. Just postcards, really, when all is said and done. And the thought gnawed at my heart: everything I had done, a collection of postcards, like a zoetrope made to resemble motion while turning in circles.

"I once worked for a short time in South America," I said, "and I lived with a family in a village at the top of the world. I was nineteen years old and I was going to live forever."

Hitoshi said: "When you remember that village, what do you remember best?"

I thought a moment. "The sound of roosters in the morning. The smell of sugar cane, like wet grass." And it all came back again, like an echo returning from across a bay, the town of Malacatos high in the Andes of Ecuador. The sound of guitars in the town square in the falling dusk. Myself at nineteen, a spectator speaking in broken Spanish. "Hey, *Gringo!*" Gringo. Gaijin. Outsider. And suddenly it seemed as though I had spent half my life as an outsider in someone else's land.

"What else?" he asked.

"Nothing. Just that: roosters, the smell of sugar cane."

"Malacatos," said Hitoshi. "It seems far away."

"No. It isn't far. It isn't far at all."

Rice fields spread before us, as flat as a table at eye level. "And you," I said. "Who are you? What places are part of who you are?" My syntax was tangled, but Japanese is a language of metaphors and it makes certain allowances. He understood what I meant.

"I trekked the Himalayas," he said. "I spent a month there, in Katmandu, in the mountains. But that is not who I am. Later, I went to India. Calcutta. Have you ever been to Calcutta? No? So many people, such energy. Beggars. The Untouchables."

"Like Japanese burakumin?"

He held up a cautionary finger. "Other places," he said, reminding me of the pact we had made. "Spain," he said. "I went to Spain. It was what we say in Japan, an 'Art Tour.' Spain and Portugal, to see Picasso, El Greco, in the original. But it isn't the art I remember best. It is the people."

He looked into the middle distance.

"I remember Nazarre," he said. "In Portugal. The women waiting at the cape for their fishermen husbands to come home. They came together every evening, when the sun is low. Like gold. They were so beautiful, these women by the sea. They are there now, maybe at this moment. Waiting. Waiting for someone. Not me." He laughed. "Too bad."

We rounded a long slow corner and the landscape shifted to the left. The far mountains were white with age.

"You know," he said, "if I had the courage, I would never have come back. I would be in Nazarre now, painting. Maybe fishing." And then he asked me, "Have you ever seen the dance called flamenco?"

"Just in the movies."

"Spain and Portugal, very different. Portugal is strong. The heart is strong. But Spain? For me Spain is like the flamenco. Women, dancing. The body is moving fast, strong, angry even. But if you look at their eyes, they are sad. The action is not the real Spain, the dance is not the real Spain. It is the eyes. That is Spain."

"And India?"

"I was alone in India," he said, as though that answered some unasked question. "I was alone, solo travel. It was before Nepal. I was sweating, my shirt is like a bath. They said to me, India has three seasons: hot, hotter, hottest." He smiled.

"Is that all you remember of India, that it was hot?"

"No," he said, and there was a long pause. "India. Calcutta. So many poor people, hands like this, out for money please. 'Rupee please, you give rupee please.' One day I was in the feeling to joke. And this little girl, she is a beggar, maybe Untouchable. She asked me many times, rupee please, rupee please. I saw her every day in front of my hotel. So I wanted to make a joke, you understand? Just a joke. So I said to her, 'Why I give you money? I am poor too. Why—'" and his voice cracked. He was staring hard at the road ahead. "—I said, 'Why I give you money? You should give *me* money, I am poor,' I said to her."

He filled his chest and let it out slowly, a long, extended sigh. I waited, but he didn't say anything.

"So what happened?" I asked. "What did she do?"

"She gave me some money."

Much is made of Japan's insularity. Too much. Commentators tend to treat the country as though it were disconnected from the rest of the world. But no nation looks as longingly or with such mixed emotions to the outside as does Japan. Japan was never a cross-roads of civilizations, it was always on the periphery, and the elements of other cultures, particularly Western cultures, have been imported painstakingly and at great cost. Today, as the world tilts toward the Pacific, Japan finds itself in the one position she has never prepared herself for: a crossroads of kingdoms, the meeting point of great cultural and economic currents. Worlds have collided and Japan is suddenly a pivotal point. It has been a trauma as much as a triumph.

The Japanese can never forget the world that exists *out there*, like a fog bank, beyond their islands' edge. It is their obsession, their neurosis, their fantasy. If Westerners have an ambivalent attitude toward Japan, then the reverse is doubly true. To the Japanese, we are legion: we are conquerors, barbarians, superiors, inferiors, dreams projected, lives unlived, icons, buffoons, the purveyors of greater ideas and nobler arts, taller, louder, faster, less refined, more sophisticated. We are all this and more, compressed into a ball the size of a fist that sits in the stomach of the Japanese.

Arrogance is always an overreaction. So is self-loathing. The Japanese have been overreacting to the West since the day the American commodore Matthew Perry sailed his Black Ships into Tokyo Bay in 1854 and forced Japan to open up its ports for trade. Until then, Japan had been cloaked in a world of shōguns and clan lords, the longest totalitarian rule in human history. Japan's vaunted insularity ended with Perry's crusade. It was date rape and it set the tone, back and forth, between Japan and the West that has continued right through to the present. If the West loves and hates Japan, Japan LOVES and HATES the West. Japan can do everything but forget us, we who exist *out there*.

The Japanese attitude to the rest of Asia is even more problematic. On the surface, they treat the rest of the continent like embarrassing country bumpkins, related only distantly to themselves. They are proud to be Japanese; they are ashamed to be Asian. This conflict runs right down the centre of their soul. India, Malaysia, Thailand, China, Korea: they lie like a stone beside the heart.

Travellers and commentators rarely place Japan in an international context because it is in their interest to make Japan seem more exotic and otherworldly than it is. We all want to be mystic explorers, but Japan is not otherworldly. Neither is it near at hand. It lies somewhere in between. Chiemi was right: Japan is caught in a permanent mid-step, one foot in Asia, one in the West.

It wasn't until much later that I recognized the convergence of the worlds inhabited by old Nakamura, Chiemi, and Hitoshi. Three people and three places. Saipan. Arabia. Calcutta. Japan as a prisoner of war, as a young woman dreaming, as an artist in motion. The world from three views: the inescapable, the unattainable, and finally, the authentic.

Japan may yet become a nation of travellers; we may yet meet her, walking the same road, hitching the same rides. Calcutta is as much a part of Hitoshi's landscape as Ecuador and the Amakusa Islands are a part of mine: the places that make and unmake us. The places that define us.

Hitoshi pulled over at an intersection. To the left, in the distance, was the angular mass of Toyama City. To the right, fields. Beyond that, mountains. I climbed out and strapped myself into my backpack. We shook hands through the car window.

"I have one question," he said. "Why do you hitchhike? It's not the sakura, is it?"

"No. It's not the sakura."

"What is it, then?"

"I wanted to find something. Something more."

"About Japan?" he said.

"Among other things."

"Then I am sorry for you." He smiled. "I didn't tell you anything about Japan."

We lingered for a moment at the contact point of hitchhiker and driver—the roadside—like people in a doorway at the end of a party.

"Any last questions?" he asked me, half in jest. "You know, Japanese ancient secrets. Such things. It's your chance."

"Yes, actually. Answer me this, it's a question that has always bothered me. Inside, in the deepest point, under all the layers, are the Japanese arrogant or insecure? I mean the kernel. The hard centre."

He gave me a shrug. "Insecure, of course."

"Did you hear that?" I said.

"What?"

"The way you said *of course*, it was very arrogant."

"Was it? Oh, I'm sorry, I didn't mean to."

"Now you sound insecure."

He laughed. "American humour," he said, but I wasn't joking.

"It's too bad you didn't get a chance to paint anything," I said.

"That's okay." He looked at the landscape that fanned out before us. "It's not so interesting."

"I thought you liked open spaces, the emptiness, wabi-sabi, all of that."

He shrugged. "Hard to paint."

15

HITOSHI DROVE AWAY and was soon lost among the gridwork of Toyama City. The road pointed north like a compass needle, and ahead of me the lines of perspective came together. I turned my face into the wind and walked toward the vanishing point.

> *early spring—*
> *a single road,*
> *vanishing*

A truck rumbled by, chased by a few cars, but other than that, the traffic on the Toyama perimeter was slight. A vehicle suddenly pulled over. It was a hatchback with a company logo on the side.

"Going north?" I asked.

Inside the car was a woman who had surprised herself by stopping. She was in her middle years, but had a bobbed girl's haircut that defied the arithmetic of age. She was all afluster. "What have I done?" she said aloud.

I opened the door and was halfway in when she said, "Wait! Stop!"

"Yes?" I was in limbo, my head in the door, my buttocks thrust out into traffic.

"Are you dangerous?"

"What?"

"I said, Are you dangerous?"

I wasn't sure I heard her correctly. "Who? Me? No, I'm not dangerous at all."

"You promise?"

"Sure."

"All right, then," she said. "You can get in."

And that was how I met the unsinkable, irrepressible, wholly undeniable Kikumi Otsugi, a woman who believed in bad men but not bad *dishonest* men. I had given her my word of honour that I would not harm her, and she was satisfied.

The car was cluttered with catalogues, magazines, stacks of brochures bound in rubber bands, road maps, file folders—as though a small tornado had recently passed through. She leaned over and shuffled some of the papers to make room for me, but all she succeeded in doing was stirring everything around. I nestled in and waited for the car to move. It didn't.

She looked over at me, then, laughing at herself, said, "What am I doing, asking a stranger into my car?"

"Would you like me to get out?"

"Oh, no, of course not," and she shook her head, less in disagreement and more as though she were trying to shake some sense into herself. "Why are you out here?" she asked. "So far from town? Is that too personal? Maybe it is. Anyway, I suppose you have your reasons. I mean, I'm curious, but it doesn't matter. Before we begin, my name is Kikumi, it means *beautiful flower.*" Then, laughing at her own immodesty, she said, "It was true once, many years ago."

"My name's William. It means *very safe person.*"

"There," she said. We shook hands and her hand felt small and fluttery in my palm, like a bird's wing. "Now then," she said. "We know each other's name, so we are no longer strangers, right? I can give you a ride."

She put the car into drive and pulled out, checking afterward to see if any vehicles had been coming. It seemed to sum up her approach to things: act first and then check later to see if it was all right.

"I know what I'll do!" she exclaimed. "I'll take you into Kurobe City. We can have an early lunch. Well, a late breakfast. Anyway, we'll have coffee—if you like coffee. I think most Americans do. Or is that just a stereotype? Who knows? No matter, I like coffee. I have a friend that speaks English. At least, she says she does. Who knows. I can't tell one way or the other. Now then . . . what was I saying?"

"Kurobe City?"

"Oh, yes. You'll like Kurobe. Very famous, you know—" she said, and suddenly pointed toward my groin. "Zippers."

"Zippers?"

She nodded gravely. "Kurobe zippers. Very famous."

We skimmed the edges of Toyama, a low, wide city of the plains framed by distant mountains. The entire area, as well as the city, was part of the regional Toyama culture. The Toyama region, according to Kikumi, was one of commerce. Prosperous, upbeat, hard-working. "Toyama women are famous," she declared. "They work. They don't just live off their husbands. Everyone says it, they say, 'Toyama women are strong willed.'"

She used the word *erai*, which is difficult to translate. The word has a slightly nasty edge to it, but it was clear that Kikumi took it as a compliment.

"Toyama women are rich—very rich. Not me, but most others are. I have one friend who played the stock market, and—you know what you should do? You should marry a Toyama girl, then you wouldn't have to hitchhike. You could take the Bullet Train, first-class—except she probably wouldn't let you. She would say, 'Save the money and take economy class.' Oh, yes," said Kikumi. "Toyama women are very strong."

"Are you a Toyama woman?"

"Yes. No. I mean, I think I am, but my husband is not so sure. Often he asks me, 'Are you sure you are really from Toyama?'"

"Maybe he married a fox?" (Foxes often assume the guise of women to ensnare men.)

"Yes!" she said. "Maybe I am a fox. You should have been more careful, to ride with a fox, it can be dangerous, but of course, I'm not a fox. We are only joking. Really, I am a—here, it is somewhere—no, that's not it—*here!* My business card. Do you see, there is some English on it. Very sophisticated, don't you think?"

Kikumi worked for a life insurance company in Kurobe, and she had been returning from a recent meeting when she saw me.

Kikumi called from her car phone and arranged to meet some of her friends at a hotel restaurant. She dropped me off at the entrance. "You get a seat, I'll find a parking spot." As she drove away, I realized I had left my backpack, my camera, most of my money, and all of my under-wear with this flyaway woman. I had often marvelled at how Japanese drivers would leave me sitting in their cars with the keys in the ignition and the motor running, but here I was doing much the same thing.

The dining room was sunny and surrounded with greenery. The menu included seafood-spaghetti, a dish that is inexplicably popular in Japan but which always reminds me of a collision, as though one waiter, carrying a plate of octopus and oysters, ran headlong into another waiter carrying pasta. The coffee bar was one of those elaborate chemistry sets where coffee is weighed out like gold dust and then boiled in beakers and poured carefully out, cup by cup. Through painstaking preparation like this, the Japanese have managed to justify charging seven hundred yen (eight bucks!) for a single cup of what is, basically, overpercolated sludge.

I choked back the java and basked in my celebrity. Three ladies, in varying ages from early thirties to late forties, were held rapt by my presence. We had a freewheeling discussion that ranged from whether perms suited Japanese women, to whether beards suited Western men, to whether Kikumi's recent decision to take up downhill skiing was well advised. The consensus on these issues was: *no, yes, no.* It turned out that Kikumi's friend Mami did *not* speak English, but she had been to Australia and that qualified her to act as translator. One of the ladies would ask Mami a question about me, Mami would ask me how to say it in English, I would tell her, she'd repeat it in English to her friends, and I would answer in Japanese. Everyone was happy.

When I told them I was heading for Sado (the distant island of the round-washtub boats) Kikumi told me the same folk story that Mr. Nakamura had told me, about lost love. But in her version the woman was *escaping* Sado, to visit a lover on the mainland. It was a slight shift in emphasis, but the difference was revealing. In one version the woman was trying to visit her exiled lover—a sad tale of sacrifice and womanly fidelity. In the other version she was simply restless and wanted to get off her island. When I asked them about this discrepancy, one of Kikumi's friends said, "It doesn't matter. In both cases, she drowned halfway across."

I wasn't allowed to pay for lunch. Kikumi waved it onto her tab with an empress-like gesture, only to have the waiter give her a strained smile. The manager soon appeared and he and Kikumi had a long, heated exchange about some other past unpaid bills, after which it was settled that (a) Kikumi was right and (b) the manager was very rude. As we left, Kikumi gave me a sour look and whispered, "Toyama men—obsessed with money. It's terrible."

Kurobe City, it turned out, *is* the zipper capital of the world. It is the home of YKK, which stands for Yoshida Kogyo Kabushiki-gaisha. The YKK Corporation has made its name and its fortune with the humble zipper. Except, of course, they aren't called zippers; that was a brand name introduced by B. F. Goodrich in the 1920s. The name *zipper* later became generic, but in the city of Kurobe, or at least within hearing range of YKK, zippers are still officially referred to, not as zippers, but rather as "slide fasteners." It seemed like such a strange industry to build a city around, zippers. I tried to imagine similar versions—the Shoelace Metropolis, the Button and Tie-Clip Capital of the World, String City—but I couldn't do it.

We swung by Kikumi's office on the outskirts of town and, as she pulled into the parking lot, she suddenly—frantically—said, "Quick! Get down!"

"Pardon?"

"Get down, before someone sees you." Her voice dropped. "I'm supposed to be working."

So I hunched over, twisting in my seat, as she parked and then said, "I'll be right back. *Don't move!*"

I sat there, all scrunched up, for a long time. Finally, when my back could no longer take it, I slowly straightened up and peered out the window. In the second storey of the office, I could see Kikumi talking with several co-workers. She was pointing to her car. When they saw me sticking my head up, they waved. I waved back. Then they began gesturing for me to get down. I saw a grumpy-looking man in a white shirt and tie appear and I quickly bobbed back down. I still wasn't exactly sure why I was hiding. Finally, a back-aching eternity later, Kikumi opened the door and said, "Hi!"

"Hi. Can I get up now?"

"No, no, not until we get out of sight. I told them I was feeling ill and that something came up at home, so I got the rest of the day off." She turned and beamed at me. "I'm going to take you to the Sado ferry terminal, what do you think of that?"

But first we had to drop by her house to fill her husband in on the day's events, and to ensure a proper alibi in case anyone called.

Her husband was a solid but soft-spoken man. He looked on with a bemused yet somehow satisfied smile as Kikumi bustled about gathering up items for our trip. He appeared to be almost pleased with what was happening, as though he were saying to himself, "Isn't that just like her to show up with a foreigner in tow and a wild scheme to get out of work. After all these years, she is still full of surprises."

Kikumi and her husband didn't catch a quick goodbye kiss on the fly as she charged out of the house—in Japan, even with someone as outgoing as Kikumi, that would be unheard of—but she did squeeze his arm, gently, briefly, as she was about to leave. It was one of the most touching gestures I had seen in a long time. Off we went in a roar of confusion.

"You want to take the ferry to Sado, right?" She tried to unfold the map with one hand and steer with the other. With her window half down, the paper was flapping up and plastering itself onto her. Rather than roll her window up, she simply flung the map into the back and said, "Don't worry. I know the way, we'll take the expressway."

"But that's so expensive." I insisted that she let me pay the tolls, which are unbelievably high in Japan.

"Don't worry," she said. "You can pay the tolls on the way back."

I smiled. "And how do you propose I do that?"

She laughed. "You're right. I never thought of that—anyway, it's all right. I'll pay the tolls because you got lunch, so—"

"But *you*—"

"*Ah, ah, ah!*" She waved my protests away with another imperial wave.

We joined the Hokuriku Expressway outside the town of Asahi. The expressway followed the sea, hugging the steep coastline and winding its way along the rocky shores of Oyashirazu. In ancient times, this coast had been an impassable barrier, and even now the expressway slipped off the shore entirely at a few points and ran above the water on elevated pylons—and we would be suspended for an instant over open sea. When the seaside toehold could not be maintained, the road plunged headfirst into the very mountains themselves.

There were twenty-six tunnels between Kurobe and the harbour town of Joetsu. The tunnels ranged in length from quick passes to gun-barrel funnels more than four and a half kilometres long. The longest tunnels had huge jet fans pulling in air to prevent motorists from asphyxiating on carbon monoxide. In and out of subterranean darkness we drove, under flickering lights, then back into the afternoon sun.

We came into Joetsu beneath frost-ridden mountains. The air had chilled. It reminded me of that haunting opening line of Kawabata's novel *Yukiguni*: "The train came out of the long tunnel and into snow country." I had passed over, into the Far North, into Snow Country. Here, on the northwestern side of the Japan Alps, cold wet air rises suddenly, creating some of the highest snowfalls on earth. Much of Japan is hot, humid, and semi-tropical. But in the north, towns disappear beneath layers of snow two stories high. Villagers burrow pathways from house to house, and the secondary roads stay closed. The population is sparse and the winters are suffocating. Even here, with the arrival of spring, the coldness lingered like patches of snow, unmelted. The northern mountains formed a wall of bad weather. There were no cherry blossoms in Joetsu.

Kikumi dropped me off at the ferry terminal. She was a bit frazzled. It had been a long ride and she was now facing the return. She wouldn't get home until well after dark. How do you properly thank someone in a situation like this? You can't.

16

I BOARDED the last ferry to Sado with time to spare. Snug and satisfied, I stood on the upper deck and watched the last-minute traffic race in. The ground crew was just about to throw the ropes free when a car came flying in, lights flashing, horn honking. It just made it. No sooner had the car rattled up the ramp and onto the lower deck than the drawbridge rose up. A trio of youthful celebrants piled out of the car, along with an American girl—well, I assumed she was American. (Hang out in Japan long enough and this will happen to you too.) They were laughing and grinning and congratulating themselves on their sudden-death timing.

The ferry had a cafeteria and a coffee shop, but for the last run everything was closed down. I bought a pack of peanuts and a can of Sapporo beer from the ferry vending machines and, as the icy mountains of northern Japan pulled away, I watched from the window as a storm rolled in toward us, low along the sea.

The sky darkened and the storm hit, strafing the deck with rain, and then—we were through. We broke free of the storm and we were out at sea, with only horizons of waves stretching in all directions. I went back onto the deck, feeling immortal. On the far edge of the sea, rising above the water like a whale's back, was Sado Island.

Night was falling and the island of Sado began to fade into darkness as we approached, becoming more and more indistinct the nearer we came.

By the time we reached Sado, Sado had disappeared.

COLD WIND

Sado Island and Tohoku

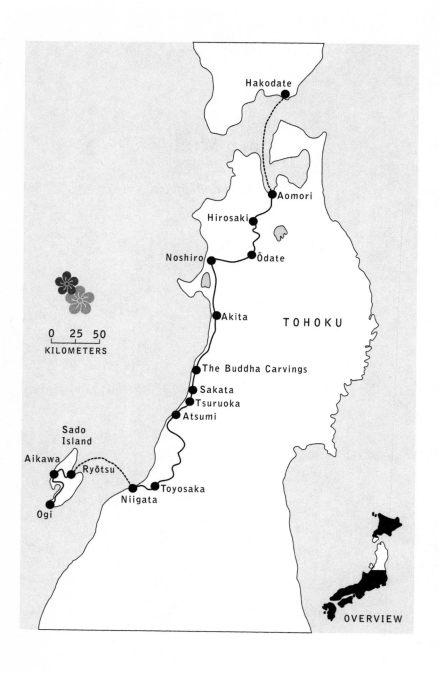

Hakodate

Aomori

Hirosaki

Noshiro   Ōdate

Akita   TOHOKU

0 25 50
KILOMETERS

The Buddha Carvings

Sakata
Tsuruoka
Atsumi

Sado
Island

Aikawa   Ryōtsu

Ogi   Niigata   Toyosaka

OVERVIEW

I

SADO HAS ALWAYS been Japan's Island of Exile.

It is a cold, distant, mythical place.

When the Emperor Juntoku led a failed revolt in 1221 against the Kamakura shōgunate, it was unthinkable to execute the Son of Heaven, even a disgraced, unruly, twenty-four-year-old ex–Son of Heaven stripped of his imperial crown. So, instead of sending Juntoku to his death for the abortive coup, they sent him here, to Sado.

In a few instances, exile in Sado was the prelude to greatness. Such was the case of the radical priest Nichiren, sent to the island in 1271.

What can you say about a man like Nichiren? He was certainly one of the most forceful personalities in Japanese history. If Kōbō Daishi was a Christlike figure healing the lame, curing the sick, and preaching inclusion, Nichiren was John the Baptist: an Old Testament–style prophet, all thunder and bluster and bile.

He was, above all, a fundamentalist. A self-described "son of an outcast fisherman," Nichiren was disdainful—and no doubt envious—of the Court Buddhism of his day, with its manorial holdings and refined airs. In sharp contrast to its gentility, Nichiren went back to basics, to the original teachings of the Buddha—and the Lotus Sutra in particular. Not only did he reject the cozy, established Buddhist orders of his day, he also denounced the esoteric seclusion of Zen monasteries.

Nichiren was the first true Japanese nationalist. He was fervent in his vision of a trans-Nippon unity, a mother tribe at odds with the rest of the world. Nichiren was acutely aware of belonging to a nation; it wasn't a particular valley or village or prefecture to which he swore allegiance. His mission was to unite and purify all of Japan. He wanted the government to create—and enforce—a unified state religion.

Between 1257 and 1260, an unprecedented series of calamities ripped through central Japan: earthquakes, epidemics, famines, floods. Nichiren took this as a sign that the end was nigh. The gods were abandoning Japan. He prophesied that these events would culminate with a foreign invasion that would conquer the nation and destroy the Kamakura shōgunate, turning the Islands of Harmony into a vassal state—unless, that is, Nichiren's obscure sect was made the official religion of Japan.

It was little more than spiritual blackmail, and the Shōgun could stand no more. Nichiren was sentenced to die by execution for insulting the rulers and inciting rebellion. What happened next is a little unclear, but legend has it that just as the executioner raised his sword to decapitate Nichiren—who was kneeling deep in prayer—a lightning bolt lashed out, breaking the sword in two.

Unnerved, the Shōgun decided instead to send the troublesome priest into exile, and so it was that Nichiren arrived on the lonely island of Sado. The small band of followers whom he left behind, who had never numbered more than three hundred, were rounded up, imprisoned, or run out of town. Their goods were confiscated and sold. It marked what should have been the end of the Nichiren movement.

For three long years, Nichiren lived on Sado, at first in an abandoned temple and later with a handful of followers who had made their way to the island. Racked with pain and in constant bad health, Nichiren nevertheless returned to his proselytizing ways, preaching the word of Buddha as he saw it and vehemently condemning all other sects. Slowly, ineluctably, he began to win over new recruits. Sado became a Nichiren stronghold, and his displaced sect—a cult really—took fresh root on this distant, windswept isle. The Kamakura shōguns had not heard the last of him.

While Nichiren was walking the backroads of Sado, news came to the capital of a Mongol army that was massing its warships off the coast of Korea. A wave of fear swept through the courts of Japan. Kublai—the Great Khan, grandson of Genghis, Scourge of Mongolia, Lord of China, Conqueror of Korea—had now turned his gaze upon the Land of the Rising Sun. The Shōgun, desperate and repentant, sent for Nichiren. His past sins hastily pardoned, Nichiren began praying day and night for the salvation of the motherland.

The summer of 1274. A flotilla of warriors, twenty-five-thousand strong, crossed the straits separating the Korean peninsula and the archipelago of Japan. They landed in waves. There to meet them were armies of the samurai lined up in formation, waiting. What happened next was closer to farce than epic.

The samurai generals, following the formal codes of Japanese culture, rode out ahead of their men to formally greet and confront the enemy. Protocol demanded a speech and a verbose challenge with much posturing and sword-rattling bravado—much like the long, tense buildups that precede a sumo bout. In Japan, opposing generals would take turns striding forth on horseback to issue a stirring bit of bombast, boasting about the strength of their army, the honour of their ancestors, the prestige of their family names, and so on. Once all the opening formalities were over—which you can still see today in the endless speeches given before any event in Japan, no matter how minor—the battle would formally commence. It was all very civilized and proper, after which there would be general carnage and bloodletting.

Unfortunately, no one thought to explain the codes of etiquette to the Mongol hordes. And let's face it, Mongol hordes are not really known for their etiquette and good manners. When the first Japanese general rode out and launched into a speech, the Mongols listened for a bit and then riddled his body with arrows. As the general toppled from his horse in mid-sentence, the samurai fell back in confusion. Clearly, this was not going to go according to plan. (And let me just say, as a veteran of many a long-winded Japanese speech, that I have the utmost sympathy for the Mongols. Many's the time I wished I was armed with my own contingent of archers to cut short the usual bloated oratory of morning meetings. "Together we must strive harder and endeavour to meet the departmental goals as outlined in the—*thwwaaaacckk! AWK!*")

With that first, ill-mannered volley, the invasion of Japan had begun. The Mongols poured in, strengthened their beachhead, and set perimeter encampments; they moved up, dug in. The battle raged in sporadic and sudden bloody engagements like a gory game of tug-of-war. And then, far from the field of battle, stirring the skies like a cauldron, the prophet-priest Nichiren called forth a wind from the gods, a *kami-kaze*, which blew through, scattering the ships and sending the Mongols back in disarray. Japan had been spared.

But Mongol hordes are nothing if not persistent, and Kublai Khan immediately laid plans for a second strike. The Shōgunate scrambled to strengthen its position and build a fleet of light, quick-running warships. They constructed stone walls along the southern coast of Japan to keep the Mongols out, much like the Great Wall of China itself, which had also been built to stop them—and had failed.

Seven years passed. The horizon darkened once again with the sight of ships approaching. It was the largest naval invasion the world had ever seen, an army one hundred forty thousand strong. The Shōgun's defensive walls contained them, barely, and all summer long the samurai armies battled back the Mongol, Korean, and Chinese soldiers. Thousands of bodies lay strewn along the coast, and the tides ran red as the clashes grew more frantic.

And then it came—again. Blowing in like a fury unleashed, a second typhoon, even greater than the first. The Mongols tried to fall back, across the strait to safe harbour in Korea, but the ships collided with each other and were sunk by the storm. More than four thousand Mongol ships went down—four thousand, mind you—taking with them over one hundred thousand men. Those left behind, or who managed to swim to shore, found themselves, in the wreckage of the storm's passage, stranded without supplies and facing a full-frontal assault by the armies of the Japanese Shōgun. What followed was a massacre. The samurai pushed the remnants of the Khan's army out onto a sandspit. Vanquished, the invaders threw down their swords and begged for mercy. They were butchered. Men died by the tens of thousands. It was a complete and utter rout, and when his few remaining ships limped back home, Kublai Khan had had enough. With the very gods against him, he abandoned his plans of conquest.

The Japanese Shōgun maintained a vigil along the coast for more than twenty years, but the Mongols never returned and the walls eventually crumbled (the ruins are still visible on the outskirts of modern Fukuoka City). Japan was the only kingdom in the Far East

not conquered by the Mongols. Indeed, Japan had never been conquered by any nation, ever, and would remain undefeated for seven
hundred years—until 1945.

Kublai Khan's failed invasions were a godsend to Nichiren. By
predicting them, and then calling forth the kamikaze to defeat them,
Nichiren had demonstrated his power and prophecy for all to see.
True, hundreds of monks and priests, the Shōgun, and even the
Emperor himself had also prayed for the gods to save their land, but
it was Nichiren who took the credit. His sect flourished. The numbers grew, the persecution ended.

Today, seven centuries later, Nichiren-shū lives on. Sōka Gakkai,
a subsect of Nichiren, has even formed its own political party, a
blending unheard of in most developed countries. Today's Sōka
Gakkai Party, heir of Nichiren, stands against corruption and for
clean government, and in its rhetoric one still hears the thunder and
echo of Nichiren's own righteous battle cry.

"I am the pillar of Japan, the eyes of Japan, protector of the
nation!" This was Nichiren's immodest boast, written during his long
exile on Sado. And it is on Sado that he is best remembered: the
prophet cast off, the voice in the wilderness, defiant and unbeaten.

Night. Falling snow. The town of Ogi was small but confusing.
Streets led you inward only to abandon you. After trudging up one
narrow lane and down another, I eventually stumbled upon a noodle
shop, which I entered with a gust of cold air, eliciting frowns and
hard stares from the patrons who sat hunched over steaming bowls.
The men looked up as though I had interrupted a conspiracy.

"Hi there!" I said.

The noodle lady shot a glance in my direction and said, more
sharply than was necessary, "No more service!" even as she ladled
out another bowl of broth and slithering noodles. I talked my way
into a space along the counter, but I had to put up with disgruntled
silence as I ate. Where was the youth hostel? *Up the hill.* Where? *Up
the hill, up the hill!* A hand waved, taking in several directions and
leaving me without bearings or welcome.

Outside, the town was deserted and the snow was sifting down,
dusting the streets and accenting the rooftops. I eventually called

the hostel from a lonely pay phone. The woman who answered—her voice as weary as might be expected of someone dealing with a simpleton—gave me directions that were only marginally more coherent than *Up the hill! Up the hill!* Sado Island is nothing *but* hills, I grumbled, and set off.

The road wound deep into a hidden valley. In the chilled white moonlight the rice fields were ridges of bone. A dog barked psychotically, almost choking on its saliva, as I approached a farmhouse. We faced off in the darkness. "Don't worry, Will. He's as scared of you as you are of him," I said, unsuccessfully trying to convince myself to be brave.

I stood there, my very presence egging the dog on to more and more outlandish threats. "First I'm gonna rip your head off! Then I'm gonna chew your skull! Then I'm gonna—" The front door slid open and a woman in an apron came out and cursed the dog into silence.

I schlepped my bag into the front foyer and signed in. The interior of the farmhouse was feathered in dust. The walls were adorned with framed jigsaw puzzles of the Rocky Mountains, and the living room was stuffed with sagging furniture. The woman took my money and then vanished into the various Escher-inspired hallways. A small child trailed after her and I was alone.

2

THE EARLY MORNING revealed a landscape of mist, muted in faded green and gold, the wisps of steam hanging low like dragon's breath across the fields. I hiked back into town, down to Ogi Port. The only business open was an agricultural co-op, but they had a coffee shop upstairs, so I sat, sipping sludge, and watched the sun break across the bay. I had arrived one step ahead of the tour buses. The town was apparently overrun at the peak season, but here in early spring, without so much as a whisper of cherry blossoms on the wind, I was the only visitor in sight.

"Next week, very busy," said the man behind the counter. "This week—nothing."

"Well, *I'm* here," I said brightly, but it didn't seem to console him.

Ogi Port is famous for the washtub *tarai-bune* boats of folk legend. These large wooden tubs, steered as they are by shifting your weight and churning the water with a single oar, are almost impossible to manage, yet the elderly ladies in their bright-sashed peasant kimonos and bonnet-like hats were having no trouble at all. The washtub boats, meant for gathering seaweed and shells, are still in use farther along the cape, but here in Ogi the tradition is kept alive primarily as a folk attraction—a sort of living theatre staged for spectators. By making a small donation, you can even try your hand at it, which I did, with the tub tilted over ridiculously to my side and the sweet little lady—her smile decidedly strained—giving me doomed advice on how to shift my weight and wield the oar. We ended up (here's a surprise) turning in circles. My shoulder was soon aching and I was feeling vaguely dizzy. The lady, her face hidden by her wide-brimmed straw hat, giggled and giggled. What I failed to achieve by sheer will and muscle, she deftly did with rhythm, taking over control and skimming us back to shore (we had spun dangerously far out to sea under my tutelage). It was a dance form, really, a swaying of semicircles acting against each other, motion through misdirection.

When we got back, another lady came bumping up to the dock and called over to me, laughingly, "She is a terrible teacher! I can teach you much better." And so off I went again, around and around and around and around and around and around. *"Jōzu desu ne!"* she cried. My arm socket was throbbing by now, and my knees were drunk on the motion, so once again I handed over control to a lady three times my age and half my height. A dozen other washtubs were waiting at the pier when we returned, and everyone agreed I was the best rower they had had all day. This buoyed my spirits slightly until I realized, as I walked wobbly away, that I was—so far—the *only* rower that day.

I was heading north on the road out of Ogi, past an automobile graveyard, when—flying around the corner—came a bright white car. As soon as the driver saw me, the vehicle came to a skidding, spontaneous stop. I didn't even have my thumb out.

"Hey, man!" a voice called out to me in what can only be described as California-cool "I remember you from the ferry boat!"

It was the same carload of energy I had seen the night before, the one that had raced the ferry and won. The driver was a tanned young Japanese man. He was wearing an earring, mirrored sunglasses, and a fluorescent orange T-shirt. Beside him was his girlfriend, an American, with tumble-brown hair and beautiful features. In the backseat, even more youthful good looks: a Japanese woman they called Abo, and beside her, sprawled out in heavy slumber, an athletic and drowsy young man named Say Ya. (At least, that was how it sounded.) I wedged into the backseat, disturbing Say Ya, who woke up, eyed me with foggy resentment, and immediately lolled back to sleep.

"My name is Atsushi," said the driver and obvious leader of the group. He turned around to shake my hand and insisted that everyone in the car do likewise. Say Ya was less than enthusiastic, waking long enough to offer a limp palm before rolling over, knees and arms forming a rubbery tangle, face into the backseat.

"He likes you," said Atsushi. "As for me, *atsui*—that means 'hot.' So you can call me Hot Sushi, if you like. All my friends do."

I was flattered that he had automatically included me in their circle, but his girlfriend Michelle was obviously not so immediately inclined. It would take her a long time to warm to me, which puzzled Hot Sushi because he had assumed—since Michelle and I were both North Americans—that there would be some kind of instant rapport between us. There wasn't. Ironically, Westerners are far more suspicious of other Westerners than the Japanese ever are. For all his exuberance and surprisingly good English, Hot Sushi was still Japanese—which is to say, trusting, innocent, and a little naive.

Michelle was from Delaware, which is apparently a city or a state or something somewhere in the United States, but I wasn't exactly sure. (Later, I learned that most Americans can't find Delaware on a map either, which made me feel better.)

Hot Sushi and the gang were ski instructors from the mainland, which explained their healthy tans and almost sexual vigour. Next to them, I looked like—well, like *not* a ski instructor. As we drove out of Ogi, Hot Sushi chatted enthusiastically about skiing, a sport that has always seemed slightly Sisyphian to me. Go up a hill. Ski down. Go back up again. So why not just stay at the bottom in the first place? No matter, I had once skied in the interior of British Columbia, which gave me much-needed credentials.

"Skiing is a rush," said Hot Sushi, and on this they agreed.

The hedonism of ski instructors seems universal. I have no doubt that this foursome would get along just fine with any other ski instructors from any other country. Hot Sushi went one better: during the winter he was a ski instructor; in the summer he flew to the island of Guam, the American protectorate in Micronesia, and taught Japanese tourists how to scuba dive. That was how he met Michelle. They both worked in Guam at the Pacific Island Club, a high-end resort with its own "swim-through" aquarium.

"Ever been to Guam?" asked Hot Sushi. "You'd like it. Lots of sun, lots of surf."

"It's like Hawaii," said Michelle, "but without the culture." Michelle had studied at a university in Hawaii and had come to Guam not long after. "Guam is a gaijin zoo," she said. "Japanese tourists go to Guam so that they can feel they went to a foreign country, but everything is geared so they don't have to speak to for-eigners and don't have to eat anything but Japanese food. Even the karaoke is in Japanese. They go to Guam to look at the gaijins."

Hot Sushi sighed, but had to agree. "It's true," he said. "Japanese want to *see* gaijins in their natural habitat. But they don't want to have to actually deal with them directly."

"You could get a job easily in Guam," Michelle said to me. "You speak Japanese. You're like a tame gaijin."

It stung, but her observation was true. Many foreigners had made entire careers out of being a tame gaijin. Japanese television was lit-tered with them.

Hot Sushi and the gang were touring Sado Island to mark the end of the ski season.

"Sado Island is dying," said Hot Sushi. "It's beautiful. But it's dying. The young people are leaving. No one is staying. It's an island of old people."

Just then, as luck would have it, we passed a young boy running beside the road, which Michelle quickly—and maliciously—pointed out. "There's a young person right there. Look."

But Hot Sushi was not fazed in the least. "Sure," he said. "But he's running to catch the last ferry off the island. It just proves my point."

The road twisted along the coast, through clustered villages where the sea and wind had leached colour from the wooden build-ings, leaving them washed-out and grey.

"This car has no radio," said Hot Sushi. "But that's okay, because I will sing for you." Michelle rolled her eyes, but Hot Sushi was undeterred. *"Do you know—where you're going to—do you like the things that life has shown you—"*

This woke up Say Ya. In spite of being a robust young man, he looked an awful lot like a grumpy child. "He's singing," he muttered. "He's always singing."

And so it was, we cruised through the rolling hills and slow curves of Sado accompanied by an off-key but spirited rendition of "Mahogany."

Where are you going to—do you know?

3

ONE OF SADO'S most illustrious exiles was a man named Zeami who lived from 1363 to 1443. Zeami was the Shakespeare of Japan. As an actor and a playwright, he codified the art of Noh theatre, fusing traditional dance with the sublime austerity of Zen philosophy. Central to his aesthetic was *yūgen*, "that which lies below the surface, that which is hidden but always present," a concept that is as diffi- cult as it is vague. Yūgen, the world beyond words, lies in the reson- ance and beauty of pure experience. It was a theory of art that was remarkably advanced for its age, especially when lined up against the literally minded morality plays that were standard fare in European courts at about the same time. ("Oh, no! Scratch the Devil is eating Lazy Child! Only Virtuous Son and Loyal Daughter can save him.")

Zeami was heralded as a genius during his lifetime, a legend of truly theatrical proportions. Mind you, it helped that Zeami—as well as being an artistic genius—was also the homosexual lover of the reigning Shōgun. In a very real sense, Zeami slept his way to the top. Alas, when the Shōgun died, Zeami lost his patron, and the next ruler was—ahem—less enamoured of the artistry of Zeami than was his predecessor. On the pretext that the upstart Noh master was hoarding artistic secrets for himself, the new Shōgun sent Zeami into exile, to the island at the edge of the world. Zeami spent his last years in obscurity, chilled to the bone and bitterly lonely. Zeami died on Sado, a broken man. His art lived on. And on and on and on and on . . . If you have ever tried to sit through an evening of Noh theatre, you will understand what I'm speaking about.

Noh has been described as "total theatre," combining as it does music, mime, dance, poetic recitals, masked costumes, and tonal chants. It is also a theatre of restraint. The tension comes not from plot but from atmosphere, much of it supernatural. The performers are usually masked, they walk with a gliding, hesitant step, and the scenes unfold like slowly transforming tableaus—all to the accompaniment of shrill flutes, sudden yelps, arbitrary drumbeats, and slow, boiling moans. Noh *is* haunting and disturbing and deep—for about ten minutes. After that, the hours slow down to a glacial pace and the movements appear to be made under deep water. It is beyond somnolent. It is boring. Profoundly, exquisitely, existentially *boring*.

Zeami's texts on Noh, once groundbreaking and avant garde, have fossilized. It is a theatre of ghosts. A museum piece. The plays revolve around the cycle of karma, of death and rebirth, and the longings that tie us to this world of illusions. Certainly, the performances proceed at about the speed one expects eternity to move.

A friend of mine was studying theatre in Japan and he was constantly trying to convince me that I did in fact love Noh. This friend—who was English, naturally (the English have an almost heroic capacity for boredom)—would drag me to touring performances and gasp and gush over the way the lead player would hold his fan. "Do you see that!" he'd say. "The lead actor is holding his fan *upside down*." My friend was, like most hardened fans, disdainful of the competition. "Noh is far deeper than the type of cheap catharsis you get from melodrama or kitchen-sink realism. And it is not simply spectacle, either. Kabuki, with its blood-and-thunder excess and extravagant costumes, is crass. But Noh . . . Noh is meditative."

"And seditative," I said.

"And yet," he would insist, all empirical evidence to the contrary, "it is very exciting. Noh operates on many levels. Underneath it is tension—this tension that is almost unbearable."

"Tell me about it."

My friend was getting exasperated. "I don't know why I even try to enlighten you. Listen," he'd say. "Ezra Pound helped translate Noh plays into English. Brecht was greatly influenced by Noh. W. B. Yeats felt that it reached new levels of suggestive art."

"Name drop all you want," I said. "It makes no difference. Noh is still Noh. It's like attending the opera or going to the dentist. You don't enjoy it, you *endure* it."

I will concede one point. The masks of Noh are sublime. The female masks in particular. (Like Kabuki, Noh is still a primarily male domain.) Poised *between* expressions, they are capable of all expressions. During performances of Noh, I have seen—though I would never admit this to my Noh-loving friend—how the masks seem to change moods onstage, so effective are the postures and gestures of the performers.

Perhaps my English friend was right. Perhaps Noh truly *is* the essence of Japanese society. Masks that have incredible depth, feelings that are restrained, emotions turned inward, silences that fester, sudden bursts, violent emotion, lifetimes of regret. Or maybe it is simply a very old and dated art form. Either way, I would not attend another evening of Noh at gunpoint.

Instead, I spent my time on Sado Island admiring masks and seething in envy over the sensual, hedonistic lifestyles of ski instructors and sun-browned scuba divers.

4

SADO ISLAND, if not lost in time, was certainly adrift in it. The villages were like fallen stacks of wooden crates surrounded by seascapes and embraced by rolling hills.

We stopped for coffee at a viewing spot along the way, and Say Ya, stretching and yawning, wandered into the tourist shop. Say Ya had to try everything, squeezing horns in the toy section, trying on hats, spinning tops, playing plastic flutes. Then, as soon as we were back into the car, he dropped into sleep as suddenly as someone under a hypnotist's command. A torrent of energy, then a nap.

"He is just like a kid," said Hot Sushi approvingly.

At Senkaku Bay we stopped to visit an aquarium, with listless fish and giant mutant crabs and stir-crazy sharks turning cramped circles. The bay itself was a deep turquoise inlet of sea amid jagged rock formations and overspills of green. We walked along a narrow footbridge onto an observation deck perched on an outcrop of rock.

Say Ya looked around and said, philosophically, "Good place for a barbecue."

As we continued up the west coast, we passed a sign near a beach: CAUTION: WATCH OUT FOR BEAUTIFUL GIRLS.

"Next week," Abo assured me. "Next week and the beaches will be filled with beautiful women."

Story of my life.

From the Senkaku Bay area, we turned inland toward a place called Kinzan, "the Gold Mountain." This was no hyperbole. In 1601, the very year that Lord Tokugawa unified Japan under his rule, gold was discovered at Kinzan. It was a rich vein, near the surface and easily separated from the bedrock. This discovery on the fringes of

Tokugawa's realm proved fortuitous indeed, for the gold of Sado funded the coffers of the Tokugawa dynasty and kept them in power for the next two hundred and fifty years. The gold of Sado outlasted the shōguns themselves. It helped fund the Meiji Reformation and it supported Japan's imperial adventures in China. Sado gold helped pay for the planes and ships that attacked Pearl Harbour, and it helped fund the winged bombs of the kamikaze pilots. Gold was still being mined at Sado right up until 1990.

At the height of the gold rush, the main site was near the boom town of Aikawa, the Klondike of Japan, a brawling community of gold miners, samurai overlords, imported prostitutes, wealthy wine merchants, assorted mountebanks, and thousands upon thousands of slave labourers. It was a major, albeit makeshift, city. Today, little is left of Aikawa to remind you of its once reckless past.

As we drove inland toward the old gold mines, the ragged green peaks called Doyu-no-Wareto rose above us. They were formed, it was said, by a gold miner enraged with greed who struck the mountain so hard with his hammer and spike that he split the peak in two. The mountain *was* split, but not by any mythical figure. It was the ceaseless mining activity of thousands that cracked the mountain.

The mines have since been turned into a sort of Disneyland of the Oppressed, with walkways built deep into the wet, chilled depths. Mannequins dressed in ragged clothes are arranged in mini-dioramas, reminders that it was grunt work, performed by slave labourers, that made the gold mines viable. The mine shafts, now a tourist attraction, were a kind of mass grave. Thousands of slaves died in these mines. Their average life expectancy, upon arrival at Aikawa, was less than four years. Meanwhile, on the mainland of Honshu north of Tokyo lie the baroque, extravagant mausoleums at Nikko, burial place of the shōguns. The contrast between Nikko and the mines of Aikawa, between two tombs, is so vast as to be obscene.

There was an awkward moment outside the Mine Museum when Hot Sushi pulled me aside and said, in a hushed voice, "Hey, man. It costs six hundred yen to enter. If you can't afford it—I mean, if you need some money, or—"

"No, no—" I waved his offer away.

Michelle eyed our exchange warily.

From the gold mines, Hot Sushi decided to follow the O-Sado Skyline Highway along the spine of the isle and then down into the port city of Ryōtsu. When Hot Sushi began to yawn, lion-like, Michelle became concerned. "Are you sure you aren't too tired to drive?"

"Tired?" said Hot Sushi. "Who—me? I never get tired. Never."

Again Michelle tried to catch him in a contradiction, and again he managed to elude her. "But yesterday you told me that you always feel sleepy."

"*Sleepy*, yes. But tired? Never."

I liked Hot Sushi. I liked the fact that you could never pin him down on anything. He reminded me, in his slightly ironic outlook and breezy goodwill, of the French Acadians of my home country. And his understanding of English nuance was remarkable as well. There *is* a difference between being tired and being sleepy.

The air was clean and alpine crisp. Sloping away on either side were heady vistas that were so absolutely spectacular we almost considered waking up Say Ya. Abo finally did, as we snaked our way down toward the eastern shore of the island.

"Yeah," he said groggily, peering out the window with one eye. "It's Sado all right."

Some towns seemed to have blown onto the shore like flotsam. Such was the case with Ryōtsu, with its shaganappy patched-up, tumble-down, falling-in-on-themselves houses with their rusting corrugated-metal roofs and sea-bleached walls. The colour of Ryōtsu was the same silvery grey of old temples and driftwood.

It was the end of the line for me. Hot Sushi dropped me off near the ferry port and gave me a pamphlet for the Pacific Island Club in Guam. "I'm in the picture," he said, pointing to a faintly recognizable dot. Diminished to a few pixels on a compugraphic imprint, Hot Sushi's smile was still visible, like the Cheshire Cat's grin, the last of his features to fade. I wished Abo the best, I shook Say Ya's sleepy hand, and I gave Michelle one of those awkward half-hug/half-handshake–type farewells that are so popular among North Americans. The four of them then piled back into the car and set off in the pursuit of experience and a never-ending present. God, how I envied them.

5

THE TOWN OF RYŌTSU, indeed the entire island of Sado, was gearing up for its spring festival of drums and horseback archery, performed at full gallop in medieval garb. The art of the Noh mask was turned into burlesque above Ryōtsu Port, where a four-metre mask was hoisted up atop a tower as a tourist attraction. "It celebrates the life of Zeami," said the man at the information desk. "And the fact that we have more than forty Noh theatres on this island, making Sado the centre of Noh in Japan."

"Do you go to the theatre?" I asked.

"Noh is very popular on Sado."

"Yes," I said, "but do you yourself attend?"

His voice dropped to the hushed tone of a dissident criticizing a military regime. "Noh is a little slow," he said, and then with a wide smile, "I prefer pro wrestling. Do you know Giant Baba? I met him once. He was very nice. I was surprised."

"But pro wrestling is fake."

"So is Noh," he said. It was one of the most reasonable things I have ever heard regarding public entertainment.

Sado Island is also home to the internationally renowned Kodō Drummers. You may know them. These are the drummers you see stripped to loincloths, muscles sheened in sweat, torsos like washboards, headbands twisted around foreheads, and a wild grimace of battle in their faces as they hammer out a war cry, the drumbeats raw and primal, until your head swims and your chest tightens as though a tourniquet were tied around your rib cage and you have to step back, head reeling, from the fire. That is Kodō.

The Kōdo Drummers of Sado Island have taken drumming to an intense, almost cultish level. The drummers perform high-speed, overlaid rhythms, and to effect this union of spirit and sound they eat together, cook together, clean together, and live together. (Most members of the troupe share communal living quarters.) If it sounds vaguely counterculture and hippyish, it's because it is. The roots of the Kōdo movement go back to the late 1960s, when the Japanese youth movement opted out of mainstream consumer society and sought to reconnect with the past. Being Japanese, their approach was anything but lackadaisical. Joining the Kōdo Drummers is like joining the Marines. It is a tough regime: up before dawn for a ten-kilometre run, near naked even in the howling depths of winter. (Long-distance running teaches you the rhythm of the human body. It also builds stamina.)

Kōdo Drummers play to the point of exhaustion, and stamina is crucial. They often perform leaning back, like a man in mid-situp, and it made me ache just to watch. They can make the drums tremble as softly as rain falling on a leaf, or come crashing to a head like sudden artillery. The drumming builds up, in waves, a hailstorm of drummers—relentless—reckless—unchained—and it rolls across the audience in volleys and echoes back again. The largest of the drums, the *Ōdai-ko*, weighs more than half a ton and is wheeled out like a creaking god at the climax of the performance. It is large enough, as they say, for a man to drown in. The drummer stands, stripped to loincloth and headband, his back knotted in exertion, and—wielding drumsticks the size of baseball bats—he pounds out a punishing rhythm, a deep reverberating *boom-boom-boom* that rattles the rib cage and alters the heartbeat.

After a demonstration of drumming at the town's public hall, I walked through a deep blue evening in Ryōtsu. The hammering heartbeat of the drums echoed in my chest all through the night.

I took a room in a ramshackle harbourside inn, where I had to wrangle with the lady of the establishment for half an hour before she would consent to renting to a foreigner. She tried to tell me she was "all full," a common-enough ruse pulled on foreigners in Japan, but an easy one to disprove. The entranceways of Japanese inns are where customers' shoes are stored, and if an inn truly is filled up, the entrance should be stuffed with shelves of shoes. In this case there was not a single pair in storage. When I pointed this out she changed tack, saying that I would have to sleep on a futon and as an American I would be more comfortable on a bed in a hotel.

It was aggravating, trying to convince this lady to take my money, and in the end I had to resort to what I call my "cousin routine." Whenever Japanese innkeepers are reluctant to rent me a room— they are afraid of misunderstandings, improper taking of baths, sudden violent murders; all understandable fears—I simply introduce myself in the following way:

> "Hello, I am the cousin of [INSERT TOWN NAME HERE]'s foreign English teacher."

As a former exchange teacher myself, I can attest to the fact that Japanese schools are simply crawling with foreigners. Virtually every high school and most junior highs have a token gaijin on staff—be he or she from Australia, America, New Zealand, Britain, Ireland, or Canada. We called ourselves GODS, that is, "Gaijins On Display," and we were looked upon by townspeople with a mix of apprehension and affection. GODS are highly visible, and everyone in town, even if they have never been formally introduced, will know of them. So when I came up against a wall of Japanese xenophobia, I simply stepped inside the circle. As the cousin of the local GOD, everything changes. Often, the innkeeper's children will materialize upon hearing this. "You are Smith-sensei's cousin?" they ask excitedly. "Yes, yes!" I assure them. "Good old Smith, how is he/she doing, anyway?"

This may seem devious and rotten and dishonest (because it is), but look at it this way: Not once have I abused my position. Several times, especially when things were going really super, I had been tempted to skip out and leave the bill on Smith's tab, but every time I have resisted the urge. After all, I may be a Travel Weasel, but I'm not some common grifter.

6

I SPENT the next day wandering Ryōtsu, its meandering streets and hard-luck homes. Some of the houses were truly remarkable: self-supporting jumbles of boards and patched-up planks that were piled like firewood. Remove one plank and the entire structure might collapse.

Late in the day, I hitched a ride out to Mano, where the exiled Emperor Juntoku lies buried. I rode with a taciturn delivery man who apparently picked me up by mistake and who seemed annoyed by my very presence. Once again I wished I was a ski instructor who summered in Guam, simmering among bodies, tanned and taut, and who was filled with hedonistic vitality. Sigh.

When you are feeling sorry for yourself, nothing perks you up better than visiting a gravesite. And if the gravesite also happens to be that of a disgraced and demeaned exiled ex-emperor whose life was far worse than your own, the experience is positively uplifting. All that was needed was a funeral procession to really top things off.

For the tomb of an emperor, Mano Goryo was remarkably understated, but then Juntoku, as noted, had been disgraced, a man who died in obscurity, far removed from his dreams of destiny and grandeur. The grave was said to be haunted by his homesick ghost, searching for an escape from this island of exile.

Not far from the tomb was the temple of Myōsen-ji, where a pagoda, centuries old, stood like an abandoned watchtower, its joinery creaking in the wind.

From the traditions of Sado, dry with dust, to the high-powered hormonal shine of latter-day technology. From the sublime to the ridiculous. From the tatterdemalion towns and fallen-away fields of Sado to the slick velocity of a jet foil hovercraft. I loved it.

The jet foil rides on blades that cut across the water, slicing through like a razor. The ship had pretensions to flight—and indeed, riding the Sado Island jet foil was as close as you could come to flying without actually leaving the water. A voice asked us to fasten our seat belts prior to departure, there was a bowel-shaking rumble from the depths, and then, well, hell, we hit warp three and screamed toward the mainland like a villain in a James Bond movie. Waves rose up to stop us, but we crashed through. Across the horizon, another storm was growing, the sky bruise-blue and roiling in with biblical wrath. What did I care, I was riding a jet foil. Ten million dollars' worth of yen for what? So we can fly a little faster, soar a little higher, and feel that extra squirt of adrenaline light up our synapses. It was well worth it.

"Jet foil, number one," said the man next to me, a salaryman intent on starting a conversation. His necktie was too tight; his neck was bulging out like a boiled sausage escaping its skin. I smiled at him wanly in what I hoped was a polite but discouraging way.

"Japanese technology, number one in the world!" he said, his smile having grown into a big insecure grin.

I sighed. He was wrong. As luck would have it, I happened to know all about hovercrafts. They were invented by the Scottish-born American citizen Alexander Graham Bell—father of the telephone—at his Canadian home on Cape Breton Island, working from an earlier design by an Italian inventor. Hovercrafts aren't Japanese; they are Scottish-American-Canadian-Italian. I considered trying to explain this to my sausage-necked friend, but what was the point? He wouldn't have believed me anyway.

Japan has never originated any major technological advance. Nothing has ever come out of Japan that has ever revolutionized the world, for better *or for worse.* Japan has given us a lot of very creative solutions to consumer needs, however. Think of the huge American boom boxes compared with the futuristic Walkman, or the ridiculous shoulder-breaking video cameras that we were lugging around until companies like Sony began developing hand-held camcorders.

"Sure, the Japanese are clever," said an American colleague, "but they aren't creative."

He was wrong. The Japanese are very creative. In fact, this is one of the most consistently creative countries I know. So are the Americans. It all depends on how you define creativity. In Japan, it's seen in terms of problem-solving, a new approach to an old puzzle. This type of creativity encourages group effort and fuzzy logic. For Westerners, it is the rugged individual with the sudden light of inspiration. Japan vs. the West. The first is practical creativity; the other, romantic. Neither view is superior, but the one is often baffled by—or even contemptuous of—the other.

The Japanese criticize the Americans as being erratic and sloppy; the Americans criticize the Japanese as being copycats. Each contains an element of truth, but neither approach is necessarily bad. The two actually complement each other.

The Sado Island jet foil bucked a ridge of waves and for one moment the ship dropped slightly, like a plane in an air pocket.

On the television set, a group of pouty teenage heartthrobs were bouncing around with excessive perkiness, insufferably cute as all pouty teenage heartthrobs inevitably are. The band's name was Cry Babies and their hair was jelled up like unusually large dandelions about to blow away. They skipped and pranced and preened and posed and moved about in what was meant to suggest dancing. But there was only a coincidental connection between their movements and the actual beat. Witnessing the spectacle, I was struck by a wonderfully reassuring thought: *There actually are people in the world with less rhythm than WASPs.*

Watching young, self-conscious Japanese college kids moving through preset dance steps—absolutely divorced from any connection to the music that happens to be playing—is a painful yet sadistically pleasurable experience. Somewhere, somehow, mainstream Japanese music got stuck in the early seventies and never recovered. They might have heart-stopping drums and larger neon signs and faster jet foils, but by God they couldn't jive their way out of an epilepsy clinic.

And on that refreshing note, I settled down and enjoyed the ride.

7

I THINK I caught Niigata on a bad day. Everything looked sullen and soiled and worn out. Even the city's smokestacks, painted in stripes like candy canes, emerged from the industrial haze like sooty sweets dug out from under a sofa cushion.

After the sparse landscapes of Sado, it was odd to be sucked into the crowds of a city again. The downtown streets were overflowing with bodies in motion. I checked into a generic business hotel, dropped off my pack, and then found a fiery Korean restaurant in which to fill my stomach. (The spiced kimchi would inflame my rectum for the next two days. No wonder the Koreans always look so pissed off.)

The weather was markedly cooler than it had been, and I found that even layering myself in T-shirts was not enough to stave off the creeping dank and cold. In search of warmer garb, I threaded my way into the rabbit hutch of retail shops that spread in tunnelled corridors beneath Niigata Station. It took a while just to find something that fit, and even then I had to settle for a hooded pullover with arms that were five inches too short, giving me that long-limbed gorilla look that women find so endearing. Fortunately, as a sort of bonus, the pullover had a bold message across the back, written in Japanese-English, or "Englese" as it is sometimes known. The message had a definite rap-music rhythm to it, and over the course of the next few weeks, whenever I was alone in front of a mirror, I took to rappin' it out loudly (with the proper angry, urban-street-gang scowly face and postures, of course). It went like this:

Piece by Piece
We Can't be Born Special
be my power
present international!
Produce Selection Since 1976
Hit It!

This is one of the most surreal aspects of life in Japan: seeing your language reduced to decoration, removed from any context or meaning, rendered into LSD musings. The Japanese approach to language—and most everything else, now that I think about it—is relentlessly deconstructionist. Everything is reduced to the bare elements and then reconstructed. It is less a form of mimicry and more one of reinterpretation. This works great with cars, cameras, and clocks but is less effective with something as organic as language.

My students in Japan were determined to reduce English to mathematical dictums that could then be reassembled. One student, who was a diligent pupil but refused to speak English with me in class, said with perfect sincerity, "It's just that I hate to make mistakes. So, first I will become fluent in English and *then* I will speak it." When I tried to explain to him that learning a language was a process and that making mistakes was a necessary, even desirable aspect of it, he politely dismissed my suggestions as being eccentric. Learn by making mistakes? Ridiculous.

The result is a nation of grammar-sharp, language-shy people. And the primary victim in all of this is English itself. When I ran into one of my high-school students in a T-shirt that read ENJOY MY BROTHER! I challenged him to explain the phrase. It was a wager, really, because I promised him ten thousand yen if he could do it. This young man was our top student, destined for one of Japan's finest universities, and he took up the challenge with confidence. "*Enjoy* is the verb," he said, "*my* is a possessive pronoun, and *brother* is the object. The subject is understood to be *you*, which makes the sentence a command phrase. The exclamation mark adds urgency." He then held out his hand for the money. "But what does it *mean?*" I said. He looked at me, utterly baffled, and said, "*Enjoy* is the verb, *my* is a possessive pronoun, *brother* is the—" Needless to say, I didn't pay him the ten thousand yen and he is still bitter about it. In his mind, he *did* explain it and all I did was welsh on a bet.

The idea that a sentence can have a meaning that is greater than the sum of its parts is hard to get across in Japan. My neighbour's wife had a favourite shirt that said LUSTY TOY, which I could never bring myself to explain to her. (For all I knew it was true. Maybe she *was* a lusty toy and proud of it. Who knows?)

Corporate Japan, with millions of dollars in resources at its fingertips, still can't come up with brand names that make any sense. English has a definite cachet in Japan, much like French once did in America, hence the irresistible urge to add a sprinkling of English on everything, from pop cans to political posters. Some of the most celebrated examples of Japanese brand names include a sports drink named *Sweat*; powdered coffee cream called *Creap*; round, chocolate plugs labelled, disturbingly, *Colon*; and a soft drink dubbed *Calpis*, a name that always suggests bovine urine to me. (I sent a package of Calpis to my friend Calvin Climie, an Ottawa-based animator, along with the note: "What a brilliant move, Cal! Marketing your own urine! You'll make a fortune. As long as you have access to tap water, the supply will never dry up.")

A lady friend of mine from Britain once showed me the tiny instruction pamphlet that came with a box of Japanese feminine hygiene products. The instructions were in Japanese, but even here the company had thought it necessary to jazz things up a bit with a display of English. At the top of the page was the stirring motto: *Let's All Enjoy Tampon Life!*

Harder to understand are the bizarre English slogans of American companies operating in Japan: *I feel Coke!* and *Speak Lark!* (a cigarette company) and *I am Slims!* (Virginia Slims). I was bothered by this—after all, you'd think that if anyone would get it right it would be American companies—but then one day I realized that these slogans were not aimed at *me* but at Japanese consumers. And Japanese consumers have all studied basic English and they can remember and recognize beginner phrases such as "I feel _____," "I speak _____," and "I am _____." That the actual slogans used make little sense is not important. They instill a sense of cool cosmopolitan awareness in the consumer and in the product. Once I realized what they were doing, these oddball phrases seemed less like a joke and more like a brilliant marketing ploy. This is also why so many mottoes use the command phrase "Let's all enjoy _____" and variations of it. This is not because it is common English (how often do you use the phrase "let's all enjoy" in a normal English conversation?), but because it is common *textbook* English, in much the same way that "This is a pen!" is such a popular English greeting in Japan.

Entire books have been written about Japanese-English. Some of it is bizarre, some of it is almost logical in a non-linear, Japanese sort of way, and a few instances are even poetic. I met an American fellow once whose greatest treasure was a small antique tea box. On the back, in English, was a list of the benefits to be gained from a cup. The list was as follows:

The Advantage of Tea

(A) on auxiliary the memory of writingses-say
(B) in increasing the prevailness of poetry
(C) For lossing the fret of mind
(D) By Assisting the discourse of gentility.
(E) With refreshing the spirit of heart
(F) On Digesting the prevention of stomach
(G) To growing the sperm of body
(H) In exempting the sadness of lone,
(I) For Driving the evilness of lone

Naturally, I immediately tried to buy the tea box from the American, but he wouldn't relent, no matter how much yen I waved in his face. It was a beautiful box as well, decorated in dragons and faded gold kanji and elaborate patterns. It still had the faint scent of tea. And who among us, in drinking a cup of Japanese tea, has not felt an increase in the prevailness of poetry? Or the prevention of stomach? And who, in turn, has not sensed the sadness of lone being exempted?

8

I WALKED and walked and walked, trying to escape Niigata City and failing. It was a muggy, cinderblock-and-concrete sort of day, the type that seems to move at half speed and double humidity. The morning traffic began suddenly, coming around the corner like the start of the Indy 500. But fortunately a small pickup truck plucked me out of harm's way just a moment before the traffic engulfed me. "Thanks," I said. The driver yawned at me.

He was a very tired, very frazzled, very fatigued-looking fisherman who kept threatening to fall asleep at the wheel as we drove out of the city. His head bobbed slowly down, his chin sagging toward his chest, and then, with a startled jerk, he was upright, gripping the steering wheel with excessive force and peering intently at the road ahead. So, as you can imagine, I talked *a lot* during the ride. "Boy, that Niigata! Some city, eh?!" Fisherman: "Hm? Oh, yeah, 's great." Then his eyelids would start to droop and my voice would become even more desperately cheerful. "How about those fish! I bet you catch a lot of fish! Tell me about the fish!"

He dropped me outside the city limits on drab, colourless plains beside the banks of the Agano, a river so thick and silty brown, you could have floated coins on it.

On hearing a lone buzz building up behind me, I turned to see a car approaching, drifting erratically across the centre line. I held out my thumb and the car slowed down to inspect me. Inside were two scruffy-looking young men. They laughed at me and returned my thumbs-up gesture as they passed. I spun around, livid, and I was about to give them a farewell, up-yours, arm salute when I saw the car skid to a stop and then lurch into reverse. It came swinging wildly back toward me, and I had to leap into the ditch to avoid it.

"Fuck you!" said the passenger, leaning over the driver and shouting down at me. "Fuck you fuck you fuck you."

I said nothing. What could I say? I stood there looking at their grinning faces until finally, in Japanese, the driver said, "So, where are you going?"

"North."

"So are we!" he shouted, giddy over such a strange congruence of events. Here I was, walking on the same side of the street as them, and we were both going in the same direction. Amazing.

"Get in!" they shouted. "Welcome, welcome. Fuck!"

They were harmless. A pair of disheveled construction workers, baggy-eyed and baggy-trousered, who had been out on a bender and were only now going home. Their eyes were bleary and red from their self-inflicted sleep-deprivation, and their breath reeked of late nights and seedy bars. "We haven't been to bed yet," the driver announced proudly. "Here! Have a beer." The sun was barely up.

The driver, who couldn't have been more than nineteen, was named Shintaro Kobayashi, though his friends called him Koba-chan. He had a thin smudge of hair on his upper lip that, in the right light, might have been mistaken for a moustache, and fine, almost petite features. His cohort and passenger was Hisao Hasegawa. Hisao—the one who kept saying "fuck you"—was in his mid-twenties and definitely the drunker of the two. He had heavier features and thick, waved hair. Hisao was Koba-chan's foreman, and he was wearing those split-toed rubber boots, still common in Japan, which give the workers such a medieval air.

Koba-chan drove without a seat belt, with his leg up on the seat and a can of beer in one hand and the steering wheel in the other.

They had spent their night bar-hopping and had ended up at an inn where beautiful young girls (or old battle-axe matrons—who could tell when you were having so much fun?) had plied them with drinks and sexual innuendoes. What began as a rowdy work-crew celebration had eventually whittled down to just the two of them. "Japanese hostess," said Hisao in sudden English. "Number one the world, sexy good! Oh, *yeah!*"

The boys had made a night of it, but though there may have been some good-natured groping (often as not, it was the hostesses who groped the customers), there had been no assignations. I could tell this because they were both so rumpled and smelly. In Japan, brothels are known as "soaplands," and the specialty is a complete lathering up, followed by a naked body wash. If a husband comes home smelling fresh and clean and well washed, his wife will launch into an attack. But if he comes home reeking of cheap perfume and cigarettes, she will relax, secure in the knowledge that any fun he had was innocent. I knew a Japanese man who was addicted to soaplands in Fukuoka, and before running home he would splash whiskey over his face and furiously puff on cigarettes and then blow smoke over his clothes.

At some point during the night, Hisao had fallen into a leaden sleep and Koba-chan had been unable to rouse him. With the dawn, the hostess had relieved them of the burdensome weight of all that yen bulking up their wallets and had then unceremoniously dumped them on the front step—literally rolling Hisao out the door. Koba-chan, it was decided, was the less intoxicated, so he was now driving Hisao home to his waiting girlfriend. It was actually Hisao's car we were travelling in. For all their slovenly attire and unwashed charm, the car was spotless and tidy.

We soon came into their hometown of Toyosaka. "Bye-bye America!" said Hisao in way of farewell. They stopped at a convenience store and loaded me up with snacks and drinks. I was just about to depart when, with a gallant flourish, Hisao decided that they would take me out of the city and onto open highway. And once we were rolling down the highway, he decided that what I really wanted to see was the construction site where he and Koba-chan were currently working. The site turned out to be a sprawling four-storey home on the edge of a rice field. The building was just a skeleton of two-by-fours, but the heavy roof was already in place (Japanese carpenters work from the top down). They pulled off the road, pointed proudly at the company logo on the large scrap containers parked out front, and insisted I climb the scaffolding with them.

The scaffolding was a rickety structure of bamboo and planks lashed together without nails, which only added to the medieval atmosphere as Hisao and Koba-chan scaled it in their baggy pants and cotton shirts, folded and tied like yukatas. Hisao's cloven-toed work boots heightened the effect. Koba-chan, meanwhile, was wearing pink plastic slippers (taken from one of last night's serving girls, by accident apparently). The slippers were several sizes too small but, even with these impediments, Koba-chan managed to scamper out across the building's frame, four stories high. He was surprisingly nimble, with only a beer and a cigarette to balance him and pink plastic slippers to supply a grip. He stood out there, teetering in the air, while I stood on the scaffolding—well, clung to it, really.

"You ever get scared?" I shouted.

"Nah." (He was young and not yet aware of his own tenuous mortality.) "Why don't you come out?" he said, waving for me to join him on the narrow rafters. I declined. He persisted.

Hisao declined as well. "Too drunk to stand," he said. "Might fall." The air was blowing through and around the building's frames, carrying with it the smell of wood shavings and dust. I looked down to the foundation and imagined myself splatting against the cement like a bug against a windshield. Then, because I am a male and very stupid, I decided to join Koba-chan on the crossbeams. I walked out, high-wire fashion, and posed, hands on hips, as I scanned the construction site. There was nothing between me and a drop of certain death except air and attitude. "Very good," I said. "Very good." But my voice was wavering and my knees started to buckle, so I retreated to the scaffolding, feeling exhilarated, manly, and foolish (not an uncommon combination of emotions).

"Anybody ever fall?" I asked, once we were back on solid ground.

"Once," said Koba-chan. "On another site. My first week on the job. I saw a man slip and fall. Did you know," he asked with genuine fascination, "that the human body—it bounces." Then, mustering all of the bravado inherent in being nineteen, he said, "We can't fear death!"

Hisao, feeling chastised by this, said glumly, "I had too much to drink. I could have fallen."

It was sad, really, that the most sensible person there was also the drunkest.

—

When I told Koba-chan and Hisao that I was following the cherry blossoms across Japan, they didn't call me sissy boy and give me a wedgie or a headlock noogie. "Cherry blossoms," they said. "Good idea." These two ruffians, these two hard-drinking, girl-chasing, rowdy boys, took my quest for flowers very seriously.

"The cherry blossoms have been late this year," said Koba-chan with a solemn nod. Hisao concurred. "It has been terrible. We haven't gone cherry blossom viewing even once."

So they decided to find me some sakura. There had to be a tree somewhere that had started to bloom. They took me first to the castle grounds of Shibata, the next city down the road, but there were no flowers there, not even a hint of pink, so instead, following a wild tip from Hisao, Koba-chan drove farther inland, into the hills, to a temple that Hisao remembered from his youth. "My dad used to bring us here."

And sure enough, there in the temple yard was a spindly tree adorned with flowers. Koba-chan and Hisao stood beside it, proudly, and urged me to capture the moment on film. They were so pleased with themselves that I didn't have the heart to say no. I snapped several slides of them clowning around and clambering about the tree, until finally I had to say something.

I cleared my throat. "Ah, guys? That's actually a plum tree."

They stopped cold in mid-clamber. "Can't be," they said. But it was. A lady of the temple came out, all smiles and politeness, to ask us to stop molesting her tree. Her *plum* tree. Plums bloom earlier than sakura in the first scrub days of spring and, although the two sometimes overlap, this was definitely *not* a cherry tree.

"Well," said Hisao, turning to the lady of the temple and clearly miffed at having his bubble popped. "Where are the sakura, then?" It was as though she were personally at fault for the fact that the Cherry Blossom Front was so late this year.

She said, "Sometimes the sakura arrive sooner in the higher mountains than they do here."

This didn't make much sense to me, but it was all the encouragement that Koba-chan and Hisao needed. Off we went, farther and farther from their original destination. What had once been a short drive home for them had now turned into a crusade. We were on a mission.

"Don't worry," said Hisao. "We'll find them."

It was a long drive, over an hour. But we sang songs and our conversation ranged over a wide variety of topics: (a) drinking, (b) women, and (c) drinking with women, the latter topic being met with special enthusiasm. The beer kept coming and by the time the sun reached its noontime zenith, I was pickled.

High above the plains, the landscape became more alpine. Forests hemmed us in. The highway narrowed and we began ascending the mountainside in a series of long zigs and sudden zags, as though following a staircase to the top of the world. My ears popped, then plugged, then popped again. The air became cold and thin.

"Are you sure there will be sakura way up here?"

"Of course!" shouted Hisao.

"Maybe," said Koba-chan.

A Shinto shrine overlooked the entire vista. Heady on the thinned atmosphere and invigorated on beer and clean air, we scaled the steps to the main building. Sure enough, there was a cherry tree out front.

It had a faint hint of blossoms, the tiniest touch of pink. This was insufferably coy for a bunch of he-men like us, so Koba-chan pulled a bud from the branch and pried it open. Inside was a delicate tuft of flower, no bigger than a pea. "Sakura!" they called out in triumph, and we all stood around to marvel at the beauty.

Flushed with victory, Hisao decided—and Koba-chan agreed— that the only thing for us to do now was to go to a hot spring and drink a lot of beer and have a long soak and find some pretty maids to dally with. *All for one and one for all!*

"There is a hot spring, farther along this mountain pass. Hot springs are great for hangovers," said Hisao, forgetting that *I* wasn't the one who had been drinking all night.

"Sounds good to me," I said.

But Koba-chan soured the mood by saying, "Shouldn't you call Akiko first and ask if it's okay?" Akiko, I deduced, was Hisao's girlfriend.

"Ask?" sputtered Hisao. "*Ask?* I don't ask, I tell!" Then, slipping again into his limited store of English, he said, "I am Japanese man! Japanese man is strong!"

We drove into the riverside village of Kurokawa and pulled over so that Hisao could use the phone.

"I'm gonna tell her I won't be back till late," he said, emphasizing the word *tell*. "Japanese man! Very strong!"

The phone call took longer than we expected. From the car, we could see Hisao gesticulating like an Italian mime, and when he hadn't hung up after ten minutes, we got out to stretch our legs. Koba-chan lit a cigarette and sat on the hood.

Hisao returned looking sheepish. "I'm sorry," he said, unable to look me in the eye. "We have to leave you here. I have to go home."

What about Japanese man number one? I wanted to ask, but I didn't. Hisao's pride had suffered enough, and it was all Koba-chan could do not to start laughing.

"But—" Hisao said, brightening suddenly. "We'll help you get a ride, won't we, Koba-chan?"

"Yes, yes," said Koba-chan. "We'll help."

"Really, you don't have to."

But they took up hitchhiking as enthusiastically as they had cherry blossoms. They "helped" me by trying to flag down traffic. They waved their thumbs in the air and jumped around, laughing, shouting, and leaping up on each other's backs. They even lunged into oncoming traffic, thumbs out, causing vehicles to swerve.

"Really, guys," I said. "You don't have to help."

"Oh, no, we don't mind, do we, Koba-chan?"

"Actually," I said, growing nervous as ride after ride disappeared, many gaping with shocked expressions as they passed, "Japanese drivers stop for foreigners, but they rarely stop for other Japanese. You see—"

Hisao tut-tutted my objections. They were having a great time annoying traffic. Their antics became sillier and sillier, but still no one stopped. Eventually the novelty wore off, and Hisao said with disgust, "I apologize. Japanese people are very bad."

Koba-chan agreed. "This is awful. They should help a foreigner like you who is visiting our area."

"Well," I said, "we tried. You can go now. Don't worry about me, I'm sure I'll—"

"But no one is stopping," said Hisao almost plaintively. "What will you do?" He glanced at his watch, thoughts of Akiko flashing panic across his face.

"Why don't I give you my number," said Koba-chan. "And later this evening, if you still haven't gotten a ride, call me and I'll come fetch you."

"Yes!" said Hisao. This was clearly a face-saving device, as well as a chance to plan a second night's revelry. "Call us and we'll take you drinking!"

Koba-chan wrote out his number and Hisao gave me a spine-rattling thump on the back. "We'll drink!" he said. "We'll see girls! I am Japanese man! Fuck you!"

I grasped Hisao's hand warmly in my own. "Fuck you, too," I said. It was a touching moment.

Within five minutes of their having left, I caught a ride.

9

According to the map I was following, Atsumi was (technically) a town, but it felt more like a village, what with the ramshackle homes and rickety piers and fishing shacks crowded in along the water's edge. Off the coast, shimmering in a cold haze, was Awajima, an island completely shrouded in seagulls. Waves rolled in from a pewter-grey sea, bringing with them the smell of salt water and the cries of reeling birds.

It was more difficult than I had expected getting out of Atsumi. The road that cut through the town banked from curve to curve with such a strong slingshot momentum that I had a hard time finding a place that was safe enough and visible enough to hitch along. Cars snapped around the bend at breakneck speeds and kamikaze angles, and with no sidewalk or guard rails to cower behind I had several brushes with death per minute.

I wasn't the only one braving traffic. A leather-faced old man walked slowly by, his hair matted in all directions and his skin creased by the sun. He was wearing blue track pants, a tattered polo shirt, and a jacket as frayed and dirty as life itself. It looked as though he had gotten dressed by crawling through a clothes hamper—which could only mean one thing: he was a widower. No woman in Japan would allow her hubby, especially an older, retired hubby, out of the house like that. I smiled at him sympathetically. He said nothing and disappeared down the road. A few minutes later, he returned carrying a bucket of fish, slopped up, tails poking above the rim, and an oily smell emanating. They were *tai*, the red-tinged sea bream that feature so prominently in Japanese celebrations. This is the fish that sumo wrestlers hold up grinningly after winning a tournament. This is also the fish that the god Ebisu keeps, tucked under his arm, as a symbol of his status as the God of Fishermen. These *tai* were much smaller than Ebisu's. One was still gasping, its gills opening and closing, drowning in air.

"Sushi?" I asked the old man as he passed. He stopped and looked at me—not in a mean way but in a rock-steady, could-chew-you-up-for-breakfast type of way—and then said, "Why are you here?"

I hate these kinds of metaphysical questions. "I'm from Canada," I said.

"Canada, Canada." He mulled this over as though it might be a place he was familiar with. "Ah," he said suddenly. "America."

I nodded. "America."

"I have never been to America," he said. "I just went to get some fish."

"For sushi?"

His eyes had drifted out of focus during this, but now he locked his gaze back on me. "What?"

"Sushi?" I asked.

"Why are you here?"

"I'm from Canada," I said, and off we went again like a dog in pursuit of its own tail. What the old man was really saying, of course, was, *Get out of my village.*

"It's not good," he said. "You shouldn't stand here like that."

"Like what?"

"Like that—here, beside the road."

Not the warmest welcome I had ever had.

Across the street, a car had stopped and the driver, another one of those leather-faced old men that Atsumi seemed to specialize in, was watching the proceedings.

"Why," persisted the first man, "are you here, beside our road?"

"I was dropped off."

"Here?" He was incredulous. "Why?"

"Look," I said. "It's really no concern of yours if I—"

"I asked you a question. How did you get here?"

Well, first the sperm travelled up through the uterus until it found the egg. "I'm trying to get to Hokkaido," I said.

"*Hokkaido!*" Now he was angry. "You are nowhere near Hokkaido.

Don't try to tell me you are going to Hokkaido when I ask you why you are here. I have lived here all my life."

It was in the middle of this increasingly belligerent conversation that the other old man—the one in the car—drove up and stopped in front of me. "Where you wanna go?" he asked without opening pleasantries or even greetings. Never had I been in a place that was in such a hurry to get rid of me.

The man in the car agreed to take me north to the next town, thus delivering me from what may very well have turned into fisticuffs. "Why are you here?!" demanded the first man even as we pulled out, leaving him behind.

"Pay him no heed," said my rescuer. "He's a fisherman," as though that explained everything.

Mr. Genzō Yamaguchi was *not* a fisherman. "I was a [something] worker. Retired now. Got an illness. They say it was [something]. But it was [something][something] else." He was trying to speak in standard Japanese, but he had a thick regional dialect that kept creeping back in. As we drove north along the coast, he relaxed, and as he did, he slipped deeper and deeper into his dialect, until I could only understand every second word. This wouldn't be so bad, except that he was a terse man and his sentences often only consisted of two words at a time, so our conversation was limited, to say the least.

He had the same stubble-chinned, salt-water-creased, just-crawled-through-a-clothes-hamper feeling about him, though he was better kempt than my earlier interrogator. At one point he told me a long, involved story, all in short bursts, about monks who lived in the nearby mountains. I nodded when he nodded, smiled when he smiled, and frowned thoughtfully when he frowned thoughtfully, but I didn't have a clue what he was talking about. The legend seemed to involve a carp, a sword, and—I think—an eggplant, but I'm not sure.

The road and the coast eventually parted company, with the road arcing slowly away inland, where a small plain lay cupped in among the surrounding hills. Mr. Yamaguchi dropped me off at an intersection that offered six possible routes. When I asked him which one went north, he replied, "Yes." When I repeated my question, stressing the word *which*, he replied, "Maybe."

—

The city of Tsuruoka had once been a castle town, but now it was a factory colony of TDR, a company that made—well, who knows what. I never did figure it out, and after the third attempt at discovering what exactly TDR produced, I gave up. Maybe shoelaces, maybe buttons, or maybe it was heat-seeking laser-guided missiles. Whatever it was, it paled next to the heavy presence of Dewa Sanzan, the Holy Mountains of the North.

I didn't go into Tsuruoka but hitchhiked around it on a wide-flying bypass that swept me across the Akagawa River and into Sakata, a sister city to Tsuruoka. Both were a similar size and layout, mirror reflections of one another.

I rode with a soft-faced, thick-lipped man named Hiroshi Endō, who introduced himself in English as a Christian seaman. I can't say I was immediately pleased on hearing Hiroshi's confession of faith. Self-professed Christians make me uneasy. They are always way too friendly and way too smiley. They are using you, of course, to propagate their faith. They don't really want to be your friends, they want to be your converters. I have always found that talking with Christian propagators is a lot like talking to used-car salesmen. They may be chummy and sugar-sweet, but all they are seeing when they look at you is another sale. (In Kumamoto City I once witnessed a wonderful encounter between two intense young Americans, one a Mormon and the other a Hare Krishna. They were locked in a polite but obviously strained theological debate when I passed by. And when I returned, *three hours later*, they were still at it, head-to-head. They were now yelling at each other about peace and love. "Oh yeah?! But what about ultimate reality, man?" "Don't tell me about ultimate reality, I know ultimate reality!" It was hilarious. It reminded me of two sand crabs locked in mortal combat, pincers shut, foam frothing up from their jaws. For all I know they are still there, spittle flying and eyes wild, in the name of God. Either that or they *both* succeeded and the Mormon went home a Hare Krishna and the Hare Krishna went home a Mormon. The main thing is this: they didn't bother *me*. If proselytizers would all just pick on each other instead of the rest of us, this would be a happier world.)

I felt none of the conversion fervour with Hiroshi. He was shy and soft-spoken, and his face was without angles or edges, as though his features had been slightly overinflated. He had a way of leaning in toward me and speaking out of the side of his mouth which made me feel as though we were doing something wrong. "There are two churches in Tsuruoka," he whispered. "Two."

I wasn't sure if he was complaining or boasting, so I made a sort of noncommittal "is that so?" noise, rather than congratulate him or commiserate. For all I knew, two churches were a triumph.

"Which church do you belong to?" he asked.

When faced with probing questions such as this ("So how much would you be willing to spend on a car today, Mr. Ferguson?") I usually respond with something flippant like, the Church of Cheap Beer and Wild Women, but he was so shy, so painfully sincere, that I mumbled something about there being a distinct lack of Presbyterians in Japan.

Mr. Endō had been a radio operator on a cargo ship and had seen the world: Australia, New Zealand, the east coast of North America, the islands and ports of Southeast Asia. He had retired just that year—not for reasons of age but for some unspecified illness—and now he was here in Japan's far north, seeking solace in the words of a distant carpenter from Galilee. The world is a strange place indeed, and the ebb and flow of religions that move around the globe like ocean currents is stranger still. Religions rise and fall, fade and overlap, from Buddhist prophets to Christian sailors, all in pursuit of—of what? Insight? Deliverance? Discipline? Sakura?

"I saw many things," said Hiroshi. "In the Philippines, I saw a man singing to the sea. In Australia, I saw kangaroos in cages." His voice was furtive, as though the vehicle were bugged, as though his life were under surveillance. "I sailed to many ports, but I wasted my youth and I married very old." (At thirty-one, it turned out; hardly a senior citizen, but a bit late for Japan.) "My daughter is a teenager now, and she looks like her mother, but everyone says she has my eyes."

"Is your wife a Christian?" I asked.

There was a slow, liquid pause. He said, quietly, almost to himself, "I go to church alone." And then, changing tack, "How about you?"

"I don't go to church. Alone."

Hiroshi dropped me off on the eastern outskirts of Sakata. I was on an overpass, above a vast marshland and a flaccid, muddy river. A white heron skimmed across the surface, but any sound was lost to the traffic that rolled by with monotonous regularity. Here too the view was dominated by the pressing mass of Dewa Sanzan, the holy mountains of Japan. Clearly visible, even from here, were sacred ski runs running down the sacred mountainsides. They looked like frozen rivers.

Cities create their own gravity wells. Hitching *in* is easy; you just relax and allow yourself to be pulled in. Hitching *out*, however, can be a nightmare. I wanted to skim the edge of Sakata, Sputnik-like, using the city's gravity to throw myself farther along, all the way to Akita.

It was tough. I couldn't ask—or expect—traffic to stop for me on the middle of an elevated bypass, but I thrust out my thumb anyway and hoped for the best.

And that's when I was captured by leprechauns.

10

THEY WERE little leprechaun people in a little leprechaun car and they spoke a leprechaun dialect I couldn't understand. There were three of them, none over five foot four and all of them dressed in tidy, freshly pressed clothes. They were the Takahashis. There was Mr. Takahashi, friendly, hunched-shouldered, cigarette-smoldering, with an expressive face that had been battered by life but not defeated. Beside him was Mrs. Takahashi, his wife, an attractive lady, very prim, who sat with her hands folded carefully on her lap. In the backseat was Mr. Takahashi's elderly mother, a tiny, thin lady.

Mr. Takahashi was full of grins and handshakes and nervous, bobbing bows. His wife was less enthusiastic. She sat as rigid as an overstrung harpsichord, and her smile never wavered. Clearly, she had not been in favour of stopping. I had seen their little car drive by three times before it finally pulled over, a common enough event in Japan, where hitchhiking is not a custom and where the driver and passengers often have hurried, frantic discussions when they see someone with his thumb out.

"It was Mother," said Mr. Takahashi sheepishly. "She said it's common courtesy. She said we had to stop, so we did."

Mr. Takahashi was an industrial mechanic with a large steel refinery. He worked swing shifts, and today being his day off, he had decided to take his mother and wife out for a drive.

The mother was delighted to have company even though my bear-size body and awkward backpack—the pack alone was larger than she was—crowded her up against her side of the car. She shared with me plums from a plastic bag, and when I was done, she held my hand in hers and patted it gently, like you might pat a sleeping baby. This was a woman who was not afraid of bears. We had a wonderfully elaborate conversation, she and I, hindered only by the fact that neither of us understood a word the other was saying. She spoke with a murky Tohoku dialect, bluesy and rich and filled with late nights and long winters. (When I asked a Tokyo friend for advice on how to speak with the Tohoku accent, he said, "Fill your mouth with mud and chew on all your consonants.") She pointed out Mount Chōkai, the "Dewa Fuji," ice-blue at the top, and told me a long, involved tale that was apparently off-colour, because at one point her daughter-in-law turned around and said, "Mother! You know that isn't true!"

But the old dear just clasped my hand and chuckled softly. "Oh, but it is," she said to me, in one of the few phrases I was able to catch. "It's true all right. I was there." And she laughed.

What had happened up on Mount Chōkai, what scandal or gossip she had imparted, was lost on me, but it helped to break the tension, and soon Mr. Takahashi's wife was laughing and gently scolding the mother, who continued to share her stories with me, as juicy as plums.

Guidebooks are great for surface-skimming—and I'd be lost without them—but to really get in and get dirty, to muck about in the back country, to really worm your way into off-track Japan, you need to travel in the company of the people who live there. Train passengers, no matter how independently they are travelling, ultimately remain spectators. Hitchhikers are co-conspirators, fellow travellers.

On the road north of Sakata, near the border of Yamagata and Akita prefectures, there lies an entire stone coast, a miniature mountainside, really, that has been carved into the shapes of Buddhist deities and saints. It is a striking landscape to stumble across, and one that was not listed in any of the guidebooks I was using: not in the Lonely Planet guide, nor in *Gateway to Japan*, nor in *New Japan Solo*.

The site, known as the Jūroku Rakan, was carved over the course of several centuries by monks from a nearby temple, carved, it was said, to comfort the souls of dead fishermen who had perished off the coast. The sculptures were like a flowing, gentler Mount

Rushmore. And the comparison to Rushmore is apt. The two contrast in several significant ways: the Japanese carvings are smaller and more fluid, shapes worked into the lay of the land; Mount Rushmore, with its granite-jawed faces blasted from the bedrock, is far more imposing.

Mr. Takahashi pulled into the parking lot and we walked down to the open-air carvings. A few sightseers were scrambling about, taking pictures, laughing, pointing out oddities and details.

A mountain of gods. I climbed up an outcrop of rock and looked out at the crash and roll of waves on the other side and then, with a start, realized that the rock I was clambering over was shaped into the form of a beggar god's face. This one sculpture was as large as a car—a Japanese car—which is to say, it was somewhat small. The entire coastal expanse, the shapes hidden like faces in a cloud, was more of a dreamscape than a landscape. The gods were emerging from the rock as you watched.

"The mountain is alive," said the grandmother in a very pragmatic, unsentimental way.

Further north, at the prefectural boundary itself, was a green park of sloping hills and grassy outlooks. We had a picnic on a small knoll overlooking the sea, and the grandmother made an effort to speak standard Japanese. She said to me, her voice as soft as a wisp of smoke, "I used to picnic over there—just over there, with my husband. I would make a bentō lunch and we would sit there." She pointed a tiny finger to a hillside. A couple was lying there now; the boy had his head on his girlfriend's lap. "Right there," she said. "Right where those two are now."

"Would you like a drink?" said Mr. Takahashi, as he offered me some sickly sweet Chinese wine—once again strengthening my resolve to seek a complete world ban on Chinese wine production. This wine—this syrup—had a certain antifreeze piquancy about it, bold yet coy, horrible yet disgusting. I am a fervent believer in the notion that countries should stick to what they do best. Japan should produce video cameras, America should produce pop stars and computers, and the Chinese should stick to producing kung fu movies and short-tempered waiters. And they should be made to write a letter of apology to every Frenchman and Italian on earth for the crimes they have committed against wine. Thank you.

When it came time to say goodbye, Mr. Takahashi had tears in his eyes. "It is good," he said, "good that we can get along like this." His wife dabbed at imaginary tears as well and then surprised everyone—herself included—by inviting me to their home whenever I came through. "We want to see you again." Yes, yes, Grandmother nodded, "and please, whatever you do, take care not to . . ." and off she went into the depths of regional dialect to places I could not follow, leaving me with the vague feeling I had just missed a very important warning.

In the end, they couldn't do it. They couldn't simply abandon me to my fate and instead Mr. Takahashi began scouring the parking lot and accosting strangers. As always when this happened, I felt very uncomfortable and vicariously embarrassed. "Excuse me, you wouldn't be going north, would you, toward Akita City? It's just that, well, we have this American who is in some trouble, you see, and, well—"

Two bird-like ladies, twittering away at the proposition, came within a giggle of offering me a ride but at the last minute declined. A husband said yes only to be vetoed by his wife, who gave us all a disapproving, sour look. Eventually a young man in a khaki-brown company uniform shrugged and said, "Sure, I can take him into Akita City."

"You can?"

"Sure."

"Thank you, thank you," said Mr. Takahashi, as he clutched the man's arm. "Thank you so much."

"No problem," said the young fellow, who was clearly warming to his role of saviour. "Do not worry. I will take care of everything."

The Takahashis waved us into the distance; even when they were specks fading into the vanishing point, I could still make out Grandmother bowing and Mr. Takahashi's high waving arm, like a man signalling a ship on the horizon.

11

DAISUKE WAS a computer programmer and yes, some stereotypes transcend national boundaries. He wore thick glasses, he had lots of pens, and he had an inordinate interest in video games. He worked for a steel processing plant that belonged to the same company that Mr. Takahashi worked for, though his office was based in Akita and Mr. Takahashi's was in Sakata. Or at least I think that is how it worked. The tangled web that Japanese corporations weave, and the interconnecting alliances and extended families they create, are something I have never been able to sort out. As near as I can tell, everyone in Japan is employed by everyone else.

Daisuke had a vested interest in giving me a ride. "I want you to explain something to me." He popped a cassette by Madonna into his car deck, and the Material Girl's coos filled the air. "What is she saying?" Daisuke had reams of tapes, filled with hundreds of English pop songs that he enjoyed but had never been able to understand. He was dying to find out what he had been listening to all these years.

The problem, of course, is how do you translate something like *"Hanky-panky, all I need's a good spanky"*?

"She, ah, wishes for someone to strike her repeatedly on the buttocks," I said, and he frowned deeply, as though considering a philosophical concept.

And how about *"Slap me with your love stick!"* or *"C'mon and ride my pony."* Pop lyrics never sound stupider than when you try to explain them to someone in another language. Most of them boil down to this: Let's have cheap, frantic sex right here on the dance floor.

We went through song after song until my frontal lobes started to ache from the exertion. Could the Spice Girls have *more* banal lyrics than they do? And how about Bryan Adams? Could this guy string together more clichés than he does? After being subjected to two hours of Mr. Adams's music—which is a clear violation of the Geneva Convention, I should point out—after two hours of this, my patience was paper thin. Every song Bryan Adams has ever written contains the word *gonna* or *wanna* somewhere in the lyrics. The ultimate Bryan Adams song would be titled: "I'm gonna wanna gonna go."

It was a very long drive to Akita. The low point came when Daisuke, apparently hoping to find something with a little more depth to it, dug up a cassette of Simon and Garfunkel and asked me to translate "Scarborough Fair" into Japanese.

"I see," he said. "So it's a shopping list."

"Basically, yes."

After that, Daisuke lost interest in translating pop songs. Instead, he wanted to talk about computer programming, a subject I knew nothing about. He then tried Formula 1 Grand Prix racing, which was even worse. I didn't even know enough about this to *fake* a conversation; he might as well have been asking me about quantum physics or English grammar. Daisuke, alas, was a true-blue fan of racing and, like most fans, he was capable of talking for extended periods of time about his topic without having to come up for air.

Having flunked out on race cars and computers, our conversation lapsed into silence. Daisuke began looking more and more forlornly at every video arcade we passed. "Do you play video games?" he asked.

"Not really—but if you want to stop, please go ahead."

"No, no," he said, smiling bravely in spite of the fact that he had picked up such a dud. "Ah, Street Fighter Two," he would say wistfully as yet another arcade floated by.

Gone were the palm trees of Kyushu and in their stead came the stunted, wind-warped pine forests of the north country. We passed stands of the trees, bent like beggars toward the road, and behind them a curtain of indigo blue: early evening on an open sea. As we approached the city, I realized that I had heard the word *akita* before. There were the Akita dogs that the prefecture was famous for, but there was something else as well: *Akita bijin.* Akita beauties.

I had entered the area of Japan where the women were said to be the most beautiful. "Is it true?" I asked, a little too excitedly.

"Of course."

This was the single best high-point apex apogee climax of my entire trip. It was like discovering the Elephant's Graveyard or the Lost City of Troy. And why are the girls so pretty in Akita? "It is related to climate," explained Daisuke with all the passion of a computer programmer. "Heavy snowfalls, long winters, not much sun. Makes the skin pale."

"And?"

"They have round faces."

"Round faces?"

"Very round," he said, proudly. "And pale."

My heart sank. Big, pale, round moon faces. Not exactly what I had in mind.

"Oh, yes," he said. "Their voices are squeaky as well. High-pitched. You know, sexy."

The Japanese image of beauty differs from that of the West, as does its image of handsome. Japanese women, for the most part, prefer clean-cut, short-haired missionary types. Tom Cruise is a sex symbol in Japan not because he is dangerous, but because he is so inoffensive. He has the bland good looks that Japanese women like so much. I tried to explain this to Daisuke, that I actually preferred high cheekbones, full lips, a deep tan, and a low, sultry voice in women, but he looked at me like I was more than a bit nutty.

This ended any attempt at guy talk. I went back to translating lyrics. Not long after this, a black-painted, right-wing van zoomed by, red sun flags fluttering as it passed us, its speakers blazing out angry rhetoric. "Exalt the Emperor! Out With the Foreign Devils!" As always, the van was manned—and I use the term *man* only in the loosest sense of the word—by young, pimply-faced Timothy McVeigh types. Only difference was, instead of being racially pure Aryans, they were racially pure Asians. What they thought of round-faced beauty versus high cheekbones I wasn't sure, and Daisuke wasn't too keen to stop them and ask.

12

WHEN I GOT to Akita, I checked into the Hotel Hawaii, a rambling, threadbare place east of the main station. I chose it from a list solely on its name; I liked the symmetry involved, echoing the Capsule Hawaii that I had stayed at in Himeji. After I dropped off my bags and bade farewell to Daisuke, I set off in search of food and pleasure.

Akita City is a northern port and it has a reputation for being a bit dodgy, but nothing I saw confirmed this. The refineries and shipping lanes are on the coast, far from downtown, and the city I wandered through had a certain rough frontier charm to it. There were even a few Western-style shopping plazas—still a rarity in Japan's smaller cities—and enough tall buildings to give it the appearance of prosperity, if not the fact. The time of day helped as well; the sun was low and golden, making the concrete blush. Bevies of girls hurried past, like leaves on an autumn wind. Akita bijin, every one.

It was into this warm sunset of a city that I wandered. My stomach was beginning to growl and I went into the first restaurant I came across, a small coffee shop where the cheapest thing on the menu was pizza toast.

Pizza toast, I should explain, is a Japanese specialty. Neither pizza nor toast, it is—in defiance of all known laws of gestalt—decidedly *less* than the sum of its parts. And as I sat, chewing and sighing (often at the same time), I reflected on how happy, how very very *happy* I was to be spending the equivalent of nine dollars for a piece of bread topped with a puddle of tomato sauce, a gob of cheese, and four thin, semi-transparent slices of pepperoni. (Essence of Pepperoni, I called it—meat that was somehow sliced one molecule thick. A remarkable feat.) My bank account was getting dangerously low. I had already exceeded my budget threefold since setting out, and the pizza toast I was now consuming reminded me of this. Which is to say, I blame the pizza toast for what happened next.

By the time I had finished my "meal" (note the ironic use of quotation marks), dusk had settled upon the city. The lights began to flicker on as I followed a small river south into the heart of the after-hours zone. It was an exceptionally bright area, even by Japanese standards of nightlife, where the motto is, "Energy crisis? What energy crisis?" There was less neon in Akita and more bulbs, giving it the appearance of a prima donna's dressing-room mirror gone mad.

The lights and laughter echoed across the water. The river looked more like a canal, with its many small, indecisive bridges hopping back and forth across the water, and with the buildings built flush against the reinforced banks. I waded into the crowds, followed the flow past pachinko parlours and noodle shops, then cut down a narrow alley until I came to a cul-de-sac bright with bulbs. This was definitely a naughty nook in a larger cranny. Side-door cabarets and soaplands beckoned. Touts in cheap tuxedos hovered near the doors in predatory holding patterns waiting for the first wave of salarymen to wander in. (Again, because I was undoubtedly reeking of AIDS, no one approached me.)

No matter. I backtracked to the main street, where couples were promenading. Crowds were milling about amid sudden, unprovoked bursts of laughter. Signs in lurid pink fair dripped with innuendo and false promises. A cinema featured posters for a movie depicting the love between a young lady and her vacuum cleaner. Another poster showed two terrified office men being threatened by a whip-wielding nurse in stilettos.

Tattered red lanterns swayed on the wind, and bands of young office ladies shouted and sang songs as they strode down the street. Equally animated bands of men rolled by the other way, and the street resembled a slow-motion pinball game, ringing with bells and whistles and flashes of strobe-lights. By now I was thoroughly impressed with Akita, a city where the women were beautiful and the nights were brimming with rivers of light.

Rather than return to the Hotel Hawaii, I decided instead to make a deeper foray into the city's nightlife—in the interests of journalistic integrity. I wanted to interview, first-hand, some of the city's famed Akita bijins. This would be tricky; I would need introductions. And this in turn would cost money for drinks, snacks, and karaoke.

This is where the pizza toast comes in. Still stinging from my undersized, overpriced dinner, I decided to cut my costs. I wanted to explore this gaudy world and I definitely wanted to meet some beautiful ladies, but at the same time I didn't want to spend a month's salary on the venture. Which is how I decided—*how I actively sought*—to become kidnapped. I followed a likely target: a group of men in navy-blue suits who were stumbling down the street. They went into a small pub. I waited outside for a few moments and then, quietly, made my entrance.

You haven't really lived until you have seen a Japanese salaryman sing the Frank Sinatra ballad "My Way." It is one of those quintessential sad sights that seem to define Japan. What an odd and yet common spectacle: a tousled salaryman, living a life of bows and stifling conformity, a man married to the company, a man who—in the thousands every year—works himself to death for the sake of the corporation, a man who has to eat shit and smile every day, a man who fuels the economic engine yet remains unsung, unacknowledged, and often openly mocked. A man like that, standing up and singing in heartfelt English: that the record should show, he took the blows and did it his way! This is something you don't soon forget.

The men were crowded along a plush couch, toasting themselves with whiskey-tinted water as they cheerfully ignored their colleague up on stage, who was quavering away about how he chewed whatever up and spat it out, and not in a shy way. Rodney Dangerfield should have toured Japan. I have no doubt he would have become a star among salarymen as he tugged on the ubiquitous, symbolic necktie. *I get no respect! No respect.*

When their compatriot sat down, another man got up to sing a spirited version of, what else, "Diana." "'I so young and you so old / Zis my darling, I been told.'"

"He wrote that for his babysitter," I said to the man nearest me. The man turned and, seeing me in the seat beside him, jerked his head back in shock. The only thing he could think to say—the only sound he could think to make—was a long, breathy "*Waaaaa!*"

Soon the entire table had noticed me and they welcomed me into their fold, insisting I sit beside their section chief, who, I quickly surmised, was top dog, so I made a point of chatting to him excessively and, when he used a few words of English, I complimented him to high heaven on being such an internationally minded chap. That was all it took. Free beer and food.

Of course, I had to sing for my supper, as is the custom. But crooning your way through "Love Me Tender" is a small price indeed for all the cold Sapporo and free snails you can eat.

My presence signalled a shift of topics. From inter-office jealousies and who was incompetent and who was not (as always, the ones who were hopelessly incompetent were also the ones, by strange coincidence, who were not present), they began to discuss violence in America. This is one of the all-time favourite topics in Japan.

The section chief was a frowny-faced man, bald, with a tight toupee. He kept plying me with beer, and then whiskey water, while the conversation took a familiar turn.

Several years ago, a young Japanese exchange student had been shot and killed in the U.S. because he went to the wrong house. An American homeowner, seeing the boy prowling around his yard, came out brandishing a gun and yelling "Freeze!" The Japanese boy, apparently thinking the man in the shadows had yelled "Please!", took a step forward and received a bullet through the heart. It was a shot heard round the world. The killing made front-page headlines in Japan—at about the same time that another killing took place: a Filipina hostess, held captive by her Japanese employers, was beaten to death. A Japanese doctor dismissed it as an accident, and no one was ever charged or convicted. The first-degree murder of a Filipina lady, and the massive cover-up that followed, were relegated to the back pages in Japan, while the death of a young Japanese boy—dead because of a tragic misunderstanding—prompted rallies, angry protests, and a public plea by the boy's parents.

My circle of Akita businessmen was also concerned, in a pornographic sort of way, with violence in America. They all had their pet theories about the matter, several of which were real eyebrow-raisers. In wit and insight, this group was not quite on a par with the Algonquin Round Table. One man declared that the problem was that all white people were, oh, what's the word, racist—a statement that was so ludicrously self-contradictory I didn't know how to respond. Whites were racist against blacks, but Japanese were not. Why? And here I quote, for it was such a memorable statement: because "our skins are slightly darker, so we can understand both white people and black people."

Another man immediately chimed in: "That's why blacks in America always riot at night. It makes them harder to see. It's very clever, don't you think?"

In the middle of witty repartee such as this, two more men arrived, and from their wobbly stance and unfocused gaze it was easy to see that they were already halfway looped. There were more introductions. A clammy face, a leer, a drunken flabby handshake. He was the Senior Vice Supervisor and he introduced me with hushed humility to the Vice Senior Supervisor, who clearly trumped everyone else at the table, and the seats were rearranged appropriately, with me sandwiched between the two men. "I have heard so much about you," said the Vice Senior Supervisor enigmatically. "Please keep up the good work."

I assured him I would and we shook hands with great sincerity. Drinks kept arriving as if on a conveyor belt, and soon the room began to sway.

I was trying to steer talk toward Akita bijin, but none of the men were interested. "It's a myth," said one. Another disagreed, but the topic wasn't pursued. Instead, the conversation, having delved into such popular topics as "America and What's Wrong With It," now moved, predictably, to "Japan and Why It Is So Wonderful."

"Japan is a small country," said one man. They all agreed.

"A poor country." They agreed.

"A poor, small country." Again, unanimity.

Japan is a poor, small country. From which they deduced that Japan is therefore "the number-one country in the world. Japanese companies are very strong. Japanese products are the best in the world." It is an odd syllogism, especially that rather tricky leap from premise to conclusion, but it is nonetheless a world view that was heartily endorsed by my hosts.

"Japan is unique," said one man, and again they concurred. "Yes, yes—unique." And they nodded their heads up and down in that unique way Japanese have, as if to say, "I agree," and then they straightened their unique neckties and adjusted the collars on their unique white shirts and drank unique whiskey on unique rocks. It was all very unique.

True, in many ways Japan is a unique country, but like a woman who *knows* she's beautiful or a man who *knows* he's handsome, it can be bloody annoying.

An older man elbowed his way in and grinned at me. Teeth. Bad teeth, like broken china. "Japan is not perfect," he said, without much conviction, "but it is good that you are here. The thing about Japan," he said, "the thing is—what you have to understand—the thing is—" He had lost his train of thought. He tried to sort it out as the conversation proceeded, then came back in with a sudden declaration: "The thing is—you can never understand Japan. Never. You're a foreigner, see? And foreigners can never understand Japan. You can't. You just can't."

Certainly not when you're pissed to the gills.

"Japanese beer," said one man. "Number one!" Which precipitated an endless list. "Japanese cameras. Number one! Japanese automobiles. Number one!" And so on. It was rapidly becoming tedious. Having drunk my fill and entertained the troops, I got up to leave. A hand clamped down on my shoulder and forced me back. "We are not through."

"Yes, but—"

It was like Zorba all over again. "Look at his biceps," they cried, squeezing my arms like fresh bread. "The gaijin is strong. How much do you weigh? What is your blood type?"

I set out to find Akita bijin and I end up boxed in between drunk salarymen. Could the evening have gone more awry than it had? By now I was sloshing my consonants so badly, all I could produce was a silly "I hafta go" type of noise which everyone ignored.

They had, by this point, decided that I was their new best friend. (The Vice Supervisorial Whatsit was convinced that I worked for the company as well, which didn't help. Mind you, he did promise me a raise next year, which I found very encouraging.) There were more drinks, more songs, more backslaps, and endless, pointless handshakes. I tried to leave several times, but every time I did, I was dragged down, liquored up, and mauled some more. They drank beer from mugs the size of rain barrels, they smoked fistfuls of cigarettes, they pried open my jaws and poured gallons of whiskey down my gullet. When we left, I staggered out as though fresh from a pummelling, ears ringing, head spinning, eyes raw red from tobacco fumes.

"Well," I gasped once we got outside. "Good night—"

But they were just warming up. They grabbed my arms and marched me down the street like a prisoner caught trying to escape. "Help me," I said weakly to people I passed. "In the name of God, help me."

My tormentors led me through a series of bars, each smaller and seedier than the last, until we found ourselves scrunched together in a piss-soaked packing crate wedged into a closet that was stuffed into a breadbox. The karaoke machine, naturally, had a microphone and an amplifier. Even worse, because they were all in a very patriotic Japanese-salaryman sort of mood, the bars they chose had traditional tatami-mat floors and low tables, which aren't a problem if you have space to sprawl, but with half the Akita male population crowded in around me, I was forced into contortionist positions, my elbows in and my legs folded up in a pretzel-shaped figure eight, much like a Yogic flyer. And oh, how I wished I could have levitated out of there. By now they were ordering Japanese gin, Akita saké, Hokkaido beer, and Suntory whiskey straight up, mixing them in my belly like Taoist alchemists seeking the elixir of life and—probably—almost certainly—death.

At some point a heated discussion broke out about my quest. "You understand the true heart of Japan," said one man, the same man who told me earlier that, as a foreigner, I could never understand the true heart of Japan. They raised their glasses. A younger member said loudly, "*This*—this is the true heart of Japan! Drinking. Singing. Friends." Which provoked an immediate response. "That is not so. We must take him to a temple, to see the plum blossoms by night!"

Soon we were back outside on some nameless side street. They were determined to show me the Real Japan. Unfortunately, they couldn't agree just what that was. One man insisted that a topless cabaret was the real Japan, another man was equally adamant that I visit a public bath, and another wanted to drink saké under the stars and compose haiku. The group dissolved into factions, and I slipped away during the confusion.

I reeled down the streets of Akita, ricocheting from one side to another, narrowly missing a plunge into one of the metre-deep gutters that plague drunkards across Japan, and finally, after exhaustive staggering, I found myself right in the centre of who-the-fuck-knows-where. The Hotel Hawaii might as well have been in Hawaii for all the navigational skills I then possessed. I wandered blindly through the city, seeking some kind of salvation.

I saw it before me in liquid purple and pastel pink, a neon oasis in a night of assassins. The name read Hotel Elegance, or Hotel With, or something along those lines. Either way, I was glad to see it. It was a Love Hotel.

Love Hotels are a bargain. For couples travelling together, they are the same cost as a business hotel but with far more space and entertainment. No reservations are necessary, though Love Hotels do often turn away *single* travellers (masturbation apparently being the only sexual act that is unacceptable to the proprietors). Lost and luckless, I decided to stumble in and try my luck.

Love Hotels are designed for people who feel that Las Vegas is too restrained. The rooms are spacious and luxurious, and shamelessly kitsch. They can be rented by the hour or by the night. When I was travelling through Japan with Marion, I became something of a connoisseur of Love Hotels. In Okinawa, we stayed in one where the entire building was shaped like a battleship (there was a large American base nearby) and the bed was a shuttlecraft. Above it, in blinking command-phrase capital letters, was the message: ATTACK! ATTACK! ATTACK! In Kagoshima, we stayed in the Mickey and Minnie Room, filled with cartoons of the famous rodent couple—which was not exactly conducive to sustained physical passion, if you know what I mean. In Beppu, we stayed in a round room with a seashell bed and silhouettes of starfish and mermaids pinned on the walls, meant to evoke an adventure on the bottom of the sea, but which induced a chest-tightening, suffocating feeling. I woke up several times and felt like I was drowning. This too was not conducive to sustained physical passion.

Still, for all their endless variation of rooms, the hotels themselves come in only three basic styles, which I have dubbed: the Park 'n' Ride, the Peekaboo, and the James Bond Secret Hideout.

The *Park 'n' Ride*–style Love Hotels are usually out on the highway or on the outskirts of town. Each room has its own entrance and its own parking stall. Couples drive in, park their cars below, and walk up the stairs to their rooms—all without having to face another person, anonymity being the prime attraction at Love Hotels. Once a couple has settled in, the phone rings, they state whether they are spending the night or just "resting." Payment is made through a slotted door, like you might in a Chicago speakeasy, again without any face-to-face contact.

The *Peekaboo*-style Love Hotels are almost like real hotels. Some even have lobbies, though no one ever seems to hang out in them. The distinguishing feature of the Peekaboo is the front desk, which is shielded with a pane of frosted glass—only the clerk's hands are visible—so that the monetary transactions are again done anonymously. These are the ones that most often turn away foreigners, simply because it is harder to slip in unnoticed.

The *Secret Hideout* style is the most common and the most fun. Everything is automated. When you walk in, an electronic voice greets you and guides you to a display panel of illuminated photographs. These are the pictures and prices of the different rooms available, from the Leather Bondage Den to the Little Bo Peep Sheep Room. Rooms that are not occupied are lit up. You pick your temporary suite of passion, press the button below it, and then go to your love nest. It will be easy to spot: a light above the door will be flashing.

The Park 'n' Ride hotels are the easiest ones for foreigners to slip into unnoticed, but the Secret Hideouts are the most entertaining. The hotel I approached was of the Secret Hideout style. I staggered in, punched the cheapest room I could find on the display panel, and made my way to the elevator. The room was a crushed-velvet, purple-wallpaper affair with a round bed—which can be maddening when you're drunk—and polyester sheets that were meant to suggest silk. A single condom was laid out on the pillow, like a mint. I looked up. Sure enough, a mirrored ceiling.

Just what I need to see while I sleep: *me*, suspended above the bed like a Macy's Parade balloon.

The phone rang, and I mumbled "overnight" when she asked me what my plans were. In this hotel you didn't pay by secret door but by pneumatic tube. A whoosh of air and a plastic canister came sliding down. I stumbled over and took the canister out, put in my money, pressed a green button, and—*whoooosh!*—off it went. A few moments later, it came back down the tube with some change and a souvenir key chain.

I sprawled out across the bed, my head still spinning in a fog of alcohol. When I opened my eyes I found myself face to face with a scruffy, ashen-faced man in a crumpled shirt and a sweaty face. Damn these mirrored ceilings. I rolled over like a walrus looking for a place to die, and found, beside the bed, a notebook and a pen. These notebooks are the most bizarre aspect of staying in a Love Hotel. Each page has a cartoon Kama Sutra of sexual positions and space for messages. Couples circle the sex positions they tried and leave notes to the people who follow. I flipped through this one and noted that the most recent entry was made that very day. The rooms are spotlessly clean and antiseptic, but figuratively speaking—the sheets were still warm. These room journal notebooks are meant to be titillating, and they are, I suppose, but I find the entire ritual a bit odd. Erotic notes to strangers. Clinical, cartoon descriptions of what you have just done to each other. I don't get it. Whenever I'm in a Love Hotel, I usually write something in the room journal in Japanese-English, just to shake things up, something along the lines of *Many times enjoy American-style happy sex play!* Tonight, still reeling and feeling queasy, I wrote nothing.

A catalogue of sexual aids and vibrating love toys, available from the front desk, was discreetly tucked in behind the headboard. The catalogue was titled, in elegantly written English, *Playing Goods for Lovetime*. But even this could not hold my interest. I crawled over to the bed's side panel and tried to turn off the lights, but managed instead to flood the room with romantic music and a swirling disco-ball effect that didn't do my vertigo any good whatsoever.

I slumped back, feeling very morose. No, there wasn't an Akita bijin beside me drinking champagne and laughing at my ready wit. No, there was no one here to enjoy my American-style happy sex play. I was in a Love Hotel. Alone. Surely my lowest point ever.

Then, just as I drifted into something approximating sleep, I realized that all my clothes and belongings were still in a room at the Hotel Hawaii, which was costing me money. Big money. Over twenty thousand yen. Having set out to save money, I was now spending over two hundred and fifty dollars for accommodation: one room for me and one for my baggage.

Personally, I blame the pizza toast.

13

OH LORDY.

I woke up with a hellish hangover and a headache of apocalyptic proportions. With a painful gait, I limped out of the Love Hotel, into the pallid streets of an Akita morning. Japanese cities by day—and especially the nightlife zones—are a lot like waking up beside someone you picked up at a bar: a bit hard to escape, or even face, in the harsh glare of morning. So it was with Akita. It proved a difficult city to leave. I walked for over an hour, past stale façades and concrete buildings, along blue-fume highways.

Akita by night had been exciting. By day, it had all the vitality of a sucked lemon. My teeth were furry, and my mouth felt as though I had fallen asleep in a dentist's chair with the suction tube on at maximum.

I vowed solemnly never to drink again. Or at least, not to excess. Or at least, not to the point of falling-down drunk. It was the Law of Diminishing Returns kicking in, the notion that if one ice cream is delicious, eating a hundred ice creams will be a hundred times more so. I had once enjoyed the flurry of festivities but, after riding a wave of drunken parties for over a month, the novelty was fast wearing thin. It had become almost an ordeal. I knew something was wrong that morning in the Love Hotel when I woke up and heard a strange, strangled noise. It was the sound of my liver whimpering. I would need to enter detox after this. My blood was so thin, my heart was pumping pure alcohol. No more, I decided. No more. Well, maybe once more, when I got to Hokkaido, but that was it.

Over breakfast (a cup of coffee and five aspirin), I watched a news report that announced, with barely restrained jubilance, that the Cherry Blossom Front had finally begun creeping up the coast. The announcer was calling for its arrival in Akita any day, but I was already exhausted with the city and was longing for the open road.

North of Akita City lay Hachirōgata-chōseiike, an odd doughnut-shaped lake. I was fascinated by this. On a map it looked like a giant moat surrounding a vast island. Up close, I discovered, it was simply a man-made lagoon that encircled flat, reclaimed farmland. I was sorely unimpressed.

I followed the eastern edge of this moat-like lagoon, through several drab little towns. Shōwa, Iitagawa, Hachirōgata, Kotōka: there was little to distinguish one from the rest save their names.

I caught a series of short rides from one town to the next. A Coca-Cola delivery man picked me up on the outskirts of Noshiro City and dropped me off ten minutes later, still on the outskirts of Noshiro City. He wanted to know how the rides were in Akita. "Good, eh?" he said, answering his own question. "Akita people are famous for their hospitality."

"Well," I said, "a lot of people slowed down to look—or even to laugh—but they didn't stop."

"They are shy," he explained.

The Coca-Cola man had dropped me off on the Noshiro Perimeter Highway in front of a Kentucky Fried Chicken outlet. I went in and nursed a cup of coffee for as long as I could, before going out and facing the road again. The toilet in the KFC had an electric seat warmer, and that is all I remember of Noshiro City.

Outside, great warheads were boiling over in the sky. My luck held, however, and I caught a ride just before the rains began—big fat raindrops that broke like bullets across the windshield.

"At least it's not snow," said the driver, a smiling, awkward young man named Norio Ito. (No relation to the other Itos I had met along the way; Japan has a decidedly limited pool of family names.)

Norio's car was in utter disarray. There were boxes stacked in the back and flour on everything. There was flour on his chin, powdered in his hair, dusted on the dash. Norio, it turned out, made *konnyaku*, a word that strikes terror into the hearts of most long-term residents in Japan. Konnyaku—translated, appropriately enough, as "devil's tongue"—is a gelatin-like substance cooked in slabs, cut into chunks, and then hidden in broth and soup as a practical joke, in amid the tofu and boiled eggs. Biting into a chunk of konnyaku is about as appealing and as appetizing as trying to chew on an especially large eraser. It looks like congealed mucus—with flecks of stuff suspended in it, no less—but without the nutritional value or flavor you would expect from mucus.

Though only in his twenties (he looked like he had barely hit his teens), Norio was now in charge of his family business. "My family has always made konnyaku," he said, though I'm not sure if it was a source of pride or penance. Then, suddenly, "*Wait!* I have a card. I do. They're here somewhere." And he began searching through his glove compartment and among his various flour-dusted boxes and even under the seats, an action that involved putting his head below the dash for extended periods of time while holding the steering wheel on autopilot with his left hand. We were slowly drifting across the centre lane when he popped up to announce—after he had swerved back onto his side of the road—that he had indeed found his business cards. They were still in their original shrink-wrap plastic, and I don't know why, but that detail struck me as being very sad. He broke the plastic and handed me one. It said: *Norio Ito, Maker of Konnyaku.* "Go ahead," he urged. "Take several. You can give them to your friends."

Norio explained carefully and at great length how to prepare konnyaku, and I pretended to listen (like I will ever want to know how to make jellied mucus). At one point, he even reached around and pulled out a foil-wrapped, rubbery brick of konnyaku and handed it to me. "A present," he said.

"Ah, thanks." And I thought to myself, How do I tell him that in the washroom stall of the Rock Balloon in Kumamoto City, a bar I used to frequent, there is the scrawled graffiti: *What is konnyaku? Where does it come from and what does it want?*

"Is it true," I asked, "that konnyaku contains animal ash to add colour?"

He giggled at the notion. "No, no," he said. "Not animal ash. Animal *gelatin*. The ash we use is from wood. Mixed with potato flour."

"Wood ash?"

"Yes," he said. "For colour. Modern companies have tried experimenting with artificial dyes, but the real konnyaku needs ash. It is a long, difficult process. And as you know, the art of handmade konnyaku is dying out."

"What a shame," said I.

"It makes it difficult to raise a family in this business."

"You aren't married?" I asked.

"Oh, no." The very notion of women made him blush. "Someday, but not yet. Still single."

He was a nice kid. He giggled a lot, in a head-bobbing way. He had probably spent a lot of his time in school getting stuffed into lockers, but he was a good kid. I felt a sort of big-brother affinity toward him.

The rain came down. Norio and I talked our way through several cloudbursts, the wipers sloshing back and forth. It was as though we were being pursued by bad weather. Behind us, a cloudbank came down in a slow wave, dissolving the landscape into ether.

The road we were on took us past an island shrine in a small lake, the torii gate made from rough-hewn logs. Farmhouses tumbled *up* the mountainsides in reverse gravity. The trees were bare, the barns the grey of old bone marrow. Dilapidated buildings, half finished and long forgotten, gave the towns we passed the archaeological feel of a construction site abandoned long ago. The only bright colours came from the wind-sock carp that were hoisted in front of homes in recognition of Children's Day, flying upstream against the wind in a personification of that peculiarly Japanese value called *gaman*, or "perseverance."

Ōdate City was Norio's home. He was supposed to drop me off there, but instead he offered to take me just out of town, and this, in turn, became an epic drive across the high mountains into Aomori prefecture.

We managed to outrun the storm. The weather broke and the rain gave up its pursuit. Outside of Ōdate there were a few marshes, some cabins, and then a thick stand of forest.

"Virgin," he said.

"Well, that's nothing to worry about," I replied. "I'm sure someday you will meet the right girl and—oh, you mean the trees."

"Yes," he said. "Virgin forests. Never been cut. This is very rare in Japan."

A thick blanket of snow welcomed us as we crossed the prefectural boundary into Aomori. The snow spread, white and pure, into the hills, and a clutch of homes loitered by the roadside, bright blue against the white, the tin roofs having melted themselves free. It was a mythic scene: vapour was rising from the highway and rooftops, as though the landscape itself were expelling ghosts.

At my urging, Norio pulled over so that I could walk out into the white. Other than a few faint falls like the one that had greeted me when I arrived on Sado Island, I had not seen snow—real snow, deep snow, snow that doesn't disappear as soon as it lands—for more than five years. Coming as I do from the original Snow Country, this was a traumatic loss. I missed snow deeply and with heartfelt sincerity. So, naturally, the first thing I did was zing Norio in the head with a packed snowball.

"C'mon," he said. "Quit it."

I got him again, *pow!* and he tried to retaliate, chasing me, flailing wildly with handfuls of snow and failing miserably. I ran into deeper banks, pelting Norio with snowballs and then laughing loudly, when suddenly the sun broke through and the world stopped. It was magnificent. Everything went quiet and sparkling. The mountain air was as crisp and clean as a celery stalk snapped in two. I breathed in deeply, filling my chest. It was like a homecoming and then—*wham!* Norio stung me in the ear with a slush ball. At almost the same moment, the snow gave way beneath me and I sank up to my waist. I could feel running water around my feet, icy cold. "Help!"

Norio came scrambling up to rescue me, which was a big mistake because, of course, my cries of help were but a ploy and I pulled him into the snow and then rolled him down the hill. He came up sputtering, and as I leaned over to help him, I got a full wet face of snow. I pulled away.

"That's not funny," I said.

"Oh, but it is," said Norio, and he shovelled some more into my face and down my neck. Which pretty much ended our ice capades for the day. I stomped back to the car with a cloud over my head and Norio trailing behind me, giggling and skipping about and flinging more snow on my head.

Grumbling about unsportsmanlike behaviour, I climbed back into the car and sulked. We began our descent into Aomori's valleys. The snow that Norio had plastered me with soon turned into cold water, soaking my shirt, trickling down my back, and chilling my wet, squishy running shoes. "I won!" he said.

"It was a tie."

"Clearly, we are using a different scoring system," he said. "By my calculations, I had victory."

"It was a tie," I said, crossing my arms and looking straight ahead. There's never a school locker around when you need one.

14

If Akita is rice country, Aomori prefecture is apple country—and boy, they don't let you forget it. Apples are embedded in fence patterns, painted on signs, alluded to at every turn. When we crossed into Aomori prefecture, everything changed as if by clockwork from rice fields to apples. Orchards, endless orchards, filled the hills and valleys with rows of gnarled, bad-tempered apple trees. It's a theory of forest personalities I developed during my many idle moments: cherry trees are wistful, plum trees are wise, cedars are mysterious, and apple trees are bad-tempered.

We came down into the wide Hirosaki Plains, slaloming from switchback to switchback, and dropping so suddenly our ears popped. In the distance, Mount Iwaki rose like a slow volcanic eruption. Traffic began to pick up as we rejoined the main highway, and a robot flagman waved us through a construction site. As we approached Hirosaki City, more and more coloured rooftops appeared, like squares in a quilt.

Hirosaki—dusty, historic, ramshackle Hirosaki—is a sort of backwoods, discount Kyoto. A northern outpost of traditional Japan, Hirosaki is a castle town, a Zen stronghold, a warehouse of artifacts. Imagine a city laid out in narrow alleys and carefully arranged blocks. Take that city and give it a couple of good shakes. Knock everything out of whack and add a layer of dust and a bucketful of history—and you have Hirosaki.

Hirosaki is the singularly most *Japanese* city I know. Not the finest or the prettiest or the oldest, but definitely the most Japanese. It is a city of neighbourhoods and alleyways. Its grandest sights are meant to be walked through, to be ducked under, sought out.

Japan *is* Hirosaki, with its contradictions and narrow alleys, the self-referential streets, the sudden dead ends, and the constant backtracking.

Everything about Hirosaki is slightly askew, and yet—like so many Japanese towns—it has its own internal logic. The variously converging and diverging lines of perspective, the carefully thought-out lack of city planning, the labyrinthine angles: Hirosaki is not a beautiful city, but it is endlessly captivating, in the true sense of the word—*captive*. Once Norio dropped me off, I was soon lost in Hirosaki's architectural bedlam. The city, it is said, was purposefully designed to be confusing in order to thwart would-be invaders. I believe it. Several times I expected to come across a haggard band of samurai invaders, stumbling blindly about, searching for the castle.

I was looking for Zenrin Avenue, and it took me all day to find it. Zenrin is a long, unusually wide street flanked on either side by wealthy Zen temples (a contradiction in terms, no?). There are thirty-three Zen temples along this one street, a remarkable concentration. A smaller, parallel row of temples runs beside it, and both converge on Chōshō-ji, the granddaddy of them all.

I spent the night in a capsule hotel near the station, and I walked down Zenrin the next morning in the early dawn, when everything was lit in watercolours. Priests swept their gates, food stalls opened up, preparing for an onslaught of sightseers, and a monk went by on a bicycle, trilling his bell. I entered Chōshō-ji Temple through its brooding wooden gate and passed the temple bell. The gate was built in 1629, the bell cast in 1306. And I thought: this gate has been standing since the days of Shakespeare, this bell has been tolling out the woes of man centuries before Columbus.

I entered the cool dark of what was once the temple kitchen. The floor was pockmarked with the memory of spiked sandals worn by samurai soldiers, and I stopped to run my fingers across it. The lady taking admission smiled at me. "Samurai," she said.

The room was stained with the smoke of countless meals and the steam of countless fires. A pot was simmering and the aroma of green tea, as heavy as incense, hung in the air. I had arrived in time for the city's Spring Festival, the only time when the mummy prince of Chōshō-ji was put on display.

"He was dug up in a schoolyard," said the small, round woman who sat beside it—him?—*it*. "The prince was very young," she said. "They suspect he was poisoned. Imported peaches, you see. Very tragic. But the prince's love of sweets may have helped maintain his body. You know, a bit like pickling him from the inside out."

The body was displayed behind glass with some of the items found in his coffin: a memorial tablet, sackcloths, a headband. After one hundred and forty years the young prince looked remarkably spry. Freeze-dried, but spry. His skin was smooth and taut, polished like beechnut, as frail as papyrus.

I stood gaping awhile at the eternally young mummy prince before wandering deeper into the temple, past the Buddhist Statuary Hall and down a "nightingale corridor" where the floor planks were tightly set to squeak as anyone approached, an early and poetic form of burglar alarm. I tried walking down it in my best ninja-soft steps— I even hummed the theme song from *Kung Fu* for inspiration—but to no avail; the singing floorboards gave me away every time.

Outside, behind the temple, lies a surprising optical illusion. The entire avenue of Zenrin appears to be on a low, flat stretch, but when you peer out you discover that it is actually built on a strategic bluff overlooking the Hirosaki Plains. The land on which Chōshō-ji was built was, in fact, the first choice for Hirosaki Castle, but the influence of the Zen monks was strong at that time and they managed to outmanoeuvre even the local warlord. In response, the lord of Hirosaki insisted that all the outlying Zen monasteries be relocated to this road so that he could keep his eye on them. This, unfortunately, only consolidated the priests' strength. I liked Hirosaki; I liked the fact that in all of the many machinations and schemes and ploys and endless intrigues, the Zen monks always came out on top. Even now, they are the wealthiest temples in the area. (And *really*, it is a contradiction in terms, is it not?)

I spent the next night in a temple. It was on the city's *other* Temple Row, Shin-Teramachi, a short walk from Hirosaki's much-photographed and often-admired pagoda. The temple was named Henshō-ji, and the view from my window was of Buddhist headstones fading into cityscape.

That view seemed to sum up everything: graveyards melting into city. In Hirosaki, past and present merge. Hirosaki is a mummy prince. A city where the merchants are poor and the Zen priests are rich. A city of graves, where even its prized pagoda was built to comfort the souls of men killed in battle.

I stood, looking out across this city of ghosts, until dusk crept in and supper was called.

15

I SPENT my next night at the Hirosaki Youth Hostel, a weary, past-its-prime building wedged into a back street. My budget couldn't withstand another night at the temple, and so, with a suitable amount of dread hanging over me, I was forced to move to a hostel. It was filled with college students, and a sign in English said *Well Come!* but there were no English speakers present. A pair of sullen-looking East Indian men were huddled in a corner speaking in dark whispers. They didn't seem to be looking for company so I let them be.

The old lady who managed the hostel took me outside to see her ducks, which were living a pampered life in a small pond beside the building. "They are very happy," she said, though how one could tell, what with a duck's limited store of facial expressions, was hard to say. They certainly looked content, waddling about, plopping into the water, quacking away. They were only for show apparently, or perhaps for eggs, because when I suggested we broil up a duck or two she gave me a look of dismay and disbelief.

A group of hostelers were organizing a trip downtown to hear the *tsugaru shamisen*, a type of Japanese banjo that is famous in this area. "It's wonderful," said one young lady after I invited myself into their conversation. "The music is very fast. Very exciting."

Her name was Midori. She smiled at me. A nice smile. A warm smile. A smile you could roast marshmallows on. Suddenly, I became very interested in the tsugaru shamisen. Midori talked on about it enthusiastically, with breathy gestures and wondrous big eyes. I can't remember much about what she said, but I do remember those eyes.

I chatted with Midori long enough to weasel an invite to the Live House Pub, a place that specializes in the local robust cuisine and its equally robust music. One of Midori's friends called a taxi and we wedged ourselves in. The driver was nice enough about it, but apparently we were being shadowed by spies, because he turned half a dozen corners, threading his way into the maze until, satisfied that we were no longer being followed, he roared down the main boulevard of Hirosaki, which was now as thick as thieves with nighttime traffic. With each turn and lurch, my leg had—accidentally at first and surreptitiously as the ride progressed—pressed up against Midori's thigh. When she didn't shift her weight, I took it as a good sign and began casually, yet in a highly erotic manner, moving my leg slightly against hers. She turned and smiled at me, and she didn't move her leg away, but when we got to the Live House she sat as far away from me as possible.

I nursed a beer and picked at my meal as a family of musicians tuned up their banjos onstage. I was soon befriended by a professor of music history who was visiting Hirosaki from Tokyo. He was a nice enough man, but his eyes were not at all wondrous.

My self-pity ended with a splash when the music began—*began* is not quite the right word. It pounced on us. It detonated. One moment there were murmurs and the smell of soy sauce and beer. The next moment there was only music.

The western half of Aomori prefecture is the home of the proud Tsugaru culture, with its own distinct dialect and music, and Hirosaki is at the heart of it. "You should hear tsugaru shamisen," said the temple priest of Henshō-ji. "That is the rhythm of Hirosaki."

And now here I was, buffeted by it. It was wilder than the drums of Sado, more joyous, more raucous, more insane. An entire family of musicians, from grandfather down to daughter-in-law, whipped up tunes like they were making meringue. It was amazing—that's the only word for it—how they managed to coax such complicated riffs and lively melodies out of a simple three-stringed instrument. It lasted for hours, then came crashing to a halt. The room hummed with silence for a moment and then burst into wild, boisterous applause.

"Thank you," mumbled the family patriarch as he mopped his brow with a hankie. "We have CDs and cassettes for sale at the cash register." He then introduced his son, the current tsugaru shamisen champion of Japan, who played a mournful, interlaid rhythm spiced with apples and mountain air.

"The sound of Hirosaki," said the music professor as he raised his glass to the stage. "The sound of Hirosaki."

My stay at the youth hostel ended when I found a private room at a small inn for less than I was paying at the hostel. It was my third place in almost as many days, and it represented a descent through Dantean degrees of travellers' purgatory: first a temple, then a hostel, and then this—a *minshuku* of mildew and lost dreams. It was the type of place where failed writers come to nurse grievances and rage at the world, where men with sinister eyes blow smoke rings across open bottles of gin. If young Ernest Hemingway or Malcolm Lowry had ever come to Japan, this is where they would have stayed.

A woman showed me to my room, where a lumpy futon awaited my arrival. The sheets, I suppose, had once been white. The wallpaper too. Perhaps. But everything had soured, faded, and turned to this: the yellow of cigarette-stained fingers, the yellow of that one little mutant toenail that grows as hard as a claw. The walls themselves sagged, as much from ennui as from age, and I dropped my bag on the floor in defeat.

The lady smiled at me. "The best room in the house," she said.

16

HIROSAKI HAS the only extant castle in northern Japan and the only one with its original walls still intact. It is also, and here I quote the official tourist brochure, "One of the Three Best Cherry Blossom Viewing Spots in Japan." Unlike most castle towns, in Hirosaki the castle does not dominate the skyline but exists, almost shyly, in a forest park, tucked out of sight. The original castle, built in 1611, had towered above the plains, but it was (surprise, surprise) struck by lightning, and a much smaller, scaled-down version was erected in its stead. The present castle dates from 1810. It doesn't exactly soar so much as it huddles, three stories high and perched on the corner of the castle wall, teetering above the moat and looking more like a watchtower than a main keep.

Spring had arrived in Hirosaki in full force. There are more than five thousand cherry trees on the grounds of Hirosaki Castle, an embarrassment of riches that seems almost baroque when at full bloom. I didn't so much enter the grounds as I swam in, through the sakura, which hung in garlands. In the park, the street lamps glowed within fountains of flowers, and crowds swirled by, hurrying to parties.

A few blossoms had already begun to scatter, falling like faint snow into the castle moat, blowing across the footbridge and stone paths. They had barely arrived and already they were leaving. Sakura, scientists insist, are scentless. Or at least very nearly scentless. A single flower has a pale perfume that is so slight it cannot be detected by the average human sense. But a *thousand* blossoms, bursting with colour and tumbling on the wind, do have a scent, faint perhaps, but unmistakable.

Sakura also have a sound all their own—the late night revelries of hanami parties. More than two million people visit Hirosaki Castle during the city's Cherry Blossom Festival, and tonight it seemed as though every one of them were on hand. The castle grounds were alive with motion. Noisy. Celebratory. A circle of office workers waved me in with much fanfare, and when I told them I had been travelling with the Cherry Blossom Front, a voice yelled out, "It's an omen! A good omen!" They asked me to present a toast to the sakura, and a ceramic cup quickly appeared and was ferried across to me. Warm saké was sloshed into it and the voices rose in laughter and mock solemnity. "A toast, a toast to the flowers! To your journey!"

My entire trip seemed to pivot on this moment.

"Tell us about your journey!" they cried. What could I say? That it seemed like a good idea at the time? That the flowers were sadder the more time I spent with them? That I had met dozens of strangers, made dozens of friends, and was still hopelessly alone? That I didn't really know what I was doing, or whether there was any point to it? There was so much to say, and yet there was nothing much to say. I raised my cup. They strained forward to hear what I would offer. "To the cherry blossoms," I said. "May we never understand them."

This was taken as a fine bit of insight and the crowd burst into rowdy applause. *"Kampai!"* they shouted, and just then a wind stirred the branches, softly scattering blossoms across the crowds. More applause, and I was just about to put the cup to my lips when I noticed that a single flower had dropped into my saké. It floated there a moment, and I was about to fish it out when the man next to me raised a hand and the crowd quieted down. "It is a sign," he said. "A lucky sign. Surely that is from the gods." There was good-natured laughter at this, but no one dared out-and-out deny it either. After all, what if it *was* from the gods, what then? "Drink it!" said a voice somewhere in the circle. "Yes," said another. "You must. Drink it, drink the flower."

I looked down and considered this small act of communion I was being asked to perform. Then, with a flourish, I tipped the cup right back, flower and all, and swallowed it in one gulp. The circle applauded and laughed. I smiled proudly and was about to speak when I felt something clinging to the back of my throat like a small wad of wet tissue—and I began to choke. I hacked and coughed and retched until my face became red. I hacked for so long, the others stopped laughing and became concerned. A man began pounding me on my back as I tried to get at the blossom with my fingers, but that only made it worse. I began to gag until finally, like a hairball, I spat it out. My eyes were watering, and when I looked at the faces around me I saw varying degrees of worry and disgust. "It—it tried to kill me," I gasped.

I was drunk on flowers. I was choking on cherry blossoms. That night, looking for someone to ground me, I called Terumi from a pay phone at the edge of the castle grounds. Back in Kyushu, the sakura had scattered weeks before and the rainy season was now dribbling to an end. The first waves of summer were beginning. I was several seasons out of step. "You missed spring in Minamata," said Terumi. "The trees behind your apartment were beautiful."

As we spoke, the sakura were swirling around the phone booth in a flurry of pink and white. I had spent more than a month surrounded by them, more than is possible, more than is natural. And it struck me then, with a deep sense of unease, that what I was doing was fundamentally *wrong*. The sakura are meant to be transitory. To try to cling to them was like trying to cling to youth. Following the Cherry Blossom Front was a denial of time, of seasons, of mortality even. It was like spraying lacquer on a lily. Like embalming a mirage. Like trying to stop time.

Back at the inn, the bathwater was tepid and yellow, and the mirror gave my skin a tallow-waxy look. For some reason, I couldn't stop sighing. I climbed the stairs to where my futon waited. The shutters had been left open and the wind was searching my room. Outside, the moon was lost in a sea of clouds. I turned out the lights and was a long time falling asleep.

17

MORNING SEEPED back in on a musty, wet scent. The blankets were cold and clammy.

I had planned on leaving Hirosaki right after breakfast, but the sky cast doubts, aspersions, and eventually rain on my travel plans. I sat in the front room of the inn with the doors opened to the street as the rain fell. Umbrellas moved past. The streets filled up with water. Vehicles crept by as slow as funeral processions. There was only me, the maid who passed through now and then, and the perpetual yawn of a television screen, the volume muted and the movements flickering frantically across the screen like the antics of a small child who knows it is losing our attention. It was one of those long, grey mornings that seem to last forever.

Even the rain was listless, falling down in sheets, letting gravity do all the work. No gusts or swirls, just a dreary constant downfall. The tea cooled, lukewarm and bitter, and the air had that dank smell of dentures and wet newspaper. The television continued to flicker, the rain to fall.

The sky didn't clear until late in the afternoon, and when it did, I decided to make my break. I had already paid for another night at the inn, but after pleading poverty and ignorance, I was allowed to leave with a grudging refund, and I hurried to pack and clear out.

Hirosaki after the rain was even more bedraggled and tattered than before. I had spent the morning studying my rail maps and had discovered a rural train station just west of a major highway. A highway that would take me all the way to Aomori City. From there, I would catch the ferry to Hokkaido.

The train rattled its way slowly east and then north, across the flatlands and through the farming village of Onoe, where I disembarked.

Everything would have been fine if I had just stayed on the main road. In the distance, at the far edge of the rice fields, I could see a tiny parade of vehicles running alongside the mountains. All I had to do was make my way across the plains, toward the mountains, to this mystery road and then hitch along it until I came to the highway. Simple.

I could have cut directly across the fields, but I decided instead to follow a small side road. I didn't walk across the fields because the rain had turned them into mud. But more important, in Japan there is a strong taboo about walking through someone else's land. When I was living on the Amakusa Islands, I once spent an evening tramping about my neighbour's place with my camera and tripod, looking for the perfect sunset shot. I carefully avoided stepping on any of the rows of rice stalks, but I left footprints all over the place. The man was enraged when he came out the next day. Police were called in. They measured the footprints, concluded that the culprit had to be the local Bigfoot foreigner, and when they found mud on the shoes in the entranceway of my house, the case was closed. I was taken down to make a formal apology to the man. It was, I later learned, like jumping someone's fence and then tracking mud all over his patio.

You *can* walk across rice fields, but only along the raised earth dividers that separate the paddies. These access strips are sort of "neutral territory," but they are also very slippery and hard to negotiate with a poorly arranged, sadistically heavy backpack on your shoulders. Which is why I chose to follow a side road through the fields instead.

Unfortunately, as I soon discovered, it was one of those roads that seems to have no sense of direction, no purpose in life, no reason to exist. It didn't connect anything with anything, it just sort of meandered around like a slack-brained teenager in a shopping mall. It headed for the mountains but then turned and took a leisurely detour through some overgrown grassy fields, then it found a small stream and followed that for a while, just for something to do. It leapt across the stream on a small bridge and loped alongside the other bank before petering out in an open field, as though tired of life itself.

I had walked for over an hour and still I was in the middle of a vast, lazy flatland. Fuming and snorting, I set off overland, walking along the balance-beam dikes that separated the rice paddies, careful not to step on the rice fields themselves. And I saw a snake. Of course. Right on my path. And when I tried to run away, I slipped off the dike and ended up with one leg in mud up to my knee and a shoe that would squish and smell of compost for days. All in all, not a good way to spend an afternoon.

When I finally made it to the highway, the sky had begun to darken with clouds. Visions of Fukui dancing in my head, I started frantically waving my thumb at anything with wheels—and I was promptly picked up by a UFO. Well, I don't know for certain it was a UFO, but it looked like one. It had throbbing purple running boards, a neon licence plate, and tinted glass. It was more than a van, it was a Love Hotel on wheels. The driver was a wiry young man with tight-permed hair and wraparound sunglasses. Beside him was his girlfriend, a chubby-faced young lady with short hair, tinted orange. (Blond dyes don't take with Japanese hair, something that Japanese women refuse to accept.)

Grateful to escape the pending storm, I crawled into the back, where the only place to sit was a plush velvet bed, beside which was a statuette of a nude cherub. I looked up to confirm, and yes, in true Love Hotel fashion, there was a mirrored ceiling. Hot damn. Japanese swingers. *Finally!*

The young man chewed a toothpick thoughtfully but didn't speak. His girlfriend, however, was bubbly with excitement. She turned right around and smiled at me with deep red lipstick. I smiled back in that suave and debonair manner that has made me famous on four continents. Unfortunately, she showed a little *too* much interest in me, and within twenty minutes I was back on the side of the road. No explanations were given; the man simply pulled over. His girlfriend became pouty and, crossing her arms, settled in for a good long sulk. At first I assumed they let me out because they themselves were turning off, but no, their van disappeared down the road straight ahead, exactly where I was going. It was the oddest encounter of my entire trip.

I stood there pondering this when it began to rain. Great spiteful bullets from Heaven, and me on an open road. It was Fukui all over again.

Swearing and kicking at my pack, I managed to wrestle my rain poncho from the secret compartment it had scurried into. I pulled the plastic poncho around me and buttoned it up to the chin just as the rain stopped and the sun burst back onstage like an actress looking for an ovation. This was followed by a new round of profanities as I launched into more of my ravings, yanking the poncho off and trampling it underfoot. (Perhaps I belong in Japan because I am at heart an animist; inanimate objects are subject to curses, punishment, exhortations, abuse. Certainly my backpack and rain poncho were inhabited by kami—stupid kami, true, but kami nonetheless.)

The next ride was with a young mother who was studying English conversation. She smiled shyly, so shyly my heart melted into a puddle-size pool of butter. It was already getting dark with intimations of night when I crawled in, and I was shocked to discover that her two children were in the backseat: a toddler in a safety seat and a two-year-old beside her. The lady drove me all the way to the Aomori ferry terminal, more than an hour out of her way and despite my pleas to the contrary. "You don't have to do this, really."

"No, no," she said (in Japanese). "I want to practise my English" (again in Japanese). "And anyway, you looked so sad out there by the side of the road" (still in Japanese). Then, with her smile showing a hint of pride, she said, "This is the first time I have ever picked up a hitchhiker."

"Can I give you some advice then?"

"Yes?"

"Don't."

She didn't understand.

"Don't pick up hitchhikers," I said. "Not late in the day when you have your children in the car."

"But you looked so—"

"Don't," I said.

She nodded. "I see."

"I'm sorry," I said. "But it's not a good idea."

"I understand. Thank you." Her voice was almost a whisper at this point. I had taken the fun out of her adventure. "It's just that you looked so sad beside the road, and I have always wanted to travel, to speak English." And for a moment I thought she might start to cry.

"I'm sorry," I said. "But you really shouldn't."

"I understand," she said. "I was foolish. I am—I am always acting foolish." She didn't say another word, except goodbye.

18

THE NIGHT FERRY was not leaving for several hours. I left my backpack at the dock and hiked into town, across the Aomori Bay Bridge, over the train tracks, and into the city centre. Aomori City, seen from atop a windy bridge suspended in space, is a remarkable sight, an arrangement of geometric shapes—circles, squares, triangles—that gave the city one of those rarest of things in Japan: a distinct skyline. Repeated throughout it, from the glass triangle ASPAM building to the spans of the bridge itself, is the shape of the letter A. A as in apple. A as in Aomori.

From such abstract heights, I descended into the city itself through a shantytown of corrugated metal shacks near the port. I eventually found the central avenue and was intrigued to see two Japanese Jehovah's Witnesses standing by the corner, impassively, as people swept by. They were holding out Japanese-language versions of the *Watchtower* in the time-honoured style of Witnesses the world over. I stopped to chat, but they had that glassy, opaque look of the firmly converted, so I wandered off. (It's a sad day indeed when even the Jehovah's Witnesses won't talk to you.)

With another hour to kill, I stopped in at a second-storey bakery / coffee shop beside a wooden Shinto shrine just off the main street. It was called the Red Apple Café, and the décor was very Japanese. Which is to say, it was a hodgepodge of French chalet, Swiss Alpine, and generic American styles. Lots of dark wood and bright lights. You know, Japanese.

I had a cup of coffee and a piece of apple pie. You have to eat apple pie in Aomori; it's like haggis in Glasgow, fish and chips in Liverpool, or Rice-a-Roni in San Francisco. The lady of the shop was a pink-faced, smiling woman who was tickled even pinker when I ordered in Japanese.

"Your Japanese is very good," she said.

"Thank you."

"And I think you understand the True Heart of Japan."

"Thanks."

"And you are very fat."

"Ah, thanks."

"And your nose. It is very big."

"Listen. You can stop with the compliments any time."

And for the record, let me state once and for all that I am *not* fat. I'm hearty in a solid, robust sort of way, like a rugby player. Really.

The ferry to Hokkaido was a floating hotel with potted plants and polished mirrors. It foghorned its way out of Aomori harbour, past the grey silhouettes of trawlers and oil refineries. On either side, the pincer claws of Aomori's northern peninsulas closed in as we slid free like a lover escaping an embrace.

I pulled my hood down and stood on the deck, face in the wind, the taste of salt water in the air. I might have stayed out there in my heroic pose for the entire crossing, but the winds were cold and I had to pee.

Inside, there was only the hum and throb of the engines and that suffocating silence of a ferry at night. Bodies were asleep at all angles, as though nerve gas had swept through the cabin. I wandered among strangers and ended up sharing a room with a cigarette-smoking, swampy-eyed man and a woman who scowled in her sleep.

INTO A NORTHERN SEA

Across Hokkaido

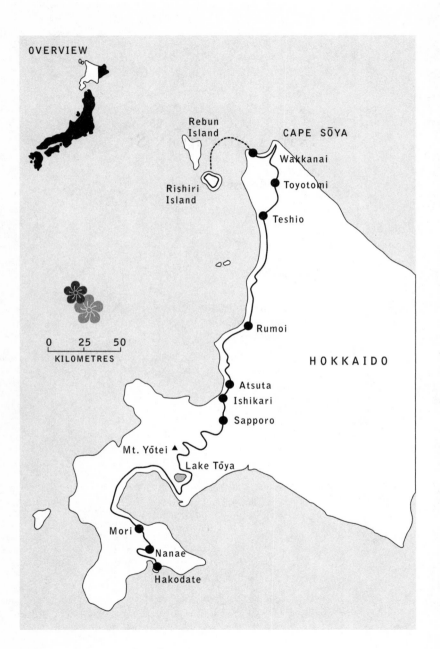

OVERVIEW

Rebun
Island

CAPE SŌYA

Wakkanai

Toyotomi

Rishiri
Island

Teshio

Rumoi

HOKKAIDO

0   25   50
KILOMETRES

Atsuta
Ishikari
Sapporo

Mt. Yōtei ▲
Lake Tōya

Mori

Nanae

Hakodate

I

HOKKAIDO IS A VAST, underpopulated island with a climate that is closer to Oslo's than to Tokyo's. The summers are short and the winters are long; this is a place that sees icebergs off its northern coast.

In many ways, Hokkaido is the least "Japanese" of all the main islands. It's Texas and Alaska rolled into one. The last frontier and the end of Japan. It was not formally colonized until after the Meiji Reformation of 1868, and even then it wasn't completely opened up by settlers until the 1880s—at about the same time that the American Wild West was at its peak, with Wyatt Earp and Doc Holliday blasting away at the OK Corral. Hokkaido even *looks* like the American West.

This is cattle country, with rolling fields, high mountains, and shimmering Texas-style metropolises. They even have their very own oppressed aboriginal minority, the Ainu. The Ainu were seafarers, fur trappers, and hunters, and though they had no written language, they passed down *yukar*, epic sagas, from generation to generation. They worshipped the bear, they tattooed themselves in elaborate— almost Celtic—patterns, they built a complex system of salmon weirs and lived in interconnecting communities along the northern riverways.

Where the Ainu came from remains something of a mystery. The consensus seems to be that they migrated from the Siberian steppes. Their skin is paler than that of most Asian people, but they are not—as many commentators purport—Caucasian. Nor are they particularly "hairy." (The fact that the Japanese describe the Ainu as being hairy—and, as often as not, "smelly"—says more about Japanese prejudices than it does about actual Ainu physiognomy.)

Although not formally conquered, the Ainu in the northern regions were brought under heel by the early shōguns. In 1669 an Ainu uprising was crushed, and for two hundred years they remained a subjugated population. It was only in the late nineteenth century that they were annexed as a people—and as an island. The Ainu were stripped of their ancestral rights, forced onto farmlands and into enclaves, and made to renounce their religion and culture. Their language was banned, and they were deemed "non-citizens."

The Ainu were not officially recognized as being Japanese citizens until 1992. Even then, the Japanese government refuses to use the term *indigenous* when discussing the Ainu (to avoid having to accept responsibility for what happened and to stave off growing demands for a land claims settlement). An important point: the Ainu never ceded their homelands nor ever acknowledged Japanese authority, making them one of the few aboriginal groups in the world that have never been offered a treaty by the people who invaded their territory. In a nation like Japan, which has decreed itself "racially and culturally homogenous," people like the Ainu simply do not enter the paradigm/mythology. At best, they are a novelty, a source of amusement. At worst, they are simply pests.

Today, twenty-four thousand people claim Ainu ancestry, but few are pure-blooded and their language is all but dead, thanks largely to a relentless and concentrated campaign of assimilation mounted by the Japanese government. The Ainu influence appears to have once extended quite far south into Honshu—the "Fuji" in Mount Fuji is thought to be of Ainu origin—but the present-day Ainu have been reduced to a tawdry tourist sideshow. Ainu elders sit stoically baring their tattoos like lepers on display while Japanese tourists giggle and pose beside them for photographs. It is very dispiriting, these human zoos, and it was one of the reasons I decided to avoid the main tourist areas around Akan Lake, once an Ainu heartland and now, well—*not* an Ainu heartland.

A stubborn renaissance of Ainu culture has taken root lately, primarily around the music, legends, and dance, but overall the situation is fragile. Australian Aborigines, North American Natives, South

American Indians—there is something in the psyche of the colonist that is unnerved by prior ownership, as we patronize, brutalize, ignore, and then wax poetic about the people we displace.

It was with thoughts like these that I entered Hokkaido to begin the last leg of my journey.

2

AT THE SOUTHERN TIP of Hokkaido lies a small hook of land anchored at one end by a dormant volcanic peak. It was here, upon this geographical anomaly, that Hokkaido's first Japanese settlement began, an imperial toehold on the great island above. The Russians had been using Hakodate Port as a landing base as far back as 1740. In 1854, Japan moved in to counter Russian expansion. Hakodate became an open city and, for one brief period, while the imperial powers moved their chess pieces into position and the fate of the northern island hung in the balance—for one brief period, Hakodate was a centre of intrigue and power.

Today, Hakodate has fallen half asleep. A threadbare, somewhat seedy city, it is one of the few areas in Hokkaido where the American influence doesn't dominate. Here the flavour is European—*eastern* European. Russian architectural styles are everywhere in evidence, even though the people are resolutely Japanese.

Hakodate is a city of endgames, where history begins and empires fade. It was here, in Hakodate, that the forces of the Shōgun made their fateful last stand. It was here, in the Battle of Hakodate, that the troops of the Tokugawa shōguns were finally defeated by the upstart civilian army of the newly modernized Emperor Meiji. It was the last hurrah of the samurai class, and it brought to an end two hundred and fifty years of the shōgun rule. In its stead was an outward-looking, imperially minded *modern* government. The Battle of Hakodate centred on the city's star-shaped British citadel, and the irony was sharp: a European-style fortress would be the last refuge of the samurai.

—

I arrived in Hakodate late in the evening, and I found a room at a bed-and-breakfast called the Niceday Inn. When I entered, the owner received me with boisterous English. "Come in! Come in!"

His name was Shigeto Saito. "But call me Mr. Saito," he said, generously. He had the face of a boxer who has seen one too many fights. Heavy, lugubrious features. (I'm not really sure what "lugubrious features" means, but if anyone had them, it was Mr. Saito.) "Welcome to my small inn. I hope you find it comfortable."

"Your English is very good," I said. "Do you study?"

"Self-taught," he said. "Completely self-taught." And then, anticipating my next question, "Why? Why so good? Because I never had a fear of foreigners. Never. I don't have a complex. Most Japanese are afraid."

"Shy," I said.

"*Afraid,*" he insisted. "But why, of all people, did I not develop a complex? Why?" We sat back to consider this. It was a question he had clearly puzzled over for some time. "I have a theory," he said after a suitable pause. "When I was a child, Russian sailors would come into port. My father was involved in business, and the Russians often came to our house. My mother was very nervous; she would hide in the back room. But the Russians liked me, a little boy. Maybe they have children also back home. Who knows? They used to pick me up and speak to me. Big hands. Loud voices. I was so small a child. But I remember it very well. Looking up at them, at their faces. Sitting on their knee. Hearing their big Russian laughter. Maybe that is why. Maybe that is why I never developed a complex. That early experience broke the barrier."

I thought this was a fine theory, and we toasted it with Japanese vodka. My liver began whimpering again, but what the hell, how often do you have a chance to be enlightened by the likes of Mr. Saito, innkeeper and self-taught speaker of English in a Russian town on a Japanese island that was taken from Ainu natives?

Mr. Saito's wife stopped in and we chatted a bit in Japanese. Mr. Saito listened with a keen ear, and as soon as his wife excused herself, he leaned over and said to me—in what would be the first and only honest assessment I would ever receive of my second-language ability—"Your Japanese is terrible."

"Um." (What could I say?)

"Your accent is very thick. That is from living in Kyushu." (The idea being, I had been infected by living amidst such a poor dialect.) "Here in Hokkaido, everyone originally came from somewhere else. We soon lost our different accents. In Hokkaido, we speak Standard Japanese. Some people say that our Japanese is the finest in Japan. You should study *Hokkaido* Japanese. And you also need to study"— we consulted a dictionary for the right word—"the prepositions. You know *ga, wa, ni, de, no.* I was listening to you speak Japanese, and it sounds like you just put them in at random."

Damn. He was on to me. I hated Japanese prepositions. I hated them with a passion, and I did indeed use them at random, much like a slot machine, hoping they would occasionally come up correct. This had also been my approach to the feminine and masculine in French, just picking either *le* or *la* at random and crossing my fingers.

"Well, I would like to study Japanese more," I lied. "Someday, I'd like to become completely fluent."

"Fluent?" He raised an eyebrow. "No, no. Not fluent. Big mistake. We Japanese don't trust foreigners who speak our language perfectly. It makes us nervous. You should improve your Japanese, but never, *never* become completely fluent."

I promised him I wouldn't. "But only if you insist," I said.

I was shown to my room. It was dormitory-style with four bunk beds and crisp sheets freshly turned down. The only other occupant that night was a large, sad-eyed beanbag of a man. He was in Hakodate for some unspecified reason and was clearly not happy with being placed in the same room as a foreigner. He put on a brave face, he even smiled at me in a sorrowful, fatalistic way, but when he battened down for the night I noticed he carefully drew his bags in around him and hid his wallet under his pillow. Not to be outdone, I did the same thing with my bags—just to let him know that I was perfectly aware of what was going on. (This is how wars start.)

Travel fatigue hit me in a wave of yawns and sighs, and I fell into sleep like a body down a well. It was a deep, rich, chocolate sort of slumber, and it lasted all of—oh, ten minutes, before I was jolted awake by the sound of an asthmatic seagull being throttled to death by a mad bagpiper. It was my roommate. He was snoring. *Loudly.* So loudly, the walls were being sucked inward with each inhalation and bulging outward with each exhalation. In between, he made this high-pitched gawking sound that set my nerves on edge. I wrapped a pillow around my head, and I was considering my options—murder, madness, insomnia—when the man stopped breathing. Entirely. I had heard of sleep apnea, but this was alarming. It lasted for long, agonizing minutes and now, damn it all to hell, I couldn't sleep because of the silence. (It's hard to drift off when you may be sharing a room with a corpse.) A few minutes later he started breathing again with a startled gasp, and I relaxed ever so slightly. With a mumbled moan, he rolled over and began releasing farts into the blankets like depth charges.

I had horrible symbolic dreams, and I woke before sunrise. I got dressed—quietly at first and then, remembering the ordeal my roommate had put me through, loudly and with much crashing about and whistling—and walked out, into the city.

3

EARLY MORNING in Hakodate. Even the very air was drowsy. I walked down among some brick warehouses as the dawn slowly filled with sounds and smells: traffic, trolley bells, car exhaust. I ended up in the city's morning market, a large, low-ceilinged building stuffed with stalls and wet smells. You could buy anything you wanted at the Hakodate market, as long as it had gills or was made of polyester.

A woman in a rubber apron, rubber gloves, rubber boots, and—for all I know—rubber underwear was hosing down a sheaf of freshly caught fish. There was that smell—that smell of fish. It fills your mouth. It's like breathing cod liver oil. "Tasty, *ne!*" exclaimed an old lady behind me, scanning the fish with a greedy eye.

Right next to the fish stall was a stand selling sweets. Is that bad market research or what? Kind of like putting a perfume factory downwind from a sewage treatment plant. I had a cup of green tea at the sweets shop, but it tasted like fish.

The further I ventured into the market, the thicker became the crowds and the narrower the lanes between stalls. Women examined floppy octopi with the critical gaze of connoisseurs. I saw every sort of slimy sea creature imaginable slopped up on tables and carefully appraised. Voices rattled and echoed under the corrugated tin roof, voices haggled, endlessly haggled, and bodies pushed past me on every turn. For the most part, Japanese markets are sorely disappointing. They are too restrained, too orderly, too reserved. But here, in the clutter and clutch of Hakodate, was a market worthy of the name. It was almost *Korean* in its exuberance and bad manners. I wandered through this smell-sodden arena like a sensory voyeur, taking in the sights, sounds, and malodorous tastes that hung in the air.

The building itself could not contain the sheer mass of the market, and shops spilled out on all sides the way that cotton will burst from an overstuffed pillow. I found a tiny café in a nook by the back alley and I decided to stop for exacting gastronomical reasons; namely, the woman behind the counter was beautiful. Stunningly beautiful.

The power of beauty to stop you dead in your tracks never ceases to amaze me. Here we were, perfect strangers, she and I, and yet my entire universe was suddenly focused on this woman. Her eyes were distant (sadly distant, I decided) and she looked as though she were perpetually on the verge of sighing. Her hair was a loose tumble of curls, an ode to a perm that didn't take, and her skin was as unblemished and smooth as warm honey. I saw myself leaping across the counter, sweeping her up in my arms, and then, reaching out for a vine placed there solely for this purpose, sailing off into the distance with her in my arms. The female urge to mother men is something that is often commented upon. The male urge to rescue women, equally as unrealistic, is one less noted. Yet here I was, no longer a lower-rung, corporate-kept English teacher in a grubby coffee shop, but Errol Flynn about to take flight. It was, it was—

"What do you want?" She was looking at me the way most people look upon drek.

"What is the least expensive thing you have?" I asked, and immediately regretted it. True, I was on a budget, but she didn't have to know that. "Or the most expensive," I said, desperately trying to salvage my dignity. "Either is fine."

I ordered pizza toast. "Nice shop you have here," I said as she went about her work. There was no response. Leaning in, I raised my voice. "I said, 'Nice shop you have—'"

"I heard you the first time. Here." She slapped down a slice of not-pizza-and-not-quite-toast. "Enjoy your meal." (I'm assuming she was being ironic.)

This woman had what writers call "a cold beauty," meaning she was beautiful but didn't respond when I tried to flirt with her.

"Well," I said as I got up to leave. "As an eccentric millionaire and close friend of Tom Cruise, I suppose I should be going."

But that isn't really what I said. I just mumbled some banality and left. She hadn't smiled once and had completely crushed my heart. For the rest of the afternoon, I kept burping up pizza fumes. It tasted a lot like fish.

4

THE HEART OF HAKODATE is the historic, time-battered
Motomachi District, which curves around the base of Mount
Hakodate. Mr. Saito, the innkeeper, insisted I borrow his wife's
bicycle to go sightseeing, and it was a good thing too. The Old Town
is spread out over a far enough distance to make walking tiresome.

"Just make sure you lock the bike whenever you park it. The
Russians are in port today."

"The Russians?"

"They steal bicycles. They take them back to Russia and sell
them. Sometimes they even steal the tires off of cars. We have to be
very careful whenever they're in town."

Jeez. From thermonuclear superpower to bicycle thieves; no
wonder the Russian hardliners are so pissed off. I assured Mr. Saito
that I would indeed watch out for nefarious bands of spanner-
wielding Russkis, and I set off.

What a wonderful place. Cobblestone streets. A beautiful Greek
Orthodox church, rising up in onion domes and spires. Winding
alleyways. Faded glory. Knocked about, meandering—Hakodate
wore its past like an old sweater. Even better, I now had a choice of
three gears: slow, very slow, and really very slow. This was a vast
improvement over the previous rent-a-bikes I had used.

I bicycled down to a crumbling old wharf where the smell of the
sea permeated the very wood and where houses were falling into
ruin, the windows cracked, the walls patched up. It was as though
the Japanese had moved into an eastern European city en masse. As
though Belgrade had been foreclosed by the bank and sold to
Japanese investors. I wobbled up and down the side streets. Parked

the bike and wandered into alleyways. Got lost. Got unlost. Got lost
again. It was like playing hide-and-seek with yourself.

A Russian man was having a futile conversation with a Japanese
store clerk over some sort of purchase. Russian is not an international language, nor is Japanese—neither is spoken much beyond
their borders—and this forced the two men to meet on neutral
ground: English. Or at least something that resembled something
that *might* have been mistaken for English.

Q: How much this is being two for each?
A: That have good tension for you. It gives four.

Q: Four? I am asking two for each.
A: Yes, yes. Many good for you.

I stood nearby eavesdropping on their increasingly surreal dialogue and tried to decide who was the worse speaker of English, the
Russian sailor or the Japanese clerk. It was hard to say. Kind of like
comparing infinity with infinity plus one.

Hakodate's prime cherry-blossom-viewing spot was at the city's
star-shaped fortress, where four thousand cherry trees were now
coming into bloom. More than one person heartily encouraged my
attendance in much the same way that people root for their home
team. *"Hakodate cherry blossoms rule! Go Hakodate!"*

Even better, for the first time since I set out, for the first time
ever, I was not assumed to be a Mormon or an American. Here in
Hakodate, everyone mistook me for Russian. I thought this was
splendid and to help it along I began speaking Japanese *with a
Russian accent.* This was more difficult than you'd think. Shop owners would narrow their eyes and ask me questions that were tinged
with suspicions waiting to be confirmed.

"Are you a sailor?" they'd ask.

"I am being from Vladivostok," I would say in what I hoped was
a suitably Slavic manner.

"Here on business?"

"*Nyet, nyet.* I am, how you say—" and here my voice would drop,
"—shopping."

"Shopping?"

"For bicycles."

It was all very entertaining, and I like to think I helped escalate international tensions ever so slightly, for which I am suitably proud.

I expanded the scope of my travels, venturing out to the international graveyards on the edge of town. There were several cemeteries to choose from: a well-kept Chinese graveyard; an overgrown Russian one; and a kind of miscellaneous, assorted-dead-foreigners one. It must be very sad to be a Belgian sailor or an Irish missionary and end your days here, dumped in the ground and categorized as "other." Normally, a visit to three graveyards in one afternoon would have left me pondering life, death, and my own (theoretical) mortality. But I was in too good a mood to let even a bunch of dead foreigners spoil it, and I bicycled back into town humming happy songs to myself.

The route I followed that day rambled across the map like an alley cat with Alzheimer's. I passed the Greek church several times, and at one point I came upon an imposing sign—in English—on a restored brick building:

> life design shop
> BLUE HOUSE
> live together with my sensitivity.
> we have abundant original for your enjoy
> life coordination.
> we, life design shop blue house,
> give aid to your self principle life style.

As near as I could figure, BLUE HOUSE was either a fashion-consulting agency or a New Age cult of some sort. Either way, I decided that my lifestyle was self-principled enough, thank you very much, and I didn't need to live together with anyone's sensitivity. Still, it was heartwarming to think of the Japanese and the Russians working together on that sign, translating from one language to the other and then back again before finally coming up with this ode to miscommunication. I pedalled away, uplifted by the thought of it.

—

Having criss-crossed Hakodate all morning, I was now ravenously hungry. I saw several places advertising themselves as "Biking Restaurants," which I took as an odd sort of specialty: cuisine geared toward cyclists. It wasn't until I peered into half a dozen of these places that I finally figured it out. *Biking* was actually the Japanese pronunciation of *viking*. Vikings ate at rowdy, communal tables laden with food. Hence, if you can follow the logic, "biking" is any large buffet-style meal. (Is it any wonder that no one understands what the hell the Japanese are talking about?) I found one Biking Restaurant that called itself the King of Kings, and—ignoring the theological implications—I went inside and gorged myself on an all-you-can-eat meat bar. That's right: *all-you-can-eat meat*. And they let *me* in. It was not a pretty sight. The manager and waitresses cowered in the corner, the other customers fled, and the cook came out and began frantically shovelling slabs of beef and lamb directly into my mouth. Every now and then I would lean back to drain a flagon of ale and roar, "More meat! Hahahahaha! *More meat!*" They had obviously never seen a real Viking sit down for a meal before, and I waddled out an hour later, satisfied beyond gluttony and having pushed the King of Kings to the point of bankruptcy.

"Come again," said the waitresses in quavering voices, fearing that I might take them up on the offer yet still bound by protocol to make it.

"Oh, I will," I said, my mouth still full, as I chewed on my last handful of sheep's flank. "I will indeed. *Hahahahahaha!*"

5

IT IS A TESTAMENT to Japanese engineering that the Hakodate cable car managed to get my heavy body up the mountain. It cost a small fortune, but I was in no condition to walk. I forked out a pile of yen and climbed on.

As the cable car groaned under my weight, I looked out across the city as the evening lights began to blink on. Hakodate's night view, it turns out, has been officially designated as one of the "Three Best City Night Views in Japan" (the other two are in Kobe and Nagasaki). Earlier in the day, however, the chap at the Hakodate Tourist Board had said in a hushed aside that really, "The night view of Hakodate is one of the best three—*in the world*—right after Naples and Hong Kong." Had he been to Naples? No. Hong Kong? No. But he had seen pictures.

Either way, Hakodate by night is magnificent, if not for the scope or brilliance, then for its striking shape. The city is built on a low neck of land, an isthmus actually, and the lights are funnelled in at the middle like an hourglass. The reflections glimmer upon water on both sides. It looks like a river of lights. Like a cup of jewels spilled. Like a wineglass filled with electric rhinestones. Like—like a woman's waist. Yes, I tilted my head and squinted my eyes. (The same technique I used to descramble adult videos.) Yes, definitely. It looked like a ruby-studded corset, slipping from a woman's body, it looked like— I stopped and cleared my throat.

"Well, then," I said as I turned and walked along the observatory platform in a jaunty way, humming lively tunes. "What a nice view!" But it was no use. In the shadows, in the corners, furtive in the half-light, I could see young, hormonally inflamed couples entwined in knots of limbs. At night, Japanese youth transform themselves into Parisians.

The Hakodate Night-viewing Observatory looked like a telescope pad used for stargazing, except, instead of stars, the gaze was directed downward, toward the city, adding to the voyeuristic atmosphere. I was standing there in the cold air, watching the night deepen and the lights become brighter, when a young woman slid up beside me.

She was staring out intently at the city lights. I sent ESP waves of charm toward her, but she evidently had her radar deflectors up. So, on the count of three, I turned and said, in a friendly-yet-exotic, American sort of way, "Hi there!"

She returned my greeting like a limp volleyball and walked away, leaving me to set, leap, and spike to an empty court. Hakodate women, I decided, were very cold.

6

MR. SAITO hailed my return with a hearty "Hello!" His face was red and he clutched a bottle of Japanese vodka in one hand and a glass in the other. "I've been drinking," he said, superfluously. "Come!" he cried. "Have some sea crabs. I caught them today when I went fishing." A steaming tray was set before him. "I wasn't even looking for crab; they just crawled into my pail. Can you imagine such luck? Good luck for me. Bad luck for the crabs." He laughed and laughed and handed me a plate.

I loathe crab. But I couldn't think of any way to decline his offer, which was generous to a fault, so I sidled up to the table and Mr. Saito, with a scholarly air, proceeded to teach me the correct way to eat them, which, if done properly, is horrible and messy and more than a little barbaric. First, he wrenched off the legs—the *hairy* legs (did you know crabs have hairy legs?)—and demonstrated how to suck the meat out. He then cracked open the backs and showed me the proper way to scoop out the (thankfully) small brains, which you lick from your fingers like pâté. "But we don't eat the lungs," he said as he removed the tiny flaps and discarded them. Why not? Well, that would be gross.

I have never felt fully comfortable eating anything that looks like a giant mutated cockroach, but with enough vodka to wash it down, I was able to eat most of my crab. Then, like a bad joke, Mr. Saito produced another. And another. The brain-scooping and lung-discarding began anew.

"Drink! Drink!" he urged. He then topped up my glass with *shōchū*, a form of alcohol so pure it shows up on some Periodic Tables.

"Someday," he threatened, "I will introduce shōchū to your country."

Fortunately, I didn't have to eat the rest of the crab because another guest arrived, a tall, gregarious American named Donner. Donner had missed a flight to Sapporo and when he tried to check into a nearby hotel, the owners had frantically fobbed him off on Mr. Saito, whose English ability was well known in the neighbourhood.

Donner was an entrepreneur. He had a smile as clean and wide as the Great Outdoors, and he had been doing business with the Japanese for almost four years. "I don't speak Japanese," he said, reciting a pet quip, "but I do speak Loud English."

Over crab and shōchū, Donner regaled us with his various misadventures in the import/export business. He had that brash confidence Americans seem to exude. "Have my card," he said, and like a blackjack dealer in a Nevada bar he pulled out a stack and dealt me one. "I have connections. Lots of connections. Japan," he said. "Tough country. Lotsa red tape. But well worth the effort. Well worth it. Profits. Huge profits. Profits the size of—of—" He couldn't come up with a metaphor big enough. "As big as—well, you know. A lot of money. Big money. You should get involved. Teaching English? Chump change. The real profit is in imports."

On and on it went, like a personal self-help video. And when he announced suddenly that he was tired (it was as though he had *decided* when he would get sleepy) a vacuum of silence followed his departure. In my heart of hearts—and oh, how I hate to admit it— I sort of, almost, *like* Americans.

"Tell me," said Mr. Saito after Donner's departure. "What did you think of Hakodate? Did you go up the mountain? Did you see the night view?"

I had indeed. He was pleased to hear this.

"There is a theory," said Mr. Saito, "a common theory, that we can understand a person by the way they look at the lights of Hakodate." It was a bit like a Rorschach test. "Some people see an hourglass: they are thinking about life and how short it is, how time passes. Other people see a fan opening up: they are very high-culture people. Others see a wineglass. Some see a river. Tell me, Mr. Will, what did *you* see?"

"What did I see?"

"Yes, when you looked at the lights of Hakodate. What did you see?"

"Ah, what you said, a river. A wineglass. That sort of thing."

He saluted my good tastes. But when he tried to foist off more crab legs on me, I pleaded extenuating circumstances. "I'm still full from King of Kings."

King of Kings? He knew the place quite well. He was friends with the owner. When I told him about the vast amount of meat I had packed away, Mr. Saito shouted with laughter. "You didn't tell him you were staying here, did you? Did you?"

"I might have."

"Oh, no!" said Mr. Saito. "I'll have to buy him a new cow just to reimburse him!" He laughed so long at this that his face became even redder, almost purple. He laughed so long he forgot what he was laughing about.

The shōchū and beer continued, and the more we drank, the more disjointed and incoherent the conversation became. Somehow we ended up talking about the war. Why does this always happen? Again, is it just me, or does every heart-to-heart talk in Japan always end up focusing on the Second World War? I wasn't even a corny pickup line in my father's repertoire when that war started. What do I know about the Second World War?

Japanese knowledge is even worse. In Japan, the bombing of Hiroshima is treated as though it were a baffling, unprovoked attack. As though the innocent Japanese were sitting around, minding their own business, when *wham!* out of the blue, the Americans decided to obliterate them. In China, meanwhile, the Rape of Nanking (dismissed as a "myth" by Japanese apologists) left more people dead than Hiroshima; and the Japanese army did it the hard way. They butchered, tortured, and raped the citizens of Nanking one victim at a time.

"I'll tell you why the Americans bombed Hiroshima and Nagasaki," said Mr. Saito. "It's because they didn't consider Asians to be human. That's why they never would have done it to a white country."

"But they couldn't have. Germany had already surrendered by the time the bomb was ready."

"There is no excuse for what happened in Hiroshima and Nagasaki, no excuse!" His voice had a sudden snap to it, and a cold fury cut through the alcoholic haze. He looked at me with a rage that was directed outward at every angle, to all points of the compass. One shouldn't talk about the war in Japan. This is one of the first rules of conversation. Every family has a litany of sorrows and a closet filled with skeletons. As often as not, Southeast Asian skeletons.

I knew this, and yet I continued anyway. Mr. Saito and I argued well into the night, arguing for the sake of arguing, like a pair of Talmudic scholars debating some fine, esoteric, and utterly irrelevant point. And nothing we said that night changed history in the least.

7

I WOKE to the familiar sound of bongo drums being played across my cranium. Death by Hangover once again loomed large as the probable outcome of my irresolute lifestyle. My journey was coming to an end, but I wasn't so much cruising to a finale as I was limping toward the finish line. I figured: Cape Sōya and then three weeks in a hospital getting a blood transfusion.

It had been decided the night before that Mr. Saito, against my better judgment and constant urging, would drive me out to the Hakodate ferry port for the arrival of the Aomori ferry. "Most of the passengers will be driving all the way to Sapporo," he reasoned. "If you hitchhike right in front of the off-ramp, you will surely get a ride."

"But what if I don't get a ride? I'll be stranded way out of town."

"That's true. What you need is a sign," he said, and he cut up a cardboard box. "This will do nicely." He reached for a felt-tip marker.

"But I've made it this far without a sign. Signs can actually *hurt* your chances in Japan. People think they should stop only if they are going to the exact destination you are holding up. One time, a Japanese friend of mine—"

"Now then," he said with the air of a man who knows his way around the world. "You must, how do you say it, *reassure* the drivers. So, let's first write your name, so they know who you are—" and in wide, thick Japanese letters he wrote HELLO EVERYBODY! I AM WILLY FROM AMERICA.

"Now then." He sat back to consider this. He had been drinking, so the letters looked a little crooked and poorly spaced, something

like a schoolchild would write. When I commented on this, he was
unfazed. "It will help you, see? Because they will think you wrote it
yourself. Very cute."

He thought a moment and said, "Now we must reassure them
that you can speak Japanese a little." So he wrote I CAN SPEAK JAPAN-
ESE A LITTLE. "And we must let them know where you are going." So
he added, PLEASE TAKE ME TO SAPPORO.

He frowned at this, and then added, I AM AN ENGLISH
TEACHER. And then, I CAME ALL THE WAY FROM KYUSHU. A pause.
REALLY, I DID.

He ended with THANK YOU VERY MUCH. I AM SORRY TO BOTHER
YOU, and then held it up for me to admire.

By this point the cardboard was completely filled with characters,
which got progressively smaller and more cramped as they neared
the bottom of the page, much like the listings posted before a sumo
tournament. In tiny English letters he scrawled across the bottom,
let's be international friends!

HELLO EVERYBODY!

I AM WILLY FROM AMERICA.

I CAN SPEAK JAPANESE A LITTLE.

PLEASE TAKE ME TO SAPPORO.

I AM AN ENGLISH TEACHER.

I CAME ALL THE WAY FROM KYUSHU.

REALLY, I DID.

THANK YOU VERY MUCH.

I AM SORRY TO BOTHER YOU

let's be international friends!

This wasn't a sign, this was a short story. It looked bad enough when
I was tipsy, but the next morning, when I found it tucked in with my
bags, it looked even more illegible and more bizarre. I discarded it as
soon as Mr. Saito was out of sight.

He was right about the ferry traffic. They *were* all heading north
toward Sapporo. But not with me. I watched with that sinking yet
oddly familiar sense of dismay that overcomes travellers with bright
schemes as car after car filed off like cattle down a chute, thumping
across the ramp, across the terminal parking lot, and then out to the

highway. No one stopped or even seemed to notice me. Perhaps I should have held up Mr. Saito's sign after all. Perhaps I should have juggled and danced. Perhaps I should have set my hair on fire and sung "Ave Maria." But I doubt any of that would have helped. I was stranded in an industrial park, miles from the train tracks, on the opposite side of the peninsula from where I wanted to be.

I walked for hours. I walked across long endless anonymous tracks of pavement, past equally anonymous houses, through a series of identical intersections, none of which were the least bit Japanese or exotic or memorable. The landscape was shaggy. The fields were shaggy. Everything was shaggy.

On a map, the highway I wanted to reach looked very near, but the reality of the matter was just so much drudgery. It was only after I examined my maps for the third time that I realized the road I was walking on, Highway 227, did not intersect with the road I wanted, Highway 5, but actually ran *parallel* to it. I had been walking alongside Highway 5 for hours.

Spouting such witticisms as "Fuck! Fuck! Fuck!" I took a short walk across some shaggy-looking, unkempt fields and soon found myself on Highway 5. I was on the outskirts of Nanae Town, which was—and here's an interesting coincidence—exactly the town I had planned on taking a train to before Mr. Saito talked me into going to the ferry port instead. In fact, just as I arrived, the very train I would have caught went rolling by at a zippy speed.

There is nothing like wasting an entire morning to put you in the proper frame of mind. I came to Onokayama Station just as a torrent of black-suited junior-high-school students came pouring out in a barrage of *"Harro's!"* and *"Zis is a ben's."*

"Piss off," I said with a growl.

The streets leading into Nanae Town were wide and flanked with tall, leafy trees. Shaggy trees. A bicycle-and-pedestrian path ran down either side of the road, making it a perfect spot for hitching rides. And so it proved. The tenth car pulled over.

Inside was a man not much older than I, dressed in a corduroy jacket and wearing a relaxed smile. His hair was slightly shaggy.

I was bracing myself for something like, "I'm only going to the end of this block, can I let you off at the next tree?" when he said, "Sapporo?"

One ride. All the way from Hakodate to Sapporo. *One ride.* It almost made up for my mindless trek across the barrenlands. I congratulated myself on being such an astute world traveller and climbed in.

8

IT WAS A DEAD-STRAIGHT, cruise-control highway of the type I hadn't seen since Canada. We blew down it like a rocket in a wind tunnel. "You know," said Takayuki, rather proudly, "Hokkaido has the highest number of traffic fatalities in Japan."

"Really? But the roads are so wide and straight," I said.

"Exactly. It is easy to fall asleep at the wheel or lose control on corners. It's too fast. Too few obstacles. Drivers become relaxed. A lot of people die."

This is not the sort of thing you want to hear when you are hitching rides.

Takayuki worked for a drugstore north of Sapporo, and within moments of introducing himself he had invited me back to his home to meet his family. A few weeks ago I would have accepted, but my funds were dangerously low, the clock was ticking, and my final destination was too near to allow—or enjoy—a leisurely detour.

Takayuki Ideta, I realized, was a perfectly normal Japanese man. He had a wife, two kids, a house, a car. He wore a necktie and he liked baseball. "You are normal," I said.

"Yes?"

"Average."

"Yes?"

"You are the first normal, average person who has picked me up."

This bothered him. "Well, I suppose I am normal—but I'm not so average." And for the rest of the trip he wore a slightly furrowed brow.

Highway 5 is a magnificent road to travel along. It skirts the edge of Uchiura Bay, and we could see right across its cold, clear waters.

Bamboo grass, thick and leafy—shaggy, really—had choked out other plants. It was everywhere. It overran abandoned farms and spilled over the edge of the road. It grew in trellises up telephone wires and it hung in vines around the poles. In southern Hokkaido, land is not so much cleared as it is wrestled free from bamboo grass. It was like a plague of crabgrass. It was *Day of the Triffids* in slow motion.

I couldn't get used to the sense of size. Everything seemed wide and open and thin on the ground. There was breathing space, elbow room, a landscape to look *through*. Nothing cramped the view, and the sky was grand and theatrical. The air seemed cleaner, too— alpine, chilled. If Hokkaido were a bottle, it would have cold condensation running down the sides.

Communities were spaced out along the bay like a supply line, small towns hugging the shore. On an island without typhoons, the homes of Hokkaido were built up against the sea. In Kyushu, they would have been washed away.

An American flag snapped in the wind as we passed through Yukumo, and I had trouble remembering where we were; my frame of reference kept slipping. The notes I took read like a drive through the foothills of my youth: *birch trees, red barns, round silos, rolling pastures, ranch-houses, chicken coops*. Men in baggy jeans. Farmers driving tractors down the road, holding up traffic. I felt right at home.

At Lake Tōya, behind a rim of mountains, there was a stark reminder that I was still in Japan, that I was still on an archipelago formed like molten pewter along a soldering joint, islands on the borders of tectonic plates: here at Lake Tōya were two very dramatic, very active volcanoes. They rose up in hammerheads, they grumbled and complained, and occasionally they coughed—deep, wet chest coughs. In 1977, Usuzan, the larger of the two, erupted, destroying a cable car and showering the lake, the valley, and the town with pyroclastic loam. The water went sludgy for weeks and volcanic mud washed up along the shore.

The smaller of the two volcanoes, Shōwa-shinzan, first sputtered out of a farmer's field back in 1943. The steaming, bubbling hole grew and grew, burning off the fields and forcing the people in the area to retreat. Today it stands at 402 metres. The lake itself is in a crater formed by a prehistoric volcanic eruption. Tōya was shrouded in mist the day I came through.

"It is a cold country," said Takayuki. "But the people are warm. I have two children, Masahiro and Satoshi, and I am glad that they will grow up in Hokkaido. It is freer. Cleaner."

We went west into the highlands, where the fields lay fallow, spread out like squares of textiles: rough canvas, unironed cotton, thick felt. Farmhouses were set high on hillocks and in among groves of trees. Takayuki was in no particular hurry to get to Sapporo, and he drove me from farm to farm, carefully pointing out which were the horses and which were the cows. "Cow," he would say. "Cow. Cow. Horse."

Then, rising up from the flatlands was Mount Yōtei, the Northern Fuji. The peak disappeared into the overcast sky.

"It's beautiful," I said, and Takayuki smiled. "The Northern Fuji," he said, more to himself than to me.

There are countless such "Fujis" across Japan, and I have seen easily half a dozen of them, so many in fact that I once referred, in jest, to Minamata City's small hill, Nakaoyama, as "the Minamata Fuji." I was taken aback when my friends took me seriously. "Yes," said one. "The Minamata Fuji. I suppose it is." Very little irony in Japan.

Of the various Fujis I have seen, the only one which lived up to its name was the verdant, perfect cone of Mount Kaimon in southern Kagoshima. The peak of Mount Kaimon rises up, green against the sea, lush and perfectly symmetrical—and quite unlike the *real* Mount Fuji, which is in essence a large scrap pile of volcanic scree. The real Fuji, with the traffic clattering by and the disgrace of factories cluttered around her hem, is dreary. Mount Fuji looks better the farther away you go. From a train, say, or, even better, on a postcard. From an airplane, it is positively stunning. (Mind you, I may be biased. I slogged my way up Mount Fuji in a fog bank, and the view from the top was about the same as you'd get if you stuffed your head in a sack of flour.)

We stopped for some of Mount Yōtei's health-restoring waters, available in conveniently priced bottles marked "health-restoring water," and Takayuki filled his tank with gasoline.

I made a feeble I'll-pay type of gesture (hands patting pockets as though searching for a wallet), but my offer was generously declined. And a good thing, too. In Japan, you might as well be filling your tank with cognac or fine perfume for the amount of money you are paying.

We came down onto the central plains, and the city of Sapporo glowed gold in the distance.

9

SAPPORO IS TOKYO NORTH, a vast, glittering love affair in the heart of Hokkaido. Sapporo is where all roads lead. I arrived at dusk and checked into the Washington Hotel, into a room without a window, and then hit the streets. I was elated. A new night, a different city. It reminded me of an axiom that Jim Drawbell, a friend of the family, used to live by: *If you are in an interesting area, in a place you have never been before, and you have twenty bucks in your pocket—you own the world.*

Night is good to Sapporo. The glass buildings shimmer, the crowds flutter past, and neon spills out in pools of light. The city has 1.7 million people in it, yet it doesn't feel crowded in the least. The streets are wide and straight; the addresses are logical—a rarity in Japan—and the main boulevard evokes images of Buenos Aires, Dallas, Houston, Calgary. Anywhere but here.

There is a reason for this. The city was laid out by an American architect. Sapporo is as American as Hakodate is Russian; there are touches everywhere, from the spacious layout to the height of the buildings, from the gaudy Pachinko USA to the splashy Hollywood Shop ("USA Movie Character Goods"), from the glass and steel to the kids with Stars 'n' Stripes tote bags.

Which makes it odd, yet inevitable, that Sapporo's most highly touted symbol would be a small clocktower, tucked in behind modern structures. It is the city's only surviving example of Russian architecture. I walked out to see this landmark, was suitably underwhelmed, and then retraced my steps back to the city's nefarious Susukino District.

Susukino is one of Japan's largest, liveliest nightlife zones. A mix of family entertainment, teenage game centres, rowdy pubs, overpriced discos, and sanitized brothels, it is all things to all people. I couldn't afford another night on the town—either financially or physically—but I could wander at will and marvel once again at the vitality of the Japanese urban night. And with my senses still humming, I returned to the windowless rooms of my hotel.

That night, I dreamt of Buddha.

He was standing beside the highway and he was holding up a sign. It read: *Hello, everybody. I am the Buddha. Please don't kill me.* Then, just when I reached him, he drove off in a small Toyota car.

There is a Zen saying: "If you meet the Buddha on the road, kill him!" This is why I gave up on Zen. It was simply too provocative a statement, one that seemed painfully contrived, like replying to the question "What is the Buddha?" with the answer "Dried dung." (An actual exchange between Zen monks.)

If you meet the Buddha on the road, kill him. Reams of commentary have been written about this statement, much of it of the esoteric angels-on-the-head-of-a-pin variety. Endless interpretations are possible. Semantics are dissected. Debates are waged. It is argued that the Buddha is not a real person but a state of mind, a catalyst to Enlightenment. If you think you have met the Buddha, you haven't. The Buddha you can see is not the real Buddha; it is an illusion. Destroy it. Other interpretations have been less esoteric: It *is* the Buddha you meet on the road, and he *must* be killed. Why? Because you have to move beyond the realm of opposites, beyond Thou and I, beyond subject and object. Beyond even the Buddha.

One thing that has always puzzled me about Zen, and indeed most Eastern paths to enlightenment, is that it always ends up back where it started. The boy searches for his ox. He finds it. The world disappears . . . and then he returns to the market, to the everyday. If Zen Buddhism is about the everyday, why depart in the first place? Why not simply enjoy the flow of characters who enter and depart, the moments that come and go?

If life is an illusion, maybe the illusion is not all that bad. Maybe the illusion *is* life. Maybe the solution is not breaking through, but pulling back, learning to embrace the illusion, learning to accept the transient world around us, learning to live among mirages.

If you meet the Buddha on the road, do not kill him. Hold out your thumb. Who knows, he might just offer you a ride.

10

SAPPORO CONSIDERS ITSELF one of the "Three Great Brewery Cities in the World," the other two being Milwaukee and Munich. You know it's true because the Hokkaido Tourist Board said so, and why would they lie?

Central Japan may be the land of saké, and southern Japan the birthplace of shōchū, but in the heart of Hokkaido it is beer that reigns supreme. The Sapporo Brewery, established in 1876, is the oldest in Japan. They produce a light blond lager that sparkles in the mouth and reconfirms my belief in God. Even better, the brewery gives free samples when you take a tour. Free tour. Free beer. Which is to say, I decided in the interest of cultural appreciation to visit the site.

I didn't understand a damn thing. There were no English explanations and I tagged along with a handful of visiting Tokyoites who had the annoying habit of saying "Is that so?" every time the guide opened her mouth. "Good afternoon, my name is Ariko." "Is that so?"

I didn't know, or want to know, the Japanese words for yeast, barley, malt, or fermentation. All I wanted was the free samples, and sure enough, once we had toured the historic red-brick building, we were seated in a hall and given a selection of beer to taste. "Excellent!" said I. "Enlightening!"

So good was the beer—and Japan makes some of the best lagers—I decided to take another tour. And another, by which time it was becoming very familiar. Same swollen copper vats, same long hallways, same tour guide, same nods, same *Sō desu ka?*'s And more beer. It was wonderful. So wonderful, I decided to go through a fourth time. But there was no one else in line, and when the guide saw me staggering up, she gave me a wry half-smile and said, "You again?"

"Is very interesting," I replied, trying not to wobble too much.

She cast a scolding look at me, the type women reserve for men who think they are being awfully clever but aren't. She was dressed in a trim red blazer and a stewardess-type hat, but she wasn't giggly or girlie at all. Her smile was ruthlessly intelligent. "Do you really want to take the tour again?" she said. "Is that really why you keep coming back?"

"Well," I said, "we could skip the tour."

She looked down at her wristwatch. "Let's just walk through it," she said. "We can talk."

I ended up spending most of the afternoon with her. She thought I kept going through the tour because I had a crush on her, and I was careful not to inform her otherwise. "I get off in twenty minutes," she said. "Meet me at the main gate."

Now, I would like to say Ariko and I drove through Sapporo in a sports car with the wild wind in our hair, spilling champagne and laughing with carefree abandon, before retiring to my hotel room (which had somehow sprouted both a view and a canopy bed) to make mad, passionate love for hours. But we didn't. What we did do was go for coffee. And we talked late into the night, sharing small confidences and comparing the separate tangents of our lives. She had been to Australia, had seen every Audrey Hepburn movie ever made—twice—and she enjoyed being a tour guide. She didn't love it, but it was all right. "You do get tired of beer after a while," she said, a statement beyond my frame of reference, akin to getting tired of air.

Ariko had a single dimple, which only appeared when she frowned or when she sat back to consider something. She was, of course, beautiful. But one gets so used to seeing beautiful women in Japan that it hardly seems notable after a while. A female friend of mine made a similar observation about California, of all places, where she got so used to seeing tanned, trim, tousle-haired men that after a while they hardly registered. Ariko looked me over and said she liked my eyes, about the only good feature I have. "Blue," she said, "like ice."

I always find it odd when other people find me exotic. It is a strange world indeed. I went back to my room in a very cheerful mood, singing my new theme song, "A Hitchhiker on the Road to Love" (Bobby Curtola, circa 1959).

My burgeoning idyll with Ariko seemed destined to turn into something more—until reality in all its pustule-pocked, wart-infested, joy-destroying majesty came bursting back on the scene. Ariko and I promised to meet again the next day (she invited me to her apartment to hear recordings of Ainu music, and needless to say I suddenly became *very* interested in Ainu music), but my time was running out as quickly as sand through a glass. Back in the real world, the *non*-travel world, I was caught up in this odd arrangement whereby I agreed to spend all day doing things that were unbearably dull and monotonous for which I was compensated financially, much in the manner of a sea lion being rewarded with a halibut. Perhaps you've heard of this concept; it's called a "job." I have never really grasped the logic behind the system, but I did know that losing one's "job" could have dire consequences in the food and shelter departments. I had already used up my paid holidays at this point, and most of my sick days, and I had even cancelled two weeks of company classes. When I called my supervisor from Sapporo, hoping to extend my furlough just a few more days—in the interests of a brewing romance, so to speak—the reception was chilled, to say the least. I practically got frostbite of the ear from the receiver. "One week," I was told. "One week, and if you are not back at your desk we will have to"—and here is where it got scary—"reconsider our options." When a Japanese company says they are going to reconsider their options, the only thing you can do is fall to your knees and beg for mercy and forgiveness.

One week. That's all I had. One week to get up to Cape Sōya and then back to Sapporo in time to catch a flight to Kyushu, but not before—please God please—I had a chance to consummate my relationship with Ariko. With any luck, by the time I got back to Sapporo, the cherry blossoms would be in bloom. (My mind was already feverishly churning up images of Ariko and me entwined on a bed of sakura.)

In my cell-like hotel, where all the rooms looked inward, I laid out several maps across the bed and counted off the mileage. My heart sank in a cesspool of despair. It couldn't be done. Even someone as cartographically challenged as I could see that. I'd be lucky to make Cape Sōya at all. In fact, I had to leave Sapporo *right now!* Swallowing the pain, I called Ariko and cancelled our date (talk about frostbite of the ear). The irony was worthy of an Alanis Morissette riff: It's like a chance for a fling, when you're already late. *Isn't it ironic.* Just when everything was going my way, I had to leave, proving once again that God can be a real bastard when He wants to be.

I left Sapporo in an understandably foul mood, taking a subway to the end of the line at Azabu Station and then walking out to Highway 231. It was already late in the day, and I wanted to clear the city and reach open country by nightfall.

Ariko didn't stay angry. She even tried to keep in touch, and for a while I received postcards and letters in carefully printed English, with the *a*'s written like those on a typewriter, with the curly bit on top. Ariko's English was pieced together like the words in a ransom note, the phrases and expressions pasted up in long, interminable strings that only occasionally made sense. "Please, many times thinking this season? Take care the hot weather."

I dabbled in fantasies: flying back to Sapporo, showing up at her door in a black cape and a Zorro mask, with a bottle of wine and two tickets to ANYWHERE clutched in my hand. But Ariko didn't need rescuing. That may have been part of the problem. She was a funny, confident, level-headed person. She liked her life and she wasn't looking for an escape hatch. I was looking for: Someone to rescue. Someone to sweep up and carry away. Someone to save.

I never answered Ariko's letters.

11

THE ISHIKARI RIVER reaches the sea in a lacklustre fashion. Slow and silted, it threads its way aimlessly through sand dunes before fanning out into a lonely, windswept delta. A red-and-white-striped lighthouse peered above the dunes and grassy hills. The waves rolled in. And low across the horizon, the sun was setting fire to the sky.

"I like it here," said Mr. Tawaraya. "It calms your mind."

Mr. Tawaraya, a quiet, elderly man, had stopped for me on the highway and taken me here—to the Ishikari delta. It was his favourite spot.

Forget Zen, I thought. Forget the mindless, repetitive rituals, the monasteries, the nonsense koans; all one needs is a windy cape, solitude, and a mind that needs calming.

So taken was I with this spot that I decided to spend the night under the protective windbreak of a grassy dune. When I pulled my pack from the back of his truck, Mr. Tawaraya became adamant. No, this wouldn't do, camping out on a beach miles from the nearest town. We wrangled over this awhile and I relented only when he began citing imaginary weather forecasts. "The rains are coming," he said in his best Old Testament voice. "Heavy rains." He hinted darkly at flash floods, fierce winds, ants, snakes, and—

"Snakes? Did you say snakes?"

We drove up the coast, looking for an inn. Mr. Tawaraya took a detour through the sand-swept streets of Ishikari Town, but the place was deserted, as though the entire population had headed out on caravan, leaving signs creaking in the wind and televisions flickering behind curtained windows. This wasn't a town, this was the *Mary Celeste*. For some reason, we were speaking in whispers.

A jogger suddenly appeared and sprinted past, down the blue-dusk streets of Ishikari, knees chopping the air, arms keeping time like a metronome. On the back of his jacket, in sharp, stylized letters, was the message JAPAN OLYMPIC SKI TEAM.

To my horror, Mr. Tawaraya drove up beside him, rolled down the window, and—as we crept slowly alongside—tried to speak to the man. "Excuse me, but my friend is looking for a room and I was wondering—"

The jogger was immediately pissed off. "Don't know," he said as he tried desperately not to lose his rhythm.

"Yes," said Mr. Tawaraya. "But you see, we were—"

"I don't know," said the exasperated young man—who did indeed look very Olympian, I must say.

"Well," said Mr. Tawaraya, as we continued to drive slowly along-side him. "We thought maybe you lived in the area and—"

"Sapporo," said the man, breathing harder, jogging faster. "Came from Sapporo."

"You don't say? You ran all the way from Sapporo, imagine that. Well, sorry to bother you. Please do your best." We accelerated away from him, but it was too late, the runner faltered and lost his stride. I looked back and saw him walking in a circle, hands on his hips, cursing.

The incident reminded me, oddly enough, of my grandmother, a wonderful old dear who passed away during my first year in Japan. One of my strongest memories of her involves hitchhiking. I was fourteen years old and Grandma was taking me down to see a chiro-practor in the town of Peace River. (I had buggered up my neck by catching an unannounced football with the back of my head.) You have to understand that this stretch of northern Canadian highway is nothing but trees, mosquitoes, muskeg, and moose. It is as wild as the Alaskan Highway, but with less traffic. As we drove down a steep hill, there beside the road was a hitchhiker, a long-haired, head-banded young man with a guitar slung over his back. This in itself was not remarkable. The North is scattered with the remains of romantic cretins who think they can hitch north and live off the land. It is a one-sided romance, alas, because the North doesn't exactly love them back with the same simple-minded sincerity. Those hippies who managed to survive usually left bitter and disap-pointed; there is nothing Rousseauian or utopian about the North.

This young man waved his thumb and, to my utter and profound amazement, Grandma pulled over. Grandma *never* stopped for hitchhikers. Yet here she was signalling right and turning onto the side of the road—slowly. Grandma needed at least a quarter-mile any time she wanted to come to a complete stop; she tended to eschew brakes and simply let air resistance and dwindling momentum do the trick. If there was the slightest downhill curve, you could be coasting for hours, if not days. For a teenager like myself, this was a painful thing to experience. One of my long-standing dreams was to attach a parachute-brake, like the kind they put on dragsters, to the back of Grandma's '72 Ford Falcon. "Need to stop, Grandma? No problem." *Whoommp!*

Anyway, by the time Grandma did finally, slowly, creakingly come to a halt, the young hitchhiker was barely a dot in the distance. I looked back and saw him running toward us, overjoyed, his guitar bouncing on his back and his long blond hair flapping.

"Wow, Grandma. You stopped for a hitchhiker."

"Well," she said, "normally I wouldn't. But it is getting late and I don't like to see a young lady out on the road after dark. It isn't safe."

"Woman? That isn't a woman."

"It isn't?"

"No, it's a hippie."

"Oh, well. I didn't realize." And then—so help me God—*she pulled away* just as the hitchhiker, panting and grinning, arrived at the side of the car. He was reaching for the handle and we looked at each other as we slid apart. His smile stayed frozen on his face, but his eyes were filled with incomprehension. I gave him a sympathetic "Sorry, but what can I do?" sort of shrug as Grandma and I left him behind.

In the distance we could see him screaming and shouting and flinging his jacket about and kicking up gravel and giving us the finger.

"Look at that," said Grandma with a tut. "It's just as well we didn't stop for him. He's a lunatic."

I loved my grandmother, I truly did. But we accrued some heavy karma that day, karma that may take several lifetimes to escape and which—even now, as a hitchhiker myself—I am slowly working off.

—

Mr. Tawaraya eventually did find me a room. We ended up driving to the next community, a small seaside village named Atsuta which looked even more deserted than Ishikari—if such a thing is possible—but which did have an inn. It was one of those small-town everything shops: a bed-and-breakfast *minshuku*, a restaurant, a liquor store, a barber shop.

"No, no, he's not on a fishing trip. No, he isn't a birdwatcher. He isn't with anyone. He's alone."

Mr. Tawaraya was negotiating on my behalf. After long pauses, much teeth-sucking, several rounds of bows, and a flutter of insincere smiles, it was finally decided that the owners of the establishment would agree to take my money.

My business card helped. "Nexus?" they said. "Very good corporation. Very good." I threw in Donner's business card as well, citing him as my personal reference. (And the cool thing is, Donner, being an American, would have gone along with it. "Sure I know him, upstanding citizen. What was his name again?")

The owner and his wife treated me with a certain guarded respect, much like people treat a tame puma. I sat alone in the dining room, turning the inn's matchbox over in my hand. Sure enough, there was a different ad on each of three sides: one for the B&B, one for the café, and one for the hair salon. All run by one family. They were the Rockefellers of Atsuta.

Word must have leaked out about my arrival, because during supper a cyclone of children came scrambling in shouting, "Is it true? Is it!" only to stop dead in their tracks with a cartoon-like skid on the cement floor.

"Hello," I said, and they scattered like birds. Feeling weary, I turned to the owner. "Surely I'm not the first foreigner to stay in this inn?"

"Well, we did have one other. An Englishman. He stayed here one night. Spoke Japanese fluently. He was walking, all the way from Cape Sōya."

I choked back my squid. "When was that?"

"Oh, fifteen, sixteen years ago. Maybe more."

"An Englishman," I said. "Walking?"

"That's right."

On this lonely coast, miles from the nearest large town, it could have only been one person: Alan Booth. Alan walked the length of

Japan and wrote a now-classic travel narrative about his trip entitled *The Roads to Sata.* I had always wanted to meet Alan, just to thank him for being a writer, but he died of cancer in 1993. He was forty-seven.

And here I was, in the very same inn. Perhaps dining at the same table. Talking to the same people he had talked to.

"The Englishman," said the owner, "did you know him?"

"No. I mean, yes. I knew *of* him. His work. He was a writer."

"Was he?" The owner smiled. Teeth of gold. "Isn't that something."

His wife had been listening and she now butted in. "He wasn't a writer, he was a student," she said. "A college student. From America. And he wasn't walking, he was riding a bicycle."

"But—"

"An Englishman," insisted the owner, and they eventually had to call on his uncle to resolve the dispute.

"He was *Australian*," said the uncle. "And he wasn't riding a bicycle, he was driving a motorcycle. Clear across Japan he was."

As quickly as my excitement had mounted, it now dissipated. Had Alan Booth stayed here? I knew for a fact that he followed this coast, but had he spent the night in this inn? Or was it someone else? It was all very confusing. That's the problem with memory, it turns into myth so easily.

That night, I fell asleep to the sound of a tired sea, pounding, pounding, pounding against the shore, like a lover past caring, fatigued. I was feeling disconnected. Untethered.

I thought of Marion, back in Scotland. I thought of Alan Booth's fight with cancer and my own quixotic pursuit of flowers.

The rains never came.

12

SOME *PÉNSEES* concerning the human thumb:

It always seemed significant to me that the sole tool of the hitch-hiker is his or her thumb, that one single digit which made civiliza-tion and human society possible. When we hold out our opposable thumb, we are displaying that which distinguishes us from all other mammals. A thumb asks and expects acts of kindness by the very virtue of being human. When we hail a taxi we use our index finger—I, the pointer, the finger of business and money. But the thumb is a free ride, bold, an affirmation. "Thumbs up!"

This was a wonderful theory, finely spun, and I enjoyed dishing it out to whoever would listen—and often without the least bit of prompting (I'm something of a philanthropist that way). Then I met a professor from Cambridge who nodded thoughtfully at my induct-ive reasoning and, with a single pinprick, punctured it like an over-inflated beachball.

"The opposable thumb is not a symbol of movement," he said. "It's a symbol of stability. A symbol of invention. Without such a thumb, we couldn't have constructed complex tools or learned to sow the ground or plow the fields or build cities. The thumb is a symbol of the settler, the townsman. It is the toe, the *big toe*, that makes us capable of upright walking. It is this toe that makes long journeys on foot possible. We rise up above the grasslands because of our big toe. It is that which made humans capable of such remarkable feats of migration. We *walked* everywhere, to the far corners of the earth. It is the big toe that is the symbol of the trav-eller. Not the thumb."

"It's the thumb versus the toe?" I asked.

"Exactly. The settler versus the traveller. The farmer versus the nomad. Our two primal urges: the nesting instinct versus the migratory." *Those who stay at home and those who don't.*

My chest slowly deflated. The thumb is a powerful, Romanesque symbol, strong, assertive, proud—but the *toe*, the big toe? Not the romantic image I was looking for.

13

THE PORT CITY of Rumoi: a gang of Russian sailors blusters by, speaking in backward r's and lower-case capitals. They are wearing genuine Russian sweaters and appropriately brooding expressions. They look like extras in a Soviet montage. "Borscht!" I said in greeting as they passed. "Kasparov Kremlin." But these Russians were clearly *uneducated* Russians, for they failed to understand me even when I was speaking their own language, and they went scowling past without reply.

What *can* you say when you meet a Russian? "Here's to the end of the Cold War, shame about your country"? "Steal any good bicycles lately?" "So what ever happened to that dialectical materialism, anyway?"

I caught a ride to Rumoi with a barber-supply salesman named Sato Isoichi. Sato was a warm-hearted man, stout and solid, with a bristled haircut and a square jaw. He reminded me of a gruff but friendly high-school gym teacher. I dubbed him Coach. We got along well, but his route took him from small barbershop to barbershop along the way, and the cumulative effect was so sad my heart started to ache. I'm not sure why, but something about getting glimpses into the lives of so many people living in obscurity, cutting hair behind faded façades where the barber poles were sun-bleached to the point of being pastel renditions rather than eye-catching totems—it was all too much. One woman in her mid-years, her hair and clothes carefully attended to, came out and waved to me in the car. Sato had been inside and had told her about me. Behind, in her tiny shop, I could see a single mirror and an empty chair. She bought one small bottle of hair tonic.

Sato was a popular man, and clearly his visit was the highlight of the week for many of his customers. Self-effacing, friendly, always making time to chat, he worked his way slowly up the back of Hokkaido and then down again once a week. He was in his fifties and had two daughters, both in their twenties, both now living in Sapporo.

I have to be careful; I don't want to paint a Willy Loman portrait where none existed. Sato lived a semi-nomadic life, true, but he was closer to Tora-san, the wandering hero of Japanese popular cinema, than to Arthur Miller's salesman. When I compared Sato to Tora-san he laughed. "But Tora-san has no children, no home. My life is not as sad as Tora's. You"—he said with a smile—"*you* are more like Tora-san."

"But I have a family, I have a home," I said a little too sharply.

"Of course you do." His voice was now conciliatory, which only made me feel worse.

Sato picked me up in Hamamasu, which was little more than a name on a map. Above Hamamasu the highway hugged the coast, at times it *was* the coast, as we went up and around a great bulge of land where seabirds nested on the cliffs.

Hamamasu North appeared (there had barely been a Hamamasu), which was a pocket of blue rooftops huddled in a small cove along the beach. Sato took me down a twisty dirt road for a better view of the sea, through a ghost town where the houses were boarded up and falling down.

Sato followed the shore north to Rumoi. Flaccid, rancid, rusting Rumoi, spread out this way and that, a city filmed in sepia where the playgrounds were patches of brown grass and the ships bled rust into the harbour. Everything needed a new coat of paint. Even the sky. Especially the sky. I felt like grabbing a can of bright yellow latex and running around madly dabbing it onto surfaces. It was such a melancholy, beat-about place. If Hakodate was Russian in style, Rumoi was Russian in its soul. Even the name sounded Russian: *Rumoi.*

The Russians were in town all right. They had graduated from bicycles and were now stealing cars. They would roll them onto ships in the night and whisk them away to Siberia, though how much truth there was in this was hard to say. If you ask me, it smacks of urban legend.

Sato gave me an informal tour of Rumoi barbershops. We drove up one dusty road and down another, and every shop looked sad and wistful. More glimpses into strangers' lives. A procession of faces and smiles from the roadside. Along the way, I saw an old man delivering newspapers in a rickshaw. A rickshaw, mind you. In Rumoi, the question was not what city were you in, but what century.

I got dropped off on the north side of town, across a flat, muddy river that sloughed its way to the sea. Concrete seawalls created a backwater, brackish and sewer green, and a miasma of swamp gas lingered in the air. I couldn't wait to get out of Rumoi.

From where I stood, I counted five lighthouses at various points around the harbour entrance. This puzzled me. There was no way Rumoi needed five different lighthouses; the bay wasn't that tricky. I couldn't help but think there was more to it than mere navigation. It was a product of yearning, a way of signalling to the world that we are still here on the far edge of a northern island, the lighthouse lights turning round and round like a prayer wheel. *Please come. Please. Please come. Please.*

14

I'M NOT SURE WHY, but just outside of Shosanbetsu I ran out of steam.

It was a small, nondescript village, just a cluster of homes really, but I felt the irrational urge to stop. To turn around. The cape was less than a day's travel away; I knew I had made it, knew I *could* make it. So why go on?

I had climbed my way up the coast, one rung at a time, from one obscure town to the other, and here, north of Shosanbetsu, my momentum had finally faltered.

The sea was throwing wild crashes of wave up across the side of the highway. They came in like cannonballs, again and again, and the trucks drove through with their wipers on. Above me, on a grassy hill, stood a lone Shinto shrine facing the sea. I walked up an overgrown path to offer a coin and a prayer. The torii was faded from salt water and time, and behind it, past the downward slope of a hill, was a small village. I sat down on the steps of the shrine.

A crow had settled on the torii gate crossbeams. The wind was sweeping through the grass, carrying the smell of dust and straw. I could hear the sea, throwing itself against the highway, and it echoed, like the sound of a distant battle.

Something moved, something just beneath the surface—like a vein under skin.

We chart our lives in graphs, in erratic heartbeats up and down. We live our lives in motion, trailing former selves behind us like the

images in a strobe-light photograph. And yet, the nature of motion—
that primary aspect of our existence—eludes us.

Through a series of logical paradoxes, the pre-Socratic philosopher Zeno proved that motion was nothing more than an illusion. But
it was Zeno's logic that was the illusion, not motion. Motion remains
a brute force—perhaps *the* brute force—of nature. The philosopher
Heraclitus, in contrast, defined the very universe in terms of motion.
"We never step into the same river twice. All is in flux."

We are in flux as well, and the same *person* never steps into the
river twice, either.

In the Inuktitut language of the Far North, the Inuit make a key
distinction between objects at rest and objects in motion. An object
that is moving extends itself across a landscape. It is a different substance, a different *thing* when it stops moving. Motion does not
describe the object, it *defines* it. When a bear moving across an ice
floe stops, it becomes something else entirely, and a different word
is used to describe it.

When in motion, you do extend yourself across a landscape. The
danger, of course, is that it cuts both ways; when the traveller stops
moving, he ceases to exist.

15

Katsuya was in his late forties, but he had a youthful, shaggy hair-cut. "I'm an English teacher," he said. "A private tutor. I also sell text-books. Here, let me give you my card." He fished one out from the inside pocket of his blazer. "You never know."

He smoked *With Class*, a brand of cigarette I knew quite well, even though I don't smoke. On the front of every pack of With Class cigarettes is printed the following message in English:

> WITH CLASS: Defined as an expression of true sophistication intel-lectuality and appreciation for equality by trend-setting independent people creating new customs for life enjoyment.

"So you're an English teacher, you say?"

"Yup." He pulled back on his cigarette like a college student latching onto a joint. "Hokkaido is all right," he said. "I'm from Tokyo originally, but I've gotten used to living out here in the sticks. It's a very conservative area. *Too* conservative. The people are behind the times."

"Well," I said, "the roads are nice. I've been travelling at record speed since I arrived."

"Do you know," he said, "that Hokkaido has more traffic fatalities per year than anywhere else in Japan?"

I gave him a wan smile. "So I've heard."

"I hitchhiked myself one summer, back in the early seventies. It was during the Vietnam War. An American GI jumped ship in Hokkaido, and a friend and I spent the entire summer protecting him, hitchhiking from one town to the next, moving all the time." He exhaled a cloud of blue death and said, "Most people don't realize how violent the anti-Vietnam protests were in Japan. They had to close the schools down. There were riots. Tear gas. Plastic bullets." He smiled warmly at the memory of it, sweet with nostalgia. "It was terrible—worse than on American campuses."

"Did you take part in the riots? The tear gas, the truncheons, all of that?"

He gave me a politician's smile. "I am a private teacher now. It is a very respectable job. I don't discuss certain parts of my past."

"What happened to your friend, the American? The one who went AWOL."

"He stayed in Japan illegally for several years, but eventually he went home. They signed an amnesty. He lives in San Francisco now, with his Japanese wife."

Katsuya had been to America, as well. "I was married at twenty, which was a mistake. We were too young. I lost my wife. I dropped out, went west—well, *east* really. You know how it is, to travel west you have to go east. I went to America. My life in Japan was smothering me and I wanted to travel. But I became involved with the wrong people—I was naive, I think—and I ended up broke, without a visa, and stranded halfway across America. Not even halfway. Utah."

"Utah?"

"A family took me in. A Mormon family."

But he wasn't a Mormon and he wasn't interested in selling me anything, not textbooks or the Word of God. He said, simply, "They were very good people. I always remember how much they helped, and now—" a grin and a shrug "—now I try to pass it along. That's why I stopped for you. I'm passing it along."

"Doling out karma, as it were."

"Something like that. So don't thank me for the ride, you should thank that Mormon family I met twenty-four years ago."

The irony was too sharp to bear.

We drove through haphazard villages, thrown together like boxes in an attic. He stopped to drop off some textbooks, to visit a student's family, to pick up a package. And the day bled slowly away.

"Tell me something," I said as we drove north into a deep indigo blue. "The Japanese. In their heart of hearts, are they arrogant or insecure?"

"Arrogant *or* insecure? *Or?*" He looked at me as if to say, Well, there's your problem. Perhaps the problem is in the question itself. "We Japanese," he said confidently, "are not arrogant *or* insecure, we are both. You know, it is possible to be insecure in a very arrogant way—and vice versa. Look at America. I have always thought that you Americans manage to be dumb in a very smart way. Very smart."

"And the French are clever in a very stupid way," I said, catching on.

"Exactly. You have to stop thinking in opposites. You have to start *uniting* opposites."

"The British?" I asked.

We mulled this over for quite a while and finally came up with "well-mannered in a rude way." It was great fun. I love labels. Especially paradoxical ones.

The sun was setting when he dropped me off. He was turning back toward Rumoi and I was continuing north. He gave me his number and told me to call him if I got stranded. It was only after he drove away that I realized I was nowhere near a town, let alone a pay phone.

I was alone on an empty highway in a cold land. Night fell like an executioner's hood. The moon, half chewed, lit up the landscape just enough to create ominous shadows and shapes. I swallowed hard and told myself to be a man. Or, failing that, a very brave child. The wind was picking up. It carried all kinds of creaks and groans and various assorted sound effects sent down from the gods above for the sole purpose of tormenting me. I tried whistling, but then I thought, what if ghosts are *attracted* by whistles. You never know, so I compromised by whistling but in a very low voice.

I'm not sure why I was scared. I had camped out on beaches and in temples and in forests, but this was somehow different. This was a highway, and there is something innately unsettling about an empty highway at night.

I kept whistling, and when a pair of car headlights finally approached, sweeping the road ahead like search beams, I took no chances. I stepped out and waved him down. He was a plant manager named—and here it gets really creepy and symbolic—Sakuraba, or Mr. Cherry Blossom Garden.

"I've been chasing cherry blossoms since April," I said, a little too cheerfully. "At last! I've found you."

This did not make him feel comfortable.

"It's a joke," I said.

"I see."

Mr. Sakuraba worked at a fish-processing plant in Sarafutsu, a small village on the northeast shore of Hokkaido, an area even more remote than that which I was travelling through. "Iceberg alley," I said, and he nodded. His village was the gateway to the Okhotsk Sea, the Japanese equivalent of the Northwest Passage. Mr. Sakuraba was on his way home from a late-night delivery and his route would take me right through the hot-spring town of Toyotomi, my last stop before reaching Cape Sōya.

"We have Russians working at our plant in Sarafutsu," he said. "Twenty Russian women and one Russian man." (Bicycle thieves *and* salmon gutters; things were looking up.)

"It's been a long day," he said. "But I have to get home tonight. Tomorrow morning, I promised to put up carp banners for Children's Festival. I have two sons," he said, and in the glow of the dashboard lights I saw his expression soften.

At Teshio, the highway turned inland.

16

THE HOT SPRINGS of Toyotomi are the northernmost in Japan. A six-kilometre detour east of the main town, the area itself is little more than a clutch of inns and red lanterns huddled around a central public bath. At night the streets were awash in wisps of steam and visitors walking through on unsteady wooden clogs. Guests were wrapped in cotton yukata robes and laughing in whispers. Every inn had its own thermal baths and its own distinct style of yukata. You could identify which hotel you belonged to by the pattern you were wearing.

I finally found a room in a dark-wood-and-white-plaster inn, a building with narrow, winding corridors and angles that didn't quite add up. In my room, I unfolded my maps and drew a thick line up the distance of Japan using a red marker, following the route I had taken.

Tomorrow I would be at Cape Sōya. Then it was a train ride back to Sapporo, an afternoon of cherry blossoms (there were now rumours of flowers to the south), and then it was back to Minamata. This seemed to call for a celebration of some sort, so I went for a walk.

It was a cold, clear night and the stars were suspended like ice crystals in dark wine. I found the Big Dipper, turned upside down in the sky, and Venus, the North Star.

Maybe life isn't one big pachinko game; endless variations in a set pattern where the house always wins. Maybe there *is* no pattern. Maybe there is no pattern except those we project onto our lives, like constellations on a field of stars. Ah, yes, Vega the Hunter. That's Orion. That's the Traveller. I remembered stargazing as a child and having the constellations pointed out. They made no sense then, and no sense now.

Toyotomi Onsen is not a large place. Walk long enough and sooner or later you will come upon the town's public bath. Inside, the sudden drop in temperature had turned the air cumulus. I soaped myself down with lather as thick as shaving cream, rinsed, and then lowered my body into the water. The shapes of people emerged from and dissolved into the mist, and my vision blurred as I tried to look at—through—into—the fog. It was like trying to focus on flux itself. Nearby was a font for drinking the sulphuric water, and I took a token, medicinal sip. It had the taste of blood and rust.

That the bath is a return to the womb, I do not doubt: a chance to float again in the oceanic state as layers of dirt and fatigue and worry wash away. You emerge, flushed and well scrubbed, with skin so clean it hurts, and your head reels and you almost fall and float away. I sat in the water as long as I could, and when I rose, steam rolled from my body and the smell of sulphur clung to me like a lover's scent.

That night, I lay awake looking at the ceiling, thinking about people and places. I remembered friends I hadn't thought of in years. I tried to make sense of my trip, my past. But it was all jumbled together like a box of slides that has fallen over and then been thrown back together, out of order. The images flashed upon the screen without rhyme or reason. Landscapes. Faces. Sunsets. Airplane wings. Tourist snapshots mixed in with still-life portraits of flowers.

I came to Japan looking for some kind of realignment. A new start. A game plan. But somehow, along the way, I had become a collector of trivia and souvenirs, writing postcards addressed to a future self who would—somehow—make sense of it all.

Deferring judgment to a later date resolves nothing, and all you are left with is a box of jumbled slides and a collection of knick-knacks and odds and ends. Here a face. There a sunset.

17

I woke to a cold grey sky. The hot-spring town was deathly still as I walked through it, and a few paltry snowflakes drifted down. What I didn't know—what I couldn't know—was that this was the advance guard of a cold front that would eventually lash out against Hokkaido and shipwreck me on an island, far from the mainland.

I caught a ride with a schoolteacher into the town of Toyotomi itself. Toyotomi had the impermanent feel of a movie set. It was the type of place where stores sell goods from the 1950s, and fashion is something you get from a mail-order catalogue. It was Rumoi without the Russian flare. Or the harbour.

Outside a small shop, a solemn-eyed six-year-old shared small confidences with me: favourite teachers, best friends, meanest bullies, that kind of thing. "Is it far?" he asked. "Where you come from, is it far?"

"No, it's not far at all."

And he walked me to the end of the street and saw me off. "Be careful," he said. "Be careful and goodbye." And that was how I left Toyotomi, walking out of town on a slow slope uphill to the gradually fading farewells of a six-year-old. "Goodbye, Gaijin-san. Goodbye."

As I set out for Cape Sōya, I felt no sense of foreboding, no premonitions—only that familiar mix of disappointment and triumph that accompanies the coming end of any journey. In light of what happened next, foreboding might well have been more appropriate.

Tomio Honda stopped for me just north of Toyotomi. He had a rough-cut, sun-creased, Jake-the-Farmhand look about him. He was a friendly man.

"Welcome to Hokkaido!" he said when he opened the door.

He was on his way to a country club to play a round of golf. Nothing unusual there. He took a shortcut, along the back roads, through sheep pastures and herds of cows. There wasn't another vehicle in sight.

"And what do you do?" I asked.

He tried to explain, but I didn't recognize the word. "I'm a teacher myself," I said.

Tomio grinned at this and suddenly switched to English. *"Cows!"* he said, pointing to one as we passed.

"Cows," I agreed.

He pointed to several more. "Cows!"

"Yes," I said. "That is correct. Cows."

"Sex!"

"Beg your pardon?"

"Cows," he said. "Cows. Sex. Cow sex!" He was now pointing vigorously at a herd and grinning.

The admittedly small section of my brain devoted to rational thought had seized up like a rusty gear. I was utterly, positively, irretrievably *baffled*.

"Cow sex?" I said.

"Yes, yes. Me. I do cow sex." His grin was now taking on a slightly demonic hint. I slowly reached for the door handle. We were coming up to a rural stop sign and the few survival skills I possessed were now kicking in like recessive genes. Run away, they whispered. Run away. I slid my hand onto the door handle and prepared to leap from the car. (I was frantically going through the fundamentals of the shoulder roll, as gleaned from high-school gym class, and berating myself for not having paid more attention.) I made my move.

The door was locked.

"Cow sex," said Tomio, his eyes shining with glee.

Well, you'll be happy to hear that the story doesn't end with me being forced to scamper about in the clover wearing a cow bell and going "moo" while the theme song from *Deliverance* plays in the background. I had just managed to discreetly unlock the door and had girded myself to leap from a moving vehicle when—like a tumbler turning in a lock—it suddenly clicked. I looked over at him.

"Are you a doctor?" I asked. "An animal doctor?"

"Oh, no." He brushed this aside with a show of modesty.

"But you help animals have babies."

"Yes, yes! Cows. Sex. Babies."

He was an artificial inseminator. "My cows," he said, pointing to one herd and then another.

I almost wept for joy. "Do you have any children of your own?" I asked.

"Oh, yes. I have three."

"And you, ah, had them—*naturally?*"

He laughed uproariously over this. "Of course, of course."

With the tension gone and my anus slowly unclenching, I became giddily, hysterically happy. Tomio and I got along famously, laughing at everything and slapping each other on the shoulder (in a strictly he-man way, you understand). By the time we reached the golf course, he had invited me along.

As I had never played the game before, it was decided we would stick to the driving range. He pulled into the parking lot and retrieved his clubs from the trunk.

"Nice place," I said.

"It's the northernmost golf course in Japan," he said. But let's face it, we were only about ten or twelve kilometres from Cape Sōya, so everything up here was the northernmost something or other.

"Form is very important," said Tomio as he teed up a ball. "Shift your left leg forward, rotate your hips, keep your chin up, your chest out, and your shoulders straight. Tilt your right knee at a forty-two-degree angle, while raising your left elbow two inches and shifting your lower pelvis over your centre of gravity. Decrease the upward velocity, slowly raise your right pinky, put your left leg in, put your left leg out, and do the hokey-pokey as you turn yourself about. And that," he said, "is what it's all about."

What a stupid sport. I took a couple of swipes at the ball, but all I succeeded in doing was sending up a spray of dirt. Rugged Canadian that I am, my technique was more slapshot than golf swing. I was digging up great clods of earth at this point, and every time I slammed down with the club, Tomio winced. His smile trembled in the way I imagine a patriot's does when faced with a firing squad. Stiff upper lip and all that.

I was sweating so hard I had to take off my jacket. I spit into my hands (a gesture Tomio had apparently never seen before) and went at it with renewed vigour. Having perfected a take-no-prisoners sort of slapshot, I began working on my wrist shot, my hip shot, and my finely tuned, scythe-like, Genghis Khan shot. I was lobbing balls in all directions, right, left, and into the next lane. The other golfers were standing back, well back, and watching with that same queasy fascination one usually gives an impending car crash.

After about half an hour of this, Tomio congratulated me on my prowess and took back his club. It was scuffed up quite a bit. On the back, in a metal sticker, was the price tag. (High-status items in Japan will occasionally have price tags that are semi-permanent and not meant to be removed.) It read: 70,000 *yen*. No wonder he was wincing. "Jeez," I said. "A hockey stick would only put you back ten, twenty bucks tops."

He smiled at me, but his eyes were full of tears.

"Shall we play a round?" I asked. "I think I'm starting to get the hang of it."

"That, ah, won't be necessary," he said.

18

TOMIO DROVE ME far out of his way, beyond the golf course, to where the road met the sea at a T-intersection. From here it was a short, four-kilometre hop to Cape Sōya. I could *see* the cape, a low slow curve of land in the distance. "I came all the way from Cape Sata," I said. "Just one last bit to go."

"I hope you make it."

I dropped several hints ("So, I guess whoever I meet next will be the very last person I hitch a ride with.") but Tomio didn't offer.

We said our farewells. "Next time," I said, "I'll teach you about hockey."

I could have walked to Cape Sōya in less than an hour, but as a matter of pride I decided to hitch.

"You came from Cape Sata?" said the young woman in the front seat, almost swooning with disbelief. *"Today?"*

I laughed. "Not today. Today I came from Toyotomi." But even that elicited gasps of wonder.

"But Japanese people never pick up hitchhikers," she said.

The car was crammed full with bags and skiing gear. Inside were three college kids, clean-cut, cheerful, and brimming with an enthusiasm I never remember possessing, even in college. The driver's family name was Kitajima, which meant "Northern Island," and the young man in the back was named Takeyuki, which could mean "Snowy Bamboo" if you screwed up the translation a bit. Up front was Yoko Tanaka, a very cute, very boisterous young lady with a big smile and dimples. I was in love with Yoko.

We went to Cape Sōya, took silly pictures, ate at a lunch counter, bought postcards, and basically goofed around. The cape itself was secondary. It was a low point, with rocks piled along it so you could go down and dip your hand into the cold north sea and say, "Here I am, at the end of Japan." At Cape Sōya you look back, toward Cape Sata in the south, across an archipelago that curves like vertebrae toward Okinawa.

In *Roads to Sata* Alan Booth suggests that the landscape around Sōya is similar to that of Sata, the idea being that nothing really changes no matter where you go. (Alan was a bit of a pessimist that way.) But this isn't true. You can drive right up to Cape Sōya and stroll down to the water. There were no cliffs or jagged rocks. These two capes—Sata to the south and Sōya at the north—are just about as different as any two points could be.

There were a few shops at Sōya, and even an inn, but little else. Other than the fact that you were at the northernmost point in Japan, there wasn't much reason to stop. Japan ends not on an exclamation point but on an ellipsis: *Sata!* to *Sōya* . . .

Yoko came bounding over, dimples ablaze. She shook my hand, squeezed it, and said with vicarious joy, "You did it! You really did it!"

19

My trio of college students took me back to Wakkanai City ("the northernmost city in Japan!"), where a reporter with the *Yomiuri*, Japan's national newspaper, was waiting.

The *Yomiuri* has the largest circulation of any newspaper in the world, so you'd think I would have been treated to dinner and drinks, but no, we held the interview in a hotel lobby.

"You travelled end to end solely on the kindness of strangers, is that correct?"

"That's right."

"No one has ever done that before?"

"Not to my knowledge."

"And you were following the Cherry Blossom Front."

"Well, I got ahead of it in Sapporo, but it should catch up to me any day."

This was a new experience for me, being interviewed. I felt like a celebrity. I felt like Alan Booth. I felt like I had done Something Significant. I was droll, witty, deep. I even joked about getting a sunburned thumb in Shikoku. The reporter took all kinds of low-angle, heroic photos of me, thumb extended, and asked me all sorts of weighty questions. We spoke for over an hour.

Why had I wanted to make such a trip in the first place? Because I wanted to see Japan, I said. Not as a spectator, but as a participant. I wanted to experience the Japanese as individuals and not as a nameless, faceless block.

My own progress was similar to that of many expatriates. Before I came to Japan, I had tremendous respect for the Japanese, but I didn't really *like* them very much. Now, after five years in this aggravating, eccentric nation; having travelled it end to end; having worked and lived and played with the Japanese; having seen beyond the stereotypes; having come up against their obsessions and their fears, their insecurities and their arrogance, their kindness and their foibles; having experienced first-hand all the many contradictions that *are* Japan, I found I did not respect the Japanese as much as I used to, but I liked them a whole lot more.

The reporter asked, "And how will you return now that it's over? Will you hitchhike back down as well?"

"No. I'm going to walk it—backwards."

There was a pause. "Really?"

"No."

"I see. So that was a joke?"

"A kind of joke."

"I see."

The reporter, packing up his briefcase and putting away his camera, happened to remark, in an offhand way, "Really, Cape Sōya isn't the end of Japan at all."

I looked at him. "Sure it is."

"It's the northernmost point *in Hokkaido*," he said. "But the islands of Rishiri and Rebun—you can see them from across the peninsula—those are the *real* northernmost points of Japan. *Ta!*" And off he went, leaving me with my stomach tied up in knots.

How could this be? I opened my map and checked. It was hard to say, but these two islands, one round and one long, certainly looked to be a nudge farther north than Cape Sōya. Everything came crashing down around me. It still wasn't over.

I ran to the terminal and managed to catch the last ferry out. If I could get to the northernmost tip of Rebun, I could say to myself, "There, I've done it. I have been to the end of Okinawa and I have been to the tip of Rebun Island. It's over. I'm done. Done with Japan."

It was only then, as the ferry moved slowly out of port, that I realized what I had been searching for: a reason to leave.

By the time we reached Rishiri Island, the decision had been made. I had only one more trip to make, across to Rebun, and that would be it. I would close a chapter in my life. This hadn't been a trip of discovery, it had been a journey of farewell. It was a sad and liberating thought.

ON RISHIRI ISLAND

THE FERRY ended its run at Rishiri Island. To get to Rebun, I would have to take another boat, two days later.

Rishiri is a Matterhorn dropped into a northern sea. It rises up directly from the water like a jagged bone, and the peak looked sharp enough to draw blood. I checked into the Green Hill Hostel, a large building shielded from the sea by a dramatic rise of land that swept up and then dropped suddenly into the water. The cliffs were filled with the cries of nesting seabirds. It reminded me of Cape Sata. It looked . . . it looked like Scotland.

And I thought to myself: It is a sign that you have been travelling too long when everything reminds you of someplace else.

A road ran along Rishiri's edge, turning around the central peak of the mountain. I decided to hitch it, completing another small circle, but after one hour and only a single, short-hop ride, I returned to the hostel and rented a bicycle.

I rode out through towns as sad and silent as graveyards. Windows were boarded up, yards were neglected, entire villages abandoned. There were no sakura, no tumbling blossoms—only the froth of sea spume that blew up across the road, spindrift and insubstantial.

It took me all afternoon and well into the evening to circumnavigate Rishiri. On the far side of the island, I stopped at a shop where the packages were covered in dust and the shelves were half empty. The lady who tended to me was very thin. She had bruises on her face, and she said she hadn't been off the island in years. She looked at me as though from across barbed wire, and when she handed me my change her fingers touched mine and I wanted to pull her in and say, "Join me! This is why I have come here, this was my purpose all along, to save you, to save me." But the moment had passed, a sword swung through mist, leaving swirls and silence and

little else—changing nothing. I got back on my bicycle and rode
wobbly away, a ridiculous figure.

At night, the hostel was cavernous and cold, filled with long hallways and sheets of ice and closets that contained entire winters.
Only a small heater warmed my room, and I spent the evening huddled in front of it. For supper, I walked into town to the only shop
I could find open. A gaunt man fed me plates of fried rice and
watched me as I sat, crouched over my meal.

An old lady whispered that there might not be any sakura at all
this year. "The flowers may die on the branch," she said, smiling
softly.

Everyone agreed it had been a very long winter.

That night, a storm rattled the windows. By morning it had turned
into snow, by afternoon a blizzard. By evening it was making news
channels across Japan.

Rebun Island disappeared like a whale into the fog, and the ferries across were cancelled. I tried to get back to the mainland but
I missed the last ferry out. The next day everything was cancelled.
Winter reasserted itself with full force, and I called my supervisor to
tell him I was stranded. He said, "We will have to reconsider our
options."

I was on Rishiri and unable to get to Rebun. The end lay out of
reach, and retreat was not possible. I couldn't go forward, I couldn't
go back. My movement had effectively come to an end; there was no
momentum left to maintain.

At Cape Sata and again at Cape Sōya, I had written in my journal: *the end of Japan*. But I would never reach the end of Japan,
because the end of Japan was unreachable. The best I could hope
for now was that someone would rescue me. All through the day and
into the night, the winds lashed my room as I sat, huddled in front
of the heater, waiting for the spring to arrive.

WILL FERGUSON spent five years in Japan. He is the author of a guidebook for budget travellers, *The Hitchhiker's Guide to Japan*, and the bestselling Canadian travel memoir *Beauty Tips from Moose Jaw*, winner of the 2005 Leacock Medal for Humour. His debut novel, *Happiness*, won the Leacock Medal for Humour and the Canadian Authors Association Award for Fiction. It was shortlisted for the Commonwealth Writers Prize: Canada and the Caribbean Best First Book, and has now been published in 33 countries and 26 languages. Will Ferguson lives in Calgary with his wife and their two young sons.

A NOTE ON THE TYPE

Hitching Rides with Buddha has been set in Fairfield Light, a modern recutting of a typeface originally designed by Rudolph Ruzicka in 1940. The reader, wrote Ruzicka, "expects nothing but to be left in optical ease while he pursues his reading."